Essentials of English Language Teaching

Essentials of English Language Teaching

Anjani K. Sinha
Former Professor and Head
Department of Linguistics
University of Delhi, Delhi

SHIPRA

Rs. 395

ISBN: 978-81-7541-876-9

First Published in India in 2017

Essentials of English Language Teaching

Published by:
SHIPRA PUBLICATIONS
LG 18-19, Pankaj Central Market, I.P. Ext.
Patparganj, Delhi-110092
Tel: 91-11-2223 5152, 2223 6152
E-mail: info@shiprapublication.com
www.shiprapublication.com

Acknowledgements

The author is deeply obliged to A.P.R. Howatt for summarizing the trends in the history of English language teaching on the basis of his *History of English Language Teaching.* He owes much to *An Introduction to Applied Linguistics* edited by Norbert Schmitt (2009). Other authors whose views have affected the author favourably or negatively have been duly mentioned in the text. The author owes quite a bit to Dulay, Burt and Krashen (1982) and to Michael McCarthy (2000) as well.

Contents

Introduction

This book discusses various aspects of the teaching of English in India. Though there are several books on the teaching of English as a second language, they all refer to general factors. They are important but we need to look at them from the point of view of the situation in India.

In Independent India, English remains a powerful language. It is a link language in which inter-state administrative transactions take place. It is the medium of higher education, including medical, engineering and professional education. Most candidates of central services choose it as their medium of examination, though alternatives are available. In many schools all over the country it is taught from standard I. Where it starts being taught at standard-III or V, privately-run English-medium public schools have mushroomed. Looking at the demand for the teaching of English, the National Knowledge Commission (2007) has recommended that the teaching of English start from class I in all schools. It further suggests that this phase of language learning should focus on using language "to create meaningful learning experiences for the child without disproportionate emphasis on grammar and rules." The commission further recommends that graduates with high proficiency in English and good communication skills should be trained to futher improve their proficiency through various training programmes. It is of opinion that training for language teaching needs to be thoroughly reviewed recognizing "the centrality of language in the curriculum." (2007:33) This book has been written keeping these developments in view and hopes to equip teacher-trainees with much needed information.

The book is divided into nine units, each unit comprising several chapters. ***Unit I*** provides background information. *Chapter 1* contains a brief discussion on the nature and role of language. It points out how human language is different from animal communication and kinesic (non-verbal) communication. It points out the nature of a language and its dialects and discusses its multiple roles in society, e.g. as an indicator of one's identity, nationality, power and gender.

Chapter 2 discusses the question of multilingualism and problems arising out of it in language teaching in schools. It treats multilingualism not as a hindrance but a resource and a strategy. It discusses the problem of multilingualism in cosmopolitan cities and bordering areas in linguistic states in India and points out how Canada, the USA and nations of the European Union are handling the question. It refers to the historical status of languages in India, the difference between home language and the language at school, the centrality of language in curriculum and the role of language teacher in a multilingual society.

Chapter 3 tells us how the language of the British islands has become the language of the USA, Canada, Australia, New Zealand, South Africa, etc. It examines how it became a second language in several countries, including India. It notes that it is taught as a foreign language almost all over the globalized world. It also discusses its growing importance in India where it is considered to be a means of upward social mobility.

Chapter 4 refers to personal and social factors that influence second language learning. Personal factors include age, aptitude and intelligence, attitude and motivation and needs whereas social factors comprise the socio-economic status of the learner, whether he/she lives in a bilingual/multilingual environment, frequency of language use, school environment and role of the teachers and peer-groups.

Unit 2 discusses the role of English in colonial and independent India. *Chapter 5* discusses various positions taken in British and independent India with reference to the teaching of English. It refers to the bilingual method suggested by Miller, Prendergast and Michael West as against the direct method adopted by British and Indian language teachers. While surveying the developments in independent India, it discusses the positions taken by the constituent Assembly of India, the University Grants Commission, the Official Language Commission, the Education Commission and deliberation by the National Curriculum Commission. References have been made to the National Policy on Education, the Programme of Action, the National Curriculum Framework and the National Knowledge Commission as well.

Unit 3 presents an overview of English language teaching. **Chapter 6** discusses philosophical (William James, John Dewey) psychological behaviorist (Watson, Thorndike, Pavlov, Skinner, Bruner vs. cognitive (Chomsky, McNeill, Braine, Lenneberg, Krashen), developmental (Piaget, Vygotsky), connectionist, prototype (Rosch) and sociological (Firth-Malinwaski, Saper-Whorf, Bernstein, Labov and other variationists') and Pragmatic approaches. It also discusses the views of modern Indians thinker' such as Vivekanand, Aurobindo, Tagore, #, Zakir Hussain, Radhakrishnan, Gijubhai Badhekha's views on education and language teaching.

Chapter 7 deals with the history of various methods of the teaching of English as a second or foreign language. It points out the change from the grammar-translation method to the direct method through rational and reform movements. It shows how most of these approaches, right from the days of Harold Palmer, are based on the structural theory of language analysis.

It shows how oral method, audio-lingual method audio-visual method and situational approach are various versions of direct method, how the limitation of structural approach led to the growth of cognitive transformational method which encouraged the creativity of the language learner. It shows how the new development led to the emphasis on communicative competence and discourse analysis. It discusses the roles of computers, mobiles and internet in language learning and teaching. Besides, it discusses the methods developed by the constructionists, Piaget, Vigotsky, N. Davies, Guttegno, Lozanov, Eldrige, Elley, Jangid, Willis, Nionoun and Prabhu. Finally it discusses the crucial question of bilingual versus monolingual method of language teaching.

Unit 4 comprises *chapter 8* which discusses some features and structures of language. It views language as a rule-governed system and discusses the question of linguistic variability and its pedagogical implications, with special reference to variety in Indian English. It discusses the organization of language at phonological, morphological and syntactic levels keeping in view the roles of universal and language-specific grammars.

Unit 5 examines how language skills are developed. **Chapter 9** examines various perspectives on teaching grammar: traditional, discriptive/structural and transformational-generative.

Chapter 9 discusses the basics of generation of sentences and how they are maniputed to put focus on one of their constituents. It compares the behaviourist approach to substitution tables with generative approach to studying the flexibility of sentence construction and how the principles operating within certain parameters generate grammatical sentences.

Chapter 10 discusses the structural approach to contrasting the structures of the second language with those of the mother tongue of the language learner and its limitations. It argues for looking at the functional-semantic rather than structural equivalence of sentences at the surface level and shows how it makes the contrastive analysis more relevant. It shows how surface differences between the structures of two languages do not cause much difficulty.

Chapter 11 discusses the errors committed by the learners of L_2 and claims that those are the focal areas. The transformational approach to errors views them as steps towards learning the correct form. They are developmental errors or 'interlanguage' and should guide the learner to move from the use of interlanguage to normal standard language.

Chapter 12 discusses skills to increase one's vocabulary by associating a word with its synonyms, antonyms, and its superordinates or subordinates in a natural class. It discusses the questions of derivation, collocational links, phrases verb, definitions, connectionism, etc. It suggests various types of word games (*antakshari*, puns, scrabbles and puzzles) to increase one's vocabulary. It offers some tips on the use of dictionaries, encyclopaedia and thesaurus.

Chapter 13 is concerned with the learning of lisening skills. Whether it is one-way listening or two-way listening, the knowledge of sounds, stress, rhythm and intonation is essential. It puts special stress on the sounds that Indian learners do not have in their mother tongues and discusses how to acquire them. The roles of language laboratory, radio, television and computer have also beeen discussed. Correct pronunciation of sounds, reduction of vowels in connected speech and importance of stress and intonation are emphasized in *chapter 14*. It makes a distinction between casual and formal speech and emphasizes the significance of turn taking and politeness in conversation.

Chapter 15 distinguishes between reading aloud and silent reading. It stresses the need for reading for comprehension. It discusses the process of skimming, scanning and skipping. It highlights the role of predictability in these processes. It points out the difference between intensive and extensive reading and shows how the latter helps one in increasing one's reading speed. It discusses how to process sentences, taking sentential cues, deletion, recoverability and cultural predictability into consideration.

Chapter 16 discusses the dynamics of writing. It covers the problems of spelling and pronunciation in English. It discusses the difference between free and controlled composition and shows how one can move from the latter to the former. The techniques of taking and preparing notes and summarizing have also been discussed. It discusses briefly the art of writing narrative, descriptive, expository and argumentative essays, letters, book reviews, dialogues, e-mails, speeches, diary and advertisement. Besides, it shows how to prepare charts and diagrams, and points out how to differentiate between good and bad compositions.

Units 6 discusses language, literature and aesthetics. *Chapter 17*, discusses different creative forms of languages including translation. It emphasises the need for and relevance of the study of literature in school curriculum. It discusses, briefly, varieties of English literature with reference to original and translated Indian writings in English. It examines three translations of the same text to make their comparative evaluation. The main focus is on the relevance of literary text is school curriculum.

Chapter 18 discusses how different forms of literature—poetry, drama, fiction—can be read and appreciated. It emphasizes the development of analytical and critical thinking in students for an effective evaluation of literature. It makes a brief reference to non-literary writings as well.

Unit 7 discusses the problems involved in the development and analysis of syllabi and texts. *Chapter 19* points out the desirability of learner-chosen texts in multilingual classrooms in such a way that the knowledge of English is relevant to the world outside

Chapter 20 discusses the theoretical issues involved in lesson planning. It talks about unit planning in terms of subject matter unit, activity unit and idea-centered unit. Each unit has motivation, presentation, explanation, application and summarization as its sub-units. It emphasizes the role of assignment in the study of what has been achieved. It offers advice to look for certain elements while evaluating the assignment. The role of sequential planning has also been emphasized. Further, it offers the unit analysis of six topics, a poem, a short-story, an one act play, a supplementary reader, a piece of grammar and a piece on paragraph writing.

Unit 8 discusses how to plan learning and teaching.

Chapter 21 discusses the roles of choral reading, dialogue, dramatization, use of puppets and marionettes, pantomimes and shadow plays felt boards and cutouts. It points out the significance of word games, quizzes, charts, graphs and maps.

Chapter 22 discusses the roles of visual aids such as flash cards, charts and pictures and audiovisual aids such as radio, television, motion pictures, language laboratory and computer. It discusses computer and mobile assisted language learning (CALL) in detail.

It emphasizes the reader's grasp of the content and asks him/her to examine the role played by its style, rhyme and rhythm, similes and metaphors, alliteration and assonance. It argues that the collocation of words and syntactic manipulations should also be examined to evaluate their contribution. The reader should be able to point out the theme of the literary piece and examine how its plot has been developed to get the theme focussed.

Unit 9 discusses language testing and assessment. **Chapter 23** discusses purposes and types of evaluation, and the reliability and validity factors on which a test is dependent. it discusses three types of test format: close-ended, restricted and open-ended. It specifically discusses the situation in India and pleads for a more transparent and reliable system of evaluation. It pays special attention to continuous comprehensive evaluation and how to implement it in our context.

The author notes that, by and large, Indian linguists interested in language teaching still believe in the old linguistic paradigm of structuralism. They have not yet taken advantage of advances in the developmental theory of language learning and in the transformation-generative paradigm. Whether they discuss English as a second or a foreign language, their emphasis is on literacy in English and not on its creativity. Even those who claim to take care of the academic needs of students do not go beyond the limits of developing four basic skills. This book tries to explore the linguistic aspect of teaching literature within the scope of second language learning. It is not enough to say what constitutes the acquisition of correct English; it is necessary to point out how the language is handled in literature and in everyday use. Discourse analysis claims to do it but it falls short of its goal in the name of concentrating on spoken English.

The change in linguistic paradigm has opened new vistas which must be availed of by the teachers of English as a second language. It is futile to claim that applied linguistics has developed its own theory of language analysis and it need not pay attention to theoretical developments. Applied linguistics, including language teaching, can ignore theoretical development at a very high cost. It is hoped that the approach adopted in this book will make one avert that situation.

While writing this book the syllabi of Aligarh Muslim University, Banaras Hindu University, Delhi University, Lucknow University Osmania University, Hyderabad University, Punjab University, Amritsar, North-East Hill University, Shillong, Gauhati University, M.D. University, Rohtak, G.G.S. Indraprastha University, Delhi Tamilnadu Teacher's Education University, Himachal Pradesh University and Ranchi University have been consulted. Special attention has been paid to the recommendations of *National Curriculum Framework* (2005), *National Focus Group on the Teaching of English* (2006) and the *Syllabus* for *B.Ed. Programme* (2015, NCERT).

We will be obliged to our readers for their comments and suggestions for the improvement of the book.

UNIT 1. BACKGROUND PERSPECTIVE

1

Nature and Role of Language

LANGUAGE—TOOL OF HUMAN COMMUNICATION

Communication means the activity or process of expressing or sharing ideas or feelings. It makes one's thought known to other people so that they understand it. It is a method of exchanging and sending information. It uses language as a tool to do so. 'Language' is a system of communication in speech or writing that is used by people of a particular country or speech community.

Language is a method of human communication, either spoken or written. It consists of the use of words in a structured and conventional manner. A *word* is a single distinct meaningful combination of sounds which is used with other words (or sometimes alone) to form a *sentence*. People use sentences, written or spoken, to communicate, and communication succeeds if they are used in accordance with conventions accepted in a specific speech community. It succeeds also because words are used in patterns accepted in that community. It succeeds because it follows the norms of that society.

VERBAL VS. NON-VERBAL COMMUNICATION

Any communication between two human beings- an exchange of words or mutually intelligible gestures, such as wave of hands- has to conform to the rules and conventions accepted or understood by all members of that speech community. If there are no firm rules, there is not any successful communication. If there are rules but they are broken during verbal or non-verbal transaction, such acts confirm the existence of such rules.

Like verbal communication, non-verbal communication is subject to community-based convention. For instance, in north India, people nod (i.e. move their heads up and down) to show their agreement and shake their heads from one side to the other to say 'no' or convey disagreement, but in south India they shake their heads from one side to the other to show their agreement and shake them with a jerk to show their disapproval or disagreement. Thus the south Indian sign for 'yes' is likely to be understood as 'no' in north India.

The study of non-verbal communication is called kinesics. It involves the movement of head, forehead, brows, eyes, nose, cheeks, mouth, chin, neck, shoulders, trunk, hips, right and left arms, hands and fingers. Each of these has its own pattern in a specific community which is visually recognized. These motion qualifiers are roughly analogous to superasegmental features of a spoken language. If they are used when oral interaction is going on, they punctuate and reinforce the verbal message and are easy to interpret. If they are used without any verbal message, their interpretation may sometimes be vague or ambiguous. Even when body movement and language are used simultaneously, it is a complex pattern; it is separable only analytically.

The human body can be twisted and turned in thousands of different ways, out of which each community selects a limited number. It is in the same way as a collection of limited number of meaningful sounds out of a vast repertory of sounds the human vocal organs are capable of making. Even when a person stops talking, he/she may not stop communicating through his/her body movement. Even if a person is completely silent and there is no body movement, his silence conveys some meaning, his/her complete disagreement with his/her interlocutor or a deadlock. Sometimes it suggests embarrassment or awkwardness.

SIGN LANGUAGE

The sign language is a system of communication with people who cannot hear, by using hand movements rather than spoken words. Like any true language, it has its own consistent modes of expression. It has a complete linguistic system which can fully communicate the utterances of a spoken language. For instance, the English sentence

Who bought the car?
Can be expressed in the American Sign Language as
Buy car who?

Each of these words is represented by a specific finger sign. The tense is indicated by separate types of hand shapes. There are two types of hand shapes for the past tense, one for the recent past and another for the distant past.

HUMAN LANGUAGE VS. ANIMAL COMMUNICATION

Most human beings who acquire language use it to express meaning. However, speech sounds are not a basic element of language. As we have already discussed, a sign language has no speech sounds but it is a language because it can be used creatively. The birds chirp, dolphins squeak and bees hum and dance but they do not have language. Talking birds such as parrots and mynahs can faithfully reproduce some expressions of a human language but they do not understand what they speak. They cannot make similar utterance on their own either. If Totaram, the parrot, can reproduce. 'Totaram wants a piece of bread' because it has been taught so, it cannot say 'Totaram does not want a piece of bread, it wants a guava'. Though it uses imitated expressions as a trained bird, it does not really understand language as an abstract concept. As Bertrend Russell aptly remarked, "No matter how eloquently a dog may bark, he cannot tell you that his parents were poor but honest."

In their natural habitat primates communicate with one another in a system which includes visual, auditory and tactile signals. Many of these signals are associated with the animals' immediate environment and carry meaning; they convey a sense of danger, aggressiveness, love, anger and other emotions. However, these sounds are highly stereotyped and carry limited meaning. They are immediate responses to a prevailing situation. They have no way of expressing their past experience or future programme which a human language has.

In recent decades scientists have tried to explore whether animals can learn a human language. In 1930s Dr. and Mrs. Kellogg exposed Gua, an infant chimpanzee, to English. Gua was raised with Kellogg's son, he picked up some isolated words but could not produce or understand any sentence. Dr. and Mrs. Hayes tried to train Viki, another chimpanzee, but he could utter only a few words with great difficulty.

Psychologists Allen and Beatrix Gardner tried to teach Washoe, another chimpanzee, the American Sign Language. She was put among hearing-impaired children. The children picked up and used the sign language fluently but Washore could produce signs for only 85 words. Psychologists Premacks tried to teach Sarah an artificial language. She could display the knowledge of certain words only when she got a cue from her trainer. Dr. Patterson taught Koko, a gorilla, to associate signs with objects and concepts which she learnt but she could not come up with any new combinations. So was the case with Nim Chimpsky. In spite of four or five years of rigorous training, none of them could come up with an expression of their own; their acts were imitative. It may be pointed out that a normal human child becomes a fluent speaker of his/her mothertongue in three to four years. The failure of these experiments gives credit to Noam Chomsky's claim that language is unique to human beings. It supports his claim that every human child is born endowed with the principles of universal grammar which enables him/her to come up with the rules of language specific grammar in course of his/her linguistic development. Though the child makes a few mistakes in the process and produces what linguists call 'interlanguage', he/she discards it in the course of his/her language acquisition.

Though there is no natural connection between linguistic form and its meaning and the relation between them is completely arbitrary (for instance, the word *mouse* and the object it refers to, i.e. a small rodent typically with a pointed snout, relatively large ears and a long tail), has a flexibility because of which it now also refers to a small hand-held device which is moved across a mat or a flat surface to move a curser on a computer screen. The use of this old signal to communicate a new expression is a novel experience. This kind of manipulation is not possible with an animal signal which has a fixed meaning.

It is because of this flexibility that words not only change their meanings but expand or contract it. For instance, in Middle English, the word *ill* meant *harmful*, now it means 'feeling unwell', 'suffering from disease'. Earlier the word '*cool* meant' of or at a fairly low temperature', now it also means showing lack of friendship or warmth towards a person, as in 'a *cool* reception'; it also means 'fashionably attractive' (as in 'This garment makes her appear cool'. In Middle English, *humour* referred to 'bodily fluid', now it is used in the sense of 'having amusing or comic quality in speech or writing'.

Unlike animals, humans keep on adding to their stock of words by inventing them (e.g. *xerox*, *google*, *fax*, *tweet*) or borrowing from other languages (e.g. English has borrowed *tikka*, *gherao*, *karma*, *yoga*, etc. from Hindi). Human languages not only borrow words, but new sounds from other languages. For example, Hindi has borrowed sounds *z* (as in *zamin* 'land', *zarur* 'essential', *zahir* 'mention', *zinda* 'live' etc.) *f* (as in *fakir* 'saint', *farmana* 'order', *fikra* 'anxiety') *q* (as in *qalam* 'pen', *qanun* 'law') *x* (as in *xatara* 'danger', *xaq* 'dust'), ɣ (as in *ɣilaf* 'quilt' *ɣulam* 'slave' etc.). It has also borrowed sentence structures (as the use of indirect speech and sentence internal relative clauses in Hindi). Such dynamism is not found in utterances of animals; they are fixed.

LANGUAGE AND DIALECTS

A dialect is a particular form of a language which is peculiar to a particular region (e.g. South American English in the USA or Scottish English in Britain) or social group (e.g. Black English Vernacular spoken by the Black Americans in the USA). Linguists hold the view that all languages have dialects and the commonly accepted standard dialect is called language. For instance, throughout Britain the standard dialect used by the mass media—radio and television—is the language called British English. Its main characteristics are its received pronunciation (RP). 95% of the English-speaking people in Britain consider the BBC English, the standard English. In Hindi-speaking regions in India the language used in books and print media and spoken by the mass media is considered to be the standard Hindi. Dakkhini is a regional dialect of Hindi. Loosely speaking, Maithili, Bhojpuri, Magadhi, Braj Bhasha, Rajasthani, Awadhi, Bundelkhandi, Pahari, Kumauni, etc. are dialects of standard Hindi. However, many speakers of Maithili, Bhojpuri and Rajasthani consider their varieties to be separate languages. Maithili is treated as a language in Nepal and Bhojpuri in Mauritius.

LANGUAGES AND SCRIPT

It is difficult to define a language in terms of its script. Sometime what appears to be the same language is considered to be different languages in different regions. For instance, Hindi and Urdu are considered to be two different languages though they have the same phonological, morphological and syntactic characteristics. The same language which is called Urdu in Pakistan is called Hindi when written in Nagari script and Urdu when written in Perso-Arabic script in India. If script is the criterion to call a means of communication language, then Santhali should be viewed as four different languages because it uses four different scripts, Nagari, Bengali, Oriya and a script invented by a Santhali who calls his script a divine gift.

LANGUAGE AND SOCIETY

Languages develop while they are used by people in a society. Social developments have their impact on them. For instance, the English as spoken in Britain is somewhat different from English spoken in the USA and Canada. Though English is spoken as the mother tongue in Australia and New Zealand as well, it has their own distinct characteristics there. English spoken in India is different from the language used in South Africa. They are called regional varieties of English. Within India itself we have South Indian English, East Indian English, North Indian English and West Indian English. They differ more in pronunciation than in their vocabulary or grammatical structures.

Even within a society, language varies because of socio-economic and cultural factors. For instance, the language of the well-educated upper and middle class British is different from the language used by the working class British population. According to the sociologist Basil Bernstein, the upper class has an elaborate code while the working class uses a restricted code. At school, upper class children are more articulate than the lower class children. In America, the white population uses a kind of standard English which is different from the 'non-standard' Black English vernacular. In India, the product of English-medium public schools uses the language differently from that of the Government-run schools.

Opinions differ in regard to the relation between language and society. Edward Sapir (1884-1939), a distinguished American linguist, observed that language acts as a socialising force and affects human thought unconsciously. Language influences concept formation. That is why speakers of one language think differently from the speakers of another language. Benjamin Whorf (1897-1941) formulated Sapir-Whorf hypothesis, according to which one's perception of the world is determined by the structure of one's native language. Later on, he put forward a weaker version of the hypothesis and used the expression 'partially determined'. Mikhail Bakhtin (1895-1975), a Russian theoretician, asserted just the opposite. According to him, social differentiation leads to linguistic differentiation. Valentin Woloshinov (1973) asserted that the linguistic sign embodies the social relationship of its users and reveals their social identity. The way we use a language in India reflects the contemporary social stratification in our society. In pre-Bolshevik Russian society, there were two second person pronouns-*ty* (the equivalent of Hindi *tum*) and *vy* (the equivalent of Hindi *aap*). When the relation between the speakers and the addressee was asymmetric, the one who belonged to the upper strata of society used *ty* for the addressee and *vy* for those who were higher in social status. After revolution, the asymmetric relation become symmetric and *vy* was used in every situation. Now that the communist regime is over, the situation has changed. Again, *ty* is the pronoun of solidarity and *vy* of power. A similar change took place in China after revolution. Such examples clearly show that the change in social situation leads to linguistic change, and not vice versa.

LANGUAGE AND IDENTITY

Identity refers to the characteristics of determining *who* or what a person is on the basis of a set of elements. It could be national, ethnic, religious or linguistic. Personal identity is the identity of the 'self' whereas social identity is the identity of a social class; it indicates close similarities or affinity between individuals of a group. It is more abstract than personal identity. It is easier to talk about the identity of an Indian individual than to discuss his/her 'Indianness'. However, it is not so difficult to talk about an ethnic identity (e.g. the characteristics of Santhals or Nagas, Sikhs or Christians). Likewise, it is not difficult to establish one's linguistic identity; it is observable. Islamic identity is a religious identity but Arab identity is a racial cum linguistic identity. However, Arabic identity is the identity of those people who speak Arabic as their mother tongue. Not all of them are Arabs. People of Turkey or Indonesia have Islamic identity but they are neither Arab nor Arabic speakers. In India, the speakers of a language called Hindi are separated from the speakers of almost the same language called Urdu. In Pakistan, they all call themselves speakers of Urdu. Language, in such cases, is confused with the speaker's religion, even though it is true that some speakers of Urdu are Hindus. Sometimes language is identified with its script. The same language, if written in Devanagari script is called Hindi, and written in the Perso-Arabic script is called Urdu. However, that also is not, strictly speaking, true. Most of the tribal languages of North East India are written in the same Roman script but they have their own identities on the basis of their vocabularies and grammatical structures. Santhal, a language of the Austro Asiatic language family, is written in Devanagari in Jharkhand, Bangla in Bengal and Odiya in Odisha but it is not confused as separate languages. Linguistic identity is, thus, based on grammatical structures and vocabulary, and not on its speakers.

LANGUAGE AND NATIONALITY

The relationship between language and nationality is very complex. At the time of partition of India, in 1947, religion became the basis of the formation of Pakistan. Like the people of North-Western parts of India, the people of the eastern part of Bangal which had a Muslim majority, opted for the new nation. However, these people, who were residents of East Pakistan demanded to be separate from it on the basis of language. They struggled for liberation and Bangladesh became a new nation in 1971. The people of West Bengal in India did not choose to merge with this new nation though they were speakers of Bengali, had the same Bengali culture and were contiguous to Bangladesh.

In Pakistan, the Balochi language speakers of Balochistan are demanding separation from Pakistan even though they already have a separate identity in the form of their own state. Cultural and economic factors seem to be behind their demand for separation and their language is a unifying factor. In Punjab of Pakistan the speakers of Siraiki want their own state on the basis of their language. Contrary to this trend is the example of the separation of Uttarakhand from the Uttar Pradesh though both the states share Hindi as their common language. In other words, language is not always a factor for the formation of a state or country, though it is a very prominent factor in the formation of one's nationality.

When two identities combine, the question of national identity becomes stronger. For instance, the Kurds of Northern Iraq, Eastern Turkey, Western Iran, Eastern Syria, Armenia and Azerbaijan speak the same language, Kurdish. Right now they are residents of six different countries but they belong to the same ethnic group and speak the same language, which gives them a strong sense of nationality and they demand Kurdistan. Likewise, the Nagas of Nagaland are demanding an enlarged state of Nagaland which would include the Naga population of Manipur and Myanmar. Nigeria is a multilingual country belonging to different African tribes. It is Christianity and the English language which hold this multicultural society together. In the six ethnic-based states in North East India, it is the English language which gives them wider mobility. Though, Nagamese, the Assamese-based creole, is their common *lingua franca*, English, and not the local language, is used as a means of inner and interstate communication; it is the widely accepted means of education.

LANGUAGE AND POWER

Language is not merely a tool of communication but a powerful means of communication. It can be used by the ruling class to share power with or to keep others under control. In ancient India, Sanskrit was used by the king to have consultation with his advisors and officers and various Prakrit dialects to issue instructions to general public and get information from them. The Muslim rulers of India used Persian as the court language and Hindustani to keep themselves in touch with their subjects. During the colonial period, the British used English as a language of administration in India. As it was the only medium of instruction in higher education, it was used to keep educated Indians informed and, to an extent, to share power with English-knowing Indians. Now that the British are gone, a mutually acceptable Indian language should have been the language of administration. It is so at the regional level but at the centre English continues as a powerful language because it is mutually acceptable to the speakers of various Indian languages. Consequently, it is a dominant language, a language of knowledge dissemination and opinion formation and has a key role in our democratic system. The upper strata of Indian society uses it to separate themselves from the lower layer of society and thereby to keep themselves exclusively in control of our political system. The lower layer of our society views it as a language of upward social mobility.

As Indian society is highly stratified, Indian languages differentiate between those who have power and those who have not. Almost all Indian languages have at least two second person pronouns, one to show the solidarity relation between the interlocutors and the other, power. In Hindi-Urdu this differentiation is made by the use of *aap* for asymmetric relation and *tum* for symmetric relation. There are two or more imperative markers (Hindi *o* and -*iye*) which are used according to the sociocultural relation between the speaker and the addressee. Even the agreement markers on the verb are chosen according to this social differentiation.

English makes no such distinction by morphological marking or agreement rules but it has its one way of exercising power and maintaining social distance. Our choice of vocabulary (e.g. *ask, request, order, command, demand* and various forms of syntactic structures (e.g. direct/indirect, active/passive, use of various modal verbs) indicate what power relation we have with reference to the addresses.

Even a language which makes no such discrimination can be used persuasively to build public opinion and consolidate power.

LANGUAGE AND GENDER

Gender in English is associated with natural association of sex; all human beings are male or female; whatever is neither male or female is of neuter gender. On the contrary, in Indian languages all nouns are either masculine or feminine, just like in French or German. For instance, the word for *turnip* is feminine, in French, in Hindi, *Shalgam* is feminine. However, there is anomaly in German; the word for *woman* is feminine but the word for *wife* (*weib*) is neuter. English has *he* (for a male), *she* (for a female) and *it* (for neutre). Hindi has only one word *wo* (he/she/it) but when it takes a verb with a masculine or feminine marker, it refers to a male or a female. The word *man* refers to a male and *woman* to a female. However, *man* is also used as a generic term, meaning 'human being, male or female'. The feminist movement is against its generic use. Similarly, it is against the generic use of nouns of common gender such as *teacher*, *scholars*, *anchor*, *dancer*, *singer*, *actor*, etc. Feminist writers prefer to use *she* for a female teacher or writer. They use *she* if *everyone* refers to a female, and *he/she* if it refers to a male or female. Since *–ster*, a female counter part of *–er*, a male suffix, had become obsolete in modern English, people use them in the generic sense and use *he* as a generic referential pronoun. The feminists prefer using he/she in its place. They are willing to use *they* instead of merely *he*. Instead of the common word *chairman*, they use *chairperson*. They consider the use of *pussy* or *bitch* for women very derogatory and the use of *she* for an automobile demeaning. They are against the sexist language and dislike expressions such as *the weaker sex* or *fair sex*. They are in favour of *salesperson* instead of *salesman* and *saleswoman*. In short, they are in favour of non-sexist, positive sexual images of women. They insist that textbooks must be written from a non-sexist point of view in order to improve the image of women. Guidelines have been prepared in order to promote gender equality through books and mass media.

Gender equality means not only to use non-sexist expressions but also to be aware of the way a woman talks or uses language. For instance, in a given situation, if a man uses (1) a woman is likely to use (2):

1. *Oh shit*, you have spoilt the milk!
2. *Oh dear*, you have spoilt the milk!

Such a difference exists in the use of adjectives, as in (3) and (4):

3. What a *terrific* idea! (male speech)
4. What a *charming/divine* idea! (female speech)

Where man use *great, terrific, cool* and *neat*, women prefer to use *adorable, charming, sweet, lovely* and *divine.*

There is difference in the choice of an imperative and use of question tags. A woman is more likely to say (5) than (6).

5. Would you close the door?
6. Will you close the door?

Men need to be more sensitive to the way women use language. The fact that some men belittle or make fun of female speech is indicative of the fact that there is social inequality in regard to the use of language by men and women. The teacher of English as a second language should make his/her students aware of it. He/she may have sexual disparity between the language of male and female in his/her mother tongue but it may not be in an identical situation. The teacher should note the difference in the categorisation of such usage and warn them against it.

The feminist movement across languages is well aware of the power of language and is trying to neutralise it. Whether it will be done permanently or in a new way of discrimination will emerge only future can tell.

In short, the use of a language differs because of social, political, ethnic or religious identity of its speakers. The teacher should not only be aware of them but warn his/her students about them.

2

Multilingualism and Language Teaching in Schools

MULTILINGUALISM: ITS NATURE AND SCOPE

India is a multilingual country. According to Singh and Manohar (1993), India has 325 community specific languages which use 25 scripts. Out of these languages, 129 belong to the Indo-Aryan subfamily, 121 to the Tibeto-Burman subfamily, 34 to the Dravidian family and 4 to the Andamanese family of languages. Two languages (Arabic and Hebrew) belong to the Semitic family and seven to other subfamilies of the Sino-Tibetan languages. Two languages (Pasto and Persian) belong to Indo-Iranian subfamily and three (English, French and Armenian) to the other branches of Indo-European language family. Three languages Nagamese, Nefamese and Kol are languages used only at the bilingual level of communication, that is, for intergroup communication.

Of the 325 languages identified by the *People of India Survey*, 199 languages are restricted only to one state or union territory (UT), 48 languages are spoken in two states/UT, 29 in three states/UT, 12 in four states/UT and 14 in five states/UT). Hindi and Urdu are spoken in 22 states. Next to them are Marwari, Punjabi, Gujarati, Nepali, Marathi, Telugu, English and Sindhi. Twenty two of these languages are specified in the Eighth Schedule of the constitution of India. According to *Census of India* (2001) 41.03 per cent people of India declared Hindi as their mothertongue, 8.11 per cent Bengali, 7.19 per cent Telugu, 6.99 per cent Marathi, 5.91 per cent Tamil and 4.48 per cent Gujarati, etc. Only 0.02 per cent declared English as their mothertongue, though approximately 200 million Indians claim to know English as a second third language. There are speakers of English among all scheduled language speakers of India. English is spoken as a second/third language by some people in almost all speech communities. In the North-East of India, 70.38 per cent Khasi speakers, 65.35 per cent Manipuri/Maitei speakers, 55 per cent Mizo speakers, 44.45 per cent Lotha speakers, 46 per cent Angami speakers and 42 per cent Ao speakers speak English as a second language. Though linguistic heterogeneity is generally found within a language family and English does not belong to Tibeto-Burman language family, it has widely spread in the North-East India because it has been the medium of instruction there for more than two centuries. It is for this reason that almost all high school graduates throughout India know English.

The linguistic diversity of India is highlighted by the large number of minor languages and the communities that speak them. According to Singh and Manohar (1993), nearly 63 per cent of the speech communities speak languages listed in the eighth schedule. Speech communities in India are by and large bilingual, some are even multilingual. However, not all members of a bilingual or multilingual community are bilingual or multilingual; only some people are familiar with a language other than their mothertongue. This diversity of languages has to be taken into account while discussing the role of language(s) across curriculum, especially at the level of high school, college and university.

MULTILINGUALISM AS A RESOURCE AND A STRATEGY

According to the 2011 census, the literacy level in India was approximately 72 per cent. The National Literacy Commission wanted to bring it up to 75 per cent. In order to meet the target, it involved the local panchayats and converged its programme with the state development programme. The elementary education is imparted through the medium of the learner's mothertongue, or a regional language with which the child is supposed to be informally familiar. At this stage the emphasis was on functional literacy. In 2005, the National Council of Educational Research and Training prepared the National Curriculum Framework for school education. It proposed that English be introduced from class III of primary schools. When the *Knowledge Commission* (2005-2007) evaluated the situation, it concluded that the school-learners cannot have access to knowledge without exposure to English. It found that the school learners who are not trained in English are always at a disadvantage when they go in far higher education. It recommended that English be introduced as a subject right from class I. It suggested that modalities be fixed for teachers' training, production of suitable teaching materials and necessary material support for the teaching of English. It emphasized the role of libraries in providing inclusive access to knowledge. Obviously the community-based information system that it wants to develop is more feasible in the local language than in English but it did not fail to emphasize the role of English as a library language. The Commission emphasized bilingualism or multilingualism even at the elementary level of education. It did not make it clear what the role of Hindi would be at this level in multilingual education. It may be that Hindi should also be introduced as a compulsory subject. It may be pointed out that both Hindi and English are needed if one moves out of one's own speech community or region, Hindi for everyday interaction and English for official purposes. It may also be mentioned that Hindi is used for administrative purpose in the Hindi-speaking region.

Researchers during the past fifty years have pointed out that multilingualism has positive effects. According to Klinger (1991), multilingualism has the following effects:

- Bilingual children show consistent advantages of tasks of both verbal and non-verbal abilities.
- They display advanced metalinguistic abilities, especially in controlling language processing.
- Simultaneous acquisition settings have cognitive advantage of being quick bilingual learners.
- Bilingual children become verbally fluent without waiting for higher proficiency.

Psycholinguists have reported that early acquisition of two or more languages is more convenient than trying to be so at a later stage, especially after attaining puberty. A person who knows more than one language can be precise and experience the world through more than one lens and that is what is pedagogically important. As many Indian children grow up in a bilingual neighbourhood, they know two languages informally before they go to school. Bilingual education consolidates and enlarges their knowledge.

Multilingualism should be viewed as a powerful resource in India which enables a person to interact with a cross section of people of various linguistic groups. A multilingual can talk to speakers of languages he/she knows and read their literature; he/she does not have to depend on translation. He/she finds it convenient to travel in the areas where those languages are spoken, interact with people and understand them better. He/she can feel close to a person if he/she speaks his/her language. In short, he/she can use the language strategically on right occasions. A multilingual teacher can handle a class better than a monolingual one because he/she can develop close relation with his/her students. In short, multilingualism empowers people better than monolingualism. Agnihotri has shown convincingly how multilingualism is an assest, rather than a hindrance, in Indian classrooms.

MULTILINGUALISM AND CURRICULUM TRANSACTION

Multilingualism in Cosmopolitan Cities

Multilingualism in India is clearly visible in all metropolitan cities. For example, according to 2001 census, in Delhi 81 per cent people spoke Hindi as their mothertongue, 7.2 per cent Punjabi, 6.3 per cent Urdu, 1.5 per cent Bengali, and less than 1 per cent spoke Tamil, Malayalam, Gujarati, Nepali, Sindhi, Oriya, Telugu, Marathi, Kashmiri and Kannada. Language-wise details of speakers are not available yet for 2011 census, but it may be on the same pattern. In Chandigarh, 68% people spoke Hindi, 30 % Punjabi, and less than 7% spoke Urdu, Tamil, Bengali, Nepali, Gujarati, Malayalam, Kashmiri, Oriya, Telugu, Marathi, Dogri and Kannada. In Goa, 57% people spoke Konkani, 23% Marathi, 5.7% Hindi, 5.6% Kannada, 4% Urdu, 1.25% Malayalam and less than 1% Telugu, Gujarati, English, Tamil, Bengali Oriya, Nepali and Tulu as their mothertongues. Kolkata, Mumbai, Chennai, Bangluru and Hyderabad present multilingualism similar to Delhi.

If we go by the principle that children ought to be taught mainly through their mothertongues at the initial (primary) level, we need schools where all these languages are used as the media of instruction. As a matter of fact, there are schools where these languages are used as media of instruction in all metropolitan cities, though most people prefer sending their children to English or Hindi medium schools in Delhi, English or Bengali or Hindi medium in Kolkata, English or Tamil medium in Chennai and English or Hindi or Marathi medium in Mumbai. Hyderabad has schools which have mainly English, Urdu, Telugu or Hindi as medium of instruction. According to Sriharirao (1993), we have a similar situation in Bhilai, an industrial city in Chhatisgarh, which has speakers of Hindi, Bengali, Marathi, Tamil, Kannada, Malayalam and Telugu in that order. I presume there is a similar situation in Jamshedpur, Durgapur, Rourkela, Bokaro and Ranchi. There are central schools in such areas which have English or Hindi medium. In so far as regional language medium schools are concerned, they are mainly run by the community-based organisations of their speakers in these cities.

PATTERNS IN UNITED STATES OF AMERICA AND CANADA

In the USA, there are bilingual schools for the speakers of minority languages such as Spanish, Korean and Vietnamese. Such schools have English as their medium of instruction but minority languages are taught compulsorily for their native speakers and one or more subjects are taught through their medium at the primary level. In Canada, in areas which have a sizeable French-speaking population, French is compulsorily taught to the native speakers of English and English to the native speakers of French. One or more subjects are taught through the medium of French to the speakers of English at the elementary levels. Similar efforts are made in some areas in France and Germany for the children who are speakers of a minority language. There is no reason why such an arrangement cannot be made in India.

It may be pointed out that the Knowledge Commission has made a similar recommendation for the teaching of English is elementary schools in India. According to it, English will be taught from class I and will be chosen as the medium of instruction for one subject from class III. The Commission has made this recommendation so that the teaching of English is integrated into the school curriculum. Teaching some subjects through English would reduce the gulf between the English-medium schools and regional language medium schools. It will give incentive to students to speak English fluently which is not the case when it is taught only as a subject. Children having their mothertongue in minority in an area will study through the medium of the majority language such as Hindi or English but will read one subject through the medium of their mothertongue, so that they can keep fluency in it and use it meaningfully.

BILINGUALISM IN BORDER AREAS OF INDIAN STATES

Indian states are divided mainly on the basis of language. Thus, Tamil is the language of the majority in Tamilnadu and Kannada in Karnataka. In the rural areas in the linguistics states, the language of the state is the medium of instruction and there is no controversy about it. However, in the border areas, children are usually bilingual. For instance, a resident of Belgaon may have Marathi, rather than Kannada, as his/her mothertongue and may like to have it as the medium of instruction. In all fairness he/she should have that freedom of choice. From standard III onwards, he/she may study Kannada. He/she should study Hindi and English, according to the three language formula. In Karnataka, a controversy arose in this regard when Kannada was imposed on all government run schools but the court intervened and the judgement was given in favour of the scheme given above. A similar situation may be there in border areas in Bihar, Bengal and Odisha, or in Maharashtra and Gujarat. A flexible language policy can be adopted in all such cases.

HIERARCHICAL STATUS OF INDIAN LANGUAGES

People in general seem to be aware of the problems arising out of multilingualism in their lives. They seem to be aware of the hierarchical status of languages. For instance, in the Maithili-speaking area in Bihar, the government has given an alternative to have elementary education through the medium of Maithili, though it is hardly availed of. Instead, people prefer to send their children to either Hindi or English medium schools. Similar is the case in the tribal areas in Jharkhand. Though Santali, Mundari, Ho and Kharia are regional tribal languages which are available as media of education at the primary school level, tribals prefer to send their children to English or Hindi medium schools. Pedagogically it is available to a person to begin education in one's mothertongue and then move to other languages but people's perception is different. In other words, the preferred language choice should be from mothertongue to regional language to national languages such as, Hindi and English but in reality it is English, Hindi or regional language and then the mothertongue. People look at the choice of languages in terms of their chances of upward social mobility. A Santali speaker thinks that his/her employment opportunity increases if he/she chooses Hindi rather than Santali, and it increases even more if he/she opts for English. However situation is different if he/she has Bengali, Marathi or any state language as his/her mothertongue. In such a case the state language is his/her first choice, English, the second choice and Hindi is the third choice. A realist teacher is well aware of the preference of the public and is guided more by it than by the policy of the state. He/she has to choose the language of the majority or the language the management of the school chooses as the medium of instruction. He/she can choose the bilingual method only if he/she is advised to do so.

The comparative prestige of languages and their value in the job market are more important factors for language learners and their parents than their psychological desirability. People assert their right to choose the languages they want to study and are not influenced by the facilities made available to them to implement the language policy of government. That is why they neglect the choice of the mother tongue.

HOME LANGUAGE AND SCHOOL LANGUAGE

The home language of children entering the school may sometimes be different from the language used as the medium of instruction at school. In fact, a class may have children of varied and heterogeneous background, so much so that their language cannot be used as the medium. In such a case, the language of the neighbourhood which children pick up while interacting with their peers should be used. Here again the willingness of one group in a community to have its children adopt the language of another group will depend upon the perception of its national or international status. In heterogeneous tribal society in the North East India, none of the mother tongues of children has a national status. In fact, some of them have no state-wise recognition; they are spoken in limited areas within the states. If speakers of such languages want their children to have education through the medium of English, it is not surprising. These children do not enter school with the knowledge of vocabulary or grammatical structure of English and they have to have a rudimentary knowledge of the language at school before they start learning any specific subject. It may be better to make them familiar with spoken English so that they take interest in activities inside and outside the classroom. It is not the case that they do not interact but they do so in a language i.e. Nagamese which they are not ready to recognise as a language. A similar situation arises in newly developed industrial areas which have heterogeneous population. But, in these areas, some kind of broken Hindi is used as the lingua franca. It is better that initial training starts in whatever form of Hindustani is used there so that there is a meaningful language interaction. Such a situation is entirely different from the bilingual areas in the USA and Canada and needs indigenous solution.

LANGUAGE AS A SCHOOL SUBJECT AND AS A MEDIUM OF INSTRUCTION

As we have already pointed out, the English language is going to be taught as a school subject from Class I in all primary schools in India. That is what the National Programme on Education 2005 suggests – where the bilingual training suggests that at least one subject (other than the language) will be taught through the medium of English after children have some acquaintance with English. It will make them learn language faster and better.

CENTRALITY OF LANGUAGE IN CURRICULUM

We have discussed various solutions in which a language is taught in a multilingual classroom. The multilingualism arising out of the migration of people of various linguistic groups is one thing, and that in a permanently heterogeneous linguistic society is another. At present people choose English as a medium of instruction in both situations. What we suggest is that the starting point should be the language children use outside the classroom and then they may be gradually introduced to spoken English. In such a case they will have a minimum vocabulary to begin with which can be developed as and when other subjects are chosen to be taught through English. The language of these subjects will enrich their vocabulary further and the practice in speaking English will make them more articulate and fluent.

QUALITIES AND COMPETENCE OF TEACHERS IN MULTILINGUAL CLASSROOMS

If a classroom consists of children who have various languages (or more than one language) spoken in their neighbourhood and it is not homogeneous from the point of view of language they speak at home, the teacher has a limited choice. He/she has to conduct the class in the language chosen by school authorities. However, if the teacher happens to be multilingual, he/she will be sensitive to the linguistic problems faced by students in participating in the classroom discussion. In fact, teachers all over India are at least bilingual; they know one dominant language and English. In case they know more languages, it is better.

We should not think that introducing English language teachers to the general principles of bilingual education and multilingual environment is enough. They should be made acquainted with the specific multilingual situation prevailing in an area and with special language and cultural characteristics of their students. Of course, their belief in the goals of bilingual education is important. Along with this, the school should have a 'linguistic profile' of individual teachers and the extent to which they are familiar with respective languages. It is important to know to what degree they utilise them at home and other domains. We must note that the teacher's attitude and behaviour about multilingualism in the classroom may have subtle influence on students. The multilingual principal of a school will be enthusiastic about bilingual education and can promote its cause a lot. Based on his/her knowledge of bilingual ability of the staff, he/she will decide which subject will be taught in which language. He/she will sort out related problems so that the programme is implemented in a balanced manner. In a multilingual situation, grouping pupils according to their bilingual potential is complex and the school organisation has to be flexible and farsighted about it. The success of the bilingual programme depends on all these factors.

To sum up, though the language situation is complex in India, it has a set pattern in a specific language region. The people who are in the central area of a linguistic state are monolingual or at best bilingual if they are educated and know English. In the border areas, they are, by and large, bilingual', they have the ability to use the language of the neighbouring state orally (i.e. listening and speaking). In cities they are multilingual.

People in metropolitan cities come from almost all over India, from other cities, villages and even tribal areas. They come for their livelihood and make necessary adjustments, including linguistic adjustment. A middle class government servant or company employee settles preferably in an area where other persons who share their mothertongue with him live. He/she knows his/her mothertongue and acquires a degree of fluency in Hindi. He/she uses English and Hindi in the office, his/her mothertongue while talking to a fellow colleague who share his/her language, and Hindi with his/her domestic helper, pedlar, vendor and tradesmen. When he/she picks up some vocabulary of that region, he/she uses English-Hindi with sprinkling of the language of that region. He/she may get used to mixing Hindi with his/her mothertongue even at home. That is true of all professionals, even a school teacher. Even a monolingual teacher becomes multilingual in such an environment. If the teacher practises multilingualism while talking to his/her students outside the classroom, he/she can establish a better rapport with them. That is a fact which is to be recognised by an academic person in such a city.

3

Expansion of English as a World Language

> You taught me language; and my profit on it
> Is, I know how to curse: the red plague rid you,
> For learning me your language!
>
> —Shakespeare, *The Tempest*, 363

THE KNOWLEDGE OF A LANGUAGE

When a person knows a language, he/she can speak it and be understood by others who know that language. The knowledge of a language enables him/her to combine sounds into words, words in phrases and phrases into sentences. Knowing a language means having the ability to produce sentences in that language and understanding them even if the person has not heard them before. This is what Noam Chomsky means by the 'creative aspect of language use'. Not every speaker of a language can create great literature but he/she creates new sentences and understands new sentences used by others. He/she may not be very innovative while using the language but can appreciate other's innovative use of that language.

THE KNOWLEDGE OF TWO OR MORE LANGUAGES

Many people in the world know more than one language. It means they can communicate in the mother-tongue as well as in some other language(s). A person who knows one language is a *monolingual*. If he/she knows two languages, he/she is a *bilingual*. If he/she knows more than two languages, he/she is a *multilingual*. A monolingual child can become bilingual or multilingual if he/she lives in a bilingual or multilingual society. Bilingualism or multilingualism is sometimes associated with migration. For instance, if a Kannada-speaking child grows up in a Telugu-speaking area, he/she is most likely to pick up Telugu as well, and be a bilingual. If he/she migrates to (or is born in) an area where Urdu is also spoken, he/she will pick up Urdu as well. But this is not the only way of being a bilingual or multilingual. One can pick up a new language (e.g. English) at school and become the speaker of that language (English) as well.

Acquiring the knowledge of two or more languages as a child is not an uphill task. Languages are structured and human beings have innate ability to recognise these structures. This knowledge is called *universal grammar*. A specific language is not a prototype of universal grammar; it differs from it to some extent because of parametric variations. As a learner has a tacit knowledge of the principles that guide a language under certain parameters, he/she understands the limits of his/her language and knows what he/she may (or may not) use. As a bilingual knows two languages, he/she knows the difference between them. But his/her knowledge of this difference depends on his/her exposure to them. Suppose a bilingual is born in a society in which his/her mother-tongue is different from the other language he/she has acquired, he/she is likely to have no clear distinction between the two languages till he/she is aware of their formal grammars. The Spanish-speaking Americans raised in the English-speaking society are likely to use "Spanglish", a mixture o Spanish and English, in which Spanish or English is a dominant element. The child may not be aware of the status of his/her language till he/she learns these languages formally at school and becomes aware of their different grammatical rules. Suppose a bilingual child is forced to be monolingual at school. For example, he/she goes to an English-medium school where Spanish is not taught at all. The use of Spanish elements in his English is considered to be 'sloppy' or 'faulty'. On the other hand, if there is influence of English on his/her Spanish, that is not considered to be so bad.

Acquiring both the languages (i.e. L_1 and L_2) equally well is not easy. To an extent, L_2 acquisition is like L_1 acquisition. Like learners of L_1, learners of L_2 construct their grammar. Initially L_2 learner's grammar is an inter-lingual grammar; it is a grammar second language learners create on the way to acquiring, more or less, a complete grammar of the target language. Interlanguage grammars do not violate the principles of universal grammar, rather they show the attempt of the learner to reach the level of the grammar of the first language learner. It is true of any language learning situation. As to how far the learner succeeds depends on his/her exposure to the language and its analysis guided by both internal and external factors.

EXPANSION OF ENGLISH AS THE MOTHER TONGUE

It was in the fifth century that the speakers of what we call 'British English' arrived in England from Scandinavia (Northern Europe) and spread to parts of Wales, Cornwall, Cambria and South Scotland where Celtic languages were spoken. After the Norman invasion of 1066, many speakers of English migrated to Northern Scotland. From the twelfth century, they started settling in Ireland as well. During the sixteenth century about 5 to 7 million people of Britain spoke English as their mother tongue.

USA

By the sixteenth century, the British started settling in northern America. By 1640, 25,000 speakers of English settled in New England. During the seventeenth century continental immigrants settled in New York and Pennsylvania. The eighteenth century saw a wave of immigrants from Ireland and Scotland. By 1790, there were nearly 4 million English speakers who were mostly settled on the Atlantic coast. The French settlers occupied the northern part of the continent, the Dutch settled in New York and the Germans in Pennsylvania. Within a generation or two, they picked up English through a natural process of assimilation. When an independent state of the USA was formed in 1776, English was declared to be the State language. By the year 2000, 215 million people (86% of the US population) spoke English as their mother tongue. Even the small minority which had Spanish or some other language as their mother tongue preferred English as their first language at school.

Canada

In Canada, the speakers of English had the speakers of French as their rivals but they dominated the scene because they were more than the speakers of French. Only recently, French was declared a co-official language in Quebec, one of its provinces.

The Caribbean Islands

The British settlers in the islands brought African slaves of different linguistic background. Their arrival led to the growth of Pidgin English which developed into Creole. However, the heterogeneous population chose their own varieties of English as their mother tongue.

Australia and New Zealand

The Australian settlement of British prisoners started by 1770. The free settlers arrived first in 1788. Since Australia became mainly the land of British settlers, English was declared to be their language. In 2000 there were 19 million speakers of English in Australia.

New Zealand, which started as a British settlement, had immigrants from other European countries as well. In 2002, its total population was over 3.8 million. They have chosen English as their mother-tongue, with a distinctive New Zealander vocabulary, and an increased use of Maori words.

South Africa

South Africa was colonised by the Dutch in 1652. The British controlled it in 1806 and their settlement began by 1820. In 1822, English was declared to be the language of law, education and most aspects of public life. It is a minority language in South Africa and is spoken by nearly 4 million people out of the total population of 34 million. Though Afrikaan is the language of the majority, English is their second language.

Besides the figures given above, English is used as L_1 by 28 thousand people in Gibraltar, 100 thousand in Grenada, 150 thousand in Hong Kong, 37 million in Ireland, 600 thousand in Liberia, 380 thousand in Malaysia, 150 thousand in Papua New Guinea, 20 thousand in Philippines, 100 thousand in Puerto Rico, 43 thousand in St. Lucia, 114 thousand in St. Vincent and Grenadines, 500 thousand in Sierra Leone, 350 thousand in Singapore, 260 thousand in Surinam, 10 thousand in Sri Lanka, 50 thousand in Swaziland, 110 thousand in Zambia, 250 thousand in Zimbabwe [as claimed by David Crystal (2003)]. According to the Census of India, 2001, 226,449 people use English as their mother tongue in India. According to Crystal, over 329 million people use English as their first language. Some African countries, which were British colonies earlier, use some English-based pidgin or creole in their daily use.

ENGLISH AS A SECOND LANGUAGE

Approximately 430 million people speak English as a second language in the world. The following table gives us an idea of how widespread is the range of its speakers:

Table 1: Speakers of English as a Second Language: World wise

Countries	*People (Million)*	*Countries*	*People (Million)*
Bangladesh	3.50	Nigeria	60.00
Botswana	0.63	Pakistan	17.00
Cameroon	7.20	Papua New Guinea	3.00
Canada	7.00	Philippines	40.00
Fiji	0.17	Sierra Leone	4.10
Ghana	1.40	Singapore	2.00
Hong Kong	2.20	South Africa	11.00
India	200.00	Sir Lanka	1.90
Kenya	2.70	Tanzania	4.00
Malawi	0.54	Uganda	2.50
Malaysia	7.00	UK	1.50
Mauritius	0.20	USA	256.00
Namibia	0.70	Zambia	1.80
Nepal	7.00	Zimbabwe	5.30

Source: Based on Crystal, 2003.

A comparison of the figures suggests that more people speak English as (i.e. 430 million) than those who speak it as L_1 (329 million). It shows how important it is to teach English well as a second language.

Number of People who Speak English as their Second Language

According to Crystal (2003: 62-65) 430.6 million people speak English as a second language all over the world. Besides, it is a co-official language in India and Ireland.

ENGLISH AS A FOREIGN LANGUAGE

No language is taught all over the world as a foreign language as English. It is taught vey widely in China, Russia, Japan, Korea, Brazil, Indonesia, almost all East European and Latin American countries. The global audio-visual market, especially the satellite TV, the internet and computer-based communication, including language-related and document handling software have made English the most dominant language of the world. It has left French far behind. According to Crystal (2003), 99% per cent of European Organisations use English as a working language as opposed to 63% French. As an international medium of science and technology, English has a more influential place than French, Russian, China or Spanish. All these factors have convinced people who do not have English as their L_1 or L_2 to opt for it as a foreign language almost all over the world.

VARIETIES OF ENGLISH

The widespread use of language has developed its local varieties in countries where it is used as a first or second language. Thus, we have America, Canadian, Australian, Indian, South African and other varieties of English. While the use of English as a language of wider communication continues to exert pressure on it towards global uniformity, the shift in its status in many countries from foreign language to second language has led to the development of a large number of local varieties. Though the trends are contradictory, they are natural. English has two main functions these days. On the one hand, it is growing as the language of international communication, on the other, it is the vehicle of national identity in many new nations which have adopted it as a language of national unity. It has encouraged the development of new forms and hybrid structures to establish their separate identity. The varieties of English can be recognised as in Fig. 1.

Earlier the print media played a vital role in maintaining a uniform standard, now it is being gradually displaced by the electronic media. Moreover, the electronic media is getting a more widespread range than the print media has. The BBC and CNN are attracting more viewers worldwide than the number

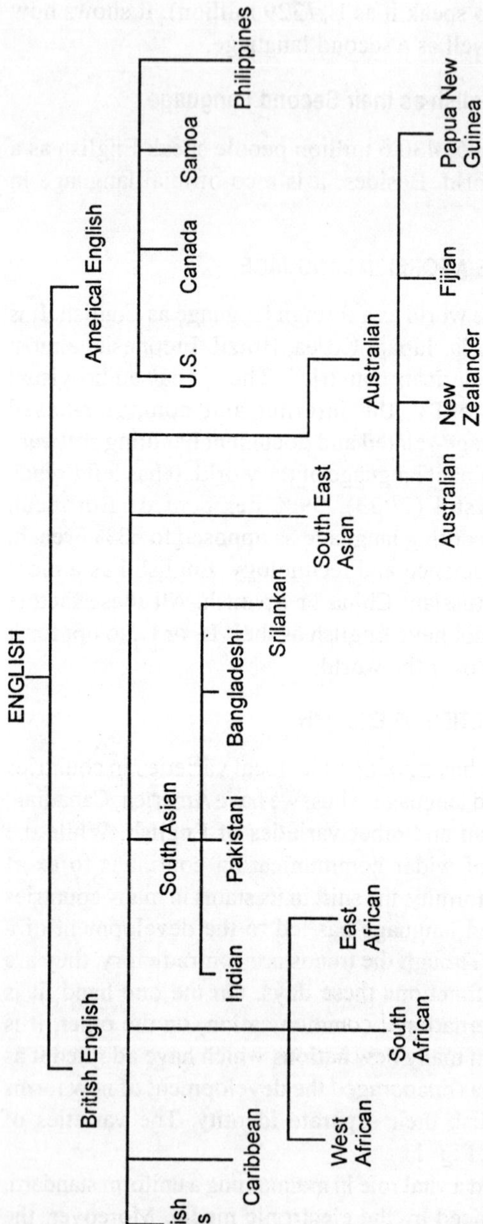

Fig. 1: Varieties of World Englishes

of readers of world's leading newspaper had. Recently AlJazeera's broadcast in English has gained international popularity though it is based on the Arab soil. Such channels are likely to act as a uniting force and maintain an acceptable standard. The growing trend towards the internationalisation of education and increasing importance of world youth culture are likely to promote the cause of international intelligibility of the language. The grip that the standard British English had over Indian English may become loose in favour of Indian and American English but the goal of international intelligibility will not be lost.

GLOBALISATION OF ENGLISH

The growth of global trade has led to the growth of transnational corporates which conduct their international activities mainly in English. The global distribution of labour has also promoted the growth of English. International joint venture in industries has encouraged the adoption of English as a lingua franca and so has the transfer of technology by transnational companies. Teleworking (i.e., working away from a central office having telecommunications) has also increased the use of English. The more business takes place over the international phone lines, the more is going to be the dominance of English as a common language. It is because of the increasing importance of English that it has become the language of upward social mobility in India. The lack of fluency in speaking English is considered a bar to certain jobs.

ENGLISH AS THE OFFICIAL LANGUAGE

Outside the countries where English is the mother tongue, it is the official language of Ghana, Uganda, Zambia and Zimbabwe. It is the co-official language in Kenya, Nigeria, Cameroon (in Africa) and in India. In these (and many other) countries it has developed through the education system. In the post-colonial era, there is no outside compulsion to use it but, along with regional languages, it is needed as a medium of instruction, especially in the field of higher education. Though it is not the language spoken by most of the population, it is used for a wide range of functions among those who speak and write it. To an extent, it has been *localised* or nativised and has developed its own innovative characteristics. Although these different varieties of English are not internally uniform, in majority of cases there is sufficient common ground to talk about a particular national variety. Its discourse style has its own indigenous flavour.

The constitution of India recognised English as a co-official language till Hindi was acceptable to all Indians. Uptil now Hindi has not been accepted as the sole official language. English is used not only for practical purposes but is a shared means of communication of people of diverse mother tongues. That way it is bonded with national consciousness and identity. It is the main link with South Indian and North East India. It keeps us in live contact with the world. The knowledge of English enables Indian citizens to have global mobility; they pick up jobs in any part of the world. They work in key positions in multinational companies and are gainfully employed in the United Nation and its various agencies.

The Role of English Medium Schools

Even in the post-colonial era, English medium education is supposed to be a better means to economic success. That is why there are more English medium schools in India today than there were during British days. Not only that, there are private teaching shops, which run courses like the *Rapidex English Speaking Course*. This book claims to teach spoken English in sixty days or so. The fact that more than ten million copies of the *Rapidex* have been sold establishes the point that Indians have realised the importance of English in personal advancement. *Rapidex* teaches spoken English through the medium of Hindi, still it fulfils the need of the aspirants of spoken English. Some so-called English medium schools are manned by teachers who are not proficient in English. Such English medium system of education undermines the attempts of the under-privileged children to improve their English. One often wonders what the best way of teaching English as a second language is: to provide better English language teachers for a period or two every day in the class or to expose them to local varieties of sub-standard English throughout the teaching hours, even if the teachers of physical or social studies may not be able to use good English in the classroom. Such a school reinforces the regional varieties of English which may not be intelligible to people from other parts of India, let alone the native speakers of English.

Challenges of Teaching and Learning English India

The key problem in the effective teaching of English in schools in India is the supply of good teachers. Well-trained teachers may not be available to teach English at primary and secondary levels. Those who have the necessary skills may like to concentrate in urban areas or gravitate to better paid jobs in India or abroad. Good teachers of English, whether they are in an English medium or a regional language medium school, can prepare students well for higher education in which the medium of education is mainly English. They must have received good training in professional language training institutes. The demands for the teachers of English as a second language is bound to increase due to the government's commitment to compulsory education and an increasing demand for English-knowing professionals in India.

As we cannot afford to bring a large number of native speakers of standard English to India, we will have to find out a viable alternative. We have to train competent Indian teachers of English who can teach and promote a brand of English that is mutually intelligible to all Indians and pave the way for those technical and professional persons who want to go out of India to render their services in specialised fields. The future syllabus of Indian teachers being trained in English will have to be revised, keeping these goals in mind. They will also have to remember that there are at least three types of learners of English in India: (i) those who want to use English in everyday life; (ii) those who want to pursue higher education in India or abroad, and (iii) those who want to be technically advanced professionals. The new syllabus will have to keep their needs in view and the newly trained teachers of English will have to work hard to fulfil their aspirations. Now that English is increasingly embedded in our education, industry, information technology and other domains, it is hard to dislodge it. It necessitates the need for a long-range planning for the teaching of English keeping its global and country specific requirements in view. The training of English language teachers should emphasize the role of English as a unifying and dynamic force in society.

4
Factors that Influence Second/ Foreign Language Learning

> The learning of a foreign language involves far more than simply learning skills or a system of rules...It involves an alteration in self-image, the adoption of new social and cultural behaviours and ways of being, and therefore has a significant impact on the social values of the learners.
> —*Williams* (1994:77)

PERSONAL PERSPECTIVE

All school-going children are exposed to several factors that affect their second language learning. In so far as learners' personal factors are concerned, we would like to emphasise three points: their age, motivation and attitude, and aptitude. Although each of these factors will be discussed separately, they affect each other in a dynamic way and it is impossible to decide what exactly their separate roles are.

Age

The critical period hypothesis, discussed on pages 68-69, is associated with the age factor. It claims that it is impossible to acquire a native-speaker—like proficiency if learning starts after the critical period. It is normally associated with Lenneberg (1967) whose conclusions are based on neurological development of the brain of the learner. Once the maturation process is completed, the brain does not function as flexibly to pick up a new language as it does before. Johnson and Newport's cognitive research (1989) supports this point of view. Their study of late learning of English by Chinese and Korean children provide evidence in their support. While younger learners have 'brain plasticity' and less inhibition, older learners have analytical ability and better understanding of grammatical rules. While younger learners are more successful in informal and naturalistic settings, older learners are more comfortable in formal instructional background.

APTITUDE AND INTELLIGENCE

Regardless of factors like age and motivation, some students seem to be better in learning a second/foreign language than others. The inherent ability to learn language is called *aptitude.* it is a combination of four factors:

- the ability to identify and remember sounds of the new language;
- the ability to recognize how words function grammatically in a sentence;
- the ability to induce grammatical rules from examples;
- the ability to recognize and recall words and phrases.

—*Carroll* (1958)

Carroll argued that intelligence should be seen as distinct from aptitude but Gardner (1983, 1999) defined intelligence as a part of aptitude. Sternberg (2002) argued that language learning aptitude needs to be defined to include creative and practical language acquisition abilities, besides memory and analytical skills. Whatever may be the relation between aptitude and intelligence, they are essential components of language acquisition abilities.

ATTITUDE AND MOTIVATION

Motivation is related to the person's drive to achieve his/her target. Gardner and Lambert (1972) differentiate between integrative motivation and instrumental motivation. The learner's attitude towards the language matters. A positive attitude motivates the learner to acquire language fast whereas a negative attitude affects him/her negatively. A learner who learns the language in a classroom may have an integrative motivation to learn but desire to get a high grade is instrumental motivation. Aptitude, together with motivation, is probably the best predictor of success in second/foreign language acquisition. Differences in learning styles and learning strategies, languages anxiety and personality factors also affect the rate of attainment. In a dynamic view of language acquisition, all individual factors interact. The mode of interaction keeps on changing while the process of language acquisition goes on.

NEEDS

It is generally accepted that motive to engage in a particular activity is based on underlying needs.

The question is whose needs should be taken into account: the institutional needs or individual needs? Curriculum developers give priority to institutional needs. They rely on information supplied by institutions which clearly define what goals the language teaching curriculum is supposed to achieve. Such an orientation marginalizes the interest of individuals and compels them to play passive, subservient roles, Tollefson (1991) denounces a covert policy based on institutional needs analysis which leads immigrants in the UK and USA to such language training that forces them to minimum wage jobs. The programmes of English for special purposes in the UK are designed to keep them at the lowest ladder. Auenbach (1995) criticises the practice of identifying learners' needs with institutional needs. He argues that the sociopolitical environment of the workplace should be emphasised as much as the attitudinal and motivational factors of the persons who are recruited for job-oriented second language learning. Jasso-Agnilar (2010) suggests the use of multiple sources and methods to identify learners' needs so that reliable conclusions could be arrived at. Language training that does not meet the needs of learners is bound to fail from the motivational point of view and similar is its fate if it ignores the social context in which the learner lives.

Maslow (1970) assumes a hierarchy of needs from the basic physical needs (e.g. food) to higher needs of approval, identification, self-esteem, achievement, knowledge, exploration, etc., the fulfilment of which leads to self-realization. All these are psychological motives. As needs refer to all of them, they involve psychological motivation and influence learning. Gardner and Lambert (1972) call needs instrumental motives. They are needed to get ahead of others in one's career, and answer questions such as 'is it necessary to get ahead in certain professional domain?' The results of a needs-analysis constitute the most important argument in favour of choosing English as a second language in India. To acquire a working-knowledge of communication skills is the basic need of a person entering a school in India. Since it is the need of every child whose parents want him/her to have it for their upward social mobility (see chapter II for details), it is a personal as well as social need.

The Knowledge Commission (2006) of the Government of India recommends "to increase assess to English language training across the population, and the promotion of English in school education at the primary level in India for increasing access to knowledge" (p. 31). It recommends the teaching of English as a language starting from class I to ensure that at the end of twelve years of schooling, every student is proficient in English, apart from the language of his/her region.

In so far as Indian context is concerned, our positive attitude towards learning English is a big factor. It is because of instrumental motivation of doing well in the classroom and competitive examinations to enable a candidate to seek admission in central universities and all India institutes of medical and technological sciences. Some students have aptitude to pursue English to gain proficiency so that they can appreciate English literature and culture. By and large, it is the urge to have better education in the subjects of their choice which motivates them to know English better. As English is the medium of education in such institutes, it gets priority over one's first language, i.e. one's mother tongue, at the time of admission. In such a case it is instrumental motivation.

SOCIAL PERSPECTIVE

Social factors play a crucial role in the second language development of the child. These factors relate to socio-economic status, bilingual environment, frequency of language use, home environments, etc.

Socio-economic Status

As discussed earlier, from the beginning of the twentieth century social perspective has been a significant point in the study of language learning. Two British linguists—B. Malinowaski (1935) and J.R. Firth (1968) focussed on the need for studying the 'context of situation' in which language is spoken. Malinowaski argued that language, an abstract entity, is manifested in different forms in different societies. Firth suggested that the socio-economic and religious backgrounds in which the speakers of a language live must be looked into. Though they did not speak anything about the second language teaching directly, the implication of their remarks are clear. A proper understanding of the second language depends upon the context of situation in which it was produced. The recognition of the fact led to the teaching of functional English to various types of learners.

In the USA, Edward Sapir suggested emphatically a close relationship between language and social reality. He observed that human beings do not live in the objective world alone, nor alone in the world of social activity as ordinarily understood. They are "at the mercy of the particular language which has become the medium for their society". He thought that "the real world is to a large extent built upon the language habits of the group".

Benjamin Lee Whorf, a follower of Sapir, drew on his ideas and examined Hopi, an American Indian language from this point of view. He concluded that "man is a prisoner of the language". His theory about the relationship between culture and language was called Sapir Whorf Hypothesis. It was welcomed enthuastically by some American linguists and criticized by others. The real significance of the hypothesis was that it emphasized a close alliance between language and the total culture of the speech community. Though it did not affect second language teachers directly, it did influence the text book writers and language planners who emphasised this relationship in the guidelines they prepared for them.

In 1960s Basil Bernstein, a professor of Sociology of Education at the University of London came up with the *Language Deficit Hypothesis.* He pointed out how class regulated the structure of communication within the family and affected the initial coding orientation of children. The pre-school children of upper and middle class used *elaborate code* and were more verbal. They were more argumentative than the children of the working class. The latter were more restricted than the former in vocabulary, sentence patterns and variety of use of conjunctions and prepositions. They had a *restricted code* primarily because of the sub-culture and role system of the family, community and work, he argued. For them, the school should bring about a change of code so that their culturally-induced backwardness transmitted through language could be reduced.

In the USA Charles C. Fries had similar attitude towards the variety of English spoken by Black Americans. He branded it 'vulgar' English and offered special programmes to improve the English of Black children. However, they did not change the situation. William Labov (1970, 1974) called their dialect 'Black English Vernaculars' and claimed that these children used it creativity. He suggested that it should be made the medium of instruction for Black children. However, his idea was not welcomed either by educationists nor by the black community. In other words, they did not feel the need for it and it was never adopted by any group. Since there is no job market for speakers of Black English, even its speakers reject it outright.

The growth of transformational-generative grammar and developmental psycholinguistics made sociolinguists think about the problem of language teaching from a new angle. Dell Hymes (1974) endorsed the concepts of linguistic competence and performance. He came up with the concept of communicative competence which involved the learner's ability to participate in the society "as not only a speaking but also a communicating member" (p. 75). In other words, a language learner needs not only grammatical competence but also how to communicate it appropriately within a particular language community. It involves ability to judge when to say what to whom in any given speech situation. In a multilingual society such as India, one has to decide when to use English in social interaction and how to do so. It is not enough to say that we need English as a code for restricted range of social interaction. Each learner has to find out what that restricted range is for him/her. The only generalised observation is that English is needed in India in linguistically diverse situations.

Studies suggest that socio-economic status of the child matters with reference to their second language learning. It has been found that the higher one's status is in social hierarchy, the better is the level of one's language acquisition. As English is supposed to be a language of higher social status in India, those who aspire to have upward social mobility, try to have, at least, a working knowledge of English. While migration of people from rural to urban areas encourages them to use an urban, rather than a local, regional dialect, migration to areas outside the region in which their standard mother tongue is not spoken leads them to choose English in many areas of everyday discourse (e.g., in office and places of public transaction). The self-consciousness that it brings can be observed in people of certain social groups aiming at a more prestigious form of language than they would ordinarily use. It sometimes results in 'hypercorrection' in their language. Those who desire to move out of the country as multinational professionals aspire even higher.

Bilingual/Multilingual Environment

If a child is born in a bilingual society where English is more important than his/her mother tongue, he/she works hard to gain proficiency in the language. We may recall how Europeans who migrated to the USA in the nineteenth century learnt English which became the first language of their children or grandchildren. A sizeable number of Koreans, Vietnamese and Chinese, who migrated to the USA after the Second World War, went through the same process. In India, Tibetan migrants have gone through the process of acquiring English and Hindi. In a multilingual society in India, where the migrant has multiple choices of a second language, he/she accepts either Hindi or English. The language of the neighbourhood in which a migrant settles down becomes his/her first choice. The community in which he lives puts a sort of indirect pressure and he/she is positively inclined towards learning its language.

Frequency of Language Use

It is generally accepted that the more a learner hears a structure, the sooner he/she acquires it. Dulay and Burt (1977) found Spanish-speaking children learning English as a second language undergoing this process and so did Larsen Freeman (1976). Dulay, Burt and Krashen (1984) report that micro-environment factors affect second language learning only when learners have reached certain points in the development of their second language. Once the learner has achieved this goal, salience (i.e. the degree of visual or auditory prominence of an expression) catches his/her attention and he/she is most likely to acquire it. If the second language is frequently used at home, the chances of its acquisition improves.

THE INFLUENCE OF THE SECOND LANGUAGE

When a child is exposed to a second language at school, (s)he may or may not be familiar with it. If (s)he has grown up in a family and/or lives in a neighbourhood where the language is spoken, (s)he is equipped with some of its structures and vocabulary. If (s)he is exclusively from a monolingual family or social environment, (s)he is completely unfamiliar with it. Even the sounds of the language, especially the sounds which are not in his/her mother tongue, are unknown to him/her. If that language is going to be the medium of instruction, it is a new situation for him/her. It is a big challenge which (s)he picks up courageously for nobody is going to be of any help to him/her outside school. He (she) has to stand on his/her own. If (s)he wishes to continue in that system, (s)he has to work hard for (s)he has to equip himself/herself fast with essentials of that language to be able to follow teachers of other subjects as well. It is this situation that an Indian child of a lower or lower middle class faces. His/her parents do not know what is in store for the child, and even if they realise it, they can be of no help to him/her. It is found that such children are initially silent inside and outside the classroom in the premises of the school if speaking in English is mandatory. As they cannot feel comfortable remaining silent, inside the premises, they either drop out or start speaking English without caring for the correctness of their expressions. Eventually they become fluent speakers though the problems involving correct pronunciation and grammar continue. Because of constant exposure to the second language (e.g. English), they catch up with other students who are from more educated family background.

If the child is sent to a school where a regional language or Hindi is the medium of instruction, he/she does not feel as handicapped while expressing himself/herself as he/she would in an English-medium school. As in such schools, English is taught just as a subject (like science or social science), (s)he does not have to struggle hard to comprehend what (s)he is taught in the class. He/she learns English mostly silently and opens his/her mouth only when the teacher asks him/her a question. In such schools, we come across two types of students learning English: those who are mostly silent and are hesitant to open their mouths and those who are extrovert and answer questions without caring for the correctness of their expressions. The latter falter but go ahead struggling while the former speak only when they are sure of themselves. Such students may use correct expressions but find it difficult to be fluent. When writing, they write slowly. In order to speak or write fluently, one has to get rid of hesitation and be natural. It can be attained only when one is determined to be so.

TEACHER

The teacher is an essential component of language acquisition process of the student. His/her voice, vocabulary, choice of words and structures, enunciation and pronunciation serve as a model for children. As to how much he/she influences them depends on several factors. If the feeling of the child towards him/her is that of admiration and affection and if he/she feels comfortable with him/her, (s)he will tend to imitate him/her unconsciously. The emotional tone of the teacher's speech and the way he/she uses it determine the feeling of the child. Younger children in primary classes are influenced more by the speech of the teacher than the children in the middle classes and the latter are influenced more than the children of the higher classes. If the teacher is impatient or intolerant towards students, they do not pay attention to what and how (s)he speaks. The use of a positive and constructive approach by the teacher improves the child's expression. His/her encouraging remarks and suggestions inspire the child; they make him/her work hard. Simple requests are more effective than threats.

PEER GROUP

As the child grows up, (s)he gets gradually detached from the teacher and moves closer to his peer group. He/she develops interest in colourful and vigorous expressions. If some of this interest is directed towards the second/ foreign language, it would be a great help. It is the period in which the child's vocabulary can grow rapidly, if his/her interests are encouraged. If the peer group uses the new language in normal conversation, it helps the child immensely.

THE SCHOOL ENVIRONMENT

An amicable classroom with paintings and charts, a good classroom library equipped with books of suitable standard, and overall congenial atmosphere make students interested in the class. The provision for adequate quantity of books and other reading materials and adequate time and motivation to use them sustain their interest. Skillful guidance on the part of the teacher and librarian helps a child to get suitable reading material and encourages him/ her to gain and enjoy satisfaction.

Since a person's language—whether first or second—is an integral part of him/her; it affects his/her growth. The full emersion programme that involves the use of the second language as a medium of instruction does not affect the development of the child adversely; rather it leads him/her to new heights, especially when the language in question is English.

To sum up, personal, social and institutional (e.g. schooling) factors influence second language acquisition. Among the personal factors are age, aptitude, intelligence, attitude and motivation. The social factors include socio-economic status of the candidate, bilingual/multilingual environment and frequency of language use. The institutional factors refer to school environment, which include factors like second language vs. mother tongue medium schools, roles of peers, and teachers and overall school atmosphere. All these have a cumulative effect on the learner. Attending an English (second language)-medium school means the full immersion of the learner in the learning environment which moulds his/her growth more than of those who are exposed to a partial immersion programme.

UNIT 2

5

English in Colonial and Independent India

Constitutional Positions and Policies

THE COLONIAL ERA

Though the East India Company was formed in 1600, it was in 1616 that Sir Thomas Roe, the British Diplomatic Representative, could meet emperor Jahangir. In 1639 Fort St. George was established in Madras. In 1661 the company took possession of Bombay from the Portuguese and in 1651 an English factory was started at Hugli. Thus, by 1670 they had a foothold in those major places which, later on, developed as cities of Madras, Bombay and Calcutta. The British had an elaborate network of civil and military services in these places to run offices. They needed Indian personnel as well and they tried to teach their employees English to communicate with them smoothly. During this period the Moghul empire declined and the British took possession of a portion of east India by defeating Mir Qasim, the Nawab of Bengal, at Baxar. After the death of Mir Jafar, Robert Clive, the governor of Bengal, was granted the diwani of Bengal, Bihar and Orissa by Shah Alam II, the Moghul emperor in Delhi. In 1972, Warren Hastings was appointed the governor of Bengal. In 1773, the British Parliament passed the Regulatory Act. Hastings was appointed the first Governor General of India and the Supreme Court was established in Calcutta. The newly expanded territory needed a large number of administrators at the lower level and all of them could not be recruited in England. Indian cadres had to be created from among those who knew some English. From the very beginning of British settlement, Christian Missionaries were running schools where they taught English, apart from religion and other subjects, through the medium of the English language. The British started a language school at Fort Williams in Calcutta and prepared standard textbooks in Hindi, Urdu and Bengali. The Christian Mission at Serampore (in Bengal) ran not only schools but also a printing press; it published the first Indian newspaper in English in 1780. In 1785 William Cornwallies became the new Governor General.

In 1833, when the Charter Act was passed, a portion of the company's budget was provided to spend on education.

As mentioned earlier, mission schools were trying to educate students by teaching English not only as a subject but also the medium through which other subjects were to be taught. In 1793, a group of teachers of English organised themselves in Calcutta with a view to expanding the role of English.

In 1797, John Miller published from Serampore, *The Tutor* or *A New English and Bengali Work*, which was supposed to be "well-adopted to teach the natives English." After introducing the English alphabet, he provided extensive lists of phonetically contrastive sets (such as *lip*, *nip*, *pip*, *rip*, *sip*) which included 'nonsense syllables' for practice (such as *chur*, *scur*, *sgur*, etc.) His word list is modern and practical which avoids all (what he considered) 'overliterate' words. The list was arranged in an alphabetical order and contained the Bengali equivalents of each word. His grammar betrayed his traditional training and contained archaic words such as *speaketh* in second person singular. The text contains dialogues related to river-boat trading, such as the following:

SERVANT : Sir, the expenses are great; the boat-hire, the mangees and dandees' wages, ghaut duties etc. from Bakurgunge amount to about four annas and the expenses from Patna come to a little more or less then five annas per rupee.

MASTER : How does the rice of Burdwan and Raur come to Calcutta?

SERVANT : In rainy season, they bring it in boats and in dry weather on bullocks.

MASTER : What difference is there in the expense of bullocks and that of boat?

SERVANT : Conveying rice on bullocks is attended with double the expense of boat.

(As quoted by Howatt, 1974: 70)

Each of these sentences was followed by its Bengali translation.

We have quoted this extract for two reasons—first, to point out the utilitarian aspect of its content which served the purpose of communication while trading, and second, to show the methodology adopted by Miller. Obviously, it was *bilingual*, perhaps to help the Bengali traders to learn and use the English version of the Bengali text. It was a pragmatic approach to enable British to communicate while trading in Bengal. Miller did not offer a textbook which was to be used at school; he offered a workbook both for British and local traders. The book was published at a time when English was taught in some schools as a 'subject'.

The budget allocation on education had no clear direction on how the money was to be used. It was clear that the British wanted the Western scientific knowledge to be known to Indians but they were not clear about how it was to be done. One view was to interpret it in the mother tongue of the learner and disseminate it (i.e. through Bengali and Hindi), and the other view was to make students fully competent to work through English. In other words, there was a controversy regarding the medium of instruction. Soon the role of English in the conduct of public business also became controversial. It was against this background that the company's Court of Directors asked Lord William Bentinck, the Governor General of India, to discharge duties by gradually introducing English "as the language of public business in all departments." This directive, issued in 1830, laid the foundation for the teaching of English as a language, i.e. a language that was not like any other subject to be taught, but a means of providing skills to serve as a tool for the effective administration of the government.

The dispute between the Oriental and Western views came to a conclusion when Thomas Macaulay (1833), the President of the General Committee of Public Instruction in India, wrote in his *Minutes* (i.e., official memorandum authorizing a course of action) that Indian languages were insufficiently rich to be used for disseminating modern knowledge, and technical advances of the West had to be communicated in a language that was already sufficiently developed for that purpose', i.e. English. However, he did not think of 'functional' English but of English language and literature so that the learners could imbibe values of Western culture. To quote him, he wanted to turn Indian youth into "Indian in blood and colour but English in taste, in opinions, in morals and in intellect". He visualized the creation of a new class of English educated Indian elite. He knew that the exposure to English literature would lead Indians to their being familiar with a new culture and would have an everlasting influence on them. He proved to be right, as can be seen in the humanitarian impact it has left on modern Indian intellectuals.

Macaulay's *Minutes* proved to be the most formative document on English in India. It led to an increase in the publication of Indian writers in English, including English literature. Today Indian writers in English are recognized in the English-speaking world, as can be seen in Indians winning Man Booker Prizes and the popularity of Salman Rushdie, Arundhati Ray, Anita Desai and other in the West.

In 1844, the Governor General declared that all government jobs would be given to people who knew English. Even for the lowest posts, people who knew how to read and write English were preferred. In 1853, the Indian Civil Services (I.C.S.) was introduced. In 1851, the first Medical College was opened in Madras. These steps further strengthened the demand for English-medium education. Sir Charles Wood's *Educational Dispatch* properly articulated the need for a wide-spread system of education through English from the primary level to the university. In 1857, the year of uprising of Indian sepoys against the British, a university act was passed that led to the establishment of Calcutta University. In 1882, the Hunter Committee, the first Indian Education Commission, was formed to report on the progress in modern system of education in India. The Government of India Resolution on Education Policy was passed in 1913. In 1917 Indians were made eligible for the King's Commission. The establishment of Royal Military College in Dehradoon (1922) and Royal Indian Navy (1926) strengthened the roots of English-medium education further. In 1937, the Wood-Abbolt Report on Education was submitted which made provision for basic (primary) education in local languages but advocated the retention of English-medium at the high school level.

During the colonial period, questions were occasionally raised about the use of teaching English in schools in rural areas. As rural people did not use English in everyday life, the question was legitimate and no direct justification could be given, except for the fact that English was the language of administration and rural people who wanted their children to take up government jobs felt sufficiently motivated to educate them in English-medium schools. Lord Curzon, the then Viceroy of India, the wrote in 1904 that English should not be introduced before the secondary phase. Consequently, Hindi or a regional language was offered as an alternative medium of education and middle school students who chose this alternative path passed out as 'middle vernacular' candidates. In Wood-Abbott Report (1937), a serious thought was given to the basic education for all in the vernacular. However, the mission schools and privately managed 'public schools' never thought of offering Hindi or a regional language as the medium of instruction at any level.

Prendergast

During the nineteenth century *Thomas Prendergast*, who served in the Indian Civil Service in Madras, wrote in 1864 a manual called *The Mastery of Languages* (or the art of speaking foreign languages idiomatically) in which he observed that small children interpreted the meaning of language by making use of other information available to them, such as gestures, facial expressions, etc. He noticed that they learnt 'chunks of language' and used them into their sentences. They used words which they did not fully understand. He thought that these chunks of words were memorized as complete units which they fluently used. On the basis of his observation, he concluded that efficient foreign language teaching system would consist of entirely memorized sentences, practised so much that they would be easily recalled. This method would help the learner to avoid inadequacy and hesitancy in his/her language and make him/her a fluent speaker. He recommended that the most frequently used sentences could be learnt in this fashion. He gave diagrams in which he showed how hundred and fifty sentences could be produced on the basis of two model sentences given at the top of the diagram.

While in India, Prendergast had himself learnt two Indian languages—Hindustani and Telugu. He knew what learning a new language was like and recommended seven steps to learn correct pronunciation and to manipulate model sentences. Though he was not a methodologist, he foresaw what the structuralists offered later, to practise substitution tables. His *mastery system* was not followed by language teachers, perhaps because he was considered to be an administrator, rather than an educationist.

Michael West

Another approach to foreign language teaching that evolved in India in the first half of the twentieth century was Michael West's *Bilingual Method* (1926). It was based on his project report with special reference to Bengal. West was critical of the system of education prevailing in Bengal which he called "the filtering system". It ensured the best products at school to filter through the system and have university education, preferably to get a government job of some appropriate kind. As the system permitted huge educational wastage, West criticised it. He thought it would be better for school children to have initial training in their mother tongue and to use that knowledge to learn English. West believed that the teaching of reading should have priority over the teaching of spoken English because most drop-outs would need the ability to read more than ability to speak English well. In order to improve this ability, textbooks had to select and distribute lexical items carefully, he argued.

West's *New Method Readers* (1927) were followed by *New Method Conversation* (1933), *New Method Dictionary* (1935), *New Method Composition* (1938) and *New Method Grammar* (1938). Although he admired Harold Palmer, he did not give priority to the *Oral approach*. His second most significant contribution was the compilation of *General Service List of English Words*, which, incidentally, coincided with the growth of the concept of 'Basic English' by Ogden. Ogden and West consulted each other at the Carnegie conference in NewYork in 1934 and the *Carnegie General Service List* had its impact on West's General Service List.

It is a significant fact that Miller, Prendergast and West, who worked in India, acknowledged the role of the mother tongue of the learners while they were being exposed to English. Though West's bilingual approach did not have much input in England, it saw, much later, a parallel development in the USA while teaching English to Spanish Americans. However, one must note that even in India, all were not in favour of Michael West's approach. As pointed out by Barnard Lott (1974: 10-11) A.P. Hawell, who submitted a comprehensive report on education in India (1870-71), regretted that English was not introduced into schools as the *lingua frunca* of the country.

Gandhi on English

These developments took place against the socio-political background provided by the national freedom movement. Mahatma Gandhi, in one of his writings, regretted:

> Our love of the English language in preference to our own mother tongue has caused a deep chasm between the educated and political-minded classes and the masses...The masses remain cut off from the modern mind.

In another essay, he observed:

> There was no other method of bringing enlightenment to the culturally retarded country side of India than by using the respective mother tongues of the villages.

Gandhi observed that the medium of instruction in India, from primary to the university level should not be English but one of the vernacular languages. He remarked that English should be taught in schools in India as a foreign language and not as a language of instruction. While talking about English as a medium of instruction, Gandhi made two pertinent points: first, it delayed the acquisition of other subjects (e.g. chemistry) because the student had to struggle in English to grasp the substance of what he was taught and secondly, he could not speak English correctly because even his teacher's English was "not without blemish".

As a consequence of national freedom movement led by Mahatma Gandhi, a parallel system or education called *basic education* was developed which adopted regional languages or Hindi as a medium of instruction but did not discard English completely; it advocated teaching it as a language. However, the basic system could not compete with the existing system even in post-Independence India.

THE POST-INDEPENDENCE ERA

Under the leadership of Gandhi, the Indian National Congress had committed itself to reorganize Indian states on the basis of language. Gandhi was in favour of Hindustani (i.e. Hindi devoid of difficult Sanskrit born words and Urdu devoid of scholarly Persian Arabic words) as the national language of India. He was not against English as a language but dead against the dominant position it occupied in pre-Independence India. He favoured Hindustani in Devnagari and Perso-Arabic scripts to keep the pre-partitioned India united but the partition of the country in 1947 changed the scenario. It changed even more after the assassination of Gandhi.

Soon after independence, Mahatma Gandhi wrote: "My plea is for banishing English as a cultural usurper as we successfully banished the political rule of the English usurper. The rich English language will ever retain its place as the international speech of Commerce and diplomacy". (*Harijan*, September 11, 1947)

A few months earlier he has written, "I love the English tongue in its own place but I am its inveterate opponent if it usurps a place which does not belong to it. English is today admittedly the world language. I would therefore accord it a place as a second optional language". (*Harijan*, August 25, 1946).

In fact, Gandhi wanted the mansion of the language of India to be built on two great pillars. The first pillar was the rich languages of the states and the second was the introduction of Hindi as a link language between the states. Gandhi favoured the redistribution of Indian provinces of the British days on linguistic basis so that the residents of each state could conduct their business in their mother tongue.

CONSTITUENT ASSEMBLY DEBATE ON LANGUAGE

In the Constituent Assembly there was complete agreement on the status of the language of the state but the relative merit of Hindi versus English as a link language was hotly debated. Mr. Gopalaswami Ayyangar thought that "English was the language on which we have built and achieved freedom" whereas for the followers of Gandhi, English was a language which was a "cultural usurper". Ayyangar proposed that English should continue to be used in the Supreme Court and High Court and in Central Offices. Another member from Madras, the Ramalingam Chettiar appealed to the Hindi-speaking people "to give up their attitude of domination and dictation and to adjust themselves". (Constituent Assembly Debate: 1375)

Some other members from the South India spoke in a similar vein. Pandit Nehru supported the draft presented by Mr. Ayyangar. He said that 'he was grateful to the English language for what it has taught us' but 'at the same time it created a great gulf between us who know English and those who did not know English and that was fatal for the progress of a nation'. "However good, however important English may be, we cannot tolerate that there should be an English knowing elite and a large mass of our people not knowing English". The attempt to bridge the gulf resulted into the passage of Articles 343 to 351 of the Constitution.

The Constituent Assembly debated for over six weeks the choice of national and (or) official language(s) of India. The KM Munshi-Ayyangar formula to have Hindi in Devnagari script as the official language of the Indian union along with the continuation of English for a period of fifteen years was adopted after an intense debate. The Eighth Schedule of the constitution provided constitutional basis for various languages. Though English was not included in the Eighth Schedule, it continued as the associate official language which gave it a fresh lease of life to preserve the cultural unity in a multilingual Indian society. The report of the Tarachand Committee spelt out its functional role.

PLACE OF LANGUAGES IN INDIAN CONSTITUTION

Articles 343 to 351 of the Constitution of India cover the relative positions of languages in India. Article 343 is framed in the most mandatory fashion. According to it, "The official language of the Union shall be Hindi in the Devanagari script". Article 342(B) permitted the continuation of English with a time limit of fifteen years. Article 345 entitled the state governments to select any one or more of the languages "to be used for all or any of the purposes of that State". Article 344 made provision for a Commission on Languages to report to the President of India on the progressive use of Hindi but it made no progress to review the progress made by the state governments for the development of regional languages to displace English at the state level. Article 351 directed the Union to pay particular attention to the development and promotion of Hindi. However, no such provision was made for the development of regional languages. The consequence was that English continued to have its dominant position in non-Hindi-speaking states. The Official Language Commission appointed by the President of India in 1955 had no definite task to inquire and recommend how the non-Hindi mother tongues were developing in these states.

The Commission reported that considerable progress was made to replace English by Hindi in Hindi-speaking states and at the level of all India employment and conduct of examination by the Union Public Service Commission. As no such development took place to replace English by regional languages in non-Hindi-speaking states, their administrators and education departments kept on using English as in the past. Even the courts in these states kept on using English to conduct their proceedings. The Language Commission felt the need for the High Courts in these states to deliver their judgements in regional languages. As a consequence of these overlaps, the non-Hindi-speaking states remained clung to the use of English. In 1955, the Government of India decided that along with English, Hindi would be used as the medium of examination for All India Services examinations and "as and when other regional languages become media of instructions in the universities up to the graduation stage as Hindi has done, the admission of other linguistic media will have to be considered". Now that regional languages have become the media of instruction up to the graduation level, regional language medium examinations are also permitted by the UPSC and other relevant agencies.

UNIVERSITY EDUCATION COMMISSION (1948-1444)

The Radhakrishnan Commission (1948) recommended that Indian languages be the media of instruction at the university level as well so that the gap between English-knowing and non-English knowing Indians was minimised.

The three language formula was evolved in 1957 which recommended that along with the state language, the official language and associate official language, a third language, preferably a south-Indian language should be taught in the Hindi-speaking areas. Thus, the status of English continued to remain unaltered.

The Official Language Commission

The Official Language Commission (1955) which recommended the implementation of the three language formula (regional language, English and Hindi) for the non-Hindi-speaking states, did not insist that Hindi-speaking states must choose a Dravidian language as the third language; from the point of view of national integration it used the expression 'should preferably choose'. As for the medium of instruction at the higher level, it observed that the universities will have freedom to decide for themselves whether they would adopt the regional languages or Hindi. The Report of the Commission was referred to by the President to a thirty-member committee of the Parliament which recommended that even after 1965 English could be used for the purposes which were to be provided specifically by Parliament by law. In 1963 the Official Language Act was passed which provided for the continuation of English for official purposes of the Indian Union. It was conceded that the process of change over from English to Hindi at the Central level could not be completed suddenly. It was a gradual process for which no rigid deadline could be fixed.

As English remained the medium of instruction in the university, many parents and teachers could not reconcile themselves to non-English medium in high schools. Since most high school changed over to Hindi or regional language medium, the English-medium schools started being opened by private managements.

Education Commission (1966)

The *Education Commission* (popularly known as *Kothari Commission*) (1964-66) recommended that the three language formula be adopted at the secondary school level, teaching the mother tongue and/or the regional language, Hindi and English. At the level of higher education, it recommended the use of one language so that students and teachers could move form one part of the country to another. It preferred to have Hindi in that position but so long as it was not acceptable to non-Hindi regions, it recommended the use of English. It unequivocally recommended the continued use of English for technical education and at all India institutes (such as Indian Institutes of Technology, management, law etc.). The commission also recommended creating institutes of research and training for teachers of English.

The Kothari Commission recommended the following curriculum for language teaching:

Table 1: Stages at which the Teaching of a Language should be Introduced

<table>
<tr><td>(i)</td><td>Lower Primary Level
(Classes I-IV)</td><td>One language: (the mother tongue or the regional language)</td></tr>
<tr><td>(ii)</td><td>Higher Primary Level
(Classes V-VIII)</td><td>Two languages: (the mother tongue or the regional languages) and Hindi or English</td></tr>
<tr><td rowspan="2">(iii)</td><td>Lower Secondary Level</td><td>Three languages: (i) the mother tongue or the regional language, (a) Hindi (at a higher or lower level), (b) English or Hindi (if English has already been taken as the mother tongue) and (iii) a modern Indian language, other than Hindi</td></tr>
<tr><td colspan="2">Note: A classical language may be studied in addition to the above mentioned three languages on an optional basis.</td></tr>
<tr><td rowspan="2">(iv)</td><td>Higher Secondary Level</td><td>Any two of the three languages studied at the lower secondary level, preferably Hindi or regional languages and English</td></tr>
<tr><td colspan="2">The Commission made no categorical recommendation at this stage.</td></tr>
</table>

(Report of the Education Commission (187-190)

The Commission observed that the three language formula be strictly observed both in Hindi and non-Hindi speaking areas keeping 'equality' in these areas in view.

National Policy on Education (1968)

The National Policy on Education (1968) recommended the adoption of the programme for language teaching as laid out by the Kothari Commission.

Though all the states agreed to implement the three language formula, they did not implement it in a uniform manner, as is obvious from Table 2.

Table 2 indicates the state of affairs in so far as the teaching of English in government-run schools is concerned. The mission schools and privately-run public schools start teaching English from the very beginning of elementary school and use it as a medium of instruction. It is introduced in Kendriya Vidyalayas (Schools run by the central government) from class I with a view to providing bilingual competence to students. The main thrust of the scheme is to equip the learner with communicative skills so that (s)he can use it efficiently as a library language at college and university levels.

National Curriculum (1985)

According to the National Curriculum for Primary and Secondary Education

Table 2: English-Teaching in India: Statewise Starting Stage

States/ Union Territories	*English Teaching Started at Class*	*No. of Years*
Arunachal, Mizoram, Nagaland, Sikkim, Tripura	1	10
Manipur, Tamil Nadu, Chandigarh, Puducherry	3	8
Kerala, Odisha, Lakshadeep, Maghalaya, Mahe	4	7
Assam, Bihar, Delhi, Haryana, Himachal Pradesh, Jammu and Kashmir, Punjab, Rajasthan, Uttar Pradesh, Madhya Pradesh, West Bengal, Andhra Pradesh	6	5

Source: Study of Language: A Report (NCERT).

(1985), the objective of learning English should be to serve the larger goals of education, i.e., the development of a pluralistic, open society, the promotion of national unity and appreciation of cultural heritage of India. The specific goals are the development of reading, writing, speaking and listening abilities. The overall goal is "to make English a tool for life-long education."

National Policy on Education (1986)

The National Policy on Education (1986) reiterated the National Policy on Education (1968) which had emphasized the improvement in the linguistic competence of students at different levels of education and suggested provisions for the study of English (as has been discussed above). It reviewed the status of implementation of three language formula and noted that it had been "less than satisfactory." It pointed out that all the languages were not taught compulsorily at the secondary stage and the attainment of competence levels of students had not been specified. It asked the Central Institute of English and Foreign Languages (CIEFL) to assure the responsibility for providing research and training inputs. It suggested that a policy should be evolved to bring about uniformity on the place of English (and other languages) in education and a direction should be given on what development should be undertaken. The education of English language teachers, which is the responsibility of colleges of teacher education affiliated to universities, should ensure the quality of teaching.

PROGRAMME OF ACTION (POA) 1992

The National Policy on Education (1986) was further revised as the Programme of Action in 1992. It reiterated that equal opportunity would be given to all modern Indian languages and three language formula would be pursued vigorously. While all three languages would be pursued at the lower levels, only two of them would be pursued compulsorily at the higher secondary level. The committee experts felt that there was no plan for learning the mother tongue where it was not the regional language and from that point of view the three language formula needed some change.

The POA 1992 emphasised micro-planning to regulate and improve language teaching at the primary level and to increase its role in secondary education. It called for the redesigning of courses to increase their relevance and utility. It stressed the importance of teacher education and suggested the development of an improved teacher education curriculum with a view to improvising new ways of language teaching. It reviewed the progress made since the adoption of National Education Policy (NPE 1986) and suggested how to increase its pace.

The National Curriculum Framework for School Education (1995) prepared by the National Council of Education Research and Training (NCERT) considered the medium of instruction a very crucial factor in determining the quality of curriculum transaction and the level of achievement.

It observed that the learner's first language was the most natural medium of instruction at least at the primary level. In the present national scenario, it accepted that English could be the medium after the elementary education in exceptional cases in the institutions where the general levels of pupil's receptive and expressive skills in English is very good. It found the current practice of imposing English as the medium on the learner right from the pre-school stage and the primary classes highly detrimental to pupils's growth. It results unproductive mugging up of text materials which is generally incomprehensible to him/her. It thought only the pupil's mother tongue should be the medium of instruction till the end of primary education.

The National Curriculum Framework recommended that English be introduced in class III and continued to be taught upto class X. The objective of its teaching should be to encourage independent thinking. Children should be motivated to interpret things and express their opinion freely. The process of globalization demands that they acquire sufficiently effective communication skills to be able to use the language purposefully. From upper primary onwards they should be continuously guided to read extensively. They should be monitored to ensure that it is implemented. It recommended that grammar should be a functional tool and the development of oral-aural skills should be emphasized.

At the higher secondary level, only one language is to be read compulsorily and the pupil is free to choose English, instead of his/her mother-tongue or a regional language. Its broad objective is to broaden the learner's mental horizon and preference should be given to the perceived needs of the learner. He/she could choose elective academic or specialised English course (e.g. English for science, technology or business).

NATIONAL CURRICULUM FRAMEWORK (2005)

The National Curriculum Framework was published in 2005 after a wide-ranging churning of ideas with pedagogies and other area '/' domain experts. In so far as language education is concerned, its primary aim was to 'promote multilingualism and national harmony' (p. 37). It observed that language teaching needs to be multilingual not only in terms of the number of languages offered to children but also in terms of evolving strategies that would use the multilingual classroom as a resource. With this end in view, it recommended a sincere implementation of the three language formula. It recommended that the home language of children be the medium of instruction. If the school does not have provisions for teaching in the child's home language at higher levels it must be used at least for the primary school education. if suggested that in the non-Hindi-speaking states children must learn Hindi. In Hindi-speaking states if children learn a language not spoken in their area, it may learn Sanskrit as well. At a later stage, classical and foreign languages may be taught, it observed.

Children have an obvious advantage if they start learning academic subjects in their mother tongue. By the time they enter school, they are well-equipped with the vocabulary and grammatical structures of the mother tongue and are pretty comfortable in articulating themselves. Their developed cognitive and communicative abilities enable them to acquire the knowledge of subjects they are taught. Even if they make errors, they need not be disturbed upto class III.

A rich exposure to the standard language and grammatical rules will improve the children's language subconsciously, it argued.

The *framework* took a pragmatic view on the teaching of English. It observed that the level of introduction of English *is now a matter of political response to people's aspirations rather than an academic or feasibility issue* and people's choice about the level of its introduction in the curriculum will have to be respected with the proviso that we do not extend downwards the very system that has failed to deliver (p. 38). It suggested that at the initial stage English may be one of the languages for learning activities and later on it may be used for reading other subjects. Looking at the success of English medium schools, it observed that English must be seen in relation to other subjects and that the gap between 'English as a subject' and 'English as a medium' must be bridged, and students should be exposed to parallel books and print and electronic media in English. It also pleaded that the approaches of Chomsky, Piaget and Vygotsky with regard to language learning be treated as supportive to explore suitable learning environment.

The *National Knowledge Commission* (2007) observed that in the current scenario, "an understanding and command of the English language is a most important determinant of access to higher education, employment possibilities and social opportunities." It pointed out that school-learners who are not adequately trained in English as a language are always at a disadvantage in the world of higher education." It found it ironical that English has been a part of modern education for more than a century and yet it is beyond the reach of most young Indians. It decided unanimously that time has come to teach English to "our people—ordinary people" as a language in schools. Its recommendation dealt with the modalities of *introducing English in schools from class I*, teacher training, language pedagogy and research support for English language teaching and learning.

The Commission recognised that nine states (of which six are in the north-east) and three union territories had already introduced English as a compulsory subject from class I. It sought to introduce it from class I nationwide, as an integrated part of school curriculum. As language teaching cannot be separated from content learning, it recommended that it should be used to teach some non-language, content subjects from class III. It would create multi-media schools and reduce the gulf between the English-medium schools and regional language medium schools. In order to meet the requirement for a large pool of English language teachers, it recommended that graduates with high proficiency in English and good communicative skills should be inducted without formal teacher-training qualifications. They should be selected through an appropriate procedure developed by the National Testing Service and then given a short-term orientation, it added. It observed that training for language programme needed to be thoroughly reviewed, "recognizing the centrality of language in the curriculum."

Since language teaching takes place not only through direct instruction but also through assimilation from environment, the Knowledge Commission desired that the classroom be equipped with appropriate audiovisual and print materials. Language learning opportunities should be created outside the classroom by forming Knowledge Clubs to discuss knowledge and extend the use of English. Such schemes would ensure that students will be proficient in the use of English at the end of class XII.

If we analyse the proposals made in the reports made by various commissions and policies adopted for English language teaching since the beginning of the colonial era, we find tremendous changes. The British introduced the teaching of English in India not only to recruit English-knowing Indians in their services to rule ever India, but to create a new class of Indians who would appreciate Western knowledge and culture and their values. They succeeded in their plan. A new generation of educated Indians came up who appreciated the value of Western mode of education and the value of freedom and democracy. The Western educated Indians wanted freedom and democracy for themselves in India which led to the formation of Indian National Congress. During the freedom movement Mahatma Gandhi realised that for a broader participation in the struggle for liberation, the masses had to be made politically aware which was not possible through English. He emphasised the value of education through Indian languages from this point of view. The leaders of national movement were not against the English language but they were aware of the limitations of having English as the medium of instruction. The British also realised it and gradually introduced Indian languages as the media of primary and secondary education.

After the independence of India, the field was wide open to switch over to Indian language as media of education at all levels but there were two main hurdles. First, teaching materials were not available for the switch over at the higher level. It was practically impossible to cope with the rapidly increasing store of knowledge in contemporary Indian languages. Secondly, Indians needed a link language to have close contact with and interaction among themselves. Till now English was serving the purpose to a limited extent. An Indian language (e.g. Hindi/Hindustani) could have replaced it but could not occupy the place of English partly because of the hostility in some parts of India and partly because it did not prove to be as flexible and accommodating as English. English continued in its position because of the need for a link language. It became a second language in field of education all over the country instead of Hindi which the framers of the Constitution of India wanted. The three language formula was implemented in such a way that Hindi got the third position in the non-Hindi speaking regions. It is a link language for limited social interaction but for a higher level of interaction, Indians need English even now.

Meanwhile a new situation has arisen because of globalisation which has opened the door for English educated Indian at the international level. Indians are now willing to move to any part of the world where they can get a suitable employment. Global companies need English educated cadres even in non-English-speaking countries because they conduct their business mainly in

English there. The situation is such that even the international labour market prefers skilled and semi-skilled workers who can carry on their day-to-day interaction in English.

All these factors have strengthened the position of English in India. After independence, the policy of the government was to preserve English as a 'library' language to make world knowledge available to us. In so far as English as a spoken link language was concerned, the emphasis was on its all India intelligibility. Efforts were made to minimise the regionalisation of spoken English so that it could be used as a language of oral communication intelligibly. Globalisation has changed that perspective and the new goal is to have *internationally intelligible pronunciation*. Hence, there is a shift in policy and there is equal emphasis on spoken English as well. The need for fluency has led to another radical change. The language pedagogies realise that teaching English as a subject is not adequate; we need to give opportunity to students to speak it freely. They think that it can be done if some other subjects could also be taught through the medium of English. Thus, we have almost reached the stage in which modern education started in India. At that time all subjects were taught through English. That was an imposed compulsion. Now we are willing to learn some subjects through the medium of English so that we have the practice of using English outside the language class.

This comprehensive view on the teaching of English in India is a welcome step and needs to be implemented by all state governments in view of the increasing demand of people to teach their children English. It is because of this demand that the number of English medium private schools is increasing. It is not a healthy sign because a large number of such schools are teaching shops which do not come up to the standard. Besides, they are not interested in improving their lot, they are commercial ventures which are disguised as "public" schools. There are some coaching institutions which teach only spoken English and use books such as *Rapidex English Speaking Course* . Since the younger generation realizes the importance of English in their life, they join such institutes readily. *Rapidix* teaches spoken English through the medium of Hindi and does not care for proper pronunciation. Still people join it because they want to speak English and seek a job in the international labour market. It is good that the Central Board of Secondary Education (CBSE) has decided to train teachers for the of speaking and listening skills in collaboration with Trinity College, London. It has decided to introduce training in these skills in all CBSE-affiliated schools for classes IX and XI in order to incorporate spoken English in its integrated English curriculum.

The successful publication of *Rapidex* suggests that a sizeable section of people wants to learn English at a 'superfast' speed. As John (2007: 161) observes, it is like a fast relief pain balm for those who do not speak English but want the door opened for migration from a backward Hindi-speaking village to the outside world. *Rapidex* runs through everyday conversational English and offers English equivalents of their Hindi counterparts. It comes with a free cassette which promises readers to be able to speak English well. It enables them to speak expressions such as 'how marvelous,' 'how disgraceful', 'well done', 'as you please', 'not a bit', etc. The fact that copies of such a book have been sold in millions points out that Indians want to learn English not just as a library and link language but as a language of everyday use so that the social gulf between the urban and rural population is narrowed. They want to earn the right to live in the city without much constraint. The mixture of economic and cultural prospects that English seems to offer allures them towards it.

There are several factors behind the wide-spread use of English as a second language in India. English continues to be the medium of instruction for higher studies in science, engineering, medical, legal and professional subjects. Even though the Radhakrishnan Commission (1949), Official Language Commission (1958) and Education Commission (1966) lamented that students fail to have a good knowledge of their subjects because they are taught through the medium of English which they do not understand well, they could not get the medium changed. In almost all Central Universities English is the medium and most of the competitive examinations are conducted mainly in English. Hindi and regional languages are trying their best to grab this privilege but they have hardly successed. In the private sector, most highly placed jobs are for English-medium products and migration for jobs abroad is impossible without English.

In India English is the co-official language for the central government and many non-Hindi speaking states refuse to have transaction with the centre in any language other than English. In North East India, there are small states like Nagaland, Mizoram and Meghalaya where numerous tribal languages are spoken and the only convenient language for administrative purposes is English. In short, English plays an effective role in inter-state communication in India.

As Kachru (1989) argues, English not only exposes Indians and other non-native speakers of English to western culture, it exposes them to their own culture. In fact, Indian English is a variety of world Englishes in its own right. It has gone through the process of *deculturation* (with reference to its native variety) and *acculturation* (with reference to Indian culture). However, we believe that Indianization of Indian English should not stand in the way of its 'international intelligility'.

> The children of independent India seem not to think of English as being irredeemably tainted by colonial provenance. They use it as an Indian language, as one of the tools they have to handle.
>
> —David Crystal, 2003:184, *English as a Global Language*

Figures 2 and 3 sum up why Indians find the English language so useful in life.

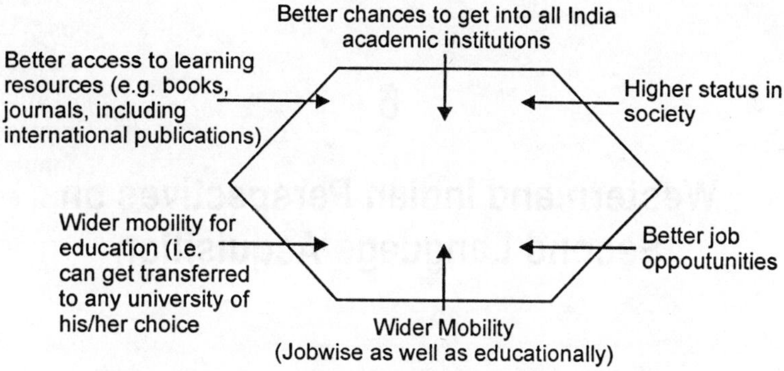

Fig. 2: External Influence on the Learning of English in India

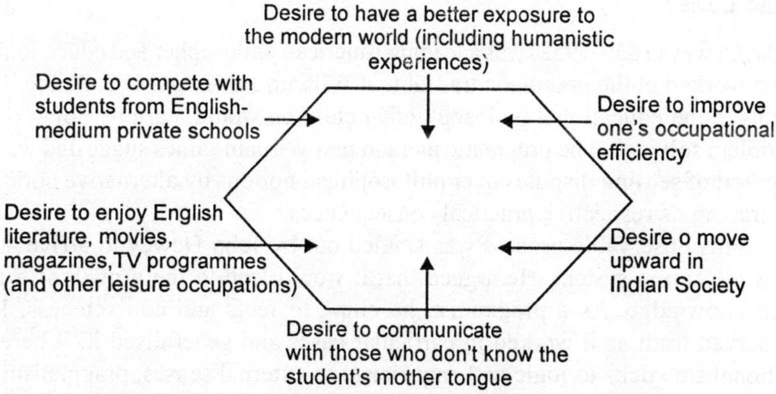

Fig. 3: Internal Factors that affect the Learning of English in India

6

Western and Indian Perspectives on Second Language Acquisition

A. PHILOSOPHICAL PERSPECTIVE

John Dewey

John Dewey (1859-1952) was a leading American philosopher and educationist who worked in the pragmatic tradition of William James and C.S. Peirce. He evolved the educational philosophy that children would learn by doing (i.e. problem solving). The pragmatic method that William James suggested was a method of settling disputes over philosophical notions by alternative notions of tracing its respective practical consequences.

This observable process was singled out by John Dewey to arrive at a new education system. He argued that it would lead to the growth of truth and knowledge. As a pragmatist, he clung to facts and concreteness. He observed truth as it worked in particular cases and generalised it. Whereas rationalism sticks to logic and empiricism to external senses, pragmatism is willing to follow a problem and find out what works best to fit every aspect of life. If knowledge acquisition is a search for truth, it is true when it works. Dewey observed that truth gives "satisfaction". He explained his views in *Reconstruction in Philosophy* (1920). He found the contemporary education "crude and primitive". It had made remarkable progress in science but lacked 'contemplative aesthetic appreciation'. The material progress it had made had produced 'a race of economic monsters' (p. 127) who were passive and inalert in "morals". What was needed was to examine the "the possibility and method of reconciliation of the attitudes of the practical science and contemplative aesthetic appreciation", he thought. The need was to balance the "real" with the "ideal". Our critical thinking should face facts. Thus exploration needs inquiry, minute and extensive scrutinising and observation. Thinking should not be treated as an escape from reality but an observation and study of reality. Thinkers should not remain aloof from practice, they should test their thought by application, he argued. Thinking should involve observation of facts, defining the problems, locating the trouble and forcing home a definite sense of what that difficulty is and where it lies.

Dewey knew that education was traditionally thought of as preparation for life, as learning and acquiring certain things which would be useful later. According to this view, childhood was a preparation for adult life and adult life for another life. The future, and not the present, was significant in education. The business of childhood education was to grow into the independence of adulthood by acquisition of knowledge and skills. And that was considered to be the end of education.

Dewey did not agree to such a view. To him, the end of education should be continuous growth, i.e. the continuous reconstruction of experience throughout life. Education is a constant function independent of age. The only substantive part of formal school education should be to render students capable of further education. They should be more sensitive to conditions of growth and more able to take advantage of them. Acquisition of skills, possession of knowledge and attainment of culture are not ends; they are marks of growth and means to its continuing. Only when people are willing to have such continued education, we will be on the path of social advancement and reorganisation. 'What we need in education is a genuine faith in the existence of moral principles which are capable of affective application", he said (1909:57-58). He argued that it should be incorporated in the educational system. He observed that teachers should have faith in it while teaching every subject and following every method of instruction.

As the goal of education is not to increase the amount of knowledge but to create opportunities to invent and discover, Dewey (1910) suggested five steps in problem solving:

(i) A degree of motivation exists in the person due to a felt need aroused by a question.
(ii) The problem is related in understandable terms, integrated and analysed.
(iii) Possible solution to satisfy the requirements of problem are proposed.
(iv) These solutions are examined for their effectiveness against the problem criteria.
(v) A 'good' solution is selected as meeting these criteria and applied.

Educationists in the USA and elsewhere adopted these criteria for implementing curriculum of development. The growth of the behaviourist theory of development added new dimensions to them but the influence of Dewey prevails even now. Cognitive psychologists who believe in divergent thinking in search of originality emphasize them even more. They emphasize the roles of problem finding, creativity and problem solving more vigrously.

B. PSYCHOLOGICAL PERSPECTIVE

Ever since the beginning of psychology, scholars started thinking about human behaviour, including linguistic behaviour. Gestalt psychology of Wertheimer, Kohler and Kuffka thought that it was the functions of mind. William James suggested that, as consciousness was the subject matter of psychology, it was a subject of introspection. It was this introspective psychology that was prominent in the first decade of the twentieth century. However, it was challenged by psychologists like John B. Watson (1912) in the USA and William Von Wundt in Germany. Watson argued that since consciousness can be analysed only by introspection (a process of looking in what happens inside us) it can never bè evaluated objectively. In 1912, he claimed that human behaviour can be studied the same way as the behaviour of animals other than man.

Watson and Behaviourism

The behaviourists were not only interested in studying what humans do but also in controlling and manipulating them. They wanted to study how they responded to certain types of stimuli. Stimulus and response can be observed under experimental control and their observations can be recorded. Watson (1914) began his work on word organisation, and observed how verbal habits are formed. The retention of verbal habits is what he called 'memory'. By 'memory' he means nothing except the fact that when we have the same stimulus again after an absence, we say the same old words we had learnt in the presence of that stimulus in the first place. The young child who learns to speak puts on his/her verbal and visceral habits simultaneously with his/her manual habits, i.e. his/her verbal, manual and laryngeal activities are organised together as parts of the total experience, he argued. A child responds in sentences to events in his/her environment and his/her responses contain elements which linguists call syntax.

Thorndike

It was Edward L. Thorndike who gave a behaviourist perspective to curriculum. His laws of learning, particularly, the law of effect and his theory of identical elements influenced the pedagogues very much. His law of effect defined learning in terms of connections between external stimuli in the environment and the overt responses to them on the part of the organism. He claimed that the connection emerges out of a trial and error process in which certain responses on the part of the organism, brought by certain stimuli, act to reward the organism. Thorndike called it "satisfaction". Learning, according to him, occurs when these connections become automatic, i.e., when responses become habits. He believed that learning is not a broad and general process but a narrow and specific process consisting of particular and specific bonds and connections made habitual through a *conditioning process*. It was as true of language learning as of learning any other subject. Under his influence, curriculum experts held the view that language curriculum should be derived from specific objectives drawn from specific skills (e.g. listening, speaking, reading and writing) and abilities found in the learner.

Another aspect of Throndike's psychology that influenced educationists, including language teacher, was his understanding of intelligence. He believed that some students are inherently more intelligent than others and they should be taught to lead the class. Others should be trained to trust and follow the leader.

In each of the Thorndikean situations, a change in behaviour springs from a contingency between some defined response and some motivationally significant state of affairs.

Pavlov

In a typical Pavlovian experiment, the behaviour of the animal is altered by the introduction of some motivationally significant stimulus, such as food. In a Thorndikian experiment, reinforcement is contingent on response but in a Pavlovian experiment, reinforcement is scheduled without regard to response. Because of it, it cannot be treated as reward or punishment in any meaningful manner. Pavlov claimed that all instances of learning could be analyzed as instances of conditioning. Pavlov uses the term conditioning in the sense of classical conditioning but sometimes for 'learning' itself.

In general, a Pavlovian situation may be defined without reinforcement to the occurrence in that situation of any particular kind of behavioural change or to the functional properties of the stimulus which are paired. What is essential is a sequence of conjunction of stimulus whose contiguity is independent of the subject's response. The only learning situation which cannot be classified unequivocally as Pavlovian is the one which involves the avoidance of an aversive stimulation.

B.F. Skinner

Skinner thought that language is something a person acquires and possesses. The words and sentences of which a language is composed are tools to express meanings, thoughts, ideas and other things that are in the mind of the speaker. The verbal behaviour has a special character "only because it is reinforced by its effect on the people". It a person says, "Please open the door" and the listener responds appropriately, a reinforcement consequence follows. How a person speaks and how the listener responds depend upon the practices of the verbal community of which they are members. Different verbal communities shape and maintain different languages in the same speaker who possesses different repertoires having similar effect upon different listeners.

In the functional analysis of *Verbal Behaviour* Skinner (1957) identified stimulus, reinforcement and deprivation as factors which control verbal response. He felt that they could be manipulated to have a desired response. He refined the theory further by emphasizing the concept of 'stimulus control' and identifying the 'controlling stimuli'; He called the 'response strength' the 'basic datum'. He believed that the verbal behaviour occurring in a given situation is fully determined; at the same time he considered 'overall frequency' an important factor, which brings in the importance of reinforcement. The three concepts—stimulus, reinforcement and response—were taken to be fundamental. They were applied to language teaching, including second/ foreign language teaching. The pedagogical development based on the approach was called the *conditional development* or *operant behaviour*. The process through which a person deals effectively with a new environment is called *operant conditioning.* Sometimes behaviourists are called environmentalists because of their belief that the environment in which a child learns a language is the strongest stimulus.

According to Skinner (1974), we are inclined to give special attention to a syntactic form because we can record it accurately simply by modelling it. The behaviourist claimed that the verbal behaviour has an independent status which linguists called structuralism. Skinner (1957) suggested that, when learners correctly produce language that approximates what they are exposed to in the input, they receive positive reinforcement and habits are formed. Hockett (1955) an eminent structuralist, observed that language is behaviour and must be taught on behavioural principles. He pleaded that as behaviour, it must be studied in terms of group norms as to usage, content and purpose.

Since habit formation in a particular language was the goal of teaching that language, pattern practice became an integral part of intensive English course in a second language teaching. C.C. Fries's *Teaching and Learning of English as a Foreign Language* (1945) contains basic patterns of English which, he claimed could be practised in three months. Another example of this type of text is A.C. Hornby's (1959) *The Teaching of Structure Words and Sentence Patterns.*

Some of the sentences for pattern practice are as follows:

1. These are the hands | of | the clock.
2. This is a glass | of | water.
3. This box is | full of | books.

In a pattern practice, the content words were not considered to be of great importance. The aim was to familiarise students with structure words and patterns. Only those non-structural parts of the language were to be used, which were related to the environment of the language learner. The restrictions on formal and situational procedures were to be emphasised, which, they thought, hamper students in habit formation. In order to find out whether certain habits were formed, variations in sentences were used with blanks, as in (4a):

4a. We talked from ____ to ____
b. We talked from morning to afternoon.
c. We talked from 9 am to 5 pm.

The blanks in (4a) were filled up by time expressions, as in (4b) or (4c).

Lado and Fries thought that students are interfered with the structure of their first language while they are trying to learn the structure of their second language. They thought of contrastive analysis of the structures of L_2 with those of L_1 to solve the problem. Such an analysis presupposed that the learners of L_2 will face no problem if the structures were similar in both the languages but they would face difficulties if the structures of L_2 were different from those of L_1. In order to overcome such problems, Fries (1942) published *Intensive Course in English for Latin American Students* and in 1946 *An Intensive Course in English for Chinese Students*. Several other manuals of this type were published not only from the USA and UK, but also from Germany and East European countries (e.g. Poland, Czechoslovakia, Russia, etc.).

Jerome S. Bruner

Jerome S. Bruner was deeply interested in child language development. One of the projects he worked on is to determine the extent to which the cultural attitude of parents influences the language acquisition of the child (Bruner 1975). In American culture, an infant is seen as someone to interact with actively and thus he/she receives a great deal of linguistic input. It is common to see parents actively involved in linguistic stimulation of their infants as if they teach them. It leads Bruner to observe that one can teach anything to any child at any age if one goes about in the right way. Piaget did not agree to it. In Piaget's work, the child is seen as developing his/her cognitive capacities through interaction with the environment but he/she needs to be flexible to deal with a changing environment (Piaget 1971). Neither Piaget nor Chomsky denied some role of cultural environment in language acquisition but they think it depends to a great extent on child's internal programming. Bruner (1975) presents a strong statement on the role of the parents.

While talking about the opportunities to acquire knowledge and competence of language. Bruner (1964:1) points out "the development of human intellectual functioning from infancy to such perfection as it may reach, is shaped by a series of technological advances in the use of mind. A person's growth depends upon the mastery of techniques and cannot be understood without reference to such mastery. These techniques are not, in the main, the invention of the individual who is growing up. They are, rather, skills transmitted with varying efficiency and success by culture – language being a prime example. Cognitive growth, then, is in a major way from the outside in as well as from the inside out. Since the development of language is a means of thinking, acquiring is a key step in the development of individual's growth. It increases his/her potential for further growth vastly, he observed.

Closely related to language development is the development of the ability to form and use concepts like 'roundness'. The development of concepts results into moving from the concrete and specific to more general and abstract. It leads to the acquisition of powerful intellectual tools which enables the individual to sort out incoming experiences. Bruner (1964) emphasised three stages by which a child learns to deal with information and form internal representation of the world.

(i) *Motor representations* from past actions (cf. Piaget's sensory motor period), (ii) *images* that stand for events in the same way that pictures do and (iii) *symbols* such as words and number which provide a means to represent experience and even to transform it. They open up the realms of intellectual possibilities. According to Bruner, the extent to which such possibilities are fulfilled depends upon the nature of the culture to which the growing individual is exposed.

In Bruner (1966), he differentiates between 'coping' and 'defending' in order to understand this impact on one's intellectual life. According to him, 'coping' respects the requirements of problems we encounter while it respects one's dignity. 'Defending' leads an individual to avoid or escape from problems for which one has no solution, in such a way that it does not violate one's integrity of functioning. There is always a mixture of coping and defending in dealing with life as one finds it.

The objective of learning is not only to master the task one faces but to master it in such a way that one would not have to learn subsequent identical tasks.

While the learning process develops in a child, initially he/she believes that thinking something and doing it are somewhat equivalent. Secondly, in his/her mind, ideas are not isolated from their motivational or emotional context. When he/she approaches the task of school learning with its highly rationalistic and formal pattern, there is a legacy of unconscious logic in his/her mind in which action affect and conceptualisation are webbed together. According to Bruner, effective cognitive learning in school depends upon effects to detach concepts from the modes of action that they evoke. The process depends upon the presence of several conditions, such as simulation, play, identification and some freedom from drive and anxiety. Bruner wants the teacher to remember that the functions of conscious problem solving can serve the interests of healthy functioning of a child's mind.

COGNITIVE APPROACH OF NOAM CHOMSKY

Noam Chomsky (1959) wrote a detailed review of B. F. Skinner's (1957) *Verbal Behaviour* in which he challenged the claim that children learn their first language by repeatedly hearing what is spoken in their immediate environment. He argued that they produce novel and creative utterances which they would have never heard in their environment. Children's creative use of the language shows that they do not reproduce what they have learnt by habit; they do not simply mimic what they hear in other's speech. Chomsky asserted that Skinner's concepts of 'stimulus', 'responses', 'reinforcement', and 'deprivation' were not relevant in the context of learning an utterance; what explains the phenomenon is the speaker's tacit knowledge of universal grammar and the rules of a language specific grammar. His critique proved that the behaviourist's explanation for language acquisition was wrong. Chomsky agreed that reinforcement, casual observation and natural inquisitiveness to imitate were important factors but the capacity of the child to generate, hypothesize and process information in a variety of complex ways were even more important. Chomsky was supported by a number of psycholinguistic research which refuted the claims of behaviourists.

The contrastive analysis based on behaviourist principles also failed to a great extent. It was reported that some L_2 learners faced problems in using structures that were similar to their L_1 structures and some did not commit errors even when the L_2 structures were different from their L_1 structures. Due to the impact of cognitive theory, the technique of contrastive analysis was changed and researchers started looking at similarity in the competence of L_2 learners rather than their performance. Approaches to the teaching of L_2 changed in course of time though some people still cling to the behaviourist approach to the extent of insisting on pattern practice.

COGNITIVE PSYCHOLOGY (DEVELOPMENTAL PSYCHOLINGUISTICS)

By 1960s, American psycholinguists had changed themselves from believing in behaviourism to working with developmental psycholinguistics. Reports showed that direct teaching by repetition and intensive practice had relatively little effect on the language acquisition of a child. Here are some instances:

1. Child : childs
   Mother : No, children
   Child : childs
   Mother : I say, children

	Child	:	childs
	Mother	:	Don't say childs, say children.
	Child	:	O.K. childs, children.
2.	Child	:	Nobody don't like me.
	Mother	:	No, say "Nobody likes me"
	Child	:	Nobody don't like me (eight repetitions of this dialogue)
	Mother	:	No, listen carefully. Say, "Nobody likes me".
	Child	:	Oh! Nobody don't likes me.

(From McNeill, 1970, 106-107)

3.	Child	:	Want other one spoon, daddy
	Father	:	You mean, you want the other spoon.
	Child	:	Yes, I want the other one spoon, daddy.
	Father	:	Can you say, 'the other spoon'?
	Child	:	Other… one… spoon.
	Father	:	Say, 'other'
	Child	:	Other
	Father	:	Spoon
	Child	:	Spoon
	Father	:	Other spoon
	Child	:	Other spoon. Now give me the other one spoon.

(Braine, 1971: 161)

In (1), the mother is coaxing the child to say '*children*', but the child is guided by his own rule of grammar; he thinks '*bags, boxes, toys, girls,* hence '*childs*'. The attempt to force the child to say 'children' is a failure. In (2) the rule of negation that the child has is different from that of his mother. In (3) the child is repeatedly saying 'other one spoon', instead of 'the other spoon'. His rule of definite description in different from that of his father.

All these examples show that the attempt at habit formation does not work. It is the child's own grammar that guides him, even though it is actually not acceptable to older people. The dialogue in (4) is similar to that in (1) in the sense that the child has a general rule in his mind and is yet to accept an exception.

4.	Child	:	My teacher *holded* the baby rabbits and we patted them.
	Adult	:	Did you say your teacher held the baby rabbit?
	Child	:	Yes
	Adult	:	What did you say she did?
	Child	:	She *holded* the baby rabbits and we patted them
	Adult	:	Did you say she held them tightly?
	Child	:	No, she *holded* them loosely (Cazden 1972: 92)

Though the adult person kept on using the word *held*, the child continued to use *holded*. The stimulus (to say *held*) was there before the child but he ignored it. It shows the poverty of stimulus argument. The mental universal grammar of the child and the language specific principle of past tense formation by adding *–ed* to the verb make him ignore the correction suggested to him. It means, he is guided by some internal process and an external linguistic input does not help him. It may be pointed out that a non-English-knowing person learning English for the first time as a second language is likely to make a similar mistake.

Developmental psycholinguists, such as Bever (1988), Curtiss (1977), Fodor *et al.* (1965, 1974, 1988), Jackendoff (1977), Miller (2003), Smith and Tsimpli (1995), Slobin (1966, 1973) and Wexler and Culicover (1980) have shown that the cognitive theory of language acquisition is an accurate replacement of the behaviourist theory. The followers of Chomsky assert that children come equipped with a set of principles of universal grammar which are subjected to parametric variations to yield language specific grammars.

1980s saw an explosion of comparative grammatical research exploiting the combination of fixed principles of varying parametric values. Their reports showed that languages, despite apparent surface diversity, could be seen as having a common fixed core. It had its impact on applied linguistics as well, especially on the study of the acquisition of a second language.

Cognition psycholinguists have proved that second language acquisition devices are similar to those of the first language. They have also worked on whether there is an interference by L_1 while a child acquires L_2. They have found that it is not necessarily the case. "Most learners of L_2 make errors in acquiring the structures of L_2 which are similar to those who acquire them as L_1. Besides, their judgment on the grammaticality of sentences of L_2 is not affected by their knowledge of L_1's (as reported in Heidi, Burt and Krashen 1984: 202).

THE CRITICAL PERIOD HYPOTHESIS

Another landmark development in the field is the emergence of the concept of critical period hypothesis of Eric Lenneberg (1967: 158). He claimed that a child acquires the rudiments of a language between the age of two and three, relatively well between three and thirteen (till the person attains puberty) and his/her ability declines after that. Later psychologists gave the examples of persons such as Isabelle, Genie and Chelsea who were cut off from the human contact for a long period since birth and efforts to introduce them to their mother tongue later on hardly succeeded.

Genie, who was brought out of isolation to human society after she was thirteen year old, could never speak English fluently. Her language remained morphologically and syntactically deficient. Such cases led psycholinguists to hypothesise that there is a limited period of development during which it is possible to acquire a language easily to normal native-like level, be it L_1 or L_2. Once this period is passed, the brain becomes less plastic and the ability to learn a language declines.

Though Lenneberg concentrated mainly on first language acquisition to make a case for critical period hypothesis, other psycholinguists worked on second language learners as well. They found that a child learns his/her second language more easily than an adult learner. It is claimed that the closure of the critical period leads to the lack of easy accessibility of principles of universal grammar to the language learner. An important view is that, though the principles of universal grammar are not completely lost in adult L_2 learner, its parametric values decrease with age. The benefits of learning L_2 at an earlier age have been reported by many developmental psycholinguists. For instance, Johnson and Newport (1989) have reported that pre-puberty L_2 learning has significant advantages. The maturational constraints, they observed, were most profound for bilinguals who tried to learn their second language after puberty. Such reports carry implications for the design and timing of programme for second language education, namely, the earlier a child is exposed to a second language, the better he/she learns it.

The conclusion that a language teacher can draw is that an early exposure to a language is ideal for a child; it is true of exposure to L_2 as well. That is why children who grow up in a multilingual society easily pick up the languages they are exposed to.

NATURE-NURTURE CONTROVERSY

Krashen

Though ability to language acquisition is biologically programmed, the internal mechanism triggers off only when it gets an appropriate language environment. It is further facilitated by other factors, such as child's upbringing, parent's education, etc. Dulay, Burt and Krashen (1984) discuss four *macro-environmental* and three micro-environmental factors that facilitate language acquisition. The macro-factors are: (i) naturalness of the language the learner comes across, (ii) the learner's role in communication, (iii) the availability of concrete representives to clarify meaning and (iv) the target language models. The *micro-environmental factors* include (a) salience (the ease with which a structure is seen or heard), (b) feedback (i.e. the listener's response to the learner's speech) and (c) frequency of occurrence of a structure.

If correction is an element of feedback, it has frustrating effect on the learner; it does not help him/her to overcome errors. If the respondent expands or rephrases the learner's speech, it has an effect. The frequency of the occurrence of a structure has a positive effect. The micro environmental factors affect second language learning only when the learner is ready to internalize a given structure.

INTERNAL FACTORS

Three internal factors—filter, organizer and monitor—operate on a second language learner. The *filter* screens subconsciously the incoming language based on the learner's motives, needs, attitudes and emotional state. The *integrative* motivation is a desire to achieve proficiency in the new language to participate in the life of the community that speaks that language, the *instrumental* motivation is the desire to achieve proficiency in the new language for utilitarian reasons (e.g. to get a job). The third motivation is for one's social group identification.

The learner's emotional states are also a part of the filter. It matters much whether the learner is relaxed or anxious while trying to learn. The more relaxed and comfortable a learner is, the better is his/her acquisition speed.

The function of the *organizer*, another subconscious process, is reflected in the transitional construction of the learner. It can be understood in terms of the linguistic complexity of the structure to be learnt or the learning complexity of the learner. The latter involves the degree of difficulty a learner experiences in acquiring a structure.

The *monitor* involves the learner's capacity to group the conscious representation of abstract linguistic rules. The use of the monitor depends on the learner's personality, his/her focus on the linguistic task and his/her formal exposure to the grammar of the language. However, the conscious knowledge of a rule does not guarantee that a learner will use it. In short, the acquisition of communicative skill depends more on filtering and organizing factors than on monitoring.

Thus, the nature-nurture controversy has been amicably resolved and it is agreed that nurture helps the natural act of language acquisition in achieving its full potential.

New Schema: Internal Processors

Based on the research in this field, Dulay, Burt and Krashen (1982) provide the following schematic diagram of language learning:

Learning Environment → [Filters → Organize → Monitor] → Learner's Verbal Performance

[From Dulay, Burt and Krashen (1982: 46)]

Fig. 4: Process of Language Learning

Though Chomsky and his followers have done a lot of work on how grammatical sentences are typically generated, processed and understood, they have not gone into what makes such sentences acceptable. The person who knows a language finds out that all the sentences that are grammatical are not necessarily acceptable to him/her. Some of them may be grammatical but not acceptable. For instance, one of the ways in which a noun phrase is expanded is to add a relative clause to it which modifies it. For instance, in the sentence *The cat killed the rat*—the noun phrase *The cat* can be modified to have a sentence such as *The cat which the dog chased killed the rat.* This sentence can be further expanded by saying

The cat [which the dog [that the man pushed] chased] killed the rat.

This sentence is perfectly grammatical but not acceptable to many native speakers because of the practical difficulty a listener faces in processing it fast. Recent developmental psycholinguists have studied sentences that are grammatical but unacceptable and also sentences that are apparently ungrammatical (because they are incomplete) but acceptable. They make a distinction between conventional meaning and conversational meaning. The latter makes a so-called ungrammatical sentence contextually acceptable. A discourse-based analysis of sentences needs both. While the conventional meaning depends on how sentences are structured, conversational meaning depends on how such structures are actually used and processed.

JEAN PIAGET'S DEVELOPMENTAL APPROACH

Sometime before Chomsky reacted to Skinner's behaviourist model, Jean Piaget, a Swiss pedagogue and psychologist, raised his voice against Watson and European behaviourists. Piaget was influenced by the works of William James, John Dewey, Freud and Durkheim and did not believe that the child's mental growth depended mainly upon quantitative addition of experience. He believed that the development of language and thought is primarily qualitative. He interpreted the three forms of knowledge-innate knowledge, knowledge gained through experience of the world and logico-mathematical knowledge—from the point of view of biological sciences and posited that "the bursting of instinct in man" has resulted in his cognitive evolution. In the *Language and Thought of Man* (1930), he argued that a child is not a miniature adult and his mind is not the mind of an adult on a small scale. On the basis of experimental proof, he showed that the child's mind evolves.

The factual basis of child's ego-centrism is provided by Piaget's investigation of the child's use of language. His systematic observation of children in his school led him to conclude that all conversations of children fall into two groups – the ego-centric and the socialised. The difference between them lies in their functions. In ego-centric speech, the child talks only about himself/herself and does not try to communicate to people around him/her. The act involves that of thinking aloud, similar to a monologue in a play. Piaget's experiments showed that the greater part of the pre-school child's talk is egocentric. Besides his/her expressed thoughts, a child has many unexpressed thoughts. At this stage the language he/she uses in basic activities is a language of gestures, movements, mimicry and words. At the age of seven or eight, he/she desires to work with others and uses full sentences. In short, according to Piaget, the sequence is as follows, from non-verbal autistic thought through egocentric thought and speech to socialised speech and logical thinking.

The basic framework of Piaget's theory rests on the assumption of a generic sequence of two opposite forms of mental activity, one based on the pleasure principle and the other, on the reality principle. Language teachers who believe in Piaget's formulation start formal language teaching at the age of five or six. However, critics of Piaget hold the view that, whether the child's talk is more egocentric or more social depends not only on his age but also on his surroundings. Children who grew up in Piaget's kindergarten had a different type of language development from those who were sent to other pre-primary preparatory schools (e.g. in the USA).

According to Piaget, the early development of language occurs because of "priori" sensory-motor constructions while the later development is determined by general principles of "assimilation", accommodation and the like. In a debate between Piaget and Chomsky, Chomsky refutes Piaget's claims. He argues that there is little reason to support that the principles of language acquisition, "have any close analogue to other cognitive systems". He cites the example given by Curtiss (1982). It was observed that Genie's linguistic ability was minimum whereas she could communicate non-linguistically (through gestures, etc.) in a very complex way. The mechanism of other cognitive development did not lead to linguistic development. Another example was given by Blank, Gessner and Esposito (1970). A three year old child had excellent linguistic ability but little ability to use language for interpersonal communication.

There has not been much impact of Piaget's theory of language acquisition on the English-speaking world and the points raised above are still being debated.

FUNCTIONALISM OF LEV SEMENOVICH VYGOTSKY

Another developmental approach was that of Lev S. Vygotsky (1934) in *Thought and Language*, which was made available to the English-speaking world in 1961 for the first time. In the words of Jerome S. Bruner (1961), he tried to save the study of language and thought "from vulgar behaviourism", on the one hand, and on the other, from "the subjective approach to mental phenomena as exclusively inner subjective conditions which can only be investigated introspectively". Vygotsky was critical of Piaget who considered autism as the original, earlier form of thought, logical thought to be late and egocentric thought as the genetic link between them. Piaget also thought that egocentric speech of the child does not fulfil any realistically useful function in the child's behaviour. Vygotsky's experiments suggested that egocentric speech assumes a very definite and important role in the activity of the child. He claimed egocentric speech to be a separate linguistic form which was a highly important genetic link between vocal to inner speech. He did not consider the drive for the satisfaction of needs to be separate from and opposed to the drive for adaptation to reality. According to him, whether the child is more egocentric or more social depends not only on his age but also on his surroundings.

Vygotsky's experiments were intended to find out the relation between thinking and speech which led him to conclude that thought and speech have two different genetic roots and the two functions develop along different lines, independently of each other. He also concluded that the close correspondence between thought and speech is characteristic of men, and not of anthropoids. In children, initially thought and speech have different roots but at a certain point of time, thought becomes verbal and speech rational. Vygotsky's investigation established that the traits of egocentric speech are at the lowest point at the age of three and at the highest point at seven. They develop in a reverse direction to the frequency of egocentric speech.

The views of Vyogtsky throw light on the language acquisition device of children. To acquire language proficiently, one has to negotiate through the zone of proximal development wherein children learn more with the support of adults around them. Vygotsky's (1962) social-cultural theory views interaction as the genesis of language. It not only facilitates language learning but is a causative force in language acquisition. He differs from most psychologists in focusing on interaction as an essential force.

CONNECTIONISM

Another psychological approach to language learning is that of connectionism. According to its latest version called Parallel Distribution Processing (PDP), the brain creates networks which connect words or phrases to other words and phrases (as well as to events and objects) which occur at the same time. These links are strengthened when learners are exposed to stimuli in specific contexts. Many studies conducted from this point of view (e.g. Ellis and Schmitt 1997, Ellis 2003) provide evidence to support connectionist account of learning. Researchers working within this framework propose that language is represented in the mind as a very large number of linguistic units which are ogranised under the law of contiguity (e.g. if A appears with B, then AB can be associated) and the law of resemblance (e.g. if C looks like A, it shares the association of A).

For instance, the word *colour* belong to the various networks. It reminds us of colours such as *red, yellow, green, blue, black* and *white*. It also reminds us of colours such as *purple* (mixed *blue* and *red*), *orange* (reddish yellow), *violet* (bluish purple), *mauve* (pale purple), *brown* (coffee colour, a combination of red, yellow and blue) and *beige* (light yellowish brown). *Indigo* is a kind of blue and *emerald*, a kind of green. It also reminds us that an object could be *colourful* or *colourless*. It could have *bright*, *dark*, *dim* or *light* colour. We *colour* something that is *colourable*. If it has been *coloured*, it is *coloured*. We think of people who are *white* or *coloured*. At a metaphorical level, we *lend colour* to something to make it true or probable but it may show its true *colour*. (See figure 5 for the hierarchy of colours).

Another type of connectionism is based on the prototype theory (Rosch 1975, 1976). If we have a hierarchy of 'birdiness'. (i.e., feature of a typical bird ought to have) and put it at the centre of a circle, *robin* is a prototypical bird, *cannary*, *sparrow* and *dove* are next to it, so we put them in its nearest outer circle. We put *crow, cuckoo* and *owl* in the next circle and *Ostrich* and *peacock* is the circle next to it. We put the *penguin* in the last circle. The less feature of 'birdness' a bird has, the further it is from the *robin.* (Figure 6)

Little research has been done on L_2 learning from the connectionist point of view. However, it is assumed that the transfer from L_1 to L_2 occurs because strong connections already established in L_1 interferes with the establishment of L_2 network. Proponents of the connectionist approach to language learning note that while frequency is "an all pervasive causal factor" (Ellis 2002 : 179), it interacts with other determinants, including the regular occurrence of the language pattern inputs.

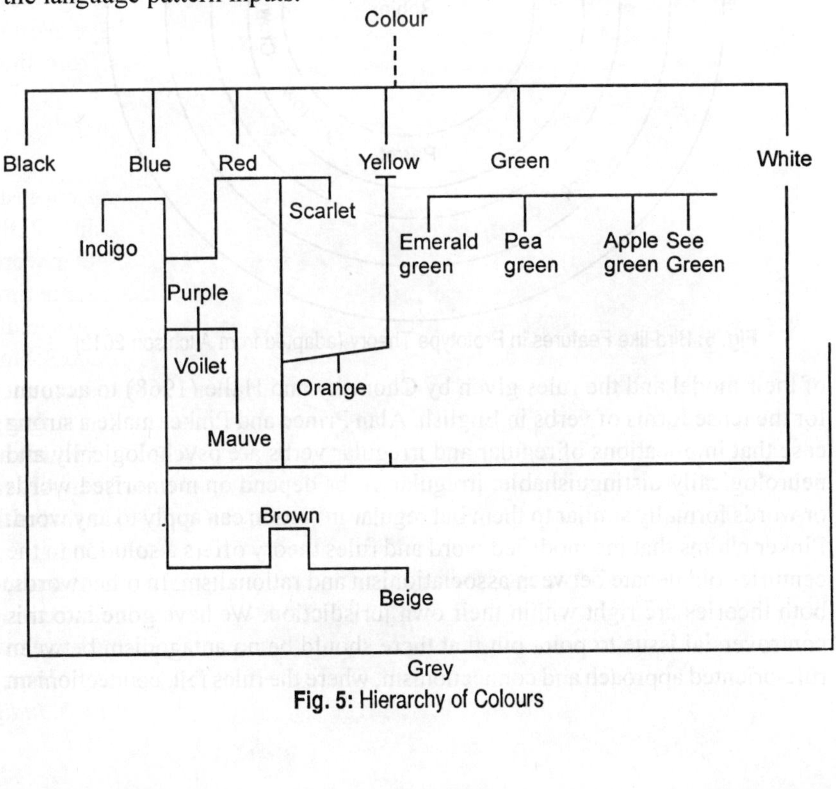

Fig. 5: Hierarchy of Colours

Connectionism differs from behaviourism in the sense that it does not believe in the thesis that behaviour (including verbal behaviour) can be explained without representing mental activity.

It differs from generative grammar the way it differs from symbol manipulations. It lacks rules organised into modules. Instead, it tries to use the law of contiguity and the law of resemblance. Rumelhart and McClelland (1986) have developed this model while discussing the past tense verbs of English.

Steven Pinker (2000: 103-117), who offers a critique of Rumelhart and McClelland, (1986) points out the problems it creates. Then he proposes a hybrid

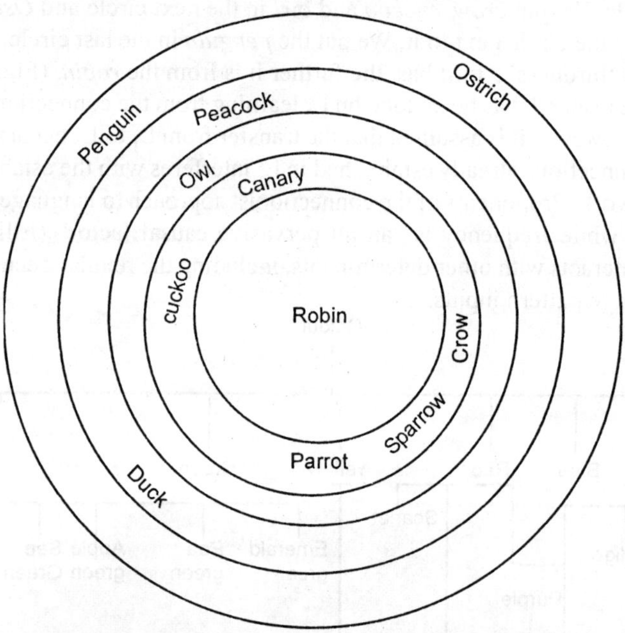

Fig. 6: Bird-like Features in Prototype Theory (adapted from Aitchison 2012)

of their model and the rules given by Chomsky and Halle (1968) to account for the tense forms of verbs in English. Alan Prince and Pinker make a strong case that implications of regular and irregular verbs are psychologically and neurologically distinguishable; irregular verbs depend on memorised words or words formally similar to them but regular infliction can apply to any word. Pinker claims that the modified word and rules theory offers a solution to the centuries old debate between associationism and rationalism. In other words, both theories are right within their own jurisdiction. We have gone into this controversial issue to point out that there should be no antagonism between rule-oriented approach and connectionism, where the rules fail, connectionism solves the problem. However, it does not mean that everywhere connectionism can replace the cognitive approach of Chomskyans.

B. SOCIOLOGICAL APPROACH

Malinowski and Firth's Contexts

Anthropology and sociology are other related disciplines that have affected our approach to the study of language learning. Two British scholars of early twentieth century - B. Malinowski (1923, 1935) and J.R. Firth (1951, 1957) focused on the *context of situation* and *context of utterance* in the process of the analysis of language. Malinowski maintained that language is an abstract universal entity which is actually manifested in different forms in different societies. Firth believed that a person is totally constrained in his/her utterance by a given social situation. The relationship of the sentence to its *context of situation* is one of the key points in his attempt to understand its meaning. The other points are its phonetics, grammar and lexicon. While describing the '*context of situation*' he thought of the socio-economic and religious settings of the society (or societies) in which the interlocutors live, their age and sex and the type of speech function they indulge in.

The context of utterance refer to the grammatical limitation on a sentence because of the configuration in which it occurs. Although they did not speak anything directly about the second language learning, their implication was clear. Second/foreign language learner has to understand the context of situation in which an utterance he/she has come across was made. As Firth was a Professor of English, phonetics and literature at Lahore University (at that time in India) for a decade (1928-1938), he must have incorporated this view while teaching in India. Though it had its impact on the teaching of English literature, the school teachers were, by and large, unaffected; they were under the influence of Henry Sweet and Harold Palmer. They believed in teaching structures and not in when to use them. While teaching literature in school, the context in which a poem or a story was written was hardly paid attention.

Sapir-Whorf Hypothesis

In the USA, Edward Sapir (1931) emphasised that, while studying a language, one should pay special attention to the role of society in which it is spoken. It was further strengthened by the theory of linguistic determinism proposed by Benjamin L. Whorf (1956). While discussing the relationship of habitual thought and behaviour to language, he asserted that every language "is a vast pattern system, different from other, in which are culturally ordained forms and categories by which the person not only communicates but also analyses... types of relationship and phenomena, channels his reasoning and builds the house of his consciousness" (1956:252). He thought that language influences unconscious habitual thought rather than limiting thought potential. Though Sapir Whorf Hypothesis influenced language philosopher and pedagogues in the USA, it did not have much impact on language teachers in schools in India.

Language Deficit Hypothesis

In 1960s Basil Bernstein, a Professor of Sociology of Education at the University of London, came up with the *Language Deficit Hypothesis*. He studied how class regulated the structure of communication within the family and the initial coding orientation of the children. The pre-school children of upper and middle class used elaborate code and were more verbal and inclined to reason than the children of the working class. The latter were more restricted than the former in vocabulary, in sentence patterns and in the variety of use of conjunctions and prepositions. They were limited to a restricted code primarily because of the sub-culture and role system of the family, community and work, he argued. For them, the school should induce a change of code so that their culturally induced backwardness transmitted through language could be reduced. However, "these children displayed low performance on verbal IQ tests and had difficulty in improving their linguistic capability. Consequently, they had general difficulty in profitting from the school" (1971:151-152).

Black English

In the USA Charles C. Fries, who was a pioneer of structural approach to English language teaching, came up with somewhat similar views on the "vulgar" English of the Black children. In 1968, A.H. Jensen elaborated the view further. A number of investigations were conducted in the USA which found that there was language deficit among pre-school and school children from poverty stricken and disadvantaged population. Cazdan (1965) argued that environmental assistance could be provided to develop their syntax. A series of specific programmes were developed for the improvement of their language skills, not only in the USA but also in Britain. However, the implications of those investigations were not applied while teaching Indian children who were also environmentally deprived with reference to English. William Labov (1970, 1974) pleaded that Black children were not deprived. They had the power of creative expressions in their own variety of English (i.e. Black English vernacular) which should be encouraged. Variationist argued for the recognition of native varieties of English outside the UK and USA. Kachru made a case for Indian English. However, it had little impact on Indian educationists. Those educationists who had sociological orientation asked the language teacher to pay special attention to them but no specific items have been suggested in the curriculum of English for culturally disadvantaged Indian children. Efforts should be made to compensate for their environmental deprivation.

Communicative Competence

The growth of transformational generative approach to language laid emphasis on two aspects of language users: their competence (i.e. ability to produce, understand and discriminate the grammatical sentences of a language) and their performance (i.e. actual use). Dell Hymes (1974) came up with the theory of *communicative competence* which involved their ability to participate in the society "as not only a speaking but also a communicating member" (p. 75). He asked linguists to study 'the communicative means available in the relationship condition, its nature and outcome' (p. 76). In short, he asked them to study language in discourse and explore the 'dimension of discourse' (p. 97), Hymes arguments were convincing and they influenced the method of language teaching both in USA and Britain. Instead of discussing the use of isolated sentences, they decided to discuss languagc in discourse.

The communicative competence approach encouraged language pedagogues to analyse how a language is structured in different context of use with a view to helping textbook writers to determine the underlying features of the text. It wanted language teachers to be more interactive with their students systematically. The discourse analysis of students' performance (oral as well as written) is supposed to lead to a better evaluation of students' performance. It is also supposed to be more sensitive to different demands that speech and writing put on the learner. Recent development in *critical discourse analysis* (as in FairClough 1995) views social context as dynamic and changing. It pleads that the text should not only be a reflection of social reality but also construct social reality.

To sum up, recent psychological and sociological approaches to language have influenced language teaching method. The social factors demand that the language to be taught must be relevant to a society in which the learner is active in life and bring him/her at par with other speakers of the language. The psychological approach helps the learner to obtain the desired objectives in a natural manner. Various developmental psycholinguistic approaches have been in search of such a method.

VARIATIONIST APPROACH

The language deficit hypothesis of 1950s brought the old controversy regarding 'standard' and 'non-standard' dialects into focus. Regional varieties of dialects had been discussed for long. What William Labov and his friends emphasised is the social variety of a language. What Bernstein and Jensen stigmatised and called handicapped expressions, Labov called a legitimate and creative dialect of Black Americans in the USA. It is a variety which is spoken and patronised by a living community. It is creative and has its own literature, Labov thought that it should be treated as an autonomous dialect. It has its own rules and the native children who speak this dialect should not be stigmatised. Those who supported the Labovian movement were called variationists. They insisted on studying the speech communities which speak such dialects. Thus developed the demand for the acknowledgement of black dialects in the UK and Africa and the varieties of English spoken in Australia and New Zealand. The variationists study the widely accepted forms of variations at the level of phonology, lexicon, morphology, syntax and discourse and examine the creative literature of their speakers. They recognise their geographical and ethnic identity on the basis of conscious awareness of their variety of language. The collection and interpretation of their data are of pedagogical importance even if they are not taught formally in schools.

GENDER BIAS AND FEMINIST APPROACH

The influence of gender on language and asymmetries of power relation have been a matter of major concern in recent time. It has affected the pedagogy of language teaching. Linguists have studied male and female accents, and the ways in which they use language. These linguistic variables have been noticed and discussed in narratives and discourse. Feminists have objected to the use of words such as *chairman*. Instead, they insist on using a gender-neutral word *'chairperson'*. They object to the generic use of *he* and want to use gender-specific word *he* or *she*. Alternatively they prefer to use *they*. Recent textbook writers have taken note of such developments. They prefer to use words and expressions which have no gender bias.

PRAGMATIC APPROACH

Many points discussed earlier in this section are assimilated in the pragmatic approach to language teaching. A pragmatic approach is not confined to the study of expressions incorporated in the text, it also studies what the text suggests pragmatically. For instance, it studies how people communicate more than what the utterances mean by themselves and how people make such interpretations. It discusses why people say or interpret something in one way and not another. It tries to find out the nature of the interlocutors and their relationship, and the circumstances in which they make an utterance.

The pragmatists are guided by Grice's conversational postulates, the use of politeness and cooperative principles. Their main perspective is based on a distinction between the linguistic form of an utterance and its communicative function. It discusses what makes a discourse socially relevant. It insists on pragmatic proficiency in language instruction. For it, they want the language learners to be exposed to pragmatically authentic teaching materials and the language teacher to be able to give pragmatic interpretation to them. *Meaning in Interaction* by G. Thomas (1995) and *Pragmatic* by G. Yule (1996) provide useful and interesting examples of such an approach.

MODERN INDIAN THINKERS ON EDUCATION AND LANGUAGE TEACHING

When the Western System of modern education was introduced to India, some Indians supported it whole heartedly and some opposed it completely. Gradually some Indians who were products of the system started looking at it critically. We may look at their views briefly here.

Swami Vivekananda

Swami Vivekananda (1862-1902) was a disciple of Ramakrishna Paramhanṣa. He was well-educated in Indian religion and philosophy and had a sound knowledge of the Upanishad, Vedanta and Purana. At the same time he had studied modern western philosophy and knew Decarte, Spinoza, Hume, Kant, Hegel, Comte, Schopenhauer and Darwin well. His study enabled him to look at the Vedanta philosophy in a new light. He believed that Vedanta inspired all philosophical trends in Hinduism. He divided the Indian philosophical trends into two groups. Dvaita (the dualist Vedanta) and Advaita (the non-dualist Vedanta). He believed that the external forces (i.e. the objective phenomena) evoke the internal forces (i.e. sensitiveness, perceptions, concepts) and they become one. This homogeneity is, according to him, the essence of one's mental development. He believed that one's spiritual and physical forces should be combined to defend one's vital interest. He believed in Karma Yoga (the philosophy of action) and argued that the knowledge of Karma Yoga exists in the mind; it guides everything, physical or mental. He believed that the circumstances of life are of decisive significance for the formation of an individual's will.

By the time Vivekananda founded the Ramakrishna Mission in 1897, his philosophical views were fully crystallised. He wanted this to be conveyed to as many people as possible and thought that one of the ways to popularise them was through education. It was through education that an individual's character could be moulded, he asserted. He said, "Education is not the amount of information that is put into your brain and runs riot there, undigested all your life; we must have life-building, man-making, character-making assimilation of ideas. If you have assimilated fine ideas and made them your life and character, you have more education than any man who has got by heart a whole library" (*The Complete Work* Vol. III, p. 302).

He criticised the modern system of education and said, "Is that education as the result of which the will is well-nigh killed out; under whose sway, why mention new ideas, even the old ones are disappearing one by one, is that education which is slowly making a man a machine?" (*The Complete Work*, Vol. IV: 490)

As he paid attention to the implementation of his views, he inspired the Mission to open Ramakrishna Mission Schools with a view to producing young men of character. Ramakrishna Mission Schools have been in operation in various parts of India for more than a century. They follow the curriculum of Central Board of Secondary Education (CBSE) or of the State Boards. Their students compete with students of other schools successfully. So far we know no objective assessment has been made to assess the extent to which they have succeeded in embibing Vivekananda's views. However, they have played a decisive role in the spread of education among girls.

Vivekananda and Language Teaching

Vivekananda rightly believed in the enormous role language plays in an individual's life. "Language is a magic form of communication; it does not require any special appliances or devices. I speak to you without touching you but the vibrations of the air produced by my speech penetrate into your ear, affect your nerve and produce a certain effect on your brain. You cannot resist it," he said (*Complete Works*, Vol. 1, P. 70).

He stressed the need to educate children in their mother tongue. At the same time he favoured the teaching of Sanskrit and English. In short, he was in favour of the use of any language which helped students in building their character and developing their personality properly.

As Vivekananda wanted to give a definite organisational form to the movement for educating the Indian masses, he attached great significance to educating people through the language they knew well. At the same time he stressed the need to enrich the knowledge available in that language by borrowing from what was available in languages like English and Sanskrit. In short, his progressive philosophical and sociological views played a decisive role in the development of modern India.

It may be pointed out that the advent of Vivekananda was after the Brahmo Samaj had its firm roots in the Westernised section of upper class Bengali society which was totally in favour of western education through the medium of English. It also coincided with the coming of Swami Dayanand Saraswati's Arya Samaj which stood for the revival of the Vedic values of Hinduism and revival of Sanskrit. Vivekananda avoided these extreme views on language and had a pragmatic approach in which both the mother tongue and English were to be used to gain knowledge.

Sri Aurobindo

The Indian Renaissance in education that began with the Brahmo Samaj and Arya Samaj and gained momentum under the guidance of Swami Vivekananda got a new manifestation under Sri Aurobindo (1873-1950). He was not only an idealist philosopher of neo-Vedanta but also an outstanding leader of the national liberation movement in India in the late nineteenth and early twentieth century. His contribution to the national educational movement was equally remarkable. He believed that education must be given a spiritual orientation so that an educated young man would lead a divine life, for his/her country, for himself/herself and for society in general. He argued that education must not provide merely information, but be "the instrument for the real working of the spirit in the mind and body of the individual and the nation". Since the principle instrument of knowledge is in the mind, education must aim at the improvement of the mind of the individual and the society, the nation and the universe, he said.

Sri Aurobindo founded the Aurobindo Ashram at Pondicherry for the evolution of a new kind of human beings who would have "higher consciousness and embody a full life of spirit". He kept this objective view while formulating his education policy. Sri Aurobindo emphasised that the goal of primary education should be the development of physical being and vital being so that a student understands both the inner world and the world outside of himself/herself. He/she must learn the right use of his/her six senses. The education of the vital being involves the discipline (*tapasya*) of power. With the increase in power, comes the liberation from the ordinary desires which lays the foundation for spiritual life, he said. The main task of physical education is to awaken the aspiration for the divine in the mind and the body, he said.

Sri Aurobindo set forth the broad outlines of his educational theory and left it for the Mother to substantiate it. As physical education is completely governed by order, method and discipline, the Mother considered sports and games as means to develop in learners good humour and self-control. It would lead to the control over one's ego, she said. The major task would be to awaken full awareness of the divine in the body. It would lead to one's mental education which aims at the acquisition of old knowledge, the discovery of new knowledge and a capacity to apply that knowledge. Neither Aurobindo nor the Mother was concerned about the teaching of many subjects. However, the Mother believed that, in order to live in a community, one has to know a language correctly, a little geography, history, modern science and rules of conduct.

The Mother recommended the teaching of English as the international language, the mother tongue, French and simplified Sanskrit. Sri Aurobindo believed that the child should be taught in his/her mother tongue but for those who want to go in for higher studies, English is indispensable. Sri Aurobindo believed in a child's free progress at school. It means that the child should be allowed to proceed with his/her own pace. Students should be able to choose their subjects of study, cultivate areas of their interest and decide to choose their examination. The emphasis was on the use of worksheets in the classroom rather than on lectures. The goal is not to prepare them for examinations to succeed and earn money but to be able to think, meditate on what they read and reflect. Free progress implies that education is merely an invitation to learning and is at best suggestive. It means to prepare students to work for personal and collective transformation, the removal of *tamas*, to have senses under discipline and to awaken *satya*. The duty of the teacher is not to lecture on these things but to present them as examples in their own lives. He/she should be a light kindling other lights, an awakened soul awakening other souls. Silent examples and casting influence were major factors in the role of a teacher, he said. The Ashram opened a chain of Mother International Schools to fulfil the educational mission of Sri Aurobindo and language teaching is a vital means to achieve it.

Rabindranath Tagore

Rabindranath Tagore (1861-1941), the only Indian who got the Nobel Prize (literature) for his poetic works, was a creative genius of many facets. He was a poet, dramatist, literary critic, essayist, artist, philosopher and educationist. In the words of Jawaharlal Nehru, "He was a beacon light to all of us, ever pointing to the finer and nobler aspects of life and never allow us to fall into the ruts…" He gave an international orientation to our nationalist movement and enriched it with his creative works in literature, arts and music. Tagore's grandfather was a close companion of Raja Ram Mohan Roy, the founder of Brahmo Samaj, and his father Devendranath Tagore its leading light.

When Rabindranath was sent to school, he felt suffocated in the 'mechanical, mountainous' atmosphere; it was 'a drain of the fluid element' of his childhood. He had to rely on his own instincts for his education. He remembered this experience when he built up Sri Niketan, a school of his dream in Shantiniketan, and gave freedom to children to find their places in natural surroundings and have fullness in their lives. He enabled them to grow up as human beings with the help of literature, music, painting and dramatic performances. He discovered that the minds actively engaged in constructive activities work fast and develope energies which seeks larger outlet in their pursuit of knowledge. He found the children always active and alert. He made an attempt to nourish their reasoning faculty to allow them freedom in the world of truth, imagination and human relationships. Unlike the children of government and mission schools, the products of his school were supposed to be sensitive to the world around them and their own selves. In the modern complex world, Tagore wanted the products of his school to be saved from the ill-temperate overgrowth of material culture, be selective and live in harmony with nature.

Tagore was in favour of the mother tongue of the child being the medium of instruction. However, he was aware of the advantage of learning English and made provision for its teaching. He attached importance to physical education and to save children from being lethargic. His students took delight in cooking, weaving, gardening, and improving their surroundings. For them, right atmosphere was more important than rules and methods, classroom teaching and textbooks. Tagore believed that in educational organisation of his type, the nourishment of reasoning faculties was more important than the geography of foreign lands. It was necessary to develop the capacity to understand people of different countries, belonging to different traditions and cultures and speaking different languages. Though Tagore was a staunch nationalist, he had an international outlook and wanted his students to develop it. International cooperation should be one of the goals of education, he said. "I represent in my institution an ideal of brotherhood where men of different countries and different languages could come together, he said. Instead of sectarian religious education, he believed in creating an atmosphere at school which was rich in the sense of being broad and secular.

Like Vivekananda and Sri Aurobindo, Tagore emphasised physical education but not for spiritual reasons but for fitness and alertness to better education. Like Gandhi, he emphasised handicraft and other manual skills not as much for economic self-independence but for artistic and aesthetic reasons. He was against the orientation of the prevailing objective of acquiring purely bookish knowledge. He favoured moral education for the all-round development of students' personality whereas Gandhi favoured it for the reasons of ethical politics. Gandhi worked for the development of an alternative national policy of education whereas Tagore emphasised both the national and international points of view.

Though Tagore was completely in favour of the mother tongue being the medium of institution, he wanted English to be taught not only for science and technology but also for access to the rich treasure of English literature. Both Tagore and Gandhi emphasised the national education to awaken national consciousness in spite of difference in emphasis on some points. These differences are manifested in the unique character of the school and University at Shantiniketan.

Mahatma Gandhi

When Mohandas Karamchand Gandhi (1869-1948), (better known as Mahatma Gandhi) came on the political scene of India, he turned the Indian National Congress from a party of enlightened educated Indians into a party of the masses. When he called for *Swaraj*, he did not mean mere political freedom; he meant self-rule by the people of India. He pointed out that the journey to *Swaraj* required vast organising ability. It meant "penetration into the villages solely for the services of the villagers". It meant 'awakening the national consciousness among the masses which was possible only when the masses were educated. Education was, thus, for him, an essential component of the political programme of the nation'.

Swami Vivekananda and Sri Aurobindo thought of an alternative education policy for India for spiritual reasons, and Tagore mostly as a reaction against his own experience of the school life. Gandhi got interested in an alternative education policy for political reasons. He believed that the ultimate objective of politics should be to have liberated human values which could be achieved by education alone. Unless all the children living in remote villages were educated, at least upto the primary level, they will not understand the real significance of *Swaraj* and will not strive for it, he thought. "Our system of education and public work must be based on provincial languages", he asserted. He pointed out that without infringing on the domain of provincial languages, "we must have a common all India medium of communication", which, he thought, should be Hindustani.

Gandhi was well aware of the vast gap between educated and uneducated Indians and wanted to bridge it. If we want a truly democratic awareness, this gap must be fitted by creating an urge among the educated privileged class to recognise the significance of working with hands. For that, he wanted to have a system of *Social Education* in which some form of socially productive work could become its integral part. He emphasised the need for it for another reason. He wanted this movement of universal primary education to be self-supporting. If children were trained in some profit-yielding production while being educated, the school would become self-supporting and teachers will not have to depend on outside support for their salary, he thought.

"My plan to impart primary education through village handicrafts like spinning and carding, etc. is thus conceived as the spearhead of a silent social revolution brought with most far reaching consequences", he wrote (*Educational Reconstruction*, 25). This approach of Gandhi, if implemented sincerely, would have strengthened the economy of the village. The production-oriented education would maintain a continuity between home and school. This well-intended scheme was implemented in the early days of independent India but it did not bring about the desired result. The schools could not become self-dependent and had to depend on government aids for survival.

Another important point in the Gandhian policy was to use the mother tongue of the child for school education. Gandhi favoured the mother tongue as the medium of instruction upto the university level so that the acquisition and assimilation of knowledge is facilitated better. He was not opposed to students' learning English. In fact, he considered it necessary to do so to have an easy access to world knowledge.

This scheme of Gandhi was put before a national conference organised by the Indian National Congress and was unanimously endorsed in 1937. It appointed a Committee under the chairmanship of Dr. Zakir Hussain to implement the programme. The Committee came up with the programme of *Nai Talim* (New Education) which was implemented by the Government of India after independence. However, it did not work successfully. The mother tongue was used as a medium of instruction throughout India, though English medium private schools were left untouched. The Gandhian principle of self-sufficiency in schools could not be fulfilled. However, the emphasis shifted to skills training and other job-oriented schemes. Increased mechanisation of agriculture and other rural economic activities have now shifted the goal of education and some of the suggestions of Gandhi have become redundant. But two important points stand out. The medium of instruction must be the mother tongue and the system of education needs to be in accordance with the development of Indian economy. Gandhi's main point – education for social reconstruction—is the corner stone of our education policy.

Dr. Zakir Hussain

Dr. Zakir Hussain (1897-1969) was a product of Mohemdan Anglo-Oriental College (later, Aligarh Muslim University), Aligarh. He joined the national freedom movement while he was still a student and became a close follower of Mahatma Gandhi. He did his Ph.D. in education from the University of Berlin and became a teacher in Jamia Millia Islamia. When Gandhi's proposal on his education policy for India was put before a national conference in Wardha in 1937, he was appointed the Chairman of the Committee which was formed to chalk out the detailed programme of Basic Education. The Committee endorsed Gandhi's policy and prepared the outlines of *Nai Talim*, (new education). It recommended the allround development of students, including physical and moral development. The students were to have a sense of dignity from manual labour, a spirit of self-reliance and firm belief in non-violence and democratic ideals. Dr. Hussain practised all these values as a teacher and, later on as the Vice-Chancellor of Jamia Millia Islamia. Under his leadership, Jamia Millia developed an excellent centre for the training of teachers who were supposed to be role models for school students.

The Basic Education Schemes, as detailed by Dr. Hussain, was picked up by the State Governments under the leadership of Congress but it slowed down when the Congress Ministries resigned during the World War II. It was implemented with renewed vigour in primary schools after 1945 but was implemented in only a few chosen secondary schools. At the university level, Jamia Millia came up with the programme of community contact and national service. It associated its students with the day-to-day management of affairs of the university, especially with the maintenance of discipline and confidence building between teachers and students. He believed in inculcating in students the qualities of fellow-feeling, the habit of working together, keeping students involved in various aspect of society. He believed in getting them inspired to work hard and sincerely in order to fashion Indian society after Gandhian thought.

Even when Dr. Zakir Hussain came to public life and became the Vice-President and then, the President of India, he did not cease to have interest in education. He often regretted the poor standard of higher education in India and wanted it to be improved. He did not like the universities to be divorced from the realities and needs of social and national life. He wanted the university to provide adequate guidance and facilities to students, especially to those who came from underprivileged unsatisfactory social and family background.

Dr. Hussain commended the public schools in India for maintaining good educational standard and invited them to have more freedom, initiative and experimentation. He asked them not to be exclusive, and enlarge their sphere of influence. He wanted them to be an integral part of national system of education and provide leadership to the programme of improvement of school education in general.

Like Mahatma Gandhi, Dr. Hussain was strongly in favour of the mother tongue being the medium of education, especially at primary and secondary levels. Later on, he became a staunch supporter of three language formula, the teaching of the mother tongue, Hindustani and English. He was in favour of having a large number of children libraries being available at schools as well as outside, in which various types of books could be made available. These books must be easily comprehensible and well-illustrated. There should be books on myths and legends, history and geography, science and technology written in Indian languages. He was not in favour of books written in controlled vocabulary. If they have a natural style, they create a natural and convenient atmosphere. While enjoying such books, children would enrich their vocabulary and power of expression. Reading books will broaden the horizon of general readers as well and make them see things in a proper perspective. He pleaded that scientific and technical books written in a simple style be made available to general public to help them develop a scientific outlook, he said.

In short, Dr. Hussain not only explained and implemented the Gandhian philosophy of education but enriched it by his own creative contribution.

Dr. S. Radhakrishnan

Dr. Sarvapalli Radhakrishnan (1888-1975) was an eminent scholar and statesman who was the President of India during 1962-1967. He served as Professor of Philosophy at Mysore and Calcutta Universities and as Vice Chancellor of Andhra and Benaras Universities. He was a professor of eastern philosophy and ethics at Oxford University, leader of Indian delegation to the UNESCO, Chairman of the University Education Commission (1948-49) and of the University Grants Commission. He was a versatile writer and wrote books on Indian philosophy to make it comprehensible to western readers. He made immense contribution to the development of new education policy in post-Independence India.

The Radhakrishnan Commission reviewed the existing secondary education system and suggested that it be of twelve years. It proposed that the graduate course be of three years. It suggested radical changes in the curriculum and introduced diversified courses. It favoured objective tests and continued evaluation. It emphasised research work in post-graduate studies and introduced the M.Phil programme as a pre-Ph.D. course work.

Dr. Radhakrishnan was strongly in favour of regional languages as the media of education. He was for the teaching of three languages — the regional language, Hindi and English at the secondary school level. He suggested that Indian languages be the media of instructions in higher education as well but also wanted English to be taught well so that western thought is constantly available to Indian students. He favoured compulsory school education with emphasis on the well-balanced development of the child. The goal of education should not be mere collection of information, it should be the acquisition of ability to think independently and develop one's full potential. To him, education is neither memorizing facts for acquiring merely technical skills, it is complete mental, physical and spiritual growth of the child, it means well-balanced development of one's personality. He observes, "Education has for its aim the complete and harmonious development of different functions of man.... Every educator must have full knowledge of the nature of the school which it is his business to bring into fullness and maturity. A knowledge of child's mind is therefore necessary for a teacher".

Dr. Radhakrishnan differentiated between *vidya* (knowledge) and *avidya* (ignorance). He thought the aim of education should be integral knowledge which possesses its object truly and securely. Nothing is external to it. "Nothing is other than itself", he observed. He thought that intuitive knowledge is immediate whereas discussion and mediate knowledge is indirect; it has symbolic or representative value. By employing intuitive consciousness, we know the object with less distortion and more actuality, he remarked. To him, knowledge and being are the same thing. That is why he argued that knowledge should be imparted in such a way that it becomes a part of one's being. *Vidya* is a way of apprehending reality. It stresses harmony and interconnection of elements which make up the world. *Vidya* is also understood as *jnana* which is the essence of reality. In short, Dr. Radhakrihsnan's conception of education was rooted in the traditional Indian approach to educational philosophy but he was equally aware of advantages of modern education and wanted it to be implemented on the universal basis in the country.

As mentioned above, Dr. Radhakrishnan wanted a regional language in

India to be the medium of education not only in schools but also at the university. However, he wanted the teaching of English to continue as a vital source of acquiring modern knowledge. At the same time he was in favour of teaching Sanskrit, together with the implementation of the three language formula. He appreciated the Gandhian system of education, specially its scheme of self-independence, allegiance to local environment and emphasis on building students' character. He was in favour of making students aware of ancient Indian culture, including the essence of Vedas and Upanishads. However, his orientation was different from that of Swami Vivekananda and Sri Aurobindo. He wanted Indian students to turn into persons who would be modern in outlook but deeply rooted in Indian tradition in regard to its basic values. He wanted teachers to be progressive in outlook, willing to encourage students to question and criticise them. He wanted them to use innovative methods of teaching to suit the changing Indian society.

Gijubhai Badheka

Gijubhai Badheka (1885-1939) was trained as a lawyer, practised law in the Badvan camp of the High Court of Bombay and was a legal adviser to Shri Dakshinmurti Bhawan. Though he was not a professionally trained educationist, he made significant contribution to the development of educational thought in colonial India. He was very critical of the highly bureaucratic education system which had no room for freshness and change. In most of the cases, in rural areas in Gujarat (as in other parts of India) there was a gap between the socio-economic background of teachers and students and between the school life and domestic life of children. Consequently, children were ill at easy at school most of the time as they did not find the learning environment friendly. The teachers too felt suffocated because they had no room for innovative teaching. Gijubhai felt the problem very acutely when his son was ready to go to school. He felt the urge to do something to change the situation, was inspired by the Montessori system and opened the first pre-primary school — Bal Mandir — under the aegis of Shri Dakshinamurti Vidyapith Bhawan. Inspired by the ideology of Maria Montessori, he expressed his views on elementary education, suggesting ways of improving it. He wrote his views in simply eloquent colloquial Gujarati with conviction and insight. He reflected on his classroom experiences and offered practical suggestions without indulging in academic jargan.

Gijubhai suggested that primary school teachers should try to learn children's psychology and offer them meaningful environment so that they become fond of their school. He recommended useful activities like storytelling, staging plays and organising games. Since games help in character building, they offer real education, he said. He wanted children to learn by doing so that they do not depend on textbooks. He was against teaching religious dogmas in the name of moral education. While teaching any subject, the teacher should concentrate on the underlying concepts and help children identify them through activities.

Gijubhai was for the change in the educational system and thought that experimentation would lead to change. He conceded that some experiments would lead to failure but that was an inevitable process. Success comes out of failures. A teaching programmes may not work the way it has been planned but it makes the teacher aware of its shortcomings while guiding him/her to further improvement and innovation. Children usually prepare themselves for the examination but they need to learn to play and read, and not focus on mere paper work, he argued.

In *Divasvapna* (1991) Gijubhai discusses how he conducted the language class by the dramatic representation of a lesson. A portion of the classroom was turned into a stage but no arrangement was made for setting the stage or procuring special dress or makeup. The students were not required to memorize dialogues. The teacher made them familiar with the story orally and gave them necessary stage directions to express them kinetically. The children enjoyed enacting the story thoroughly and it was not necessary for them to memorize its contents. The grammatical lessons on number, gender, case, pronouns and agreement were presented as word games. They were made familiar with the gender of words with the help of cards. On one side of a card was a word, on the other side was its gender. The children looked at the cards one by one to familiarize themselves with the gender of words (e.g. *horse: male, bitch: female, hen: female, bull: male, etc.)* Then they were given two boxes. One box contained the words of the masculine gender and the other, those of the feminine gender. Students were asked to pick up one word from each of the boxes and form couples (e.g., *cow: ox; horse: mare; cock: hen, etc.).* They were asked to tell the gender of the word *student.* Some said male, some said, female. They responded the same way about the word *teacher.* Since these words could be wither *male* or *female,* they belonged to the *common* gender. The students were asked to differentiate between names of entities which have life (i.e., are animate) and those which don't have life (i.e., are inanimate). They were told that in English only animate entities were either masculine or feminine; All inanimate entities were either masculine or feminine; all inanimate entities were of neutral gender. Thus, the word game made them familiar with the gender system of English and they did not have to memorize them by rot. Gijubhai discusses in detail how students could be made familiar with various grammatical categories while they played various types of word games (*Divasvapna* 1991: 50-59)[1].

1. In *Divasvapna* Gijubhai, presumably, discussed examples from Gujarati. We have presented examples from English to make them relevant in the context of this book.

One of his experiments was to do away with the hackneyed timetable. He divided the day into activities — games and stories. His writings opened the doors of possibilities to make primary education enjoyable and beautiful. One may not like all ideas of Gijubhai equally but one will not fail to be inspired to explore one's own new ideas in search of meaningful alternative ways of teaching.

One of the after effects of Gijubhai's work has been the study of cross cultural variations in psychological processes of learning. Researchers have tried to identify specific situations of cultural differences in the psychological processes of learning. Several interesting methodological strategies have been used to ascertain the reasons for cultural differences, explain them and draw conclusions to tackle the problems of children of multiple cultural backgrounds in a classroom. While the results of those research activities are made available to primary school teachers, Gijubhai's arguments that the self-introspection of teachers is of utmost value remains valid. Experiments in multicultural classroom can lead to greater appreciation of cultural differences in a complex society such as in India. An appreciation of differences by a teacher can enrich the life of children with tolerance and appreciation of diversity.

The Western perspectives on education, with special reference to second language teaching, can be looked at from philosophical, psychological and sociocultural points of view. From the point of view of modern philosophy, the chapter summarizes briefly the views of William James and John Dewey which emphasize the creative urge of children to encourage their problem-solving ability. Though their basic philosophy was over-shadowed by logical positivism of late nineteenth and early twentieth century, the orientation it gave to curriculum development continued even during the hay day of behaviourism. Psychologists such as Watson, Thorndike, Pavlov, Skinner and Bruner kept the objective of encouraging problem solving in view to enhance children's intelligence.

The behaviourist theory of language learning believes in habit formation and recommends structural drills to form sentence construction habits. It also believes that some features of first language differ from those of the second and this difference obstructs the acquisition of second language correctly. It recommends that, while hearing a second or foreign language, special attention should be paid to such differences.

The developmental theory of Chomskyan transformational generative grammar asserts that the process of L_2 acquisition is identical to the process of acquiring L_1. Its followers propose a new model of processes of learning in which the language environment plays a crucial role but so are the roles of filter, organizer and monitor. It is suggested that filter and organizer are subconscious processes whereas monitor is a conscious process. The subconscious processes may lead to 'interlanguage' which the monitor modifies, giving the learner the skill to correct verbal performance.

While Chomsky believes in the in-born ability of a child to learn a language, Piaget thinks that language acquisition is a process which moves from an egocentric to a socialised stage. Vygotsky's approach believes in the concept of inner speech which is an internal mental exercise which is improved by external social uses. According to him, the learner's acculturation is a crucial factor.

Connectionism is a new version of classical associationism which believes that language is represented in the mind as linguistic units. These units are activitated when the learner is exposed to stimuli in specific contexts. The prototype theory of word-association with superordinate and subordinate units is an example of connectionism.

The modern Indian views on education, including language teaching, comprise those of philosophers like Swami Vivekanand, Aurobindo and Radhakrishnan, sociopolitical thinkers like Rabindranath Tagore and Mahatma Gandhi and academic activists like or Zakir Hussain and Gijubhai Badheka. They all emphasize the need to give a new orientation to the modern education system in India and highlight the importance of spiritualism and morality. They want the system to help Indian children in developing a wholesome personality and to be able to think on their own about the knowledge they acquire and accumulate. They want children to develop a healthy national outlook but not ignore their responsibility to the world. While Gandhi thought of educational reconstruction for all sections of children of Indian society from the national point of view. Tagore and Radhakrishan wanted them to imbibe the basic values of Indian culture. Dr. Zakir Hussain and Gijubhai Budheka were pragmatists who thought about ways to assimilate Indian values in our education system. They contributed to educational methodology in their own ways.

All of them wanted education to be impartial though the mother tongue of the child, up to the highest level, if possible. None of them minimized the importance of teaching English but they did not want it to upsurp the position reserved for the mother tongue or national language. They were all reacting to the colonial system of education and the role of English in it. They could not visualize that Indians would demand the teaching of English for their social enhancement even in independent India, even though they recognized the increasing significance of English as a world language.

Eclectic Approach

The language teacher operates within the generative framework when he/she teaches transformations and manipulation of syntactic expressions. He/she follows structuralism when he/she insists on structural drills and on connectionism or parallel distributed processing when he/she relates words to other words. An eclectic approach to language teaching welcomes all these steps.

7
Teaching English as a Second Language
Various Methods

SYSTEM, METHOD, APPROACH, STRATEGY, DESIGN AND TECHNIQUE

A *system* is a carefully designed or formulated plan or procedure to be followed while doing a certain kind of work. It is a set of principles or procedures according to which something is organized or done.

A *method* is a particular procedure of doing something, for instance, teaching, which is regular, orderly and definite in thought or exression.

An *approach* is a way of dealing with a situation or problem. It is a way of thinking or doing a particular task.

A *strategy* is a plan of action designed to achieve a long term goal or fulfill an overall aim. It is a skill in managing or planning, especially by using a strategic scheme to achieve some purpose.

A *design* is a plan or drawing produced to show the look and function or working of an object. It indicates purpose or planning that exists behind a fact, an object or an action. It is a plan or sketch to work from.

A *technique* is a way of carrying out a particular task. It is a scientific procedure to carry out an operation. In general, it is a method or manner of accomplishing some tasks.

In language teaching we talk about the direct or bilingual method, the oral method, the audio visual method, etc. We adopt the deductive or inductive approach to discuss linguistic data. We have a psychological, sociological or socio psychological approach, the communicative approach, etc. The expressions *approach* and *method* have overlapping uses. Some people talk about the situational approach and some about the situational method.

TEACHING A SECOND LANGUAGE IN ANCIENT INDIA

Teaching a second language – whether it means another language of the same country or a foreign language – has a centuries-old long and diverse history. In ancient India, natural languages (variants of *Prakrit*) developed as languages of everyday discourse and Sanskrit became a language of scholarly and polite courtly discourse. It was taught as a second language but people did not feel any difference. Perhaps, initially, no attempt was made to teach Prakrit formally but Sanskrit was taught by teaching the well-established rules of its grammar (as in Paniṇi) and a well-recognised lexicon (as in *Amarkosh*). People from abroad – from South East and East Asia and from neighbouring West and Central Asia—who came to Taxila, Nalanda and other centres of higher learning, learnt Sanskrit and Pali to understand lectures and discussions on philosophy, religion, politics, administration, and various other subjects. Unfortunately, there is no written record of how they learnt the language(s) of scholarly discourse. When Muslims came to India from various Islamic countries, they brought Persian with them and adopted it as a new language of administration. When the British arrived in India, they found both Sanskrit and Persian flourishing as languages of scholarly discourse. In south India, they found Tamil occupying a similar place. In centres of learning, the emphasis was on learning the skills to read and interpret the texts for which listening and speaking skills had to be acquired as well.

Early immigrants in India acquired the local language of the area in which they settled and they got assimilated in the local population. When Muslim immigrants came in contact with the local population, their mutual contact gave birth to a new language – Rekhta or Hindvi – out of which Hindustani grew up; in course of time, it developed into Hindi and Urdu. Sanskrit, Persian and Arabic were taught, not through the medium of local languages, but independently, by teaching their grammars and vocabulary. They followed a monolingual method, as the grammar of local languages did not stand in the way of acquiring these languages of higher discourse.

TEACHING ENGLISH TO IMMIGRANTS IN THE UK

The British of the early days were taught Latin, as Sanskrit was taught in India, by exposing students to grammatical rules and lexicon – and helping them to read Latin itself. In the sixteenth century, the reformation brought about a radical change and people's interest developed in teaching English formally. After Norman invasion, French became a prestigious language in England and was learnt by those who wanted their cultural and social advancement. The educated upper class learnt French, Greek and Latin at school but not through the medium of English.

After the Reformation, a little over four hundred thousand Protestants from France, Spain and Italy migrated to England who felt the need to learn English for their survival. Jacques Ballot, a French immigrant, wrote *The English Schoolmaster* in 1500, which contained a detailed account of English alphabet and pronunciation, and some rules of grammar to enable the new immigrants to learn reading and writing in English. The dialogues in the text contained scenes of shopping, social gathering and conversation. John Floria, who was a private tutor of Italian to aristocratic families in London, also wrote two small books on English. He discussed spellings and pronunciations of some English words and wrote some practical dialogues in English on fanciful topics. Georg Mason, a French merchant, wrote a small book on English which had dialogues concerning business and women. There were several books by foreign writers on the teaching of English as a foreign language but none of them made the kind of impact that John Wallis' did.

MILLER'S BOOK ON TEACHING ENGLISH TO BENGALIS

From the Indian point of view, the publication of John Miller's *The Tutor* in 1797 was unique. "It was a new English and Bengali work, well adopted to teach Bengali natives English". It introduced English alphabet, a list of phonetically contrastive sets (like lip, nip, sip, rip, pip, etc.), a list of words with their Bengali equivalents and some traditional grammatical notes. The dialogues were concerned with commercial activities and each English sentence was given its Bengali equivalent in a parallel column on the same page. It was the first empirical effort to introduce English to those Indians (especially Bengalis) who had business relations with the British.

GRAMMAR-TRANSLATION METHOD

During the eighteenth century, the concentration was mainly on the foreigners settled in the UK and the method to teach them English was to make them familiar with pronunciation, vocabulary and rules of grammar of English and then expose them to various types of dialogues. However, it did not remain indifferent to the well-established system of teaching classical languages like Greek and Latin which emphasised making learners familiar with the rules of grammar. They applied this knowledge to the interpretation of texts with the help of dictionaries. This method was suitable for well-educated people but when it was applied to schools, the texts were replaced by examples of sentences denoting various grammatical categories. These books were graded and examples were given for each stage. Each new lesson had one or two new grammatical rules, a short vocabulary list and some practice – examples to translate (e.g. from English to German and vice-versa). Franz Ahn's French course book, *A New, Practical and Easy Method* was published in 1834. It was a huge success. Its lessons were arranged in short, easy sections. Each odd numbered lesson gave a grammatical note with a paradigm, some vocabulary items and a set of sentences to be translated into the mother tongue (e.g. from French to English). Each even numbered lesson contained mother-tongue sentences to be translated into French and had no teaching point. The grammar and vocabulary were simple but the sentences were disconnected.

Another successful book based on the grammar-translation method was H.G. Ollendorff's book on German. He based his lessons on "interaction". Each lesson had a question and an answer which showed the relation between interrogative and indicative sentences. His main emphasis was to put grammar in a conversational style.

There were other text-books based on grammar-translations method which were more grammar-oriented. They gave full declensions of nouns and verbs and took number and gender into consideration. Such text books were heavily loaded with grammatical points. Though they were more comprehensive than the books of Ahn and Ollendorff, the latter were more in demand than them. The main problem with all of them was that they concentrated on analysing the language rather than using it.

Jacque Joseph Jacotot, a teacher of French as a foreign language, was struck by the irrelevance of explanation in textbooks available in the grammar and translation model. He argued that the function of a language teacher was to respond to the learner, and not to direct and control him by explanations in advance. He believed in the philosophy of self-help and in the dictum that one should learn one item thoroughly and relate it to everyday event. Though he could not have much impact on language teaching method, he raised issues which opened the door for a new approach.

THE RATIONAL MOVEMENT

Claude Marcel pleaded to make reading the first priority in the foreign language teaching. He made a distinction between 'impression' (i.e. reception in modern terminology) and 'expression' (i.e., production) and talked about four skills of language study: hearing, speaking, reading and writing. He ordered *impression* (i.e. hearing and reading) over *expression* (i.e., speaking and writing). He pleaded that the analytical method could bring the learner closer to the object of study than the synthetic method which paid attention to principles and rules. However, in keeping with the trend of his time, he paid more attention to reading than hearing. It created the impression that he did not care for pronunciation which is why the proponents of the reform movement did not pay much attention to him.

THE MASTERY SYSTEM

One of the key nineteenth century reformers, Thomas Prendergast was an officer of the Indian Civil Service in Madras where he learnt Telugu and Hindustani. His mastery of languages (or the *Art of Speaking Foreign Languages Idiomatically*) was published in 1864. He observed children learning a language and found that they learnt readymade chunks of language and used them in complete idiomatic sentences with fluency. However, if an

Englishman wanted to learn Telugu or Hindustani properly, he had to have an organised mind and an ability to fit the chunks of expression he had picked up into basic sentences he knew already. He emphasised the conscious mastery of sentences rather than understanding of structures. He was against the intervension of the language teacher when the learner was trying to express himself/herself.

Francois Gouin, a pre-reformist, believed that people expressed their experience in sequence and a language-learner should be encouraged to describe his/her experience in sequence of small sentences. Earlier, he had tried to learn German through grammar-and-translation method and had miserably failed. Later on, he applied the 'series' notion to his problem in learning German and succeeded. He applied the idea as a language teacher in the institution that he founded and succeeded. His method became a standard technique in the direct method of language teaching. What came immediately after Gouin was the Reform Movement.

THE REFORM MOVEMENT

The Reform Movement was started in the late nineteenth century. It began with Viëtor in Germany, Passy in France, Jespersen in Denmark and Henry Sweet in England. The peak period of its development was between 1882 and 1904. In 1894, Sweet's *The Practical Study of Language* was published.

The Reform Movement was based on three basic principles:

(i) In any study of language, speech was primary.
(ii) The centrality of the connected texts was the kernel of the teaching-learning process.
(iii) The adoption of the oral method was an absolute priority in the classroom.

It was argued that the overburdened students should get relief by the abolition of written homework and exercises and the spoken language should be the only work done in the classroom. The reform was to begin with the accurate description of speech based on phonetics and conducted by trained phonetician-teachers. The learners' pronunciation was to be correct before they moved on to the text.

The overemphasis on phonetic transcription was criticised in some circles but nobody objected to the use of a connected text. As teachers were fed up with the absurd example-sentences of the grammar and translation method, they all welcomed it. It was further suggested that the language of the text provide data for grammatical rules rather than be used to provide examples for the rules learnt previously out of context. The language being taught was to be used for the classroom communication.

The Reform Movement offered a scientific approach to language teaching with increased importance given to phonetics. Paul Passy organised the 'Phonetic Teachers Association" which eventually led to the formation of "International Phonetic Association (IPA)" and the evolution of a standardised international phonetic script. Sweet wrote *Primer of Phonetics* (1890). *The Sounds of English* (1908) and *The Practical Study of Language* (1908). He firmly believed that "all study of language must be based on phonetics". He provided an analytical framework for the acquisition of an accurate pronunciation of English. As he believed in the psychological theory of associationism, he pleaded for forming and maintaining a link between linguistic elements within the language and that in the outside world. As the text had a big role in the success of the Reform Method, its selection and grading attained utmost importance. His methodology consisted of five stages:

(i) the mechanical stage, which stressed good pronunciation;
(ii) the grammatical stage;
(iii) the idiomatic stage;
(iv) the literary stage (i.e. stage for the study of literature)
(v) the archaic stage (where philological questions were discussed).

The first three stages comprised the basic course. After learning the pronunciation and grammatical details of the given text, its vocabulary was to be dealt with. The last two stages were devoted to the literary and philological aspects of the text. Sweet's great merit lay in developing a theoretical framework for English language teaching which allowed a distinction to be made between the objective selection of course contents and their gradation. Like Jespersen, he was strongly opposed to practising with disconnected sentences and uninteresting and monotonous material.

Another person who belonged to this school of thought was Harold E. Palmer who tried to provide a scientific foundation for language teaching. He did not find any of the prevailing method "wholly" satisfactory.

NATURAL METHOD

The Reform Movement of Henry Sweet, Jespersen, Passy and Viëtor led to the evolution of the Natural Method which held the view that interaction was at the core of natural language acquisition. In 1693, John Locke had observed that people learn language "for ordinary intercourse and communication of thought in society and for that purpose, the original way of learning a language by conversation was to be preferred as proper and natural". Natural Method of learning language through conversation was championed even before the nineteenth century by Locke and Montaigne. The upper class people engaged private tutors to teach their children a language through conversation but this method was not adopted for teaching large groups of students. It came into use under the impact of Johann Henrich Pestalozzi who offered lessons in a language through objects. His student Gottieth Heness, who migrated to the USA, taught German to children at Yale by applying the object-lesson technique. Heness and Lambart Sauveur, his collaborator, started giving lessons in language without grammar.

The Sauveur-Heness School of Modern Languages caused a great deal of interest in the USA. This method was called the Natural Method which furnished "the most philosophical introduction to the study of languages" (Kroch, 1887). Kroch noted that even in the second language teaching to adults, the Natural Method depended on very common place topics which found favour with the new immigrants from the non-English speaking European countries to America. They did not need traditional scholarly knowledge of English; they found the conversational approach on common topics more useful. This approach was further developed with intensity by Maximilian Berlitz who built-up a network of language schools on this line, first in America and then in Europe.

Berlitz's Approach

Berlitz's approach was simple and straightforward: the target language was to be used directly in the class and there was no possibility of using translation under any circumstances. There had to be a strong emphasis on oral work and there was no scope for offering any grammatical explanation. The question-answer technique was to be used to the maximum. It was a system which teachers as well as students found very stimulating.

The Berlitz's English course was in two parts, each subdivided into two sections. The opening section of Part 1 had objects in the classroom whose names were used while practising sentences with the verb *to be* and adjectives such as *small*, *big*, *thick*, *thin*, etc. Parts of the body and clothings were used next with prepositional relationships. Some lexical verbs were used next. After that the alphabet was introduced. In Section 2 of Part 1 simple texts were used, containing everyday conversational utterances. In Part 2, the concentration was on questions and answers in the second language without ever using the mother-tongue. Berlitz used reference books written in a simple, systematic and orderly manner.

THE DIRECT METHOD

Berlitz's associates used the term 'The Berlitz's Method' to refer to his approach. However, it was popularly known as the Direct Method. Nobody invented the term but it emerged somehow as opposed to the traditional grammar-translation method. In that sense, it is a cover-term which includes the Reform Movement as well as Berlitz's method. It covers the terms such as the Oral Method and the Natural Method. It insisted that listening was best learnt through listening practices, and speaking through speaking practices. The learning process of an utterance was directly associated with the objects and actions demonstrated in the classroom. The grammar was learnt indirectly, rather intuitively, not by learning the rules but by providing direct practices in listening and speaking. The meaning was acquired through visual perception, by using sensory experience. It may be called a *monolingual approach to teaching a second or foreign language.*

In Europe and the USA, English was taught as a foreign language to those whose mother tongue was some other language but wanted to have proficiency in listening and speaking English. The Direct Method proved to be of great help to them. There were people in Asia, Africa and Australia whose mother tongue was not English but came under the colonial rule of the British. They had to remain in contact with the native speakers of English for administrative and commercial reasons. The British introduced a new system of education in India. They made provision for two types of schools, some schools had English as the medium of instruction whereas others were permitted to have elementary education through local languages. However, in all schools. English was a compulsory subject. At the university level, English was the medium of instruction. In short, it became imperative for Indians to acquire the knowledge of English, both spoken and written, but in most cases the emphasis was on the written language to enable people to familiarise themselves with the knowledge available in English. As lectures at the university level were delivered in English, some knowledge of spoken English was also needed. Two British scholars – Harold Palmer and Daniel Jones - did pioneer work to emphasise spoken English, and therefore, direct method of teaching English in India.

Harold Palmer

Harold Palmer's *The Scientific Study and Teaching of Languages* (1917) attracted Indian teachers of English who studied at the University of London. They were, also exposed to Daniel Jones' *The English Pronouncing Dictionary* (1917) and the *Outlines of the English Language.* Palmer's *Oral Method of Teaching Language* brought Indian teachers of English in contact with the Direct Method. *His English through Actions* (written with his wife Dorothee Palmer) and sequence series exposed them to the Direct Method even more. Though Lawrence Fawcett was not a member of the Jones-Palmer team, he developed the first large scale direct method course – *The Oxford English—* in 1930s which was published by the Oxford University Press. E.C. Eckersley's *Essential English for Foreign Students*, published during the same period, proved to be another popular text book written under the influence of Direct

Method. He kept the utilitarian purpose of his students in view and combined simple, everyday dialogue with the language needed to talk about English. It had a relaxed and lively atmosphere and remained very popular for nearly thirty years. The real problem with Direct Method was that it needed teachers who were highly proficient in spoken English, which was not always possible in the third-world countries.

Basic English

In 1930 C.K. Ogden published *Basic English* which had a vocabulary of 850 words, of which 600 words referred to things, 150 to qualities and 100 to operations which included compulsory verbs, prepositions, articles, demonstratives and conjunctions. He used BASIC for 'British, American Scientific, International and Commercial Words'. The basic system depended on reducing the number of words to a minimum and extending their use to a maximum extent. The criticism against it was that it produced unnatural English and did not have simple words of everyday life such as *like*, *want*, *understand*, etc.

The controversy about the selection of words led to the statistical approach to lexical selection. It was argued that the basic words of English as a second/foreign language should not be different from those of English as the mother tongue.

THE AUDIO-LINGUAL METHOD

The audio-lingual method was an outgrowth of the direct method because it also emphasised the spoken language as its primary teaching objective. In its earlier phase, the gramophone played a role in language teaching, as in Harold Palmer's work in Japan while teaching English. But it did not prove to be very popular. Later on, American linguists such as C.C. Fries, Nelson Brook and Robert Lado played a big role in developing audio-lingual method for pattern drills. It believed in the behaviourist theory of learning. It viewed second language learning as a mechanical process of habit formation. It was assumed that (i) habits are strengthened by reinforcement, and (ii) foreign language habits are formed most effectively by seeking right responses.

Fries' Oral Approach

Fries called his method the 'oral approach', audio-lingual or 'aural-oral method'. Its popularity spread from the USA to Europe after the Second World War and it became very popular in 1950s and 60s. During the period learning took place through drills.

THE AUDIO-VISUAL METHOD

The audio-visual method also gave the spoken language its first place. It became prominent in 1960s, especially because of its new technology of producing visual information. As Volga Rivers (1968) observes, it need not be listed as a separate category simply because it used visual components such as pictures and films as useful aids. They were used not just for presentation but for repetition and reproduction. The audio-lingual and audio-visual methods were initially developed in the USA, primary at the English Language Institute at the University of Michigan. It derived its strength from the descriptive – structural approach developed by C.C. Fries and his associates. The teaching method to be practised in the language laboratory was based on structures selected from a graded syllabus. These efforts were better organised than the earlier attempts of Palmer. The role of the teacher became less prominent in a language lab than it was in a classroom. The language lab played a central role but made the exercise relatively dull.

Fries called his approach the Michigan Oral Approach. In many ways it was similar to Palmer's Oral Approach. Both emphasised the acquisition of good speech-habits by language learners in the early stage of second language learning. Both used sentences to teach grammar and emphasised practising them. However, there was a difference. Palmer based his data on his intuition as a language teacher whereas Fries based his data on the findings of contrastive analysis. Fries' *Teaching and Learning English as a Foreign Language* (1945) was considered to be a major contribution to the field. Students were supposed to have the speech habit training before being exposed to structure drills and pattern exercises, which were to be established in their mind. For that purposes, he kept the vocabulary to a bare minimum. The approach was eventually called structural.

THE STRUCTURAL APPROACH

The Structural Approach, which was developed at the University of Michigan, encouraged the publication of *Intonation of American English* (1966) and *Phonetics* (1967) by Kenneth L. Pike, *Morphology* by E.A. Nida (1946-49) and *Linguistics Across Culture*, by Robert Lado. Fries's book on the teaching and learning of English became popular. Besides, *Language Learning*, a journal published by the English Language Institute, had a number of articles by Hill, Twaddell and many others which helped the development of the new method. The American government gave substantial financial support to this programme because it needed trained teachers to teach English to people in East and South East Asia. It was adopted by the language training programme of the Foreign Service Institute of the US and was supported by the National Defence Education Act of the US in 1959. It was funded by the Fulbright and Rockeffer foundations. Consequently, separate English teaching courses appeared for the speakers of Mandrin Chinese, Bahasha Indonesia, Korean, Thai, Vietnamese, Persian, Turkish and Serbo-Croatian. The Centre for Applied Linguistics was opened in Washington, DC to engage scholars in doing research on teaching English to speakers of various languages and on teaching their languages to Americans. Thus, teaching a foreign language got a boost not only in the USA and UK but in other countries as well, especially in countries which developed close economic and political ties with the USA after the Second World War.

The UK did not lag behind in organising such programmes. A.S. Hornby was the first editor of *English Language Teaching*, a journal founded by the British Council, which published papers on teaching English as a second language. After resigning from its editorship, he compiled the *Advanced Learner's Dictionary of Current English.* It proved to be a standard work of reference and showed the collocational contexts in which English words are normally used. In 1954, his *Patterns and Usages in English* was published which proved to be a very helpful pedagogical grammar. He published *Oxford Progressive English for Adult Learners* the same year. The book had lessons based on Direct Method and thus it followed Sweet's tradition of connected texts. His last work, *The Teaching of Structural Words and Sentence Patterns* was a reiteration of the Oral Method.

The work done by Hornby was supplemented by his colleagues in the UK. E.V. Gatenby's *Direct Method English Course*, W.S. Allen's *Living English Speech* and *Living English Structures*, and Gimson's *An Introduction to the Pronunciation of English* made solid contribution to the cause of teaching English as a second language.

THE SITUATIONAL APPROACH

Hornby's situational method is to be noted for its careful selection and grading of language patterns and vocabulary, its emphasis on pronunciation and the importance it attached to the text. It emphasised not only the oral work in the classroom but also the significance of introducing well-formed, standard sentences of English. The combination of the two enriched the language teaching programme.

In spite of common points discussed above, there is a difference between the British and American approaches. The British approach to structuralism was situational, it was fundamentally based on the fortuitous emphasis on context of utterance and context of situation whereas the American approach was purely structural, it had emphasis on the formation of speech habits and constrastive analysis of the learner's first and second language.

BILINGUALISM AND THE GROWTH OF WEST'S NEW METHOD

We have already seen how in 1797, John Miller wrote *The Tutor* or *a New English and Bengali Work*, well adapted to teach Indians (especially Bengalis) English. His was the first bilingual approach within the grammar-and-translation method. During the early phase of the Direct Method, Thomas Prendergast, who served as a civil servant in South India and learnt Hindustani and Telugu, proposed the Mastery System which concentrated on patterns to construct sentences out of prefabricated expressions in English.

Michael West

However, none of them made an impact of the type Michael West did while working in Bengal. His *New Method Readers* were a new step based on his experimental experiences. He found that most students who started school education dropped out before they completed high school. He wanted them to have the "surrender value" of whatever English they had learnt. He thought that teaching spoken English, as Palmer had recommended, was not as valuable to them as teaching reading, which gave them access to information.

West thought about how to improve children's reading habits. The first step was to simplify the vocabulary by replacing scholarly words by common place words (e.g. *state* for *plight* and *way* for *mode*). The second step was to control the lexical distribution so that the new words are not compactly packed. It enabled children to read faster. He prepared *New Method Conversation*, *New Method Composition*, and *New Method Dictionary* to aid his programmes. At the vocabulary level, students were made familiar with nearly 1500 words. The second priority was to concentrate on skills and the third to move on to strategic reading, with emphasis on the technique of scanning.

West's last book came at a time when initiating the correct pronunciation was emphasised all over and the slogan of 'reading first' became out of tune. His bilingual method did not get many supporters but his work on the lexicon led to the statistical approach to lexical selection which ultimately prepared the ground for English for special purposes (e.g. Science, Medical, Engineering, Business, etc.)

THE COGNITIVE TRANSFORMATIONAL METHOD

The structural method to teach English as a second/foreign language became dominant during the Second World War and remained unchallenged till 1950s. In 1957 Noam Chomsky published *Syntactic Structure*. In 1959, he wrote a critical review of B.F. Skinner's *Verbal Behaviour* in which he challenged the behaviourist theory of language learning by habit formation. He argued that people have an in-born ability to learn their mother-tongues and they use the same ability while learning a second language. In 1964 he published *Aspects of the Theory of Syntax* in which he made a distinction between competence (what a person knows about the language) and performance (how he/she uses that knowledge). In 1966 he addressed the North East (US) conference on the teaching of foreign languages in which he emphasised the importance of the psychology of language teaching over its technology. The process of language learning is based on abstract rules that are an innate part of one's intellectual organisation, he argued. He talked about the underlying principle of universal grammar and how they operated within certain parameters.

Krashen's Approach

Based on the insights of Chomsky and his colleagues and backed by cognitive psycholinguistic research, a number of scholars have worked on aspects of second language acquisition. Among them, Marina Burt, Heidi Dulay and Stephen Krashen are pioneers. In *Language Two* (1982) they arrive at the following conclusions:

1. There appears to be innate learning processors which guide the acquisition of second language. The *filter* and the *organiser* processes work subconsciously while the *monitor* takes care of conscious processing.
2. Exposure to natural communication in the target language enables the subconscious processors to work well. The better the exposure to the learner, the quicker and more comprehensive is the learning.
3. The learner needs to be exposed to the comprehension of the natural language.
4. A silent phase of exposure to the language is beneficial.
5. Conscious learning of grammatical rules has a place in the second language learning.
6. Certain structures are acquired only when the learner is ready for them.

Based on these observations, the practitioners of this approach recommend that the student be exposed maximally to natural communication. The teacher is to have a silent phase at the beginning of the instruction programme. He/she is supposed to use concrete reference to make the new language understandable to the beginners. He/she should keep some time reserved for formal grammar lessons. The dialogues used in the classroom should be socially useful. He/she is not supposed to refer to the first language of the learner while teaching the second. The classroom atmosphere should be relaxed and students should not feel embarrassed if they make mistakes.

Role of Creativity

The influence of Chomsky is visible when teachers emphasize the creative use of language in the classroom. It is provided by a natural communication situation in which the focus of the listener is on the message conveyed and not on the form of the message. However, it does not mean that the form should be completely ignored. It simply means that when a learner is answering a question, he/she should not be stopped and corrected. Correction comes when the teacher provides the learner with exposure to natural language. Selinker called the transitional language of the learner 'interlanguage'.

One of the most important points in the new approach is the *monitor*. Krashen (1975, 1977) proposed the construction of the monitor to account for a number of perplexing phenomena that he observed in adult learner's performance. Some young children start speaking the second language well though they have no conscious knowledge of the rules of grammar whereas some adult learners consciously have the knowledge of the rules of the language but they cannot use the language well for communication. As both the organiser and the monitor are agents of second language acquisition, they interact and affect the performance of the second language learner. While the organiser processes only language, the monitor is a general cognitive processor.

Comprehensive Input

Krashen's (1983) listening-based method of teaching depends on the notion of 'comprehensive input'. He asserts that acquisition can take place only when the listener understands the message in the target language. He claims that all teaching methods that work utilise the same fundamental principle of providing comprehensive input. In short, the outcome of second language teaching depends on how far the teacher has succeeded in maximising the comprehensive input rather than explicit explanation and exercises. Krashen and Terrell (1977) call their approach *Natural Approach* which aims at rapid acquisition of listening comprehension as well as speaking skills. The Natural Approach is different from the Natural Method of Sauveur-Heness discussed above.

COMMUNICATIVE COMPETENCE APPROACH

Chomsky's notion of competence was modified by Dell Hymes (1974), a sociolinguist by professon. He believed that it was not as important for a second language learner to learn how a language is structured as how it is used. While Hymes agreed to Chomsky's "creative" aspect of language, he differentiated the generative power of language from the appropriateness of language use. Every speaker of a language, including a second language, has a tacit knowledge of language use, and that is what he meant by one's communicative competence. He asserted that it should be the goal of language education, and acceptability should be its guiding principle. Being sensitive to the context is a key point in language use which brings one to the concept of appropriate creativity.

The Context of Language Use

The theoretical point that Hymes raised brought him closer to the development in second language teaching in Britain. Based on the Firthian tradition, Michael

Halliday and his colleagues developed the *systemic-functional grammar*. The aim was to develop a coherent view of the functional relationship between linguistic systems and their communicative values. This new scheme of thought asserted that the core of language lessons is the communicative activity itself. David Mackey and others wrote *Language in Use* (1971) and Halliday and Hasan, *Cohesion in English*. W.H. Widdowson (1978) wrote *Teaching Language as Communication*. Widdowson pointed out that the central point a teacher should have in view is how to prepare materials to guide learners to the awareness of communicative conventions operating in the kind of discourse they would be concerned with.

National Syllabuses

The communicative approach attempts to integrate the linguistic activity of the second language learner with a wider programme of language learning. It attempts to relate it to the objectives of the course as in the syllabus. It emphasises "using English to learn it" rather than "learning English to use it". This insightful approach brings the learner to the threshold level and is based on the analysis of the communicative needs of the learner. One offshoot of this approach was the immersion programme which made the learner immerse in the second language. John Munby's *Communicative Syllabus Design* (1978) and D.A. Wilkins' *Notional Syllabuses* make efforts to produce syllabi from that point of view. The notional approach is basically functional and English for Special Purposes (ESP) has been designed keeping various *registers* and discourse analyses in view. It has resulted in the publication of books such as *English in Physical Sciences* (GBS Allen and H.G. Widdowson), *English We Use for Science* (Close), *Engineering Discourse and Listening Comprehension* (Cadlin and Murphy), *Doctor-Patient Communication Skills* (Cadlin *et al.*), *English for Business* (BBC) and many such books. Christopher Brumfit's (1984) *Communicative Methodology in Language Teaching: The Role of Fluency and Accuracy* in an important book in this field and so is Brumfield and Johnson's *Communicative Approach to Language Teaching.*

DISCOURSE ANALYSIS

The use of discourse analysis for language teaching is a recent trend. It has emerged because of language teacher's growing interest in the process of meaning creation in real situations where texts alone are not found sufficient; and settings, participants and goals of interaction become important. An important study of spoken discourse is Sinclair and Courtland's *Towards an Analysis of Discourse* (1975). From a smaller unit of interaction (question-answer-feedback) they move to a larger unit called 'exchange' and then a still large unit called a 'transaction'. Sinclair and Courtland's examples are well-ordered and tightly constrained by the classroom setting. However, casual conversation in the real world is often messy and needs a more sociolinguistically inspired approach. Efforts to translate discourse analysis with pedagogical guidelines have resulted in Cook's *Discourse* (1989), McCarthy's *Discourse Analysis for Language Teachers* (1991) and McCarthy and Carter's *Language as Discourse: Perspective for Language Teaching* (1992). Calci-Murcia's *Grammar Pedagogy in Second and Foreign Language Teaching* (1991) stems from learners' communicative needs. It is the assembly of a corpus of material relevant to those needs.

In recent years a trend has emerged to examine language more and more in its real context of use and to bring to center stage the participants and their social world. It has focused on the idea of language as a discourse rather than as sentences and that has heavily influenced the second language teaching.

Computer-Assisted Language Learning (CALL)/Mobile-Assisted Language Learning (MALL)

We have already seen how advance in technology has led to the adoption of audio-lingual and audio-visual methods in second language teaching. However, every institution that taught English as a second language could not afford to have a proper language laboratory. The relatively recent development of personal computers and their use for pedagogical purposes have opened the door for Computer-Assisted Language Learning (CALL). Similar is the advantage of Mobile-Assisted Language Learning (MALL). Now it is possible for a learner to work on his computer at his own pace. Computer technology has facilitated the incorporation of audio and video inputs in learning programme. The most popular programme, called the *interactive programme* can be tailored to the needs of specific learners and keep track of their progress.

Corpus

The use of computer technology for data collection has made a large scale data base possible. Such data are called *corpora* which are now used by lexicographers and textbook writers. The corpora of spoken discourse highlight the distinction between spoken and written discourse. The best research on corpora has made distinction between various registers (e.g. between the languages of fiction, academic discussion and social discourse). From these corpora, the teacher can select authentic data for use in the classroom, whether he/she chooses to appreciate the method recommended by the followers of Chomsky or Dell Hymes.

Constructionist Approach

The most recent development in the method of second language teaching is the growth of *construction* method, a post-Chomskyan descriptive approach. It is based on computer-generated data base called *corpus.* It has provided numerous insights into the working of language Perhaps its most important outcome has been the description of a vast amount of lexical patterns. Evidence from *corpora* has led to the development of very useful learner's dictionaries. It has highlighted the difference between the spoken and written discourse. it has emphasized the fact that natural spoken language is largely phrasal. New descriptive grammars have been made available which have authentic examples of various grammatical structures; they have been called *construction grammars*. The theory of language acquisition and use, such as Tomasello's (2003), is called *constructionist*. It shows how collocation patterns (e.g. *black coffee, hot coffee*, *cold coffee*, *coffee shop, coffee cup, coffee house*) is acquired. It shows how lexical patterns lead to formulaic sequences.

The constructionist approach emphasizes the interdependence of grammar and lexis at three levels: formal, semantic and functional and asserts that grammatical regularity and acceptability are conditioned by words. Lexical phrases are conventionalised form-function composites and have more idiomatically determined meaning than we get by putting them together by rules. The problem is that these numurous phrasal units cannot be adequately accounted for by models consisting of abstract rules of syntax. There is considerable evidence that they are learnt first as unanalysed chunks and later as particular grammatical patterns. That is why the proponents of this theory insist on teaching how these chunks interact with each other at the discourse level.

The construction grammar takes the position that certain words fit certain patterns. It is not the case that any word will fill any slot in a construction. A good example of this model is Adele Goldberg's constructionist approach to argument structures. The theory has been explained by Charles Fillmore, Paul Kay and Mary Catherine and Conner (1998) in *Regularity and Idiomcity in Grammatical Construction* and by Laura Michaele and Krued Lambrecht (1996).

Two more factors need to be referred to. Some scholars agree that social and contextual influences that affect interpersonal discourse must be looked into to find out the extent to which they can affect second language learners. In other words, they want the pragmatic perspectives on language use examined. As pragmatics is a discipline which investigates different aspects of complex relation between the linguistic meaning and contextual interpretation of an utterance, it must be paid attention to. The impact of psycholinguistic research on the second language learning process cannot be ignored either. It is argued that even preconscious stages of language-learning can be examined to evaluate a learner's readiness to learn an item and his/her willingness to communicate. The study of dynamic nature of language acquisition and use will prove increasingly helpful to language teachers and learners. In short, the problems of second language learning and acquisition are being looked at from various angles, which may lead to further improvement in the technique of language learning and teaching.

SOCIO-CULTURAL APPROACH

Vygotsky

In all communicative approaches, it is assumed that a learner cannot learn a language by just acquiring words and grammatical rules; he/she has to actually use the language in a meaningful context. Vygotsky argues that the meaningful context must be a socially meaningful interaction. He differentiates between the actual developmental level and proximal developmental level. The actual developmental level refers to what a child can perform independently and the zone of proximal development level is reached when the child learns something with the help of someone else. He believes that language allows the learner to self-regulate the process of learning which results into self-directed speech. Not only children but also adult learners of L_2 talk to themselves while solving a difficult task. However, as language is of social nature, language learners grow intellectually only when they interact with people in their environment. It is only this interaction that allows a variety of internal developmental processes to operate which depends a great deal on language. According to the socio-cultural theory of language learning, it is a dialogical activity, either with the self, as in a private speech, or with peers or experts.

Scaffolding

Scaffolding (Verbal guidance which an expert provides to help a learner perform a specific task) is central to Vygotsky's concept of socio-cultural theory. It provides learners with relevant and precise information in the environment at the right time to help them solve a problem. It is not something that happens to a learner as a passive recipient; it happens with a learner as an active participant. It includes verbal collaboration of peers as well. The information, thus supplied, makes a stepwise solution possible . If the communicative theory aims at language acquisition, the socio-cultural theory aims at participation in language interaction. In other words, this theory stresses contextualisation of the language and engagement of the learner with others in L_2. However, since such instructed learning takes place in the classroom, the opportunity to learn by participation in the community is scarcely available. The artificiality of the classroom activity cannot be a substitute for real interaction. It is for this reason that some academic institutions arrange for international exchange programmes which bring students into contact with the native speakers of a foreign or second language in their community.

THE TOTAL PHYSICAL RESPONSE (TPR) APPROACH

In *Receptive and Productive Skills in Foreign Language Learning*, N. Davies (1978) explained the subtle points of this theory. He puts the receptive skills first in teaching and learning process. He argues that listening is a place to start learning a language, as listening skill is the first to develop. The learner is supposed to learn carefully so that he/she can distinguish between correct and incorrect expressions. Davies prefers reception to production because of the disappointing results of practising production in initial stages of learning a language. James Asher (1986), in his *Learning through Action: The Complete Teacher Guide Book* suggests that learner should remain silent in the beginning and carry out orders of the language teacher. In other words, he wants to start with one-way, non-reciprocal listening, even though the fact is that most of our everyday listening occurs in two-way interaction: someone who is spoken to responds.

According to Asher's scheme, the learner is supposed to listen to the teacher's instruction and silently perform the task assigned to him/her. He/she learns by successfully performing the task. It is an instance of task-based language learning.

Seely and Romijn (1993) propose four major stages in TPR (Total Physical Response) which are supposed to take care of (a) use of single unrelated commands, (b) action series, (c) action with dialogues and (d) action of role playing. These steps will lead the class to TPR storytelling, i.e., production of speech.

Listening processes are complex and listening comprehension is difficult in L_2. Besides, a certain level of linguistic proficiency is required to handle listening comprehension. It includes a minimum level of knowledge of the features of the sounds of grammatical systems of the language at the sentence level. It is not clear how the proponents of total physical response propose to tackle these basic issues.

THE SILENT WAY

The main feature of this approach is that the learner himself/herself solves the problem he/she is confronted with and the teacher remains silent. In the beginning, students are shown coloured rods to get exposed to various colours and, threby, learn the abstract concept of colour. Celeb Guttegno (1972) explains in *Teaching Foreign Language in Schools: The Silent Way* how to proceed further. He claims that the method does not depend entirely on one's cognitive learning ability, it is not purely linguistically inspired either. It is a holistic approach which increases one's self awareness. It gives satisfaction to the learner and provides him/her further incentive to learn. The learners feel responsible as a group for the learning task before them; the teacher acts as a counsellor.

The theory draws strength from the psycholinguistic research of Lenneberg (1967) who points out the phenomenon of understanding language without speaking it and discusses the significance of the silent period. It is supported by the findings of Ervin-Tripp (1974) in which she refers to the English children in a Swiss school where the medium of instruction was French. These children gained comprehension but no speaking ability in French.

The theory got some enthusiastic support in the beginning but has been eventually marginalized. Its most influential and beneficial effect might be that solving the problem gives satisfaction to the learner and is, thereby, an incentive to learn.

THE PROGRAMMED INSTRUCTION (PI)

The Programmed Instruction is a way of language teaching that allows the learner to work independently, without any teacher. The learner is assisted by some learning aids of mechanical nature, e.g. computer, mobile phone, tape recorders, videotape, television, etc.

The course is divided into closely linked small units called 'frames'. Each unit is followed by a small multi-choice test. The learner comes to know of his/her achievement immediately after the completion of each unit. If the learner selects the correct answer, he/she proceeds to the next unit. If not, he/she is supposed to consult an additional remedial unit.

The best known models are linearly ordered and have branches. The programme is graded, assuming that there is a precise description of the language to learn.

In 1960s a lot of emphasis was given to this programme in the USA. However, since the approach is based on Skinner's formulation of language learning, the rejection of his behaviourist theory made it relatively unpopular. Certain aspects of phonetics can be learnt by using this approach in second/foreign language teaching in a basic language course. Information and Computer Technology (ICT) can be profitably used, especially CALL and MALL.

In the US the programme was considered to be a panacea for all foreign language teaching problems but the results were disappointing. It was claimed that such a theory would produce only imitative language behaviour in the learner which was not absolutely correct. It was proved that there need not be a direct link between the programmed instruction and behaviourism; it may accommodate the most diverse linguistic theories. It has been claimed that it is in direct proportion to the concreteness and specificity of a subject; the more abstract and varied the subject is, the more difficult it will be to programme it. Since language is used for communication; in a truly communicative situation, the reaction of participants is hardly predictable; natural language communication is not really programmable. Even then certain subskills can be acquired by programmed instruction. For instance, some aspects of phonetics and syntax can help the learner acquire tools which could help him/her to have fluency in a relatively short time. Most writers conclude that a combination of programmed instruction and practice in natural language interaction could be the best solution. That is why, some linguists prefer to use the term 'Programmed-Assisted Instruction'.

The application of programmed instruction depends on the skills that are taught. For instance, the programmed teaching of oral production skills depends on the ability of the learner to discriminate between sounds. As many L_2 learners are not proficient enough to discriminate L_2 sounds from their L_1 sounds, the problem remains unsolved.

These days people are interested in using computers for programmed instruction. CALL programmes have been developed to take up more specific problems of L_2 learners by using computational analysis. These programmes deal with grammar and vocabulary. Listening and reading comprehension and translation skills are yet to be finalized. So long as computers do not analyze human speech well, programmed instruction cannot be used to evaluate oral proficiency well.

SUGGESTOPEDIA

Suggestopedia has been proposed by George Lozanov (1975) as an alternative method of second language teaching. It is an attempt to give full scope to all cognitive learning abilities by eliminating all affective elements in a tightly controlled situation. It aims at avoiding the learner's mental blocks by means of making the learner listen to music. It creates a hypnotic situation in which the learner is put in a pleasant learning environment. He/she sits on a comfortable chair and listens to soothing music. The teaching material is indirectly suggested to him/her without any direct intervention by the teacher. Lozanov's psychological experiments have demonstrated that the method is effective for the learning of vocabulary. In so far as an L_2 learning model is concerned, it resembles the *processing model*. It has not succeeded so far in catching the attention of language teachers.

IMMERSION LANGUAGE TEACHING

In immersion programme a part of the curriculum is taught through the medium of the second language, i.e., for some subjects the second language is used as the medium of instruction. It has been successfully implemented in Canada, esp. in Ontario, where English-speaking children are taught some subjects through French. This programme is different from other programmes in the sense that the emphasise is not on teaching French as a subject but on using French while teaching other subjects and thereby, exposing the language functionally to students. There is little teaching of grammar or rules, the language is learnt while using it. The programme was introduced in the areas in Canada which were bilingual. As English is the first official language of the state, the French-speaking students have to learn English compulsorily which they resented. The government decided to use French partially as the medium of instruction for the English-speaking children who formed the majority. The parents agreed. The programme is successful because of the positive attitude of the parents, their wards and the government. From the methodological point of view, it is an interesting step because it enables English-speaking students to have a sound knowledge of French indirectly. Since they come form a bilingual region, bilingual education does not appear to be a burden to them. As Swain and Lapkin (1982) point out, learners in immersion programmes and schools with bilingual streams outperform learners in traditional classes in the second language.

CONTENT AND LANGUAGE INTEGRATED LEARNING (CLIL)

A new approach to language teaching has emerged out of the immersion programme which is called *content based instruction.* The Europeans call it the *Content and Language Integrated Learning* (CLIL). In this approach, the language to be learnt is used to teach other subjects. Under this scheme lessons are delivered in the second language; it is used to carry out all tasks. As the focus is on the message rather the language, the learner listens carefully in order to learn the subject that is taught through it. The evaluation of the Canadian scheme shows that students reach a fairly high level of fluency but show a lack of accuracy and correct use of grammar. Now the French immersion classroom has incorporated the formal instruction of grammar as well. Consequently, the learners are fortified with a normal dose of grammar.

The immersion programme has enabled the children of the minority languages in some countries to have instruction in their own language, though most subjects are taught through the medium of the national language. For instance, in Bavarian, the Turkish children of the minority group are taught some parts of the curriculum in Turkish and in New Zealand Maori children have Maori as the medium of instruction for some subjects. Denmark has provision to teach some subjects through German in German-speaking areas. The European Union has welcomed this scheme for other member countries as well. Some experts, for instance, Wallace Lambert (1990), have criticized the scheme because it places minority children "into another form of psychological limbo." On the other hand, developmental linguists, who, like

Chomsky (1968), believe in setting "a rich linguistic environment" for L_2 learners are in favour of creating a situation in which L_2 learner are immerged in the language so that they pick up the L_2 rules intuitively.

THE WHOLE LANGUAGE APPROACH

The whole language approach is the methodology of teaching English as L_2 developed in Eldrige (1995), Elley (2001) and Jangid (2005). It emphasises the significance of story-reading (as against reading stories as a text). The teacher reads out a story aloud, which is repeated by students as a choral reading as well as reading individually. The repeated regular reading is followed by retelling the story orally and later on, by writing it by students. It not only increases their reading habit but enables them to acquire the use of words and expressions without trying to cram them. Regular story telling leads to an all-round language acquisition; it increased students' skills in listening, speaking and writing as well. Thus, what begins as a pre-reading activity for students becomes regular reading, speaking and writing activities.

THE TASK BASED APPROACH

The task-based approach has been developed by N.S. Prabhu (1987) during the Bangalore project. It is a reaction against the traditional form of language learning and teaching in India and the type of situational teaching practised here. The real ground for rejecting them is the refusal to recognise the classroom as a 'real' situation in its own right. He argues that a real classroom uses activities that are proper for classrooms; it focuses on educational tasks. If learning needs performing a task, teaching means helping students in performing the task, for instance, making the plan for a house. The classroom activity involved developing a dialogue in which the teacher asks students to tell what a classroom should be like. The learner's responses to teacher's questions are as of learners, and not of the person who uses his/her knowledge of the outside world.

The validity of task depends upon its usefulness as a means of learning the language. The classroom, for example, serves as a communicative educational setting in its own right.

Prabhu's original list of task includes (a) information gap activities, (b) reasoning gap activities (e.g. working out time tables etc.) and (c) opinion gap activities (e.g. the responder's preference). Jane Willis (1996) lists six main tasks: listing, ordering and sorting out tasks, comparing, problem solving, sharing personal experiences and creative tasks. Noonam (1995) talks about ten types of tasks, including predicting, discerning conversational patterns and comparing. Thus, the concept of tasks varies considerably. However, the basic pattern of task is the same pre-task, task cycle and language focus. The task-based learning uses communicative language teaching in a greater range of classroom activities.

KEY ISSUES

While surveying various approaches to teaching a second/foreign language, we have been confronted with two key issues:

i. Should the second language be taught through the medium of the first language or should there be a direct exposure to L_2?
ii. While exposing students to L_2, should the focus of the learner and the teacher be on the form or the content of the material that is discussed in the class?

BILINGUAL VS. MONOLINGUAL APPROACH

The second language teaching began with the grammar-translation method which was essentially bilingual; the learner had to comprehend the material he/she read and translate it into his/her mother tongue. The Reformist and champions of the Direct Method decided to keep the mother tongue out of the picture. All lessons in L_2 had to have L_2 as the medium. Whether one believed in situational, structural, functional, audiolingual or communicative method, one believed in the monolingual approach. Michael West gave priority to the teaching of reading over that of speaking and favoured a bilingual approach. However, he did not have much impact outside India. During the late twentieth century, a different kind of bilingual approach emerged in the form of immersion programme. According to it, in a bilingual situation some contents of the curriculum could be taught through the medium of the second language. It is argued that such an exposure to L_2, i.e. the use of L_2 for knowledge acquisition, helps the learner in learning it fast and fluently. However, research reports have shown that the learner is not able to use the language accurately, though the developmentalists believe that a rich exposure to L_2 in its natural setting will lead one to have a better knowledge of L_2 both in terms of fluency and accuracy. Recent research e.g. by Kroll and Dijkstra (2002) suggests that translation from L_2 to L_1 is faster than from L_1 to L_2 because the former involves accessing lexical level language connections whereas the latter requires concept mediation. If the conclusion is correct, what the learner acquires through the medium of L_1 is easier to convey in L_2 than to convey in L_1 what he acquires through the medium of L_2.

In the USA, partial bilingual education has been recently arranged for Chicano, Latino, Philippino and Chinese children, not as a programme for the disadvantaged but an experience in multicultural and multilingual coexistence. In India, the Knowledge Commission, which has recommended the teaching of English from class I, has suggested that one of the content subjects be taught through English from class III. If implemented, it will lead to the adoption of bilingual education on a large scale. However, this provision does not mean that it recommends the use of the mother tongue to teach English. .

The question of form-focused instruction is another hot issue. Recent research has shown that communicative approach to language teaching, which focuses more on contents than on the form, is not sufficient to help learners become either completely proficient or accurate in the second language. For instance, Norris and Ortega (2000) have looked at the effect of grammar instruction on L_2 learners and concluded that focus on form does make a positive difference. The experiments make clear the difference between the implicit learning (in which the learner discovers the rules) and explicit learning (in which either the teacher or the textbook explains the rules). It is now believed (atleast by some leading scholars) that reactive intervention by the instructors has a positive effect on learners. It draws their attention to linguistic features that appear to cause problems. In short, due attention should be paid to contents as well as form. We may conclude that providing a mixture of meaningful input and some implicit or explicit instruction on form may be the most effective method of teaching a second language. This conclusion contests Krashen's claims that explicit rules that are learnt do not lead to acquisition.

To sum up, teaching English as a second or foreign language has a long history. It started with the grammar-translation method for which one needed some understanding of the rules of grammar, a dictionary (preferably bilingual) and a text book that had to be read and understood (most likely in the mother tongue of the learner). There was a reaction to this method; people needed a reform, a natural way to acquire the language which led to the oral method (or direct method) of language teaching. It focussed on spoken English, as accurately as possible. It needed a well-trained teacher in the classroom, preferably a native speaker of English. It was not an impossible task for an immigrant in the USA or UK to find such a teacher but then the domain of English expanded. There came up new colonies where some English-speaking non-natives were to be prepared for meaningful interaction in trade and commerce, public administration, spread of modern education and knowledge. What was needed was not a mere knowledge of correctly spoken English but the ability to read, understand and assimilate knowledge available in English. What is needed now is the development of competence in a range of styles in English for education and social and public life. In a country like India, it is necessary to shape (or reshape) the knowledge of English for a fairly extensive practical purposes. In our country English is bound with the process of one's development at most levels and English language teachers and policy makers need to be sensitive to this aspect of our life.

The Grammar Translation method was discarded because it ignored the first two elements of language learning-listening and speaking. The Direct Method which emphasized them proved to be beneficial to the non-English-speaking immigrants in the USA and other English-speaking countries. it succeeded because there was no dirth of native speakers and those who chose to teach English were properly trained. However, when it came to teaching English in third world countries, it became a problem to find phonetically trained teachers of English on a large scale. Locally recruited and trained teachers did not always prove to be efficient enough to teach spoken English. The structural approach did not succeed in changing this situation. The situational approach attempted to enliven the environment of language teaching by creating the right ambiance. However, it could not motivate the learner as much as was needed. The communicative approach emphasized the functional aspect of language learning which led to the discourse-based approach but it has its own problems. It is a fact that oral discourse does not present an ideal form of the language. As it is full of incomplete and inaccurate expressions, it gives a distorted impression about the language to the learner. The remedy lies in adopting well-formed discourses and presenting them to the class orally and, later on, in the written form. It is important to expose students to natural rather than contrived, communication in English which meets national and global needs.

The fact that every child has creative ability to learn a language should inspire the textbook writers and teachers to create situations in which it can be fully exploited. The developmental approach to language learning provides a viable option. It means the learner should be given ample opportunity to develop his/her ability to learn the language. Those who believe in it should not hesitate to take advantage of advanced technology. Audio-visual aids, especially computers, should be used to provided the natural environment. It is not possible to send all learners to the countries where native speakers of English live but it is possible to videotape their verbal and non-verbal communications and present them to the class. The silent way approach and suggestopedia have limited scope but the immersion language teaching is practical. If English is used as a medium of instruction for teaching one subject or more in non-English-speaking countries, it will provide a natural environment to children to use it as an instrument to convey their thought and experience. It can be used successfully whether the approach is structural or developmental. For the reasons given above, we favour the adoption of developmental approach combined with our own version of the immersion programme.

In India English is the language of upward social mobility. It provides geographical mobility from one Indian state to another, and from India to distant countries. As English has emerged as an international language, English-speaking professional Indians and workers who migrate even to non-English-speaking countries in search of jobs, find an opportunity to move around the world and interact at social, industrial and cultural levels. There was a time when Indian teachers of English were in search of a variety of English that would be intelligible to all educated Indians. Globalisation has changed our perspective and we need speakers of English as a second language who can be intelligible to the wide world. For that, we have to rise above the current controversy regarding English as spoken by the British and Indians. We should find suitable means of teaching the language to meet our requirement completely. Perhaps a spoken discourse based on British English will not meet our requirement. We need an eclectic method which uses teaching materials from diverse sources – both oral and written – within the broad framework of cognitive developmental approach to language learning.

Table 3: Development of English Language Teaching Methods

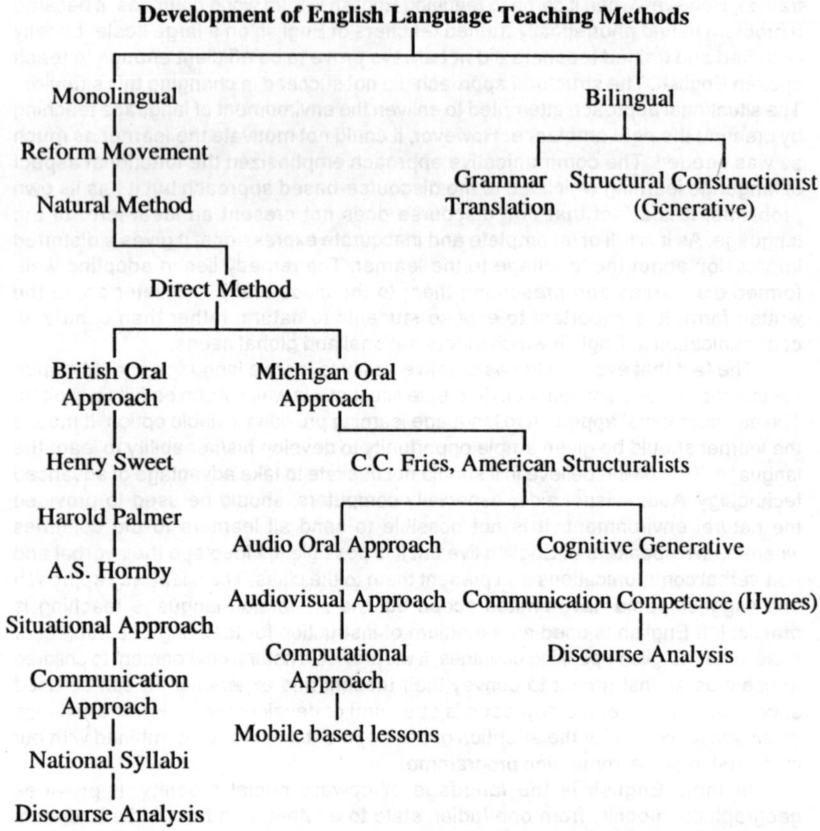

UNIT 4

8

The Linguistic System

FEATURES OF LANGUAGE

So far we have discussed that

- Language is a means of communication, oral as well as written.
- It consists of the use of words in a structured and conventional manner. In other words, the words of a language are structured and they are well-defined. It also means that these structures are accepted in the speech community in which it is spoken by convention.
- The relation between linguistic forms and their meanings is arbitrary but their arbitrariness is accepted by convention.
- Every language has creativity, i.e. all grammatical level-words, phrases and sentences- are productive.
- Language helps its speech community in parsing it and transmitting its culture.
- The sounds in a language are fully distinct. For instance, the only difference between the pronunciation of /p/ and /b/ is that the former is voiceless and latter is voiced but when they are used as parts of a word in English, they are very different; *pun* is entirely different from *bun* because of the difference between /p/ and /b/.
- Words of a language have syntagmatic (horizontal/sequential) as well as paradigmatic (vertical/substitutional) relation. In other words, they have chain and choice relation.
- Every level-phonological, morphological and syntactic- is rule governed. The rules are according to certain universal principles of grammar and vary according to the parameters applicable to a specific language.

STRUCTURES OF LANGUAGE

Every language can be analysed at the levels of phonology, morphology and syntax. Language consists of sentences and the syntactic level is the key to the understanding of all other levels of language as a whole.

At the syntactic level, we discuss the arrangement of words and phrases which create well-formed sentences. A *sentence* is a set of phrases (or words). It is complete in itself. It typically consists of a subject and a predicate. It conveys either a statement, or a question, a command or an exclamation. If a sentence has only one finite verb, it is a simple sentence. If it has more than one, it is either a compound or a complex sentence. In such a case, a simple sentence which is its constituent is called a *clause*. A compound sentence has a main clause and a coordinate clause. A complex sentence has a main clause and one or more subordinate clauses.

A *sentence* consists of a noun phrase (the head of which is a noun) and a verb phrase. A verb phrase may have a noun phrase attached to it which may be either its object or complement. A noun phrase may have an adjectival phrase in it and a verb phrase may have an adverb phrase in it.

A *phrase* is a group of words which together has a particular meaning and forms a part of a sentence. Phrases are named after their heads. Thus, we have a noun phrase, a verb phrase, an adjectival phrase, an adverb phrase and a prepositional (or postpositional) phrase.

A *word* is a single, distinct meaningful unit of speech or writing, which is used with other words to form a phrase or sentence. It is a single conceptual unit which is written with space on either side. It may be a root word or with its inflected form which indicates grammatical markers attached to it.

A word may be a bare root (as *child, write*) or its inflected form (as *children, writing*). When the inflected form is separated from a word, the units are called *morphemes*. A morpheme is the minimum meaningful unit of a word which cannot be subdivided into other meaningful units. (the word *children* has two meaningful units: *Child+ ren* (plural).

A *morpheme* can be split into *phonemes*. Each phoneme present a distinct sound in a specific language. Two phones may be allophones of a phoneme or distinct phonemes. For instance, /p/ and /pʰ/ are allophones of /p/ in English but two separate phonemes in Hindi-Urdu.

LANGUAGE AS A RULE-GOVERNED BEHAVIOUR

All languages are governed by rules. We call them principles in modern linguistic theory. A rule operates in a language guided by a parameter. For instance, a rule of syntax says that all sentences must have a subject. It is a rule of universal grammar which every human being has in his/her mind inherently. The rule is applicable to English but not to Hindi. It is because of the *pro-drop* parameter which says that some languages may have *pro* (i.e. invisible, zero) subject. For instance, in (1a) *in this room* indicates location.

When this expression occurs in the subject position in (1b), *the room* becomes the subject of the sentence in English. (2a) in Hindi is like (1a). In (2b) *is kamre men* occurs in the subject position but it does not become a subject NP; it remains a locative. It is because Hindi is a *pro*-drop language but English is not.

1a. There are two hundred people *in this hall.*
1b. *This hall* accommodates two hundred people.
2a. *Do sau log is kamre men aa sakte hain* (two hundred persons in the room come can).
2b. *Is kamre men do sau log aa sakate hain* (this room in two hundred persons come can).

A rule of English morphology states that all countable nouns can be made plural by adding *–s* or *–es* to it, as in (3) and (4) respectively.

3. These *dogs* are domesticated.
4. These *mangoes* are very sweet.

Since *rice* is an uncountable noun, it cannot have a plural. That is why (5) is correct but (6) is incorrect.

5. Basmati rice has sweet fragrance.
6. *These rices are very expensive.

As to when a noun will take *–s* and when *–es* is also governed by rules. For instance, when a noun ends in a consonant, it takes *–s* to have its plural (as in *dog*, dogs); when it ends in a vowel, it takes *–es* (e.g. buffalo, buffaloes).

The rules of a language may have some variations depending on who speaks it and where. For instance, it standard English, *furniture* is a mass noun; it is uncountable and does not need a plural marker. We can say *these pieces of furniture* but not *these furnitures*. However, in Singapore English, we find *a lot of furnitures* (Jenkins 2015; 142). As noted by Trudgill and Hannah (1982, 2002) we have plural of *furniture*, *fiction* and *evidence* in colloquial Indian English as well.

LINGUISTIC VARIABILITY

If a language is spoken in various regions, it has regional variations, for instance, British English, uses *to fill in a form* whereas American English uses *to fill up a form*, British English uses *to protest against* whereas American English uses just *protest*. Where British use *transport*, Americans use *transportation*. When British says *racialist*, Americans use *racist*. British use *cooker, dress, cinema* and *push chair* whereas Australians use *stove, frock, picture theatre and stroller* respectively in their place. In short, variations exist in the regional varieties of English at the level of lexicon, grammatical structure (morphological as well as syntactic), phonetic as well as semantic. They lead to linguistic diversity. Learners of English as a second language need to be sensitive to such variations while reading the literature of a particular country and listening to a foreigner.

Regional variation may be similar to ethnic variation. For instance, in West African English, the standard present perfect *I have gone* is replaced by *I done go* or *I done gone* as it is in Black English Vernacular (African American English). *He ain't done it* is used in place of *he has not done it.* African American English uses double negatives for a negative expression. For example, the Standard American English *He does not know anything* becomes *He does not know nothing. He is gone* becomes *he gone.* The point is that African American English is different from the standard American English and that difference is rule-governed. We can generalise that in African American English—

(a) the copula is not used
(b) double negatives are used for single negation and
(c) present perfect is indicated by a verb in the past participle; *have* is not used.

THE PEDAGOGICAL IMPLICATION OF VARIATION

Initially American pedagogies thought that African Americans were "culturally deprived" (cf Karl Bereiter 1965, Jensen 1969). Figenbaum (1975) thought that "by comparing the standard English structure to be taught and the equivalent or close nonstandard structure, the student can see how they differ. The instruction should include practice in sorting out standard from non-standard. The practice can be provided when both standard and non-standard are used in the class. For many students, the sorting out is the beginning of a series of steps from passive recognition to active production (p. 147). He suggested that the teacher could, for example, write the following two sentences on the board:

7a. He work hard.
7b. He works hard.

The teacher would then ask how the two sentences differ and which one is non-standard. Asking for the students' observation will make the activity more interesting, he thinks. He suggests that it would follow by an identification drill and a discrimination drill. While the former will enable the student in recognising the correct form, the latter will enable him/her in distinguishing between standard and non-standard forms. Apart from these, Feigenbaum suggests translation drill and response drill. In a translation drill, the student translates a non-standard sentence into a standard sentence. In a response drill, the attention of the student is focused on the grammatical feature that marks the standard form.

These drills are oral drills which elicit oral responses from students. They are intended to encourage them to reorganise and produce complete, natural sentences. The goal is to enable students to have a control of oral standard presentation of grammatical structures. The same technique can be used to make them aware of standard pronunciation as well. Such drills are of moderate intrinsic interest after the initial novelty is worn off. The drill is best conducted for a brief period; it may not always succeed in the production of standard English. As the student hears people around him/her using the so-called 'non-standard' or 'incorrect' form, he/she may start doubting the relevance of what he is taught. Feigenbaum thinks that repetitive use of the correct form in the class will have a permanent effect on the student but the situation is not so simple. There may be areas in which the form the student is using is grammatically correct but it is a non-standard form in a given context. For instance, an Indian student of English is well aware of the present perfect and simple past forms of English but he/she is not aware of when to use them aptly. He/she uses present perfect for simple past if he/she is referring to an immediate past event, i.e. uses it in the sense of 'near-past'. However, that is not correct – Present perfect is used in English if an events happened in the past but its impact is still there. If somebody went out an hour ago and has not come back yet, we can say, 'He has gone out' but if he has come back, we should say, 'He went out an hour ago and has come back'. *Has come back* means he is here right now. If we do not know whether he is still here, we will say "He went out an hour ago and has not come back". In short, structural drills may be of some use to learn a correct structure, but if the correct structure is already known, its correct use needs some explanation of its role in the discourse'. It is a challenging task because in the oral English, most Indians do not use it correctly and the data input is more in favour of incorrect usage them correct usage.

VARIATION IN INDIAN ENGLISH

The spoken Indian English differs from the Standard British and American English at some points at many levels. The problem is easier to solve at the level of lexicon than at any other level. The students have to be aware of the words that are used more often in Indian English than in British English. For example, we may look at the following:

8. | *Indian English* | *British English* |
|---|---|
| almirah | a chest of drawers |
| as such | consequently |
| colony | residential area |

eve teasing	teasing girls
hotel	restaurant, café
jawan	soldier
police firming	shooting by police
stir	demonstration, agitation

To make students familiar with the internationally acceptable synonyms is not a serious pedagogical problem but to make them conscious of the fact that the following words have no plural is:

Aircraft, litter (N), secrecy, evidence, information, poetry, fiction, alphabet, etc.

The teachers may make students practise these words only in singular in drills but they hear their plural forms being used all around. It makes students feel that the plural forms can be legitimately used. The only solution seems to be that the teacher uses the singular form whenever the student uses the plural form.

The teacher should pay special attention to the overuse or underuse of particles/prepositions with the verb. For instance, Standard English uses *dispense with* rather than *dispense*, and to *strike out* rather than *strike*. It uses *accompany* (without *with*), *combat* (without *against*), to *fear* (without *of*) and to *return* (and not *return back*). The standard British and American English use *to be adapted to*, *to be baffled by*, *to pay attention* to and *to tear up* (rather than *adapted in*, *baffled with*, *pay attention* and to *tear off*.

The Standard English does not use *since*, in place of *for* (e.g. *for two hours*, rather than *since two hours*). It does not use the future tense in a conditional clause, i.e. it uses (9b) rather than (9a):

9a*. If I will go, I will do it.
9b. If I go, I will do it.

It does not use the progressive form of the verbs to indicate a habitual action, i.e. it uses (10b) rather than (10a).

10a*. He was having two cars.
10b. He had two cars.

It uses the perfect progressive form, instead of the simple past with time adverbial.

11a.* He lived here for the past ten years.
11b. He has been living here for the past ten years.

It does not use the verbs of physical and mental perception in the present progressive form.

12a.* I am seeing/smelling/touching it.

12b. I see/smell/touch it.

There are two ways of looking at the problems. What Trudgill and Hannah (1982, 1985) accept as examples of "Indian English (a variety of world 'English'), Quirk (1990) considers examples of "inadequately learnt version of correct native English" (1990). Without getting into any controversy regarding non-native varieties of English (e.g. Indian English), we would like to state that Indian learners of English take both varieties as evidence of reality about the variation in English and expose themselves to both. They would pick up Indian English anyway, whether the teacher likes it or not. However, they must know what native (British and American) English is and understand and use it in international discourse.

What is true at the lexical and syntactic levels is also true at the level of pronunciation. The teacher should try to take students to the level where they become nationally intelligible. At the same time they should be able to listen to internationally acceptable pronunciation. In India, they can get away using |th| and |d| for |θ| and |ð| respectively, but in order to be understood internationally, they should acquire |θ| and |ð| and know where and how to use them. Students will not be able to do so if their teachers are not able to articulate them correctly. It is essential to acquire these sounds not only when we go abroad but also when we listen to international news channels and watch international movies and television programmes (The acquisition of English sounds will be discussed in detail in Chapters 13 and 14).

LINGUISTIC SYSTEM

According to Chomsky (2000:10) every language has a system of computational operations which involves three kinds of elements:

(i) The properties of sound and meaning, called 'features'.
(ii) The items that are assembled from these properties, called lexical items, and
(iii) The complex expressions constructed from these lexical units (called phrase, clause and sentence).

THE ORGANISATION OF SOUNDS

Sounds of a language are either vowels or consonants. English has the following consonant sounds which can be organised according to the place and manner of their articulation:

manne	*bilabial*	*place labia dental*	*alveolar*	*palate velar*	*palatal*	*vela*	*pharyngeal*
plosive	p, b		t, d			k, g	
fricative		f, v	s, z	ʃ,ʒ	tʃ, dʒ		h

affricate			#	
nasal	n	n		ŋ
liquid		l, r		
glide	w	l, r	j	

- It has the following front vowels:

i: (as in *see*), *I* (as in *sit*), *e* (as in ten), *x* (as in *cab*)

- ə (as in *about*), ʌ (as in *cup*) and ɛ (as in *fur*) are central vowels. a: (as in)

- *a*: (as in *father*), ɒ (as in *got*), ə (as in *saw*), *u* (as in *put*), ʊ: (as in two) are back vowels.

- *ey* (as in *say*), əʊ (as in *go*), *ai* (as in my), əi (as in *boy*) aʊ (as in *now*), ia (as in *near*), *e∂* (as in hair and ə∂ (as in pure) as diphthongs. A *diphthong* consists of two vowels spoken in such as sequence that they sound like one. Individual sounds are segments. *Suprasegmentals* are features of an utterance other than the consonantal and vocalic elements. English has *stress* and *intonation* as suprasegmental features. It has syllables. Each syllable contains a consonant (e.g. k as in *Cat*) or a set of consonants (e.g. sch as in *scholar*) followed by a vowel (e.g. *cut*, *scholar*). Words with one syllable are monosyllable, those with more than one syllable are *polysyllabic* (as *cat* and *scholars* respectively).

The smallest discrete segment of sounds in a stream of speech is a *phone* (e.g. |p| in pen). A phonetic variation of a *phoneme* is an *allophone*. For example, in English |p| is a phoneme which has two allophones, |p| and |ph} (e.g. |p| in *spun* and *pun* respectively). The smallest combination of phonemes that forms a meaningful unit is a *morpheme*. It is the minimum meaningful unit of a word. The word *read* is a morpheme because it cannot be split into further meaningful units. The word *reader* consists of two morphemes, *read* and *–er* (which denotes a person doing a specified activity). Since *read* can be used independently, it is a *free morpheme*. As –er can be used only when it is attached to a word, it is a bound morpheme. Word formation is a process which involves a free and one (or more) bound morpheme(s). If a bound morpheme is attached in the beginning of a free morpheme it is called a *prefix*. For example, in *unhappy*, *un* is a prefix. If it is used at the end of a word, it is a *suffix*. In *happiness*, *-ness* is a suffix.

Word formation is a productive process; it enriches the vocabulary of a language. In English, *nation* is a word to which we can add a suffix *al* and have a new word *national*. We can add –ize to *national* and have a new word *nationalise*. We call add *–tion* to the new word and have *nationalization*. If we add the prefix *anti* to *national*, we get *anti-national*. If we add *de-* as a prefix to *nationalize*, we get *denationalize* from which we can have *denationalization*. The suffix *–at* makes the noun *nation* an adjective (i.e.

national), the suffix *–ize* makes the adjective a verb and the suffix *tion* turns the verbs into a noun. Thus we have

$$[_N[_V[_A[_N\text{nation}]_N\text{al}_{Adj}]\text{izc}]_V\ \text{tion}]_N$$

When words incorporate prefixes and suffixes, they undergo internal phonological changes, we can see it in the process of formation of new words from *nation* |neiʃn|, e.g. *national* |næʃənl|, *nationalize* |næʃnəlaiz|, *nationality* |næʃənæləli|, *nationalization* |næʃnəleizeiʃn|. We may note |əi| becoming |æ| in the process of word formation. This is an example of phonology-morphology interface. These are specific examples of English but the process of word formation and word internal phonological changes are universal processes.

UNIVERSAL GRAMMAR

Universal grammar is a theory of initial cognitive state which has a richly structured linguistic system. It is a theory of linguistic invariance which expresses the universal properties of natural languages. They are biologically necessary universals that are determined by our in-born language faculty. As the biological endowment for language is constant across the species, we are not specifically predisposed to acquire the language of our biological parents, but to acquire whatever language is presented to us initially in childhood.

Universal grammar is a set of language invariant principles and parameters. A particular grammar (i.e. the specific grammar of a language) can be derived from universal grammar by fixing the parameter in a certain way. For instance, the principle that every lexically realised noun phrase must have a case is universal and so is the provision that the case will be assigned if the NP is properly governed. Even if an NP is not overtly case-marked, it is assumed to have a case if it is properly governed. It means that the case theory is intertwined with the government theory. The development of the principles of universal grammar has led us to the conclusion that human languages are much more uniform than was previously thought to be.

Universal grammar has provided a new way of looking at language acquisition. Acquiring a language means fixing the parameters of universal grammar on the basis of experience. The child interprets the incoming linguistic data through the analytical device provided to him/her by universal grammar. He/she fixes the parameters of the system on the basis of the analyzed-data which is his linguistic experience. Thus the acquiring a language means selecting those which match experience and discarding the other options. Under this understanding of universal grammar, 'learning by forgetting' seems to be an appropriate answer to the acquisition of linguistic knowledge.

FROM SOUND TO MEANING

According to Chomsky, a linguistic information fall into two categories –

phonetic and semantic. The former is the product of the sensory motor system, the latter of the conceptual intentional system. Acoustic and articulatory phonetics try to understand how the sensory system produces phonetic representation and interprets sounds. Semantic representation determines the meaning of an expression. However, it is much more complex than phonetic representation. The understanding of an expression is at the LF (logical form) interface. It represents a complex system of knowledge which is an essential part of innate biological endowment. The system at the interface invites many questions, the question of conceptual system, of the use theory of meaning, a causal theory of reference, etc. In spite of these complexities, human thought is interpretable in terms of other systems of mind involved in thought. It is remarkable that a limited exposure to language in highly ambiguous circumstances enables children to understand the meanings of words and sentences. It is far beyond anything that modern comprehensive dictionaries and grammars convey. For this reason, Chomsky considers semantic representative "innate and universal". It is for such reasons that we consider our linguistic system complex.

UNIT 5. DEVELOPING LANGUAGE SKILLS

9

Perspective on Teaching Grammar

For a common man, learning the grammar of a language means learning how to speak, and write correctly in that language, but what do we mean by correctly? The word *correct* means 'free from error' and *error* means 'the state or condition of being wrong'. In short *correct* means 'right' and *incorrect* means 'wrong'.

According to the traditional view, the correctness is determined by what is 'right' or 'wrong' from the point of view of authorities and that is what should be acceptable to a common man.

PRESCRIPTIVE GRAMMAR

According to a prescriptive grammarian, a grammar consists of a set of actual or presumed notions about the correct usage of a language. He/she would assert that people must say *It is I*, and not '*It is me*', '*Whom did you see*? and not '*Who did you see*?', '*none of us is perfect*' rather than '*none of us are perfect*'. He/she would prefer *I do not remember to whom I loaned the book* to *I do not remember whom I loaned the book to,* and *he/she felt bad about his/her loss*, to *he/she felt badly about his/her loss*. The prescriptive grammarians believe in the doctrine of rules as laid down in the a traditional grammar. They believe in recommending how people should speak. However, their dos and don'ts are not important anymore because most people think that one should learn the language as it is rather than as it ought to be .

DESCRIPTIVE GRAMMAR

The descriptive grammarian believes in the doctrine of general usage. For example, he/she prefers *who* to *whom* in the objective form in question and does not mind using *badly* in '*I feel badly*'. The doctrine of usage believes in the doctrine of appropriateness. A consistent use of the doctrine means that every newcomer to a speech community needs to learn how appropriately an utterance is used in that community. One may argue that it would lead to acceptance of various local dialects or varieties of a language and would result in the decline of the concept of cultivated speech, understood and acceptable everywhere. This objection is met by the argument that a completely consistent adherence to the idea of general usage leads to an agreement on a standard language which will keep on improving in expressiveness and effectiveness. If the speaker is reasonable in his/her expression and aims at precision and fullness of meaning, the doctrine of appropriateness leads to the doctrine of linguistic norm.

For the teacher of grammar, the doctrine of linguistic norm seems to be the best option. He/she ought to have a disinterested attitude towards the controversial issues of usage and yet be able to make a critical evaluation of the language in use. *The Oxford Dictionary of English* (2005) defines grammar as "the whole system and structure of a language or languages in general, usually taken as consisting of syntax and morphology (including inflections) and sometimes also phonology and semantics". This definition covers the scope of descriptive linguistics adequately.

Descriptive grammars believe in looking at sentences in terms of their structures. Words are combined into phrases and phrases, into sentences. Most descriptivists split words into two or more morphemes, which are the smallest meaningful units. A free morpheme can stand on its own in a sentence (e.g. *boy*, *eat*) but a bound morpheme is always attached to a free morpheme (e.g. *-s* in boys, *eats*, *-ing* in *eating*, *en-* in *enable*).

Teachers who believe in structural approach use substitution tables in the class and ask students to choose a word from each column to form a sentence. For instance, we may look at the pattern of substitution in Table 9.

Table 9: Substitution Table: This/That/It Construction

This	is	John's	book
That	was	Mary's	face
It		his	nose
		her	hand

Students are supposed to make sentence such as:

1. This is John's book.
2. That is Mary's face.
3. It is his/her book/hand, etc.
4. It is her hand, etc.

Different kinds of structures need different kinds of substitution tables. For example, we can have a look at tables 10 and 11.

Table 10: Substitution Table with *Too*

The ceiling fan	is	too	high	for	me	to	touch
The suitcase			heavy		you		reach
The drawer					him		lift
							move

Table 11: Substitution Table with *Enough*

John	is	tall	enough	to	touch	the ceiling
					reach	that point
		wise			understand	it
					get	the point

The tables show the difference between the occurrence of *too* and *enough* in a syntactic frame. Though both of them are intensifiers, *too* occurs immediately before the adjective and *enough*, after it. Though substitution tables have their relevance, in some contexts they fail to show the relationship between the constituents. For instance, both *eager* and *easy* occur in identical syntactic frame, but they do not have identical relationship.

Table 12: Substitution Table with *Eager* and *Easy*

NP	Verb	Adjective	Infinitive
John	is	eager	to please
		easy	

TABLE SHOWING IDENTICAL STRUCTURES

John is eager to please can be paraphrased as 'It is John who is eager to please (someone)', whereas *John is easy to please* can be paraphrased as 'It is someone who finds it easy to please John'. In the first case, John is the logical subject; in the second he/she is the logical object. Just paying attention to the pattern without considering underlying relationship is erroneous and misleading.

There are several other difficulties in relying on a structural grammar. For instance, it cannot account for syntactic ambiguity in (4).

4. Flying kites can be exciting.

The structural approach will just show that the expression *flying kites* is a combination of a gerundial adjective and a noun; it cannot suggest that it can refer to either '*kites that are flying*' or '*the act of flying kites*'. Its binary approach leads to bifurcating a sentence into two phrases, a Noun Phrase

(NP) and a Verb Phrase (VP) and then these phrases into further subdivisions till we have only one lexical item under each node. It also runs into problems. For instance, in (5) what will be the binary division of *John or Bill*?

5. John or Bill will go there.

Whether we divide it into *John* and '*or Bill*' or *John or* and *Bill*, we have a problem; neither '*Or Bill*' nor *John or* is a constituent.

Construction Grammar

Recently new descriptive theories of grammar have come to light, for instance, cognitive grammar by Longacre (1987) and Construction Grammar by Fillmore, Kay and O'Connor (1988), George Lakoff's (1984, 1999) and Goldberg's conceptual structure (2006). They highlight the point that constructions integrate form and meaning at various levels of complexity, from the level of morphology of words to phrases and clauses.

The construction grammar holds the view that certain words follow certain patterns which cannot be adequately described by rules generated by generative grammars. They need to be described adequately. Such descriptions are based on the rich data available in corpus linguistics, for instances, in British National Corpus, the Oxford Word List, the Brown Corpus, the Lancaster. Oslo-Bergen Corpus and the Helsinki Corpus of English Texts. These corpuses provide frequency lists, concordance packages and lexical concurrence patterns. These patterned grammatical structures have strong preferences for use. For instance, *start* and *begin* are synonymous, but there is a difference in use. *Start* is more frequent in spoken English and *begin* in the written literature. We may say 'He *started* the story by narrating a series of events and it *began* well. We can say she *started* the journey but not *'began'*. The constructionists insist on capturing such difference in grammar. They think, it can be done only by describing the collocational restrictions on words and not by rules. Only future can tell how adequately they can represent and account for all the data available in their corpus.

Such problems created crisis in the structural approach which led to an alternative approach called transformational generative grammar.

GENERATIVE GRAMMAR

The transformational generative grammar has passed through three phases. The first phase (Chomsky, 1965) talked about underlying structures from which surface structures (i.e. actual sentences) are derived by applying rules to them under certain conditions. At that time Chomsky called them 'constraints'. This phase may be called the combinatory stage. The second phase was called Principles and Parameter theory (earlier known as the Government and Binding

Theory) which was explained in Chomsky (1981, 1982, 1986 a, b). It was claimed that human mind has the inborn ability to have a set of principles (such as theta theory, case theory, control theory, binding theory and bounding theory) which are applied for the generation of sentences of a specific language, subject to certain parametric variations. For instance, there is a null subject parameter which permits certain languages to have a sentence even without a subject. But as English is not subject to null-subject parameter, its every sentence must have a subject. If no subject is available, *it* is substituted in its place. For instance, (6a) is not a sentence of English but (6b) is,

6a.* ... is easy to please John.
b. It is easy to please John.

Alternatively, *John*, the object of the sentence, can be moved to the subject position to have (6c).

6c. John is easy to please.

The third phase in the generative theory is the emergence of the Minimalist Programme (Chomsky, 1995, 2000). The principle and parameter phase opened the door to account for grammatical variation while the Minimalist phase tries to answer questions on factors leading to grammatical adequacy. It suggests that the computational system (i.e. syntax) is central to language and offers the optimal solution to the central task of language relating to sound and meaning. LF (Logical Form) is what feeds it with cognitive components that deal with intentions, beliefs and other forms of conceptual knowledge; PF is what grammar contributes to the sound structure of the language.

According to Chomsky (1995), the language determines a set of derivations which converge at the interface levels, it yields a representation satisfying FI (full interpretation) at that level. It converges at both interface levels, PF and LF, otherwise it crashes. The derivations are due to *select* and *merge*. After the derivation is spelt out, no further selection is made. If a consituent is lacking in some features, it is motivated by greed to move in search of those features, otherwise it procrastinates, i.e. it remains in its original place. In *John is eager to please*, John remains in its original place because all its requirements (e.g. case assignment) are satisfied but in '... *easy to please John*', *John* moves upward to the subject position to get a case, which is supplied by the agreement features of the verb *be*.

The operations offered in the Minimalist Programme are simpler than those offered by Principles and Parameters Theory or the *Aspects of the Theory of Syntax* but since they are theory-oriented issues, it is not necessary to discuss them with students at the high school level. However, the generative approach can be successfully adopted to show the relationship between sentences such as in (7-12):

VARIOUS WAYS OF EXPRESSING THE SAME THOUGHT

7. John bought a new sofa set from the furniture shop.
8. It was John who bought a new sofa set from the furniture shop.
9. It was a new sofa set that John bought from the furniture shop.
10. It was from the furniture shop that John bought a new sofa set.
11. What John bought was a new sofa set from the furniture shop.
12. What John bought from the furniture shop was a new sofa set.

Students may be told that all these sentences convey the same thought but there is a difference in emphasis. (7) is a neutral statement of fact, (8) emphasises *John*, the buyer, (9) *a new sofa* set and (10) *the furniture shop*. Likewise, there is a shift in emphasis in (11-12). (11) brings 'the new sofa set' in focus and so does (12).

SOME TOPICS THAT NEED TO BE FOCUSSED

Given a sentence, such as in (13), questions can be asked as in (14-16) to highlight a point:

QUESTION FORMATION

13. I think John saw a tiger in the mango grove.
14. What do you think John saw?
15. Where do you think John saw a tiger?
16. Who do you think saw what in the mango-grove?

It may be pointed out that (14-16) are possible questions but not (17) or (18).

17.* What do you think who saw in the mango grove?
18.* Where do you think who saw a tiger?

It may be pointed out that all the NP slots can be filled up by question words but they cannot move, if the first question word is to be crossed. Thus, (19) is all right but (20) is not. In (20) *where* crosses over the first question word *who*.

19. Who saw what and where?
20.* Where who saw what?

This point can be discussed in a higher secondary class to explain how the movement of question words is constrained.

AGREEMENT BETWEEN SUBJECT AND VERB

There are several ways in which some notions of generative grammar can be fruitfully explained. For instance, students can be told that the verb agrees with the head of the subject noun phrase which may not necessarily be at the end of the noun phrase. For instance, in (21) the head of the NP is at its end but in (22) it is not.

(21) Hundreds of crows were flying back to their nests in the evening.
(22) The performance of the three actors was very funny.

In (22) the head of the NP is *performance*, and not *actors*.

The Agreement involves only the number of the head of the NP and the verb.

- The following words are singular and when they are used as subjects, they take singular verbs:

each, either, neither, one, everyone, everybody, no one, nobody, anyone, someone, somebody.

Each of the students *has* a personal computer.
Everyone of the group *wants* to join the I.I.T.
Nobody wants to own the guilt.

- We may note that the prepositional phrase that comes between the subject and the verbs does not affect the agreement rule, even though it is a part of the NP phrase that contains its head.

- When *none* or *any* occurs as the subject of the sentence, it may be treated either as singular or plural, depending upon whether the speaker is thinking of one entity or many. For example:

None of the players *was* injured.
None of the players *were* injured.
(= *No players* were injured)
Any of these documents *is* reliable.
Any of these documents *are* reliable.
(= All these documents are reliable)

- The words *some*, *all* and *most* may be used either as a singular or plural depending upon whether they refer to something singular or plural.

Some of the books *were* lost.
Some of the mustard *was* left in the bowl.
Most of the *book* was interesting.
Most of the *books* were interesting.

- If a noun phrase is added to the subject noun phrase with *as well as, together with, in addition to, including*, the agreement rule is not affected. The verb agrees with the subject noun phrase. For example,

The captain as well as the coach *was* happy.
Ratan, together with his friends *has* gone to the movie.
John in addition to his brother, *is* a vegetarian.

- Most compound subjects joined by *and* are plural and take a plural verb.

The pen and the wallets are on the table.
The car and the truck have just collided.

However, if a compound subject is treated as one unit, it takes a singular verb.

The principal and secretary of the Governing Body of the College *does* not agree to the proposal.

• Singular subjects joined by *or*, *nor*, *either or neither nor* are treated as singular and take a singular verb.

Neither John nor his father likes it.
Either John or his father has gone out.
John or his brother is a revolutionary.

• When two subjects are joined by *or*, *nor*, *either or neither nor* and one of the set is singular but the other plural, the verb agrees with the nearest subject.

Either John or *his parents are* wrong.
Neither John nor *his mother likes* it.

• When the subject comes after the verb, as in a *there* construction, the verb agrees with the subject.

There *is only one student* in the class. There *are thirty students* in the class.

• If the subject is a collective noun, the verb will be singular or plural depending upon whether the noun is treated as a group or individually.

The managing committee *was* unanimous in its views.
The managing committee *were* divided in their opinion.
These details of the agreement rules in English cover almost all situations.

Agreement between a Pronoun and Its Antecedent

A pronoun agrees with its antecedent in number and gender.

23. *The man* expressed *his*/*her opinion forcefully.
24. *The woman* differed in *her* opinion from the man.
25. *The city* is proud of *its* mall.
26. *The students* differed in *their* opinion.

In (23) *his* agrees with *man*, in (24) *her* agrees with *woman*, in (25) *it* agreed with *city* and in (26) *their* agree with *students*. In such cases the agreement involves the number of heads of NPs and the possessive pronouns that refer to them.

VERB PHRASE

If we separate the subject NP from the sentence, the left-over forms the Verb Phrase. A verb phrase consists of a verb (with its auxiliaries, if needed) and its object complement (if the verb is transitive) and adjunct. An intransitive verb does not need an object complement but a transitive verb does, as in (29-30)

29. John *slept* well.
30.* John slept Judy.
31. John ate a mango.
32. John gave a mango to Judy.

In (29) the verb *sleep* is intransitive. It does not need an object complement, which is why (30) is ungrammatical. In (31) *ate* is a transitive verb and needs an object. In (32) *gave* is a ditransitive verb and needs two objects. *A mango* is the direct object and *to Judy* is an indirect object. (32) can be rephrased as (33) in which the indirect object precedes the direct objects.

33. John gave Judy a mango

An object complement is different from a predicative complement, as in (34).

34. He/she seemed a very nice fellow.

Here *a very nice fellow* is like an adjective complement, as in (35)

35. He/she seemed very nice.

Adjuncts can occur with transitive as well as intransitive verbs. In (29) it occurs with an intransitive verb, in (36), with a transitive verb.

36. He/she drove his/her new car *very carefully.*

Here, *his/her new car* is an object NP and *very carefully* is an *adverbial* adjunct. The adverbial could be an NP (as in 37), a PP as in (38), a clause as in (39) or a tenseless clause as in (40)

37. He/she came *this morning.*
38. He/she came *at 7 am.*
39. He/she came *when I was asleep.*
40. He/she came early *to avoid rush hour traffic.*

A clause can be used as a subject or an object or an adjunct, as in (41, 42) and (43) respectively.

41. *That he/she came so early* surprised me.
42. He ate *whatever I served him.*
44. He/she ran away *when the rain began.*

Apart from the subject-verb agreement features, an important aspect of the verb in the verb phrase is that it must have an appropriate tense.

GRAMMAR IN CONTEXT

Sequence of Tense

The sequence of tense can be taught better with the help of a written text. For instance, it can be used to show the difference between the simple past and past perfect, as in (44):

44. The door *opened* and she *looked out* and *saw* her husband. She *came* to him affectionately and *put* her arms around him. He *stood, smiled* and *said* nothing. He *had met* her in America and *had waited* to fall in love with her.

All verbs, except the last two, are in simple past tense because they refer to actions that occurred in the past in a sequence. The last sentence uses past perfect; the two verbs (e.g. *had met, had waited*) refer to past actions completed before some other past actions or events (e.g. *stood, smiled, sent*). The verb *has escaped* in (45) refers to a past action but is in the present perfect because its impact is on the present.

45. "He is an American from US Navy", he *spelled* it out... He *has escaped* and that is why he *is wounded.*

The man spoke in the narrative in the past and that is why past tense has been used for his utterance. In his speech, he says he *has escaped* because even though the act of escaping happened in the past, its impact is there on the present (i.e., he is there). Similarly, the contrast between the Simple Present and Present Progressive can be shown, as in (46):

46. "I *realise* you *are saving* my life again", he told Sadao.

The man realises what Sadao was doing for him, and he uses the present progressive. He uses *realise* for himself because it is a verb of perception and cannot have a progressive form.

Similar examples can be found for other tense forms. Their use should be explained by the teacher always in a context. For instance, though the subjunctive mood is rarely used in the present day English, we have sentences such as in (47-48).

47. ... there he had found Hana and had felt he would love her *if it were* at all possible.
48. The strange thing is *if the man were* a thief, I could turn him over to the police.
49. It would endanger all of us *if we did not give* this man over as a prisoner of war.
50. It would be best *if he could be quietly killed.*
51. I guess *if all the Japs were like you*, there would not have been a war.

WORD ORDER

Word order is another aspect of grammar the teacher should pay special attention to. A declaration sentence has a subject-verb-object word order. Usually a direct object precedes an indirect object, as in (52) but a change of order is possible, as in (53):

52. He/she gave the book to me.
53. He/she gave me the book.

Another kind of change in word order is compulsory in *there* – construction, as in (54-55).

54. There seems to be a snake in the garden. (e.g. A snake is in the garden)
55. There is a mobile on the table. (e.g. a mobile is on the table)

In (54-55) *there* occpupies the position of the subject which occurs as the complement to the verb.

The same pattern is followed if a sentence begins with an empty *it*, as in (56)

56. *It* is a roller ball pen that I want.

The change in word order is obligatory in the following type of sentences, (called Pseudo-cleft sentences), as in (43).

43. What we need is a new football. (e.g. we need a new football)

The word order of an interrogative sentence is different from that of a declarative sentence.

If a question is to be answered in *Yes* or *No*, the sentence begins with its first auxiliary, as in (58).

58. Has he/she been in Mumbai for long?

If such a question has *be* or *have* as the main verb, it comes to the beginning of the sentence, as in (59-60).

59. Is he/she sick?
60. Has he/she enough money?

If a question has a *wh* word, it begins with that word and is followed by the auxiliary of the main verb, as in (61-62).

61. *Who is* he/she talking with?
62. *What does* he/she want?

As the subject of the imperative sentence is understood to be *you*, it does not appear in the sentence which begins with the verb, as in (63).

63. Wait for me.

The word order of an exclamatory sentence is also different from that of a declarative one.

Usually it begins with *how* or *what*, as in (64-65).

64. How nice of you!
64. What a magnificent building!

In short, each type of sentence has a fixed word-order, but sometimes the order is changed for emphasis, as in (66):

66. Bananas I like; apples I do not.

When a question is put in the indirect speech, there is no change in its word order in so far as the subject and the verb are concerned, as in (67).

67. I wanted to know what he/she was looking for.

Place of an Adverb Phrase

An adverbial phrase which modified the whole sentence occurs usually at the end of the sentence but sometimes it may occur in the beginning, as in (69):

68. He/she came to me early in the morning.
69. Early in the morning, he/she came to me.

Frequency adverbials never come in the beginning of the sentence, as in (70):

70.* Rarely he/she complains.
71. He/she rarely complains.

Usually an adverbial phrase is added to a verb phrase at its end as in (72).

72. He accepted the proposal *completely*.
73a.* He *completely* accepted the proposal.
73b.* He accepted completely the proposal.

(73a) and (73b) are incorrectly because the adverb has been used wrongly. However, in some cases (as in 74-76) it can precede the verb.

74. He will *definitely* do it.
75. We can *scarcely* ignore her.
76. I can *barely* follow you.

Word Order in a Verb Phrase

A verb phrase (VP) consists of a verb followed by an object noun phrase (if the verb is transitive) and an indirect object noun phrase (if the verb is ditransitive). The adverb phrase comes at the end of a verb phrase as shown in (68-69). The verb is the head of the verb phrase. In short, the preferred word-order is a follows:

77.	*Head of the Verb phrase*	*direct object*	*indirect object*	*Complement/ adjunct*
	gave	the book	to me	in the library, this evening

When the direct and indirect objects change their place, it is as in (78)

78. gave me the book in the library this evening

We may note that the direct object does not need any function word (i.e. a preposition) to connect it to the verb; indirect objects (e.g. *to me*) and adjuncts do (e.g. *in* the library). In other words, they usually occur as prepositional phrases.

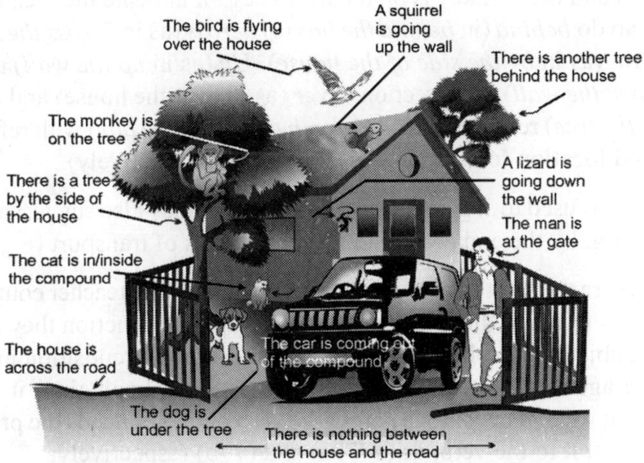

Fig. 23: Prepositions showing Location and Direction

Prepositional Phrases

A prepositional phrase is a group of words that is headed by a preposition. What follows it is a noun phrase (e.g. *at the open door* or *at it*). In short, a preposition governs and precedes a noun phrase. It establishes a relation between a verb and a noun phrase. It may establish a relation between a noun phrase and another nounphrase as well (e.g. the boy *in* the classroom). *Of* is the only preposition that does not connect a verb to a noun as in *of the book, nine of the eleven students, the status of the man, the coming of the film star, the singing of the national anthem*.

The function of a prepositional phrase is determined by the function of the preposition that heads it. For instance,

- *At, on, in, inside, within,* and *out of* indicate location (with reference to place or time) (as in Figure 23);
- *out of, into, from, to, up, down, through, towards,* and *back to* indicate direction;
- *for, to, during, since* express duration of time, of these, *since* refers to a specific time when something starts.
- *Above* and *over* refer to higher than the specified location; *below, under, beneath, underneath* refer to lower than the specified location, etc.
- *Between* means across the space separating two objects or regions, and *among* differentiates three or more parties.

- *With* means accompanied by a person or thing; it indicates an instrument with which an action could be performed.

In figure (23) on page 137 the man is *at* the gate, the cat is *in/inside* the compound and the monkey is *on* the tree.They all indicate the location of the entities. So do *behind* (in *behind the house*) *across* (as in *across the street*) by the side of (as in *by the side of the house*). *Up* (as in *up the wall*) and *down* (as in *down the wall*) are direction. *Over* (as in over the house) and *under* (as in *under the tree*) refer to an entity (i.e. *the bird* and *the day*) with reference to a specified location (e.g. *the house* and the tree respectively).

- *By* is used to suggest an agent (by him); it may also suggest a deadline (e.g. by the end of the month) or a means of transport (e.g. *by* car)

These are the most frequently used prepositions. The teacher could explain their uses in terms of the type they belong to and the function they perform.

The subject noun phrase is never introduced by a preposition in English. When the agent of an active sentence comes in its beginning, it needs no preposition; when it becomes a part of the verb phrase, it needs the preposition *by* to connect it to the verb, as in (79a) and (79b) respectively;

79a. *Salman Rusdie* wrote Joseph Anton.
79b. Joseph Anton was written *by Salman Rusdie*.

Word Order in a Noun Phrase

Just as every verb phrase has a fixed word order, so has every noun phrase. A noun phrase begins with a determiner which is followed by an adjectival phrase. The head of the NP is placed immediately after it and it is followed by a modifying prepositional phrase, if any. The relative clause follows the head noun which it qualifies but if the NP has both a relative clause and a prepositional, modifier, the relative clause follows the prepositional phrase. Thus, a noun phrase which has all the potential constituents will be as in (80)

80. [This [beautiful [jacket] [from Kashmir] [which I bought in Delhi]

• order :	[*det.*	[*adj.*	*head noun*	*prepositional phrase*	*relative clause*

The adjectival phrases occur in a fixed order, as in (81)

81. A [beautiful small new round brown Italian leather] jacket.
• order : *det. [appearance size age shape colour from where material]* head noun

Determiners and Pre-determiners

Besides *a, an* and *the*, which are traditionally known as *articles*, there are deictic expressions, such as *this*, *these*, *that*, *those* and expressions such as *what* or *which*, as in *what* book or *which* book and *every*, *each*, *either* (as in *every*, *each*, *either*, book) that are known as *determiners*. The possessive is another determiner. No two determiners occur together is a noun phrase. Hence we have *the book* or *which book* but not* *the which book* or* *which the book*. However, we have expressions such as *all the men* or *both* the students where *all* and *both* are pre-determiners. A pre determiner precedes the determiner as is clear from (82). The preferred order of the NP is as in (82) :

82. *Pre-determiner* +	*determiner* +	*adj. phrase* +	head noun...
e.g. some of	his	less known	books

• If an indefinite noun begins with a consonant sound, it takes *a*, if it begins with a vowel sound, it takes *an*. Thus we have *an apple*, a *mango*, an *honourable* gentleman, a *European traveller. Honourable* begins with a consonant letter but the sound |h| is silect, it is pronounced as |ɒnərəbl|, i.e. with a vowel sound and takes *an*. Likewise *Europe* begins with the letter 'E' (a vowel) but is pronounced as |juərəpi:ən| (i.e. with a consonant sound and takes *a*.

• If the noun is a definite description, it is preceded by *the*, as in (82).

83. They are new students.
The students are very friendly.

The first sentence in (83) describes the students, i.e. *new* students. When the same Noun Phrase is repeated in the next sentences. It becomes a definite description (with reference to the fresh sentence) and needs the definite article *the*.

• Proper names are not preceded by *the*, but if a name is a definite description, it is preceded by *the*, as in (83);

84. *the* USA, *the* UK, *the* Suez canal, *the* Ganges.

We have deliberately elaborated some grammatical points which grammar books do not pay much attention to but are necessary for writing correct English. Other items of grammar may be followed as prescribed in the text book. Usually the text books contain grammar exercises based on a lesson at its end. They should be strictly practised in the class with reference to their occurrence in the lesson. However, a few points need to be emphasized.

In terms of frequency count, articles (*a*, *an*, *the*) other determiners (*this*, *that*), conjunctions (*and*, *or*, *if*, *that*, *which*), various forms of verb to *be* (*is*, *are*, *was*, *were*, *will/shall be/been* and prepositions (such as *of*, *in to for*, *with*, *on*, *by*, *at*, *from*) are used very frequently in English and all of them should be paid attention to in the class.

The teacher needs to point out the difference between a preposition and a particle attached to a phrasal verb so that students can understand the ambiguity of sentences such as in (85):

85a. He/she decided on the boat.
85b. He/she decided [on the boat].
85c. He/she [decided on] the boat.

In (85b) *on* is a part of the prepositional phrase *on the boat*, whereas in (85c) it is a part of the phrasal verb *decided on.* (85b) refers to the place where a certain decision was taken and (85c) refers to making a choice out of several alternatives. The teacher will come across several phrasal verbs while going through a prescribed literary text and should explain their significance. According to the British National Corpus, verbs such as *say, know, get, go see, make, think, take, come, use, give, want, find, mean, look, begin, help, become, tell* and *seem* are more frequently used than other verbs. Students should be made familiar with their combinations with various particles.

TEACHING GRAMMAR TO THE LEARNERS OF ENGLISH AS L_2

Stephen Krashen (1985) believes that the grammar of a language is acquired subconsciously. He suggests that a learnt grammar does not convert into the acquired grammar that the speaker uses. Conscious knowledge of language rules is an additional asset. Wilga Rivers (1964) points out, "Analogy provides a better foundation for foreign language learners than analysis" but it is not necessarily so. If a second language learner lives among the native speakers of English, Krashen's observation seems to work. A discourse-based approach works in such a case. However, teaching English as a second or foreign language in India has a different problem. Here one has to base oneself mainly on the written discourse available to students in text books. In such a case, it is necessary to explain the grammatical points available in the text citing similar other examples. Explicit grammatical teaching is essential only when some forms or structures are urgently needed to enable students to express themselves but are not available in the prescribed text. For instance, English is not a pro-drop language and consequently it needs a sentence with *it* as the subject when a content-word subject (such as *John*) is not available. Such cases are hardly pointed out in a text book. As it is a frequently used in conversation, it cannot be ignored.

Likewise, the question of word order is ignored but it is a vital issue. If the teacher pays attention to increasing the language awareness of students, a great deal of problems would be solved. If the student is aware of what is needed in a context, for him/her an explicit explanation of the rule is easy to appreciate.

HOW TO HANDLE THE TEACHING OF GRAMMAR

Various approaches have been suggested to handle the teaching of grammar. Some hold the view that grammar is best learnt when students are engaged in understanding the meaning of the text they are going through. For instance,

Krashen and Terrell (1983) hold the view that grammar is learnt subconsciously. Some linguists such as Norris and Ortega (2000) believe that it must be taught explicitly while some others claim that children learn the grammar of a language implicitly whereas adult L_2 learner need the rules of grammar explained to them. The followers of Chomsky believe that knowing a language, including the second language, involves some kind of knowledge of the grammatical rules of the language. The teacher's task is to help students develop this grammatical sensitivity. In other words, he/she should demonstrate his/her own awareness of the syntactic patterns of the language that are being taught. He/she should encourage students to process sentences consciously. They may be able to construct complex sentences without being aware of their complexity. The teacher could help them monitor their endeavoures to understand them.

The results of the second language acquisition research point out that grammar is not acquired linearly, i.e., it is not the case that the learner acquires one structure and then another and so on. New structures are not mastered one by one, rather they enter the learner's interlanguage as needed. It may take time to get them properly assimilated. It is an interactive process. The teacher can facilitate students' ability to assimilate new forms and structures by using them more frequently and explaining their intricacy, if necessary. Obviously, it cannot be done successfully if these items are introduced in decontextualized forms. When students are made to do isolated grammatical exercises, they do it mechanically which does not guarantee that they will be able to use them appropriately in a communicative interaction situation. Learning is perfect only when the learner can use the learnt items freely and confidently. The teachers' job is to guide students to achieve this goal.

However, there are problems inherent in this situation. Students may not easily come across some structures because they are not used frequently in ordinary discourse. In such a case, the teacher has to contrive a situation in which the use of such structures is necessary. Secondly, students may find it difficult to handle a structure and avoid it. The teacher has to make a note of such structures and use them tactfully so that they catch the attention of students. He/she can choose a text the context of which makes the use of targeted structures obligatory in a natural manner. It can be done only if the teacher is innovative and alert. If the recommended text misses a grammatical item that is needed by students for self-expression in verbal interaction, a supplementary text should be used keeping their needs in view.

Our views on the teaching of grammar has changed over years and so has our awareness of current and idiomatic usage in the language. As the teaching of grammar is a complex and multidimensional task, it requires the teacher to be sensitive to the needs of the learner as well as the nuances of the language. In short, the teacher should have an eclectic approach and take advantage of advances in the generative grammar, the communicative competence approach and discourse analysis. Grammar should be treated as a tool for the understanding the structures of the language rather than an instrument to learn the language.

To sum up, English grammar should be taught in the context of a written text in an L_2 classroom by illustrating the grammatical points with sentences from the text.

- Alternatives to a given sentence should be pointed out, where necessary.
- Special attention should be paid to function words and their usage while reading a text.
- Sequence of tense, narration and word order should be specially discussed while going through the text.
- The teacher should use his/her knowledge of generative grammar in the class without discussing any theoretical issue.
- Prescriptive grammars should be avoided in order to get rid of redundant rules.
- Emphasis should be on current, idiomatic usage.
- Functional English should be preferred to literary English. (Here 'functional' refers to 'functional variety of standard English').
- The doctrine of linguistic norm is probably the best ground for teaching English as a second language.

10

Contrastive Analysis

Structural and Generative Approaches

Contrastive analysis of two languages is considered to be an endeavour to rationalise foreign language teaching. Charles C. Fries (1945), an American structural linguist, tried to apply its principles to the teaching of English as a foreign language. He observed, "the most effective [teaching] materials are those that are based upon a scientific description of languages to be learnt, carefully compared with a parallel description of the native language of the learners" (1945:9). Robert Lado (1957:3) agreed to this proposal and said, "Textbooks should be graded as to grammatical structure, pronunciation, vocabulary and cultural content. And grading can be done after the kind of comparison we are suggesting here". Accordingly, the Centre for Applied Linguistics of the Modern Language Association in America in Washington, D.C. commissioned the Contrastive Structure Series with a view to describing similarities and difference between English and other European languages. Under the series, W.G. Moulton (1962) published *The Sounds of English and German* and H.L. Kufner (1962) *The Grammatical Structure of English and German.* Similar books were published on the sound patterns of English and Spanish, and English and Italian. These publications set the trend and a lot of research was done on English and East European languages at centres of language studies in Warsow, Prague Poznan, etc. In India, some work was done on English and Indian languages, though none of them was so comprehensive. These works were done on the taxonomic (i.e. Bloomfieldian) model of language description. Those who work according to this model, keep comparison and contrast limited to the surface structures of sentences.

The contrastive analysis hypothesis is based on the assumption that (a) language learning is habit formation, (b) the habit formation of the second language acquisition is as different from the formation of habit during the first language acquisition as L_1 is different from L_2. As recent research has shown, these assumptions are open to question. Ravem (1974) studied the acquisition of *wh* questions by Norwegian students and compared it with their acquisition by English-speaking children and found that the process of acquisition was the same in both cases. Ervin-Tripp (1974) studied the acquisition of word-order in French by English-speaking students in a natural setting with that of the same in their mother-tongue and found that "both first and second language learning was similar in natural situation' (P. 126). Neither Ravem nor Ervin-Tripp has claimed that the acquisition of L_1 does not interfere in any way with the process of acquisition of L_2; what they have emphasised is that other things being equal, the process of acquisition of L_2 is similar to that of L_1.

Since mid-nineteen sixties the transformational generative theory of language analysis has been available and people who work according to this model look at sentences beyond the surface level. The concept of universal grammar motivates them to do so. For instance, if we compare an English sentence [as in (1)], with a Hindi sentence [(as in (2)], we find that the English sentence has no overt case marker which the Hindi sentence must have.

1. This room has thirty students.
2. is kamare *mẽ* tees chhatra hãi
   (This room in thirty students are).

However, both sentences have the same underlying case, namely, locative in the begining. A generative grammarian would, therefore, generalise that the locative - marker 'in' is deleted (or is not manifested) when the phrase occurs in the subject position in English but it is not so in Hindi. On surface, there is only one difference between Hindi and English, i.e., Hindi marks the case with a postposition and English, with a preposition, as in (3) and (4).

3. tees chhatra is kamare mẽ hãi
4. Thirty students are in the room.

Ever since the Principles and Parameter version of the generative grammar has emerged, a lot of work has been done on comparative and contrastive syntax. For instance, as Sinha (2016) has shown that both English and Hindi have sentential complements as objects as in (5-6).

5. John wants *that Bill should leave the room.*
6. John chāhtā hai ki Bill kamare se chalā jāe.
   John wants that Bill room from leave.

However, when the object clause is moved to the subject position, it become the subject in English but not in Hindi, as is obvious from (7) and (8) respectively.

7. That Bill should leave the room is John's desire.

8.* ki Bill kamare se cala jai ye John cahta hai.

However (8) can be rephrased as (9) in Hindi.

9. yah bāt ki Bill kamare se calā jae John ko pasand hai
   [the matter [that Bill room from leave] John wants.

In other words, in English *that -S* can be the subject complement of a sentence but in Hindi it cannot; we have to give it the form of an *NP* $[_{NP}$ Yah bat [ki S]$]_{NP}$.

In English, the case marker is lost if the beneficiary (i.e. indirect case) occupies the position of the direct object, as in (10b).

10a. John gave the book to Judy.
  b. John gave Judy the book.

But in Hindi, the case marker is retained in both positions, as in (11 a, b)

11a. John ne Kitāb *Judyko* dī
11b. John ne Judyko kitab dī

Every sentence in English must have a subject; if the slot for the subject is vacant, it is occupied by an empty *it*, as in (12 b).

12a.* — is easy to please John.
12b. It is easy to please John.
12c. John is easy to please.

Either *John*, the object of *please*, is moved to the subject position of *is easy* or the position is filled by *it*, but it is not so in Hindi; it does not need an empty (pleonastic) subject, as in (13).

13. John ko	khush karana	asan hai
John to	please	easy is

In short, comparing and contrasting sentences under the Chomskyan model takes care of more facts than does the grammar which is confined to only surface sentences. Burt and Dulay (1975) give several examples of how the knowledge of the two languages (i.e. the mother-tongue and L_2) can be creatively used to enable students to acquire a second language.

The points discussed above bring the question of equivalence between the structures of two languages to our attention. While formal equivalence can be established relatively easily, functional-semantic equivalence is difficult to set up.

For instance, both *at* and *on* are translated as *par* in Hindi which obliterates the difference between the two. *At* expresses location or arrival at a particular position or place; as in (14-15).

14. He is at the station.
15. The train arrived at New Delhi junction.

On the other hand, *on* means 'physically in contact with (and supported by) a surface, as in (16).

16. The pen is on the table.

Unless we mention the functions of *at* and *on*, the distinction is not clear; their translation equivalents lead us nowhere. *In* and *into* have *mẽ* as their Hindi equivalent but they are functionally different. *In* expresses the situation of something that is (or appears to be) enclosed by something else, as in (17a) whereas *into* expresses movement of someone or something with the result that it becomes enclosed or surrounded by something else; as in (17b).

17a. He is in the room.
17b. He went into the room.

The postposition *se* in Hindi does the functions of *with*, *from* and *by*. *With* indicates the instrument used to perform an action, *from* indicates the place from which a motion or action starts and *by* identifies an agent performing an action, as in (18), (19) and (20) respectively:

18. Usne chhuri se seb kate
    he knife with apple cut
    He cut the apple with a knife.
19. Ye gari Delhi se Mumbai jati hai.
    this train from Delhi to Mumbai goes.
    The train goes from Delhi to Mumbai.
20. Ye kam usse nahiĩ hoga.
    this work by him will not happen.
    This work will not be done by him.

Numerous examples of this type can be cited to illustrate that literal equivalents of words do not serve the real purpose of contrastive analysis.

Fries and Lado suggested that second language teaching can be planned better if we use the results of contrastive analysis of languages. Nickel (1971) argues that it can be more useful in teaching L_2 to adults or grown up children than to young children. Undoubtedly, it is useful for a second language teacher because it predicts the putative areas of difficulty to which he/she should pay special attention. It can also guide the designers of second language texts. However, it cannot be the only guiding factor. The results of tests administered to L_2 students point out that motivated students pay special attention to difficult and unfamiliar areas, and have little difficulty in understanding the structures of L_2 though they are different from the structures of L_1.

There are many factors which facilitate second language learning. The personality of the learner has its effect. Persons with lower anxiety level learn faster than those who tend to be tense and very anxious. Besides, there are other factors such as tendency to be outgoing, capacity to empathise and analyse logically. If these factors are positive, a new structure of L_2 does not bother the learner much.

The age of the learner is another important point. The younger the learner is, the easier it is for him/her to pick up a new language. An approach based on contrastive analysis does not pay attention to these factors. Psycholinguists such as Brown (1973), Slobin (1971), Smith (1985, 1999) and others have shown that L_2 acquisition process is similar to L_1 acquisition process. Ravem (1968) and Milon (1975) have pointed out that L_2 errors of children are similar to the errors committed by those learning English as the first language. It implies that a child learning English as L_2 is not affected much by his/her mother-tongue. All these researches have minimised the role of contrastive analysis in L_2 learning. Any way, it has never been demonstrated that course materials based on contrastive analysis are more effective than course materials based on other principles.

Nevertheless, there has been a revival of the procedures of contrastive analysis at an abstract level based on the principles of generative grammar. Such studies are being applied to machine translation and have proved useful for translations in general.

To sum up, contrastive analysis states that a learner's first language interferes with his or her learning of second language and that it is the major obstacle to successful mastery of the second language.

- It holds the view that where structures in L_1 differs from those in L_2, the habit of L_1 will affect the production of L_2. They could happen at the levels of phonology, words, phrases and sentences.
- A comparison of structures of L_1 and L_2 could predict the areas of difficulty in learning L_2.
- Those who prepare text books and plan lessons could keep the predicted problems in view and so can the classroom teachers of L_2.
- Research has not substantiated these claims fully. Recent work suggests that L_2 learning is similar to L_1 learning and the surface difference between the two languages does not cause much difficulty.

11

Error Analysis

To err is human. —*Alexander Pope*

The word 'error' means 'the state of being wrong'. It is synonymous with 'mistakes' which primarily means 'an act of judgment which is wrong or misguided'. It is specially used for a word which is not correct or accurate. 'Lapse' is a brief or temporary failure of concentration, memory or judgement. It indicates a decline from the standard. 'Slip of the pen' means 'a minor mistake in writing' and 'slip of the tongue' refers 'to a minor mistake in speech'. For instance, if one used *pain kills* for *pain pills* or *pain killers*, it is a slip. The use of *fatal flows* for *fatal blows* and '*board and room*' for *room and board* is a slip of the pen (or the tongue/speech). However, if one is not able to correct such expressions in spite of being told that they are not correct, it would be wrong to label them as examples of mere slips of the pen (or speech); they are errors. If the speaker (or writer) of a lapse is able to correct wrong expressions used by him/her earlier, it may be treated as a slip of the pen (or tongue); if he/she is not able to do so, it may be treated as the example of an error.

Corder (1967) makes a distinction between 'mistakes' and 'errors'. According to him, mistakes are unsystematic whereas errors are systematic. The former occur due to strain or other psychological conditions whereas the latter occur because the learner has failed to acquire the items

Language teachers are used to pointing out mistakes in the speech or writing of students. Traditional teachers correct them in the class and warn their students not to make them again. They repeat the relevant grammatical rules when several students make the same mistake and ask them to be careful. They make no difference between errors and lapses. They do not describe the types of error they come across nor do they generalise them on their basis.

THE STRUCTURALIST APPROACH

The structuralists believe in describing errors category-wise. They separate the lexical errors (i.e. wrong use of words) from grammatical errors and discuss the latter in detail. For instance, errors in the use of articles are listed as follows:

A. i. Wrong use of *a*
  a. Use of *a* in place of *an*
  b. Use of *a* in place of *the*
 ii. Overuse of *a* (where no article is needed)
 iii. Underuse of *a* (where *a* was needed but not used)

B. i. Wrong use of *an*
  a. Use of *an* in place of *a*
  b. Use of *an* in place of *the*
 ii. Overuse of *an*
 iii. Underuse of *an*

C. Wrong use of *the*
  a. Use of *the* in place of *a*
  b. Use of *the* in place of *an*
 ii. Overuse of *the*
 iii. Underuse of *the* (Sinha, A.K., 1967)

Likewise, errors of prepositions are discussed itemwise. For instance, errors involving the use of *at* are discussed as follows:

i. Wrong use of at
  a. Use of *at* in place of *on*
  b. Use of *at* in place of *upon*
  c. Use of *at* in place of *in*
  d. Use of *at* in place of other prepositions
ii. Overuse of *at*
iii. Underuse of *at* (*ibid*)

Errors involving tense are usually split into two groups: (a) wrong tense forms and (b) wrong tense usage and each of them is discussed separately. Likewise, errors involving agreement and forms of pronouns, adjectives and adverbs are discussed separately.

Apart from wrong use, overuse and underuse of grammatical features, cases of double markings of the same grammatical aspects are also noted. For instance, in (1) two features of past tense formation are found.

1. I *did* not *went* there.

Here, the *do* support, which is used in negative formation, has been used in the past form; at the same time *went*, the past form of *go*, has also been used. Likewise, in (2) two singular marks (e.g. suffix-*s* and the present tense singular of *do*) have been used.

2. He *does* not *knows* the conductor.

In (3) the negation-marker is used twice.

3. He did *not* give me *no* money.

In (4) the object is retained in its position and topicalized as well.

4. That is the girl *whom* I saw *her*.

Thus, the structural analysis goes on adding to the error-types.

As the structuralists believed in the behaviourist theory of language learning, they considered it a process of habit formation. A grammatical error was taken as an example of failure to form a correct habit. The contrastive analysis approach to errors was to match them with the items predicted as the areas of difficulty on the basis of a comparison between the structures of L_1 with those of L_2. It recommended more structural practices to get the relevant features stuck in the memory so that no further error was made.

This approach was simplistic and did not account for all errors. For instance, both English and Hindi have subject-verb agreement rules, which apply only once in a sentence. Then, why did errors like the one in (2) were made and why was it doubly marked? The gap between the errors projected by contrastive analysis and actual errors forced the error analysts to think afresh. Chomsky's (1959) critique of Skinner's work questioned the very foundation of behaviourists' habit formation theory as an account of language learning.

THE GENERATIVE-TRANSFORMATIONAL APPROACH

Chomskyan generative-transformational approach and Piaget's developmental cognitive approach highlighted the mental makeup of learners as a central force in the learning process. Consequently, new attempts were made to offer explanations for errors made by language learners. For instance, it could be pointed out that the person who used (2) knew the negation formation rule of English (i.e. the verb needs a *do* support if it does not have an auxiliary and *do* occurs before the negation – marker *not*, but he did not note the point that the main verb remains unmarked for agreement when the marker is attached to *do*. Likewise, the person who used (3) knew that the negative marker is attached to the auxiliary *do* which carries tense but forgot to make the main verb unmarked for tense.

Just as in a *wh-* question, in a relative clause formation, the word for the relative clause markers (e.g. *whom/who*) occurs immediately after the noun to which it is attached. The person who used (4) knew it but forgot that the objects NP after the verb in the relative clause was to be deleted because it has already got its copy in the beginning of the relative clause. In short, the generative approach enables one to think of a correct sentence and how it is formed and then compare it with the erroneous sentence in terms of the components of a rule which the user has failed to apply.

The traditional approach will treat (5) as a failure to form a negative sentence properly. In its view, the sentence in (2) is of the same type.

5. He knows not the answer.

However, a generativist will treat (2) differently from (5). In (2) the negative formation rule has been applied partially because it ignores the point that once the agreement and tense markers are attached to the auxiliary *do*, the main verb becomes unmarked. (5) on the other hand, misses many steps of negative formation: (i) it does not apply the *do* support rule, (ii) it does not transfer the features of tense and agreement to *do* and it places *not* after the main verb whereas it should have been before the main verb. In Hindi the main and auxiliary verbs, if any, remains in situ (i.e. as it is), as in (5) but (5) is not the result of the influence of Hindi because in Hindi also the negative marker precedes (and not follows) the verb. In brief, the generative approach goes through the details of steps which the language learner has taken and points out the steps he/she has missed. Its recommendation for the correction of the error is drawn from the steps the speaker of the erroneous sentence has not taken. In some cases, he/she has to concentrate on the wrong step he/she has taken. In other words, the explanation for errors lies in drawing the correct inference based on reasoned arguments and empirical evidence.

The contrastive analysis-based explanation is confined to surface structure comparison between the structures of L_1 and L_2 but, as has been shown in the previous chapter, it is not satisfactory. The Hindi postposition *par* has two equivalents in English: *at* and *on*. However, if a man used (6) for (7), he is confused between the domain of usage of *on* and *at*; it is an intralingual problem.

6.* He is on the gate.
7. He is at the gate.

At refers to location of a particular point or position whereas *on* refers to somewhere in the general surface area of a place and suggests contact with that area. Since a man cannot possibly be in contact with the general surface area of the gate to stand on it, (6) is inadmissible. However, (8) is acceptable because a cat can be in contact with the surface area of the gate.

8. The cat is on the gate.

In brief, both logical and functional aspects of the item should be taken into account while considering the appropriateness of a sentence.

GLOBAL AND LOCAL ERRORS

Burt and Kiparsky (1972) and Burt (1975), who approached the analysis of errors from the generative point of view, divided errors into two groups: local and global errors. Local errors are errors that affect single element (i.e. constituent) in a sentence and do not hinder communication significantly. For example, sentences (1-7) ae examples of local errors and so is (8):

8. Why we like each other?
   (for, why do we like each other?)

Global errors are those errors that hinder communication significantly, as in (9-11).

9. English language use many Indians
   (for, Many Indians use the English language)
10. He will be rich until he marries.
    (for, He will be rich when he marries)
11. Students' proposal looked into the principal)
    (for, Students' proposal was looked into by the Principal)

The idea of putting errors into two groups – local and global—is correct but Burt's definition of local errors is not very accurate. (10) contains only one constituent error but it is global in the intended sense.

(12) is a global error in the sense that it conveys the opposite of what it is supposed to convey but is formally correct in another context.

12. The teacher was helped by the students.
    (For, the students were helped by the teacher)

However, (13) is a good example of global error.

13. The teacher was helped the students'.

The reader of the sentence is not clear whether it is used in the sense of (14a) or (14b):

14a. The teacher was helped by the students.
14b. The teacher helped the students.

Out of the context, the erroneous sentence (13) is ambiguous but in a context it is either for (14a) or (14b).

Burt *et al.*, who believe in relative seriousness of errors, have assigned different numerical points to different categories of errors. For example, all errors involving plain function words such as articles, prepositions, conjunctions, adverbs) are assigned one point whereas verbs with grammatical endings (–ed, –ing, –en, –s) are assigned two points, and all possessives are assigned three points. However, there does not seem to be any sound basis for such evaluation. No psycholinguistic research has come to defend such a system. If at all such an evaluation is done, it should be on the basis of syntactic and semantic complexity. For instance, a sentence with right hand embedding in English is less confusing than the one with the middle embedding, as in (15) and (16) respectively.

15. It was widely noted [that John criticised the book (before he read it)].
16. That John criticised the book before he read it was widely noted.

The generativists advocate that language acquisition strategies consist of rules and if an error occurs in a sentence, it means that a rule has been wrongly applied, omitted or not applied at all. For instance, if someone says (or writes) *hers pajamas* (instead of her *pajamas*) the rule for the use of predicative possessive has been wrongly used. Instead of it, the rule for the use of *her* (as a possessive) should have been used. If someone says *her teeths* (instead of *her teeth*), he/she has overused the plural formation rule and applied it to a word which is already the plural form of *tooth.*

MODERN USAGE

The language teacher should be aware of recent changes in modern English. For instance, in modern English, (17b), in which *who* has been used in place of *whom* (as in 17a), is a completely acceptable sentence.

17a. Whom do you want to meet?
17b. Who do you want to meet?

When *whom* moves to the subject position, it becomes *who.*

The past tense and past participle forms of *cast* is *cast*, as in (18).

18. He was cast in the same mould.

On the same pattern, the past of *broadcast* is *broadcast* but now *broadcasted* is also used, as in (19), though *telecast* has no alternative, as in (20).

19. This news was broadcasted in the morning.
20 This news was telecast in the morning.

There are some other irregular verbs which are being regularised. Similarly some nouns which had irregular plural are having regular plural forms now. The plurals of *corpus* are *corpora* and *corpuses* and if a student uses *corpuses* he/she should not be marked wrong. Sentences such as in (21-22) in which prepositions have been stranded are considered perfectly correct now.

21. Who did you vote for?
22. Which book are you referring to?

However, not all sentences with stranded preposition are acceptable, as is clear from (23).

23.* Which way is he annoying her in? (for, 'In which way does he annoy her)

Prescriptive grammars declare all sentences with stranded prepositions incorrect or, at least, inelegant but that is not true of modern English. All speakers of English use stranded prepositions. Indian teachers of English ought to take note of such developments. They should not consider such expressions used by their students as ungrammatical.

Recent developments have made us realise that the role of the first language of learners in the acquisition of second language is rather limited. The first persons to report this fact were Dulay and Burt (1977a) who found that nearly 5% errors reflected the effect of learners' first language. Most recent research reports confirm this conclusion though the proportion of errors due to learners' first language differs. The general conclusion that can be drawn is that majority of errors made by second language learners are not inter-lingual but developmental. It has also been found that adults learning English as a second language make more inter-lingual errors than children.

The research in India on error analysis suggests that bulk of errors involve the use of articles, prepositions, correct tense usage, word-order and agreement. In so far as the usage of tense is concerned, the problem areas are the distinction between simple present and present progressive, simple past and present perfect, past perfect and simple past, and progressive and perfect progressive. The choice of an appropriate modal verb is also a problem. The correct word order is a problem in the reported speech which has an embedded question in it. In spoken and written communication, the learner tends to avoid complex structures rather than use them and make mistakes. Such areas include sentences with optional movement of constituents (such as in extraposed, cleft and pseudo-cleft sentences). The use of phrasal verbs is generally avoided by learners. In so far as the lexicon is concerned, the main areas of difficulty are the inappropriate choice of words and collocations.

INTERLANGUAGE

While trying to speak correctly in a second language, the learner may not be able to do so in his/her first attempt though he/she tries to achieve the goal. Thus, a speaker may say (24a) or (24b) instead of (24c), or he/she may first say (24a), then (24b) and finally (24c).

24a. Why you not like ice cream?

24b. Why you do not like ice cream?
24c. Why don't you like ice cream?

(24a) and (28b) are attempted products of the targeted norm. Pit Corder (1967), in his paper on the significance of learner's errors, argued that second language research should follow the example of first language research and view the learner's development as the development of underlying linguistic competence. Systematic errors may be viewed by the researcher as learner's current transitional competence. They reflect the learner's attempts to make sense of the input to which he/she has been exposed. He/she has made a distinction between input (i.e. what the learner is presented with) and learner's intake (i.e. what the learner actually takes). The personal transitional system possessed by an individual learner is different from that of another. Though learners at school are put in grades or group, individual learners may be at different points along a common route.

William Nemser (1971) proposed that the second language learning should be seen as a succession of evolving system that takes the user nearer and nearer the target system and further away from the source system. The learner creates a series of system, which he called '*approximate systems*' that take him/her closer and closer to the system used by a normal native speaker.

Selinker (1972) considered utterances such as in (24) examples of *interlanguage*. His approach is similar to that of Nemser. He considers it a stage in the process of language acquisition. It can be observed and analyzed to find out how much a learner has acquired and what strategies need to be adopted to concentrate on what ought to be learnt but has not been learnt yet. While using the interlanguage, the speaker concentrates on the message, and not on the correctness of the message.

The concept of interlanguage has radically changed our way of looking at errors. Earlier, we concentrated on what the second language learner had failed to learn. Now we concentrate on how much the learner had acquired. In (24a) the learner has acquired the devices of using negative and question markers, in (24b) he/she has learnt how to construct a negative sentence and (24c) he/she has learnt how to frame a negative question. Each utterance offers evidence of some learning though it is only in (24c) that the norm has been achieved. The concept of *interlanguage* enables one not only to describe an error from a positive point of view but also to speculate on what underwent in the mind of the speaker and what motivated him/her to make such an utterance. Krashen (1977 a, b) uses the term *monitor* for the internal system that appears to be responsible for conscious linguistic processing. He argues that the linguistic knowledge that one gains through monitoring can be used to consciously formulate a sentence and to correct one's own utterance. The editing function of the monitor helps one in self-correction; it can be effectively used to take remedial measures to remove errors.

The mere capacity to recognise interlanguage does not guarantee that the learner will achieve the goal of using a normal sentence nor does the scope of the use of the monitor. Much depends on the learner's personality, and his/her focus on the linguistic task. It is in the context that the role of the teacher becomes important; he/she can formally expose the learner to the grammatical point to make him/her aware of what is yet to be learnt.

FOSSILIZATION

In spite of all precautions, *fossilization* occurs where errors become firm like fossils. It suggests a stage in which development stops in spite of repeated exposure to the item to be learnt. Fossilized errors are hard to remove because they are often based on false generalization. For instance, both *for* and *since* are used to indicate a period of time; *for* when the starting point of time is not specified and *since* when it is specified. Some learners stop at the first generization and do not differentiate them on the basis of the reference to the point of time, producing sentences such as (25):

25*. He has been living in Delhi *since* thirty years.

It is hard to get rid of fossilization without the expert help of the teacher.

However, fossilization is a controversial topic. Some L_2 learners gain fluency in written and spoken English but retain this non-native accent and linguists are divides in their opinion in calling this habit fossilized. In many parts of the world, where English has become a second language, some local characteristics have developed and if does not seem to be right to call them instances of fossilization.

To sum up, errors are to be differentiated from slips of the pen or tongue and looked at positively as evidence of how much the learner has acquired.

- The structuralists' attempt to collect and categorise errors points out what types of errors a learner makes but it is descriptive. It does not suggest why the errors are made.
- The generative approach to errors explains the nature of errors and how and why they are made.
- To view an error as the evidence of interlanguage learning is the positive way of analysing how much a learner has learnt. It implicates how much needs to be learnt. The monitoring system tells us how consciously linguistic learning process works. It helps the learner in self-correction. It also tells the teacher what remedial measures to take to facilitate learning and how to eradicate fossilized errors.

12

Helping Learners to Enrich Their Vocabulary

Words, Words, Words in Songs and Stories
If only I Understood them. —*Pete Seiger*

VOCABULARY

The word *vocabulary* refers to the body of words used in a particular language. It is also called *lexicon.* It comprises words of all types, words which refer to concrete objects, action and events as well as abstract concepts such as *truth, virtue, idea, knowledge,* etc. We need a large stock of words to communicate in a language. However, we are told that if we knew a hundred function (structural) words (such as *is, of, and, the, be,* etc.) and hundred most frequently used content words, we can recognise nearly half the words we come across in English.

Now-a-days it is not difficult to have a frequency count of words in English. The British National Corpus., the COBUILD Corpus and other corpora are available for corpus analysis. Frequency of words is one of the considerations in selecting a word in a text at the initial stage of teaching English as a second language but it is not the only consideration. The most common words do not differ greatly from one type of text to another. However, one cannot depend solely on them to speak or write reasonably natural English. Much depends on the context in which the language is used. One chooses a word on the basis of its lexical meaning, collocational restriction on it and its appropriateness in the context. For instance, we utter the word *say* to say something but it cannot be used in all contexts. We *tell a story, state a fact, announce an event, declare war,* and *express one's feeling.*

VARIOUS TYPES OF VOCABULARY

Every person who knows English has several overlapping and somewhat interwoven vocabularies. The commonest words of the language are known to all. Some words are used in formal setting and some in even more formal situations. The number of words one recognises and comprehends is greater than the number of words one has to use in any form other than in reading. The types of vocabularies which need to be considered in educating a language learner can be discussed under four headings:

(i) *Understanding Vocabulary:* The words recognised and comprehended through listening and reading.
(ii) *Speaking Vocabulary:* The words used in the course of ordinary conversation and the words the individual understands and can draw upon when the occasion arises.
(iii) *Writing Vocabulary*: Informal words used in personal correspondence, notes and diaries, and the words used on more formal occasions, such as in examination and professional writing.
(iv) *Marginal vocabulary*: Words a person can interprete from context and words which are known because of one's knowledge of word formation (prefixation, suffixation, compounding, etc.)

Some pedagogues differentiate between "incidental" and instructed vocabulary. Such a division is artificial. Vocabulary is acquired during listening and reading. Whether it is an intensive reading or an extensive reading, it does not matter. What matters is to have familiarity with the word one comes across and ability to use it in an appropriate context.

Words and their meanings are learnt at first, on the oral basis. Only after a person starts reading, (s)he begins to gain new words and new concepts. As his/her knowledge of the language develops, his/her potential to use more words also develops. His/her writing ability has all those potential words at his/her disposal. S(he) can understand some of the potential words from the context. Whether (s)he can use them depends upon the frequency of occasions(s) he gets to be familiar with them.

WHAT VOCABULARY TO LEARN

A high school student needs to learn essential words and phrases of everyday use. Verbs such as *know*, *get*, *see*, *make*, *think*, *take*, *come*, *use*, *give*, *want*, *find*, *look*, *mean*, *begin*, *become*, *help* and *see* are essential because they are most frequently used. So are the phrasal verbs formed out of them.

SYNONYMS

Each of these essential words has (near) synonyms which can also be learnt. For instance, *get* has synonyms such as *achieve*, *acquire*, *attain*, *gain*, *earn* and *obtain*. *Get* is a comprehensive verb. A person *gets* whatever he comes to possess or experience with or without any effort. A person *gains* or *acquires* something he/she has strong desire for. To *obtain* implies some kind of activity or desire on the part of the obtainer and *secure* means that which is difficult to obtain. A person *earns* what he gets as a return for his/her labour but he/she may get even that he/she has not earned.

As one word leads to another word semantically, to paraphrase the word in a sentence may lead a person to another word indicating the same sense.

A game can be played to show agreement of opinion by replacing a word with its synonym.

1. A: "The teacher *erased* a line from the passage.
   B: 'Yes, he *expunged* it'.
2. A: He is very *industrious.*
   B: 'Yes, he is *diligent*.'
3. A: He *encouraged* you to join this course.
   B: 'Yes, he *inspired* me'.
4. A: 'He *believed* me'
   B: 'Yes, he had *faith* in you.'
5. A: 'The prospect for the future looks fairly *dim.*
   B: 'Yes, it is hopeless'.
6. A: The glow of the flame was *dim.*
   B: 'Yes, it was fairly *light*'.

Some synonyms which are frequently used are: *large/big, fresh/new, cold/ chilly, warm/ tepid, correct/ right, crazy/ stupid, deny/refuse, fix/set, friend/ buddy, many/several,* etc.

A word game of the type given above could be easily played.

ANTONYMS

Another way of enriching one's vocabulary is to think of its opposite. For instance, the opposite of *open* is *close*. When *open* is used as an adjective, its opposite is *closed* (as in an *open/closed door*). The opposite of *take* is *give* and that of *begin* is *end*. Some words get their antonyms by adding a prefix to them, (e.g. *happy-unhappy*; *possible-impossible*; *able-unable*); some by adding suffix to them after removing the existing suffix, e.g. *harmful-harmless*; *colourful-colourless*; *careful-careless*, etc.

Games involving antonyms can be played to show disagreement. If one student says 'it is hot', the other responds by saying, 'No, it is *cold*'. Likewise, the game may continue.

7. A: 'It is *soft*'.
   B: 'No it is *hard.*'
8. A: You are *rich.*
   B: 'No, I am poor'.
9. A: The world is *flat.*
   B: 'No, it is '*round*'.

10. A: This table is *large.*
    B: 'No, it is small.'
11. A: 'This shirt is *expensive*'
    B: 'No, it is *cheap*'.
12. A: This room is *rectangular*
    B: 'No, it is oval'.
13. A: This food is *delicious.*
    B: 'No, it is *unsavoury.*'
14. A: His remarks were *adverse.*
    B: 'No, they were *favourable*'.

Some frequently used antonyms are: bright-dull, high-low, right-wrong, young-old, sweet-sour, full-empty, same-different, fit-unfit, push-pull, light-dark, light-heavy, cooked-raw.

They can be used in a word game involving anonyms.

DERIVATIONS

A root word can yield several words if suitable prefixes and suffixes are added to it. For instance, from the word *mean* (in the sense of 'signify'), we have the words *meaning*, *meaningful*, *meaningless.* When we add a prefix or suffix or both to *able*, we have *enable*, *unable*, *ability*, *inability*, and *ably*. From the word *system*, we have *systematic* and *systematically*, *unsystematic* and *unsystematically*. In short, we can add prefixes and suffixes to frequently used content words (nouns, adjectives and verbs) to increase our vocabulary.

APPROPRIATE COLLOCATIONAL LINKS

Expressions such as *precious stones*, *crunchy cereals*, *juicy fruit*, *icy cold*, *hot-tempered*, *hot favourite*, *hot news*, *soft-spoken*, *soft copy*, *soft cover*, *hard bound*, *hard cover*, *hard disk*, *hard currency*, *hard core*, *hard pressed*, etc. are frequently used in a set pattern, they could be introduced to students on appropriate occasions. Emphasis should be put on acquiring often-used 'prefabricated expressions and formulaic sequences' (i.e. multi-word items) such as *think, think aloud*, *thinking*, *think fit*, *think nothing of it*, *think tank*, *good-for nothing*, *goody-goody*, etc.

PHRASAL VERBS

Another way to increase one's vocabulary is to pay attention to phrasal verbs occurring in the text. For instance, from *come*, we have phrasal verbs such as *come about* (happen), *come across* (meet), *come along*, *come back*, *come between* (interfere with the relationship of two persons), *come down* (collapse), *come forward* (volunteer oneself), *come of* (descend from), *come on*, *come over*, *come round*, *come under*, *come up*, *come upon*, *etc*. There are several phrasal verbs with *go*, *give*, *take*, *get* and *become* which must be taken note of.

ONE WORD FOR A LONG EXPRESSION

There are words which have no synonyms at the level of words; they need to be defined or explained. For instance,

- the action of buying and selling goods and services is called *trade* and the person whose profession is trade is a *trader*. The sale of goods to be public in relatively small quantities for use or consumption (rather than for resale) is the *retail* (trade). A person or company involved in wholesale trade, especially one supplying goods to a particular trade is a *merchant*. A person who moves from place to place to trade in small goods is called a *pedler* and a trader in street is called a *vendor*.
- A person who studies at university or school or other places of education is a *student*, a person who teaches, especially in a school is a *teacher*, a university teacher is a *professor*, a person who gives lectures professionally at university or a centre of higher education is a *lecturer* and one who teaches something is an *instructor* (e.g., a physical training instructor). A university teacher ranking below assistant professor is also an *instructor*.
- An expert in *physics* is a *physicist* and one who is a qualified doctor in medicine is a *physician*. The person who practises physical therapy is a *physical therapist*; he/she is also called a *physio*.
- A person who prepares food, a dish or meal, is a *cook*. A person whose profession is making and selling bread and cakes is a *baker* and a person who is a professional cook in a hotel or a restaurant is a *chef*, especially if he/she is the chief cook.
- An electronic device which is capable of receiving information (data) in a particular form and of performing a sequence of operations in accordance with a predetermined variable set of procedural instructions (programme) to produce a result in the form or information or signals is a *computer*. A person having sufficient knowledge and skill to be able to use computers is *computer literate* or *computerate*. To convert information to a form which is stored or processed by a computer is to *computerize*. Thus, one word leads to another and a little mental exercise in this direction can enrich one's vocabulary. We can go on adding to a list like this.

WORD MEANING

Dictionaries give us general and specific meanings of words. The general meaning of *baby* is 'a very small child' including a very young animal. Its specific meaning could be 'a thing regarded with affection or familiarity (e.g. *this baby* (with reference to a car) *drives very smoothly*), or a lover (often used as a form of address). As an adjective, it means 'comparatively small' (e.g. *buy a baby car*). *Baby blue* means pale shade of blue and 'baby blues' means 'blue eyes'. A '*baby carriage*' refers to 'a pram' and '*baby bloom*' means 'a sudden increase in the birth rate'.

HOMOPHONES

As a verb *mean* means 'to signify'. As an adjective, it means 'unkind or unfair'. As a noun it means 'the quotient of several quantities or average'. These are three separate words; they are homophones. Students could be made aware of such words when an occasion arises. In short, words have different kinds of relations among themselves.

Connectionism

Psycholinguists who believe in the theory of connectionism explain these relationships in terms of network of interconnected simple units.

For instance, word *milk* reminds one of milk products such as *cheese, butter, ghee, yogurt, curd, cream, pasteurised milk, toned milk, dry milk, milk powder*, etc. It also reminds us of *milk food, milk products, milk pudding, milk chocolate, milk cake and milk shakes. Cream reminds us of ice cream and cheese, of ricotta cheese, cheese burger, cheese cake, cheese cloth, cheeseboard and cheese straw. Milk also reminds us of milk man, milk booth, milk bottle and milk processing plant.* It reminds us of *cow, buffalo, goat, dairy farm, dairy man, dairy maid, dairy product*. We can see that there is a network of words around the word *milk* and most of the members of these network (such as *cheese, milk product, milk processing*) have their own networks. Besides, the word reminds us of idiomatic expressions such as 'milk from something' and 'milk something for all its worth'. It reminds us of the idiom, milk of human kindness, as well.

The main point of the connectionist model is that it associates features with features. This enables grouping synonyms together because synonymous words have similar (or the same) features. Similarity is accountable for with the mind storing different words with similar sense together, it also accounts for different forms of the same word (e.g. *eat, ate, eaten*; *drink, drank, drunk*; *use, used, using*, etc.). It also accounts for the fact that the words of generic group can be put together. For instance, *red*, *white*, *black*, *blue*, *green* are under one superimposed group of *colour*. Even words like *bright* and *dim* are associated with colour. The word *starved* is associated with *hungry* and so are *thirsty*, *food* and *eat*. The word *salt* is associated with *pepper* and so it is with *taste* and *shaker*. The word *bazzar* is associated with *merchant*, *customer*, *vendor*, *peddler*, *buyer*, *seller* and names of commodities available in the market.

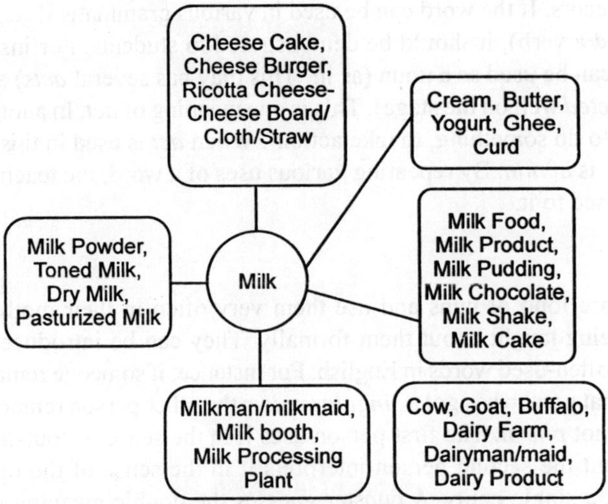

Fig. 22: The Domain of Milk

Another way of remembering a category of words is the prototype theory (Rosch 1986) which puts a group of words together on the basis of their family resemblance. For instance, *lemon* resembles not only *lime* but also *orange*, *tangerine*, *grapefruit*, *mausami*, *kinu*, etc.

WAYS TO INCREASE ONE'S VOCABULARY

One can increase one's vocabulary by linking a new word to the words one knows already. It can be done in terms of its synonymy or definition if synonymous words are not available. For instance, to give way to someone is to *yield*, to stop resisting an enemy or opponent or to submit to the authority is to *surrender*, and to examine someone or something closely is to *survey*. A person who works without being paid is a *volunteer* and an officer employed to ensure that official rules and regulations are obeyed is an *inspector*.

Word Games

Word games can be played in the class and students may be prompted to give the synonyms and antonyms of words, as has been shown on p. 159-160. They may be given a simple word and asked to derive other words from it. For example, given the word *play*, one can think of *playful*, *player*, *playmate*, *playground*, *play time*, etc. One can even think of *play a game*, *play a trick*, *play with fire*, *play it cool*, etc. They may be taught how to play anagram and *antakshari*.

Repetition of a new word which students come across in a text and its various uses is another way to increase one's stock of words. If a new word is used in a sentence in the class, students are made familiar with the structure in which it occurs. If the word can be used in various grammatical ways (e.g. as a noun and a verb), it should be demonstrated to students. For instance, the word *act* can be used as a noun (as in 'This play has several *acts*) and a verb (e.g. He *acted* well on the stage). This is one meaning of *act*. In another sense, it means 'to do something, to take action'. When *act* is used in this sense, its noun form is *action*. By repeating various uses of a word, the teacher can get students used to it.

Puns

Children are fond of puns and use them very often in their mother tongue without being taught about them formally. They can be introduced to puns involving often-used words in English. For instance, if someone remarks about a singer, that person has got a *singular voice*; the other person remarks, Thank God, it is not *plural*. The first person uses it in the sense of 'outstanding' or 'unique' but the second person interprets it in the sense of the opposite of plural, i.e. a single entity. A punster guesses the double meaning of a word fast and gives an unexpected twist to the other person's remarks. For instance, a person talks to his neighbour about his newly born son:

'I suppose the new baby is the *king* in your family' to which the other person replies.

'No, he is the *prince of Wails*.

The pun is in the interpretation of *'Wales'* as *'Wails'*.

Scrabble: In a scrabble, some letters of a word is given and people are expected to guess the word. In some cases, the meaning is given to help the person guess it correctly. For examples:

	l	w				'on all occasions' (answer is always)
d		y	'opposite of wet' (answer, 'dry')			

In other cases the meaning is not given, for examples:

	p	p			(answer: '*apple*')
	o	r		d	(answer: '*world*')

Puzzle: In a puzzle, students have to fill up the blanks with letters in such a way that the desired words are obtained. The letters are put in some spaces and the rests are to be filled up by the person who tries to solve the puzzle.

For instance:

	A		E
E		E	

Left to Right
1. a story full of action
3. to prepare something

Downwards
1. What is measured in minute, hours and days.
3. A large area of water surrounded by lake

Answer:

T	A	L	E
I		A	
M	A	K	E
E		E	

Puzzles could be as complex as the standard of students who will solve them.

Finding Connected Words

One way to enrich the vocabulary of language learners is to look at the problem from the connectionist viewpoint.

The teacher may point out a *chair* in the classroom and ask student to name the types of chairs they know about. He may get responses such as *sofa chair, easy chair, folding chair, lawn chair, cone chair, plastic chair, wooden chair, steel chair,* etc. *The table* in the classroom may remind students of *study table, dinning table, drawing table, dressing table, end table,* etc. It may also remind them of *stool, desk* and *tripod*, on which we put things.

The teacher may ask students to name other objects they sit on (or, in) and get responses such as *sofa, couch, bench, seat* and even *morha* or *mudda* (for which there are no English equivalents).

The teacher may put all these names on the writing board in the class and tell students that they are all pieces of *furniture* which comprises objects (or movable articles) that are used to make a room suitable for living or working. It includes objects to sit on, to put things on or in (e.g. *almirah, cupboard, drawer, etc.*) or to relax on (or in) such as bed. They can be classified as in Figure 23.

Finding Matching Words

Students may be given two sets of words in a random order and asked to prepare a set of matching words. It could be matching a set of synonyms (e.g. *essential* matches *vital* and *crucial*) antonyms (e.g. *ampty* matches *full*) or collocations (e.g. *cool headed, hot tempered, cool and calm*).

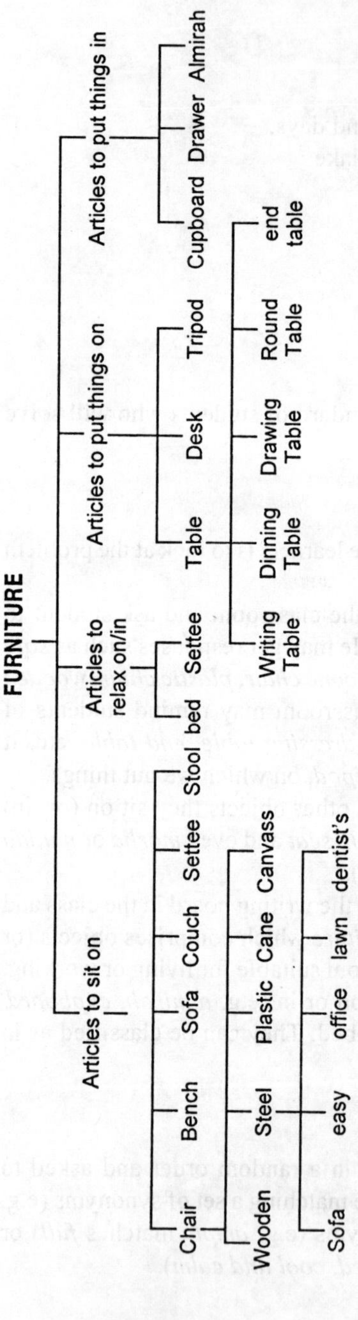

Figure 23: Pieces of Furniture

UNDERSTANDING THE MEANING OF WORDS

Dictionaries: Monoligual/Bilingual

The best way to know the meaning of a word is to use a dictionary. While learning English as a second language, one is confronted with the choice of a dictionary. Should one use a monolingual dictionary (English-English) or a bilingual one (e.g. English-Hindi)? In some cases the choice of a bilingual dictionary makes the task of knowing the meaning easy. For instance, an English-English dictionary will describe *pomegranate* as 'a spherical fruit with a tough golden-orange outer skin and sweet red gelatinous flesh containing many seeds'. Though it is an accurate description, it is tough for a student of junior classes to understand. An English-Hindi dictionary will give *anaar* as its equivalent which is easy to understand for a child who knows Hindi. However, monolingual dictionaries have their own significance; they describe a word and, very often, use it in a sentence which is a useful aid to learners, as in *Oxford Advanced Learner's Dictionary.* On tactical ground one can recommend a bilingual dictionary for consulting equivalent terms for names of objects, and a monolingual dictionary for other cases. Students can consult a dictionary when they are reading on their own and no helping hand is available. In the classroom, the teacher can help.

ENCYCLOPAEDIA

An *encyclopaedia* is a book or a set of books which contains information on many subjects or many aspects of a subject. It is a dictionary with encyclopedic material, i.e. comprehensive knowledge. In case a teacher feels that the dictionary does not have all the information (s)he needs, s(he) should consult an encyclopedia. *Encyclopaedia Britannica* is a very reliable source of information. It has 30 volumes and is alphabetically arranged like a dictionary. It is available on the internet and also in a CD ROM pack.

The *Reader's Encyclopaedia* provides a great deal of information. It contains information on plots and characters in famous fiction, summaries of longer poems, brief biographies of writers, mythological, classical and Biblical allusions, literary terms, etc.

If we consult a dictionary and an encyclopaedia for the same word, the difference between the two becomes very clear. If we look up the *Oxford Dictionary of English* for the word *moksha*, it notes the following points:

> Moksha/mɒkʃa/noun (mass noun) (in Hinduism and Jainism) release from the cycle of rebirth impelled by the law of Karma.
> The transcendental state attained by this release. Origin: from Sanskrit Mokṣa

The dictionary has given the pronunciation of the word in the phonetic script, its grammatical category and two meanings. It has also noted that it is a borrowing form Sanskrit.

The same word has the following entry in Encyclopaedia Britannica:

> Sanskrit *moksa* (release), also called *mukti* or *apavarga* in Hinduism and Jainism, the ultimate spiritual goal, designating the individual soul's release from the bonds (*bandhan* of transmigration). The soul, once entered upon a bodily existence, remains trapped in a chain of successive rebirths (*samsara*) until it has reached perfection or the enlightenment that allows its release or *moksha*. The methods by which release is sought and attained differ from school to school, but most schools consider *moksha* to be a person's highest purpose in life.

A comparison of the dictionary entry with that of the *Encyclopaedia* makes the difference clear. While both entries clarify the meaning, the Encyclopaedia provides an explanation which the dictionary does not.

Thesaurus is a book that lists words in groups of synonyms and related concepts. *Roget's Thesaurus of English Words and Phrases* (1852) is the first thesaurus. Other thesauruses published since then are modelled after it. Thesaurus is the best source to find synonyms of a word.

If we look at a Thesaurus for the word *listen* we find the following entry:

> *Listen, attend, hark, harken, hear, heed, list.*
>
> To *listen* is to make a conscious effort or endeavour to *hear*. We may *hear* without listening or we may listen without hearing. In *listening* the ear is intent upon the sound, in *attending* the mind is intent upon the thought. To *hear* is simply to become conscious of sound. To *heed* is not only to attend but remember and observe. *Harken* is obsolete, *list* is poetic.
>
> *Antonyms: be deaf to, ignore, neglect, scorn, slight.*

In short, the thesaurus gives the synonymous of a word and differentiates its shades of meaning. It also gives its antonym.

Students should be encouraged to guess the meaning of a new word from the context in which it is used in a text. Guessing the meaning of a word is a good mental exercise. Sometimes one's guess may go wrong; it can be verified and corrected with the help of a dictionary or a person who knows better. In several cases, meaning can be deduced from the form of a word. For instance, if one knows the word *notice*, one can guess the meaning of *noticeable*, *notice board*, *notify* and *notification*. As mentioned above, given a word, one should be able to guess its derivatives.

USE OF CARDS

A device that is used in Western countries to understand the meaning of a word is the use of cards. On one side of the card, a word is written or printed, on the other, its meaning is given. One is supposed to look at the card to be familiar with the word and its meaning. The teacher can encourage students to prepare their own cards, if they are not readily available in the market.

ARCHAIC WORDS

The senior secondary textbooks used in India include literary pieces written in the distant past. For instance, the *Literature Reader* recommended by the CBSE has a piece from Shakespeare's *Julius Caesar*. It has words such as *hurtled* (clashed), *lusty* (strong), *puissant* (powerful), etc. While students need to know their meanings, they must be told that these words are no longer used in modern English. Archaic and obscure lexical items may occur in a text but they are not to be used now. Similarly, archaic grammatical expressions (such as *'the most unkindest cut'*, i.e. the use of double superlatives) should be avoided. However, the metaphorical words must be discussed in the class if they occur in the text, because metaphors are an integral part of a language, and they do not become easily outdated.

Since the learner's proficiency in the language depends on the size of the vocabulary he/she has at his/her disposal, the teacher must have a well-thought out plan to help him/her with his/her vocabulary. The plan should be based on the awareness of high frequency of words. The teacher should have a strategy to make students learn how to deal with them.

To sum up,

- Since one's proficiency in language depends on how to cultivate one's habit of using most frequently used words, the teacher should help students in expanding their vocabulary.
- It can be done by learning new words, their synonyms, antonyms, derivatives and collocational links.
- Words can be stored in mind by connecting them in various ways.
- One should consult dictionaries and also try to guess the meanings of new words from the contexts in which they are used.
- To get accustomed to new words, students should be encouraged to play word games and use cards with words and their meanings printed on them. Repetition of words used in sentences in a context is a well-tasted technique to get used to new words.
- Obscure and archaic words must be avoided in use.
- Students should be assigned tasks of filling in the blanks with appropriate words in the context and with matching words.
- They should be encouraged to create word-families and asked to name the members of the families of fruit, vegetables, garments, furniture, footwear, etc.
- 'Pre fabricated patterned' expression and 'formulaic sequence' should be paid special attention to.

13

Teaching Listening: Issues and Strategies

'He that hath ears to hear, let him hear'.

—*The Bible*

To *hear* means 'to perceive with the ear the sound made by someone or something'; to *listen* means 'to pay attention to a sound'. Listening involves making sense of a spoken language, which is normally accompanied by other sounds and visual input. It is a bundle of related processes which includes recognition of the sounds produced by the speaker, perception of his/her intonation pattern suggesting focus of information, interpreting the relevance of what is said in the current context and so on. In a normal situation, all these factors operate smoothly and the comprehension of what one listens to is easy. But all situations are not normal. Sometimes there is disturbance in the environment and acoustics is poor. Sometimes the speaker has an unfamiliar accent, especially when he/she speaks a language which is foreign to him/her or to the listener. Sometimes the speaker is very fast and the listener has to ask him/her to repeat or rephrase his/her utterance. The listener has to make an additional effort to listen to what is said if the situation is not normal. Even in a normal situation, a fluent speaker uses assimilation (such as saying*/gʌmmt/* for '*government*'), elision within the word (as in *tamprari*/for *temporary*'), or in the vicinity of word boundaries (as in */go: wei/* for '*go away*') and other such devices in connected speech. All these factors make it imperative to treat listening as an active process in which the listener is supposed to be as alert as a speaker. Just as a speaker uses not only words, phrases and sentences but also prosodic features, such as stress, intonation, rhythm, loudness, etc. to convey his/her ideas, the listener has to pay attention to all of them to grasp and interpret what is conveyed.

LISTENING IN A NORMAL ENVIRONMENT

Any programme of teaching listening comprehension has to take note of the situations given above. In majority of natural situations, there is no chance of slowing down the flow of information reaching the ear. For instance, while listening to a lecture, a play, a movie, a TV programme or a radio broadcast, the listener has only one chance to hear what is spoken; he/she has no control over the rate of delivery. Even in a face-to-face conversation, communication is disrupted if the listener asks the speaker to repeat what he/she has just said. It is as true of listening to an utterance in one's mother tongue as in a second or foreign language. It is desirable that the listener is exposed to a wide variety of utterances discussing familiar topics and to normal conversational styles. The second language learner may be exposed to tapes, records, films and other audio-visual aids to practise listening. These aids may be graded but natural. Listeners may be exposed to a simple conversation or speech in the beginning and then to lessons of increasing complexity.

TYPES OF LISTENING

There are two types of listening: one-way listening and two-way listening. They interact with two principle functions of language: transaction and interaction. While transaction is concerned with the transfer of information, interaction refers to the maintenance of social relation. Virtually all communication involves both the elements. However, in a particular situation, one may be more prominent than the other.

One way listening is important in an academic setting, such as listening to lectures and lessons in schools, which are normally full of cognitive contexts. Listeners of such one-way communication listen in order to learn and take notes of what they have heard. Listening to radio or television is a different type of exercise. It may have exposure to a formal script (as in a news bulletin) or an informal discussion (as in a commentary on sports).

The two-way listening is more interactional than the one-way listening; it is listening and speaking. It involves dialogue or discussion. In this mode, a listener is a potential speaker. He/she has to process what has been said and respond appropriately. He/she has to be quick and alert, ask questions about what he/she has not comprehended well and get his/her doubt removed if he/she thinks he/she has missed or wrongly heard a point. Whether he/she has a right to respond or intervene depends on whether he/she has been addressed directly, or is a mute listener or an overhearer.

PROCESS OF LISTENING

There are two processes of listening: 'bottom up' and 'top down'. The bottom up processing involves putting together the parts of what is being heard in a linear fashion, in a sequence. It is a must at the acoustic level, for example, to differentiate between similar sounds. The top down processing goes from the whole to parts, and focuses on interpretation of an utterance rather than recognition of sounds, words and sentences. It makes the listener active; he/she relies on what he/she knows to make sense of what he/she hears. The prior knowledge and experience that he/she has in his/her memory is called on when he/she tries to comprehend what he/she listens to. It consists of content schemata (networks of knowledge on different topics) and rhetorical schemata (i.e., the knowledge of the organisation of discourse on a topic). It enables the listener to guess the rest of the message on the basis of the part of the message he/she has already comprehended. He/she puts them together and makes inferences (i.e., listens between the lines) to get a complete picture.

A competent listener uses both 'bottom up' and 'top down' processing to have an effective comprehension of the spoken language. Successful listening depends on the listener's ability to gather information from both processes.

However, the successful use of these two processes depends on cultivating some 'enabling' micro skills. In order to recognise prominence within utterances, one should be able to:

- discriminate sounds within words, especially phonemic contrasts;
- distinguish between strong and weak forms, i.e., note phonetic changes at word boundaries;
- identify use of stress, pitch and intonation patterns (for noting information units and points of emphasis).

Once a listener acquires perception of these points, he/she can formulate the content of an utterance. In other words, he/she can deduce the meaning of words (including unfamiliar words), infer implicit information and link between propositions. He/she can identify, maintain and update the content by looking at the context and guessing the intension of the speaker.

IMPROVING LISTENING SKILLS FOR ENGLISH AS A SECOND LANGUAGE

A second language learner can improve his/her listening skills by paying attention to the following points:

Sound Contrasts

One of the important ways of improving listening skills is to hear and appreciate sound contrasts within words. Speakers of almost all Indian languages are familiar with plosive sounds such as /p,b; t,d; k, g/. They do not exactly use English /tʃ, d3/ but can hear the difference. Many of them have difficulty in differentiating between /ph/and/f/and/v/and/w/. Some speakers of Indian languages cannot hear the difference between /s/and /ʃ/, /d3/and /z/, and /z/and /3/. The teacher may show the difference in the point and manner of articulation of sounds as shown in figure 7 on p. 173. He/She should make them familiar with the difference between them by exposing them to contrasting sounds, such as the following:

(i) *phil* 'pill' vs. fil 'fill', '*phein*' 'pain' vs. '*fein*' 'fain'
(ii) *vain* 'vine' vs. *wain* 'wine'; *vest* vs. *west*
(iii) *si:* 'see' vs. *ʃi:* she'; *si:n* 'seen' vs. *ʃi:n* 'sheen'
(iv) *dʒest* 'Jest' vs. *zest* 'zest'; dʒəun 'Joan' vs. zəun 'zone'
peidʒ 'page' vs. peiz 'pays'; reindʒ 'range' vs. reinz 'rains'

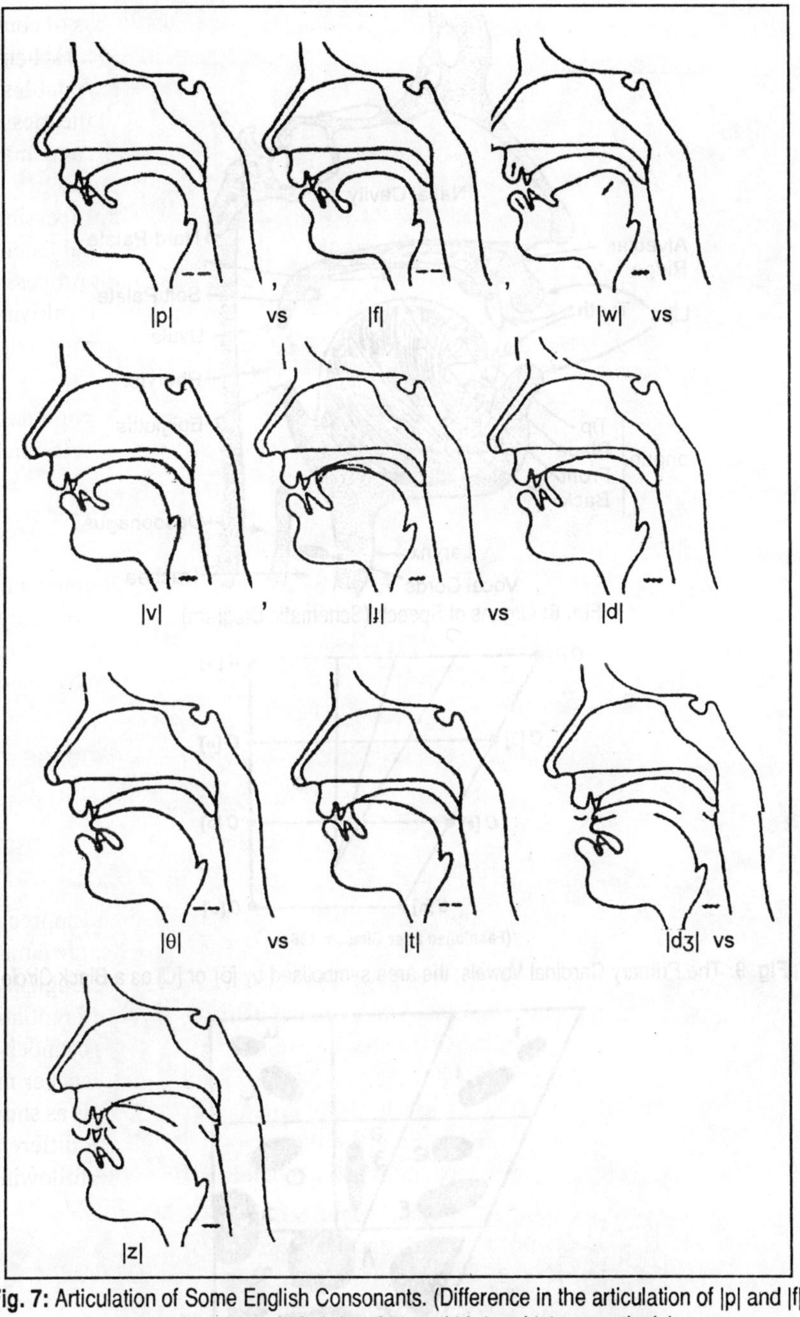

Fig. 7: Articulation of Some English Consonants. (Difference in the articulation of |p| and |f|, |w| and |v|, |ɹ| and |d|, |θ| and |t|, and |dʒ| and |z| respectively)

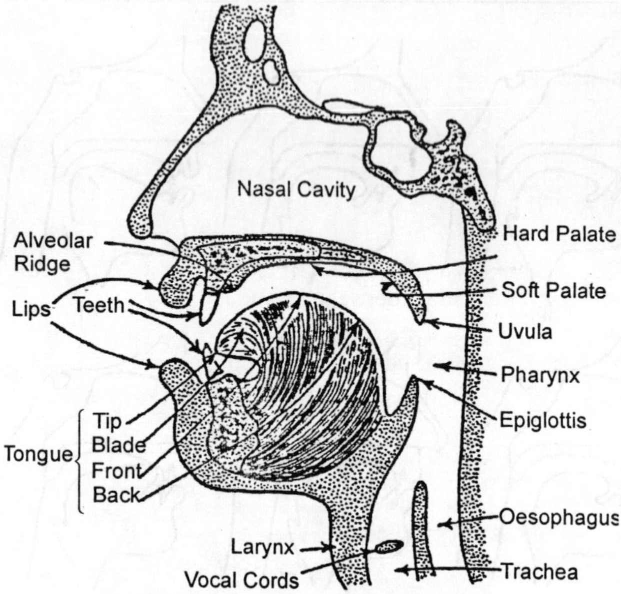

Fig. 8: Organs of Speech (Schematic Diagram)

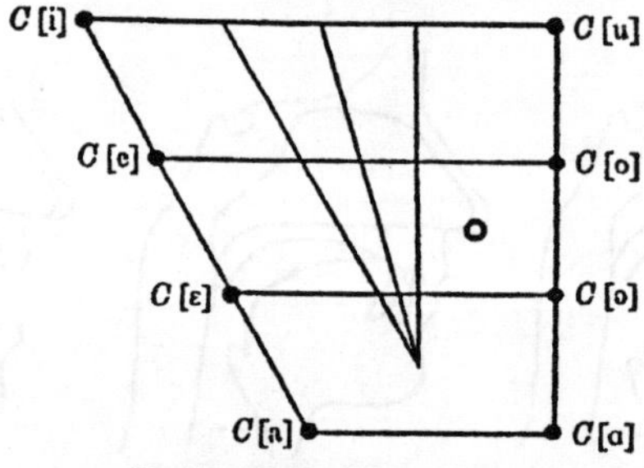

(Fashioned after Gimsom 1964)

Fig. 9: The Primary Cardinal Vowels; the area symbolised by [ë] or [Q̈] as a Black Circle

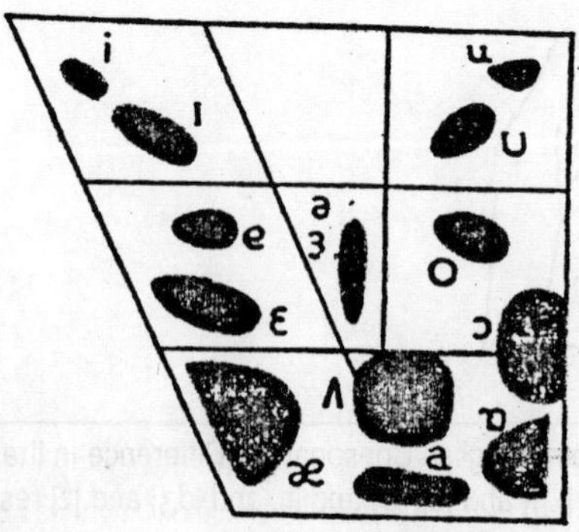

Fig. 10: Vowels in Indian English

(v) kənfjuʒn 'confusion' vs. kənfjuʃn 'confucian'

(vi) *leʒə:* 'liesure' vs. *ledʒə:* 'ledger', *viʒn* 'vision' vs. *pidʒən* 'pigeon'

There are two consonants /θ/ 'th (as in *thing*) and /ð/ 'th (as in *these*), in English which are unfamiliar to Indians; they hear them as /th/ and /d/respectively. The following minimal contrasts pronounced correctly will make them familiar with the difference between /θ/ and /t/.

(vii) *θri*; 'three vs. *tri:* 'tree'; *θik* 'thick' vs. *tik* 'tick'
θɔ:t 'thought' vs. *tɔ:t* 'taught'; *θru:* 'through'tru: 'true'

(viii) contains the constrast between |ð| and |d|
ðen 'then' vs den 'den'; ðeə* there' vs deə* 'dare'
ʌðə 'other' vs. ʌdə 'udder'; ðəu: 'though' vs. dəu 'dough'

Sentences such as the following can be used to hear the difference between /t/ and /θ/:

1. I decided to plant *three lemon trees*.
2. I could not *trust* the main *thrust* of his argument.

Sentences given in 3-5 can be practised to hear the difference between |θ| and |d|.

3. They called me *that day*.
4. I do not *dare* to go *there*.
5. By *then* they will be in their *den*.

Indian learners of English ought to cultivate the habit of differentiating between |e| and |ei|, |ei| and |æ|, |æ| and |əi| and |ɒ| and |əʊ|

The teacher can make them used to the sound contrasts in the following pairs:

(i) *get* 'get' vs *geit* 'gate; *let* 'let' vs *leit* late; *wet*' wet' vs *weit* wait
(ii) heit 'hate' vs hæt 'hat'; meid 'made' vs mæd 'mad'
(iii) bæk 'back' vs baik 'bike'; sæt 'sat' vs sait 'sight'
(iv) *nɒt* 'not' vs *nəʊt* 'note', *gɒt* 'got' vs *gəut* 'goat'

They may practise the following sentences:

6. *Let* us not be *late*.
7. Please *tell* me an exciting *tale*.
8. I *hate* this *hat*.
9. They *plan* to buy a new *plane*.
10. They *sat* down at the *site*.
11. He *bought* a *fine fan*.
12. I have *got* your *goat*.
13. It is *not* in the *note* you have given me.

Figure 8 on p. 174 shows the speech organs whereas Figure 9 presents the cardinal vowel diagram. Figure 10 presents the positions of English vowels in Indian English; it may be compared to the positions of cardinal vowels.

The following list of examples presents the most common words, first in their unaccented (normal) weak forms and secondly in their less usual accented strong form:

Table 4: Accented and Unaccented Function Words in Connected Speech

	Unaccented	*Accented*
a	/ə/	/əɪ/
am	/m, əm/	/æm/
an	/n, ən/	/æn/
and	/ənd, nd, ən, n/	/ænd/
are	/ə/ + consonant	/ɑ:/
are	/ər, r/ + vowel	/ɑ:r/
as	/əz/	/æz/
at	/ət/	/æt/
be	/bI/	/bi/
been	/bin/	/bi:n/
but	/bət/	/bʌt/
can (aux.)	/kən, kn/	/kæn/
could	/kəd, kd/	/kʊd/
do (aux.)	/dʊ, də, d/	/du:/
does (aux.)	/dəz, z, s/	/dʌz/
for	/fə/+consonant/fər, fr/ + vowel	/fɔ//fə:r /
from	/frəm/	/from/
had (aux.)	/həd, əd, d/[1]	/hæd/
has (aux.)	/həz/, əz, z, s/[1]	/hæz/
have (aux.)	/həv, əv, v/[1]	/hæv/
he	/hr, i:, I/[1]([hi])	/hi:/
her	/hə, a:, ə/[1]	/hɜ:/
him	/hIm/	/hɪm/
his	/ɪz/[1]	/hɪz/
is	/s, z/	/ɪz/
must	/məst, məs/	/mʌst/
not	/nt, n/	/nɒt/
of	/əv, v, ə/	/ɒv/
shall	/ʃəl, ʃl/	/ʃæl/
she	/ʃr/([ʃi])	/ʃi:/
should	/ʃəd, ʃd/	/ʃʊd/
there (indef. adv.)[3]	/ðə/+consonant /ðər/ + vowel	/ðɛə/ (rare) / ðɛər/ (rare)
to	/tə/+consonant	/tu:/
than	/ðən, ðn/	/ðæn/ (rare)
that (conj. and rel. pron.)[2]	/ðət/	/ðæt/ (rare)
the	/ðɪ/([ði])+vowel / ðə/+consonant	/ði:/ „

Source: Adapted from Gimson 1964, pp. 240-241.

PROMINENCE OF A SYLLABLE IN A WORD

Stress, pitch, quality and quantity of a syllable make it more prominent than its neighbouring syllables in a word. For example, in the word *examination* /igzæmi'neiʃn/, the syllable /nei/ is more prominent than the other syllables and gets the primary stress. The listener should be made aware of this fact. He should be enabled to judge that next to /nei/ is the prominence of /zæ/; /ig/ is less prominent than /zæ/ and /mi/ is less prominent than /ig/.

Pitch-change is another important factor which marks the distinction between words, for instance, between |impɔ:t| as a noun and |im'pɔ:t| as a verb. There are several words where pitch change marks the change in the grammatical category. For instance, we may look at Table 5.

Table 5: Change in Grammatical Category and Stress

14. *word*	*as a noun*	*as a verb*
absent	'æbsənt	æb'sent
conduct	'kɒndʌkt	kən'dʌkt
desert	'dezət	de'zə:t
export	'ekspɔ:t	iks'pɔ:t
object	'ɒbdʒikt	əb'dʒekt
progress	'prəʊgres	prə'gres
project	'prodʒekt	prə'dʒent
record	'rekɔ:d	ri'kɔ:d
subject	'sʌbdʒikt	sub'dʒent

There are several words of the type which differ in pronunciation because of change in stress; they indicate change in the grammatical category of the word.

Elision

Some words are subjected to elision (i.e., a process of gradation) in spoken English. For instance, *recognition* /rikəgniʃn/ is pronounced as |rekəgniʃn|, *cigarette* /sigəret/ as |sig'ret| and possible |pɒsəbl| as /pɒsbl/.

Reduction of Vowels

The reduction of unaccented vowels (i.e., vowels which do not have primary accent) is a special feature of English and the listener should learn to pay special attention to it. For instance, he/she may note the pronunciation of *na* in nation |neiʃn, national /næʃnəl/ and nationality /næʃnæliti/. (See Table 4 on p. 176)

Stress and Rhythm in Connected Speech

In a connected speech, unaccented a |ei| is pronounced as |ə|. The listener may pay attention to a recorded piece or listen to a television programme (especially news bulletin) in English to get himself herself exposed to these features. We may note that *am* |æm| is pronounced as |əm| or |m|, *are* |a:| as |ər|, can |kæn| as |kən|, *could* |kud| as |kəd| or |kd|, do |du:| as |dʊ| or |də| and does |dʌz| as |dəz| or |z|

Intonation

Getting the correct intonation of the speaker is an important task for the listener. Intonation is closely related to sentence-stress, but it is not always so. In some cases, it is one of the elements of stress, the other being loudness and length. It marks the direction of the shift (i.e. movement from one tone to another) between syllables and the general movement of the voice up and down. Generally the movement from one tone to another takes place between syllables but sometimes the voice slides from one tone to another while pronouncing a syllable.

Rising-Falling Intonation

The rising-falling intonation pattern looks like this: _⌐¬_

For instances, in (15), the sentence-stress is on *hear*, it rises and then falls.

15. I said I couldn't hear you.

In (16)

16. What is the matter ?

the voice slides down from the high on /mæ/ to the low note within the syllable.

Rising Intonation

The rising intonation is normally heard at the end of a 'yes/no' question. The voice goes up to a high note on the last sentence-stress and the syllables which follow the rise are also pronounced on a high note, as in (17-18):

17. Does he want to take any bike with him?
18. Will you have sugar or lemon with tea?

Persons whose native tongue is not English may have difficulty in pronouncing a *wh* question with the proper rising-falling intonation; they may use the rising intonation instead. However, if they are exposed to the difference between a *wh*-question and a *yes/no* question as spoken by a native speaker, they may mark the difference in their intonation.

In contrast and comparison, special attention is paid to both the ideas being compared and contrasted. The first one is given a non-final high note, as in (19-20).

19. He writes better than I do.
20. The new book is not as good as the old one.

There are many intonational patterns, other than these two, which are at times used by the native speaker of English. The listener who is not a native speaker of English may get used to them by practice. However, he/she has to remember that the variation in intonation does not always depend upon the grammatical construction and logic; it depends on the mood and point of view of the speaker as well.

Rhythmic Pattern

A remarkable feature of English is that the utterance is delivered as a series of close-knit rhythmic group intervals of time. Consequently, the speed at which the unstressed syllables are uttered depends upon their number occurring between two strong beats. However, all the unaccented syllables between two strong beats may not be uttered with equal rapidity. Those following the strong beats of a stressed rhythmic group tend to occupy slightly more time than those which precede the strong beats. Besides, the rhythmic grouping or unaccented syllable generally correlates with grammatical word-clusters. A rhythmic division does not normally fall within a word pattern, but several words may combine to form one rhythmic group. We may note the rhythmic groups, based on a strongly accented syllable in (21-22):

21. They all said | they would go.
22. Did you understand | what they said?

In (21) both *they* |ðe:| will have the weak form /ðə/, and *would go* /gəʊ/ , will retain their normal forms.

In (22), *understand* |undə:stænd| and *said* |sed| are the key words around which other words rally.

One nice way to acquire the ability to listen to the rhythm is to listen to the compact disc (CD) of a nursery rhyme. For instance, we may listen to (23), or (24):

23. Baa, baa,|black sheep||
    Have you|any wool?||
    Yes sir|yes sir||
    Three bags|full||
    One|for the master||
    And one|for the dame||
    And one|for the little baby||
    Who lives|down the lane.||
24. Mary, Mary|quite contrary||
    How does|your garden grow?||
    With silver bells|and cockle shells||
    And pretty maids|all in a row||

Usually children are exposed to nursery rhymes in their elementary classes.

Those who start English as a second or foreign language late, may not have that privilege but they may be exposed to nonsense verses of Edward Lear, such as the following:

25. There was|an old man of Calcutta,
    Who perpetually ate|bread and butter;
    Till a great bit of muffin|on which he was stuffing,
    Chocked|that horrid old man of Calcutta.
26. Who, or why, or which, or what|Is the Akone of Swat?
    Is he tall or short,|or dark or fair?
    Does he sit on a stool|or sofa or chair
    Or squat,
    The Akond of Swat?

THE PURPOSE OF LISTENING

People listen to an utterance with a purpose, though sometimes they have to listen to unwanted expressions. However, it cannot be denied that listening with a purpose achieves better results than a purposeless listening. The more significant the listener's purpose is, the more carefully and efficiently one listens. If one listens for *specific details*, one concentrates on every point the speaker makes. If one listens for the *gist* of what the speaker is saying, one filters out the unnecessary details and concentrates on the substance of what the speaker says. Suppose we are listening to the announcement made at an airport about the flights taking off from that airport, we are interested in every bit of information about the flight we would take. We would like to know the gate number we are supposed to go through to reach the plane and the exact time of the arrival and departure of the plane. The announcer announces such details about several flights scheduled around that time but we ignore them altogether. In fact, we do not hear beyond what we need to know and that is what is done by all passengers waiting at the airport.

We follow the same pattern while listening to the radio or watching a television programme. However, when an announcement that concerns us is made, we become alert and pay full attention to it. Language learners should be exposed to such electronic media programmes and be asked comprehension questions to find out how much they have grasped. If some portions of the programmes are not understood in spite of paying full attention to them, the teacher should find out the reasons. Is it because of failure to follow the language, if so at what level? Remedial practices could be arranged to help remove such weak points. It is because the listeners have come across many unknown words, the teacher should try to enrich their vocabulary. If it is because the subject is completely unknown, measures should be taken to improve their background knowledge.

LISTENING STRATEGIES

Learning to listen comprises not only to develop the ability to listen to sounds in words and sentences distinctly in a classroom or language laboratory, but also to listen to and comprehend natural utterances in any situation. Research in listening strategies has led to the development of 'a strategy based approach to teaching listening comprehension'. Learning strategies are divided into cognitive, meta-cognitive and social strategies. The *cognitive aspect* involves listening to the text in a context and summarising it mentally or by taking notes. It involves making prediction or inference on the part of the listener from not only the text of what he/she hears but also from the voice of the speaker and his/her body language. The listener elaborates what he/she hears on the basis of his/her personal experiences, knowledge of the world, prior academic learning and from imagination. While listening, sometimes he/she stops to think about the meaning of what he/she has just heard and usually takes a mental note of it.

At the *meta-cognitive* level, the listener pays attention to the overall message by taking note of the familiar words, the specific parts of the message and its information structure. He/she monitors his/her comprehension and concentrates on what his/her mind preserves. He/she checks his/her interpretation against the background of whatever he/she has predicted and knows and considers appropriate in the context. At the *social level* he/she takes note of who is speaking to him/her and for what purpose. He/she asks for clarification and/or repetition of a point, where necessary. Skilful listeners use these strategies in combination, varying their use according to the needs in a specific situation.

Researchers who have tested second language listening technique of persons of various background report that five factors are associated with successful listening:

- problem solving (guessing and monitoring their guesses)
- planning and its elaboration (preparing to listen and access success in listening)
- avoiding mental translation,
- personal knowledge (i.e. self-perception as a listener), and
- direct attention (i.e. ways of concentrating on aspects of the task)

METHODS ADOPTED BY TEACHERS

It is difficult to gain insight into the way the listener has reached his/her interpretation, even if one comes to know what he/she has understood. However, it is important for the language teacher to figure out some sort of listening problems. Unless he/she does so, he/she is not in a position to help the student of listening comprehension to do better. The investigators who have worked on how learners achieve understanding have noted that they use three main methods; 'observation', 'introspection' and 'retrospection'. Numerous studies have been done to find out specific trouble spots in the process of comprehension but even the most controlled experiments have not been able to pinpoint the state of listener's mental model. The observation method can be supplemented by introspection, in which the listener may be asked to introspect on the problems he/she faced at the time of listening. According to Ross (1997), some students were stuck on keywords they were unfamiliar with while the better ones actively searched for better clues to get the message, though they were also worried about unfamiliar words.

The third method of retrospection encourages the listener to recall the experience of comprehending the spoken words. The method is based on the memory support (i.e., being exposed to the recording of the original conversation). Each of these methods has some inherent limitations but there is no harm in using their judicious combination. In fact, such a combined method is being used by researchers to find out how individuals listen and how they deal with problems of comprehension.

FACTORS THAT AFFECT LISTENING

The following facts that affect listening adversely may be noted:

- The speech rate of the speaker is fast.
- The accent of the speaker is not familiar.
- The speech contains unfamiliar words
- The speech is grammatically complex.
- It contains many embedded structures.
- It contains complex pronominal references.
- The topic is unfamiliar or very complex.
- It contains unfamiliar sound contrasts and phonological tactics.
- It contains irrelevant details.

When the listener comes across unfamiliar words while listening, he/she is confronted with a tricky situation. If he/she decides to look them up in a dictionary, he/she has to wait till the speaker stops, otherwise he/she is likely to miss the next point the speaker is making. All he/she can do is to guess the meaning. He/she can predict it on the basis of which he/she has understood so far. The context of utterance may predict the approximate meaning of the words that have been used. It is a guess work and guesses may be wrong. Perhaps the listener can guess the kind of vocabulary the speaker is likely to use as soon as he/she knows the topic on which the speech is likely to be. In such a case he/she can prepare himself/herself by looking up the meanings of expected words. But, suppose such a word is used in a conversation, it is two-way listening. In such a case, he/she can request the speaker to clarify his point by paraphrasing his/her remarks.

Another semantic problem may involve making sense of a connected speech. As is mentioned earlier, in a connected speech function words are used in reduced forms. The listener can go through the list of reduced expressions (as given on p. 176) and remember what they stand for. We may recall that the reduced form of *has* is *s* or *z* and so is that reduced form of *is* or *his*. In such a case only the context can tell the listener whether the speaker has used |z| for *is*, *has* or *his*.

For teaching listening comprehension, authenticity of text is an important factor. However, Widdowson (1979) differentiates between authenticity and genuineness and argues that a text must be genuine, i.e. it must contain the sort of language typical of that genre in actual use: it does not matter whether it has actually been used. A text could be genuine even if it has been 'invented' for teaching purposes. Authenticity could be the end of language teaching but not necessarily the means. Realistic (rather than 'real') texts could be used to help learners to respond appropriately. In order to make instruction successful, the teachers has to make his/her preparation thoroughly effective. At the end of the lesson, a diagnostic test should be administered to find out how much has been learnt in a listening course and what remedial measures have to be taken.

ROLE OF LANGUAGE LABORATORY

We have already pointed out that tapes, films, records and live broadcasts can be used to expose the second language learner to listening comprehension. As to how much the listener has acquired can be easily recorded in a language laboratory, if a two-way approach is adopted. The remote access system enables a student to listen to the recorded material, and answer the questions posed on the master tape. The audio laboratory allows the learner not only to listen to the tape and hear his/her own response over the headphones but also to record both questions and answers on tape by means of a tape recorder installed in his/her booth or a nearby cabinet. He/she can then play back his/her own response which he/she can compare with the correct response recorded on a different track of the same tape. However, a secondary school student learning English as a second or foreign language needs an adult professional/supervisor who will direct the drill session. He/she will make the learner detect the difference between the sounds which are on the master tape and those which the learner has produced. There is evidence to show that a better result is achieved if the student has the opportunity to hear the recording of his/her own voice in juxtaposition to the correct voice on the tape. It is a fool-proof technique but this facility may not be available in most of the government schools in India because of budget limitations, lack of infrastructure facilities (separate rooms for each group of learners, proper equipment and supervisory staff, etc.). However, the goal should be kept in view and facilities made available, wherever feasible.

MEASURES TO IMPROVE LISTENING

Teaching listening comprehension in a second language is a difficult task and should be taken up seriously. The recent decision of the Central Board of Secondary Education (CBSE) to introduce measures to improve listening skills in English of students of classes IX and XI in all-CBSE affiliated schools is a welcome step. Now that it has become an integral part of English language curriculum, the situation is bound to improve.

TRAINING TO LISTEN IN A GRADED MANNER

Listening instruction must start with the initial exposure of students to learning English as a second language and continue upto every level at school. It should be specially emphasised at the secondary level. By this time students acquire knowledge of reading and writing in English and a high level listening programme is urgently needed to support these skills. As listening is a significant medium of learning a language, it must be paid special attention to. It is subject to training and improvement. A proper training to listening comprehension is a must for an all-round language acquisition. It is said that it is the privilege of wisdom to listen and all of us must desire to have it.

LISTENING PROBLEMS OF SCHOOL CHILDREN

One difficult task for some children is to learn when to give full attention and when to give marginal attention to what the teacher is saying. The period during which a young child can listen attentively is short at first. It gradually lengthens as (s)he gains experience and becomes secure in the classroom. It is desirable for the teacher to note the child's listening span and adjust himself/herself accordingly. If the teacher is unduly persistent to hold the child's attention to his/her listening beyond what he/she can do comfortably, the tension thus created holds in the way of good listening. Free conversation in the classroom can keep children relaxed.

RADIO AND TELEVISION PROGRAMMES

Listening to radio or viewing television can make children patient while listening, for they take the programmes as they come. An extensive study of the time children spend on watching television in approximately 24 hours a week. It suggests that children could view programmes which improve their listening comprehensibility. They may discuss at school what they have viewed at home and thus develop wholesome listening ability.

SIGNIFICANCE OF LISTENING

Asher's *Total Physical Response Method* (TPR) claims that listening is an effective way of learning a second language. It emphasizes learning through physical action. In the beginning the teacher uses single, unrelated commands which the students are supposed to obey, commands such as '*open the door, hold the knob, stand at the door*, etc. The student understands the meaning of the sentences in the process of performing the acts. The next step is to give instructions which lead to several interrelated actions. After they are carried out, they are followed by dialogues based on natural action. Finally, the children are led to active role playing and then to TPR story listening. This method of task-based language-learning gradually leads the learner from the learning skill of listening to that of speaking. An interactive CD-ROM called *Live Action English* is available to guide the teacher and learners who choose to follow this method.

While explaining his notion of "comprehensible input", Krashen claims that listening is motivated by the need to get message out of what is heard. L_2 learners acquire a new language when they hear it in meaningful contexts. Based on his/her knowledge of whatever he/she knows about that language, he/she makes sense of whatever is new. Krashen (1981) claims that all teaching methods utilize the same fundamental principle of providing comprehensible input. However, he does not explain what the dimensions of comprehensible input are. Even then it is important that he emphasises the significance of listening in this context.

DO'S AND DONT'S ON LISTENING

In order to listen better one should *avoid*, while listening

- preoccupation
- day dreaming
- prejudice
- wrong attitude
- self-centeredness
- close mindedness
- jumping to conclusion without listening to the whole utterance
- stereotype thinking, and
- passive listening which produces no reaction on the listerner

In order to make listening an active process, one should look for the main idea and avoid being distracted. One can ask the speaker to slow down and seek repetition and clarification, if necessary. One should pay attention to speaker's pauses and kinetics because utterance is often followed by visual images.

Listening is like information processing (IP). It demands listener's attention and thus involves controlled processing. The L_2 listener should try to move from controlled processing to automatic processing as he/she does while listening to a message is one's mother tongue. It can be acquired through practice.

To sum up, listening involves making sense of

- spoken language in a normal environment.
- One-way listening (e.g. to a lecture at school) and two-way listening (e.g., in a conversation) are equally important.
- For successful listening one should be aware of the phonemic contrasts, strong and weak forms, stress, pitch and intonation patterns of English. The stress and rhythm in a connected speech should be paid attention to.
- Listening strategies include cognitive, meta-cognitive and social strategies.
- The teacher should observe how students speak, and ask them to introspect and retrospect while going through listening comprehension.
- The authenticity and genuineness of the text used in the listening should be paid attention to.
- As far as practicable, language laboratory should be used to improve listening comprehension.
- Training in listening comprehension should have graded texts.

[For materials and resources for developing the listening skill, see chapters 21 and 22.]

14

Teaching Spoken English

Talking and eloquence are not the same;
to speak and to speak well are two things,

—Ben Jonson

Oral language activity involves listening as well as speaking. Usually speakers and listeners are involved in simultaneously producing and processing utterance. The speaker has to pay attention to how the listener receives the message and the listener has to see what the speaker tries to communicate by utterances and gestures. A speaker has to take account of who he/she is speaking to and for what purpose and the listener has to pay attention to what the speaker is saying and why. Both of them have to consider the context of utterance. One of the most important aspects of conversation (i.e. oral interaction) is that it takes place in a cultural and social context. People speak to convey the meaning of what they speak and the meaning of their utterance assumes some nuances from the context.

SPEAKING CASUAL/FORMAL ENGLISH

The native speaker of a language grows up not only listening to an utterance but also interpreting it for its proper comprehension. All he/she learns at school is its formal aspect, the difference between a casual conversation and a formal interview, and between the narration of an event or experience and a public speech with a definite end in view. The speaker of a second/foreign language does not have that advantage. He/she has to learn to speak that language in a real or an artificial situation. The child of an Indian migrant in the UK or the USA may learn the English language formally at school, but he/she is exposed to it most of the time at the market place, at playground and in other normal environments. An Indian learning to speak English in India may not have the facility of exposure to the language at home or outside school. If he/she is a first generation learner of English, his/her parents may not know the language and he/she cannot speak to them in it. Even at school, he/she may have to face either of the two situations. If he/she is in an English-medium school, he/she is exposed to English all the time in all classrooms. Some such schools insist that their students speak English inside the school premise all the time. Such students are "soaked" in the English language atmosphere and learn to speak it pretty soon. Some others, who do not use English outside the classroom, take more time to pick up speaking it. Some students who don't attend English-medium schools are exposed to English only when it is taught as a subject. They take longer time to pick up speaking English. There is yet another type of schools where English is introduced after a few years of schooling and is taught through the medium of a none-English language (e.g. Hindi or Punjabi). The students of such schools take a very long time to speak English; they learn it much later than to read and write. The variation in the pattern of exposure to English as a second/third language accounts for the time the student takes to speak English but the difficulties they face are similar, if not exactly the same. They have to learn to listen to spoken English and then try to speak whatever they have learnt. In other words, listening and speaking go together at any stage of exposure to a new language.

SPEAKING ENGLISH AS A SECOND LANGUAGE IN THE CLASSROOM ENVIRONMENT

Teacher's Spoken English

Speaking English as a second or foreign language in a classroom environment may have some problems. One of them is the way the child is exposed to the new language. If he/she depends on the reproduction of the recorded voice of the native speaker, it is good. If he/she depends on the voice of the teacher to imitate, its standard is entirely dependent on the acceptability of the teacher's spoken English. In case he/she speaks a regional variety of Indian English, he/she may not be intelligible to people from outside that region. The minimum that is required of him/her is an all India intelligibility. However, one should aim at the acceptability of the learner's spoken English at the international level. Indian government has sought the collaboration of Trinity College, London to assess the speaking and listening skills of Indian teachers of English. The aim is to prepare a large number of Indian teachers who can speak some sort of internationally acceptable English. In other words, the focus is on the teachers' spoken English. If it improves, it will be an acceptable model for students.

Speaking in a Natural Environment

There is another aspect of a classroom situation. Even if a student listens to the taped material and practises new patterns, he/she may not be able to respond correctly if he/she is asked a question which is not included in the given patterns. There are several ways of asking and answering a question and all of them may not be presented in the classroom for drill. If a foreign language is taught in the class to prepare students to communicate, these facts cannot be ignored. If speaking is one of the objectives of teaching the language, the student must be able to respond intelligently to what someone has told him/her in that language.

The Teacher's Role

There is another difficulty in learning speaking in the classroom. In case a student does not speak correctly, the teacher tends to stop him/her to correct. If the learner is very young, he/she may not mind it, but in case he/she is an adolescent or adult, he/she hesitates to speak because she/he is afraid of being stopped. He/she is always in search of a proper pattern and fails to express what he/she needs to say in a particular situation. His/her performance is not satisfactory if he/she is not flexible. Even when his/her expression is correct, if he/she speaks excessively slow, he/she is not ready for a normal conversation. In such a situation, the student should be trained to accelerate his/her speed. Instead of being a hindrance, the classroom environment should encourage a student to speak freely in a natural manner.

Classroom Activity

Usually the teachers of spoken English tend to emphasise pattern practices in a classroom situation. Enthusiastic champions of drill use it to the exclusion of other techniques which are needed to produce free responses. The teacher must insist that students engage themselves in the follow-up work by creating sentences which are relevant to them presently. In the initial stage the students would find it difficult to do so because of their exposure to a narrow range of structures and limited vocabulary. However, if the teacher makes an effort to take his/her students out of their narrow range of development, the latter may be able to produce new combinations of the known structures and lexical items. In the classroom, the teacher must play the role of a moving consultant who is available to help when students find themselves in difficulties. Of course, the complexity of materials which the students are supposed to discuss freely is dependent on how far they have proceeded through the course of study. Effort should be made to take them as the foundation and build up new structures on them. In short, the classroom activity should be a facilitator rather than a rigid regulator.

CORRECT PRONUNCIATION

An important aspect of speaking involves the proper production of utterances in a language while communicating, which means not only the knowledge of individual sounds but also of how they are combined into words, phrases, and sentences. It consists of the knowledge of stress, intonation and rhythm, and how they work in a connected speech. Some of these concepts have already been introduced in the chapter on listening. However, we will refer to some of these points again to remind the learner how to speak properly in English.

CONSONANTS

Teachers of English in India know that the English sounds |θ| and |ð| do not exist in Indian languages and they are replaced by |th| and |d| respectively in the speech of most Indian speakers. It makes them unintelligible to listeners of English outside the sub-continent. The teacher should try to pronounce the sounds separately and then in words and explain that θ and ð are continuants whereas |t| and |d| are stops. While pronouncing |θ| and |ð|, the tip of tongue touches top teeth whereas it touches the teeth ridge while pronouncing |t| and |d|. (Please see the relevant figures on p. 173). After showing how they are produced, the teacher should pronounce them in minimum pairs such as the following:

1. Thank – tank, theme – team, thick – tick, thin – tin, thigh – tie, thinner – tinner, thought – taught, death – debt, fourth – fort, math – mat, faith – fate, with – wit, both – boat.
2. their – dare, then – den, they – day, those – doze, though – dough, lather – ladder, other – udder, worthy – wordy, loathe – load, seeth – seed, wreathe – read, breathe – bread, soothe – sued.

At the next stage, the teacher could make them practise the contrast in sentences with contextual clues, as in the following:

3. I do not *dare* to go *there*.
4. He *loathes* carrying big *loads*.
5. By *then*, the tiger was in the *den*.

The teacher may also try to have sentences with both the sounds in them, as in (6-10)

6. He was absent *th*is af*t*ernoon.
7. I will *t*ake any*th*ing you *ba*ke.
8. He is in the ba*th* *t*ub.
9. I *t*rust his *thi*rst for knowledge.
10. He *th*inks they s*t*ink.

While talking about improving listening skills, we have talked about the difference between |f| and |ph|, |v| and |w|, |s| and |ʃ|, |dʒ| and |z| and |ʒ|. Some minimal pairs have been given on pages 172 and 175. The teacher has to demonstrate in the class that |p| and |ph| are voiceless stops; when they are pronounced, the lips are closed; |f| on the other hand, is a bilabial fricative; it is produced by the movement of the tongue from the lower lip to the upper teeth. The student may be shown the contrast between *pool* and *fool*, *praise* and *phrase*, *prose* and *froze* and |*pʌn*| and |*fʌn*|. (See the figures on p. 173). The sentences such as the following may be used to practise the contrast:

11. The chie*f* wants it chea*p*.
12. He had to lea*p* to get the lea*f*.
13. He *f*ainted when he smelt the *p*aint.
14. My cli*ps* fell off the cli*ff*.

The contrast between |v| and |w|, which hardly exists in many Indian languages, may be shown by the minimal pairs in (15).

15. Veil-wail, vent-went, vest-west, vet-wet, viper-wiper, veered-weird, and vault-walt.

Students may be shown that |v| is a voiced continuant which is produced by the movement of the lower lip to the upper teeth whereas |w| is produced when lips are rounded. The sentences such as (16-18) can be used to show the contrast in a context:

16. His *verse* is getting *worse*.
17. The *veep* began to *weep*.
18. We get fine *wine* from this grape *vine*.

The contrast between |dʒ| and |z| can be shown by the minimal pairs in (19-22).

19. Jest-zest, change-chains, gauges-gazes, jealous-zealous, rage-raise, fudgy-fuzzy.
20. The *bars* were on the *barge*.
21. The *zealous* lover was very *jealous*.
22. He was *fussy* about his *fuzzy* arguments.

The student must be told that |d3| is an affricate and |z| is a fricative; |d3| is pronounced when the front of the tongue touches the hard palate and |z|, when the tip of the tongue touches the tooth ridge.

The contrast between |s| and |ʃ| can be explained by showing that |s| is produced when the tip of the tongue touches the tooth-ridge (as in *see*) and |ʃ|, when the front of the tongue touches the hard palate (as in *she*).

The contrast between |s| and |ʃ| can be shown, as in (23):

23. sell-shell, sake-shake, same-shame, said-shed, sin-shin, sign-shine, sun-shun.

The difference can be contextualised, as in (24-27).

24. Did *she see* the ship?
25. The red *sign shined* in the moonlight.
26. *Sh*e sells sea-*sh*ells on the seash*o*re.

Some students may have difficulty in differentiating |v| from |b|, as in (27).

27. vest-best, vote-boat, curb-curve, van-ban and vail-bail.

They should be told that |v| is a fricative whereas |b| is a plosive; |v| is pronounced when the bottom of the lip touches the teeth ridge, and |b| when it touches the upper lip.

Some students may confuse between |d3| and |j| . They should be shown how |d3| is an affricate and |j| is a continuant, though both of them are produced when the front of the tongue touches the hard palate. The following minimal contrast can make them aware of the difference:

28. jet-yet, jello-yellow, gam-yam, jeer-year, joke-yoke, juice-use.

They can be used with a contextual clue, as in (29-31).

29. Has the *jet* come here *yet*?
30. It *jar*red the whole yard.
31. A bad y*olk* is no j*oke*.

The sound |ʒ| is a palatoalveolar fricative which is different from |z| or |d3|. The teacher should point out how it is produced. It does not occur in the initial position in any English word. It occurs, in the middle of a word (as in pl*eas*ure, le*isu*re, m*eas*ure, co*nfus*ion) or word finally (as in *prestige*, *barrage*, *range*, *beige*).

It can be contrasted with |d3| as in *leisure-ledg*er or |z| (as in *fusible* |fjuzəbl| - *confusible* |kənfjuʒəbl|). The rest of consonantal contrasts are familiar to Indian learners of English and are not difficult to pronounce.

VOWELS

In so far as the front vowels in English are concerned, most Indian learners have no difficulty in differentiating between |i| and |I| (as in *beat* and b*i*t) in Indian languages what differentiates them is their length though there is a difference in their place of articulation in English. What sounds like a long |e| is, in fact, a diphthong (as in *day* |dei|). The diphthongisation is more in British English than in American or Indian English. In Indian English, as in British, |e| (sometimes transcribed as |ɛ|, is pronounced without any pressure on the tongue. The tongue touches the spot where the lower front teeth joins the teeth ridge. The sound |æ| is pronounced when the jaw is lowered quite a bit, until the mouth is almost as wide open as it can be without making a muscular effort. The highest possible touch is made between tongue tip and lower tooth ridge to pronounce |æ|. The students can learn to pronounce the difference between *pin*, *pen* and *pan*, between *laid*, *led* and *lad* or between *shell* and *shall*.

Among the back vowels, the difference between |u| and |ʊ| is easy to make (as in p*oo*l and p*u*ll, f*oo*l and f*ull*) but the difference between |ɒ| (as in |pɒt|*pot*, |əʊ| (as in *boat*|bəʊt| and |ɔ:| as in |bɔ:t|*bough*t) will have to be learnt. The teacher should show how these sounds are pronounced. In order to pronounce |ɒ| the tip of the tongue lightly touches a point as low on the floor of the mouth, so that the back of the tongue is raised just a little in the throat. In order for the lips to assume the position for |əʊ|, the jaw is raised a little. The tongue remains in the same position as in |ɔ| but bunches a little more towards the back of the mouth. The |ɔ| sound is easily confused with |o| but for the production of the latter, the lips form the shape of the letter O. It requires that they be rounded more than for |ɔ|. The resulting opening is a little circle about half an inch in diameter. The jaw is raised still more and the bunching of the tongue at the back of the mouth is greater. |o| is diphthongised in British English, and is pronounced as |əʊ|. The teacher should demonstrate the difference by contrasting *not* with *naught* and *bought* with *boat*. The first needs |ɒ|, the second and third |ɔ| and the fourth |o| or |əu|. (See the relevant diagrams on p. 173).

Examples such as in (32-37), can be used for practice:

32. Did you g*e*t a new g*a*te?
33. I h*a*te this h*a*t.
34. He b*ough*t a new b*oa*t.
35. It is n*o*t in the n*o*te.
36. Don left home at d*aw*n.
37. I heard a *sh*out followed by a *sh*ot.

Among the central vowels, |ə|, |ə:| (or ər in American English) and |ʌ| may be contrasted. They are neutral and relaxed vowels. The sound |ə| is formed with the lips slightly parted over almost their entire length. The tongue lies relaxed on the floor of the mouth and usually neither its sides nor its tip touches anything (as in *a*b*ou*t, *a*ff*e*ct, and the weak forms of *a*, *an* and *the*. |ə:| is articulated with the centre of the tongue raised between half-close and half-open. No firm contact is made between the tongue and the upper molars and the lips are neutrally spread (as in b*ir*d, h*ear*d, w*or*d, n*ur*se, w*or*k). |ʌ| is produced with a considerable separation of the jaws and with the lips neutrally open. The centre of the tongue is raised just above the fully open position and no contact is made between the tongue and the upper molars (as in s*u*m, s*o*n, l*o*ve, m*u*ch, s*u*ch). Students need to be told that in a connected speech |ʌ| is often weakened and spoken as |ə|. Thus, |bʌt| is spoken as |bət|, but in words like |kʌt|, the vowel is not weakened. Sentences such as (38-40) can be practised.

38. I ran fast b*ut* missed the b*us*.
39. The b*u*g was in the j*u*g and the j*u*g was on the r*u*g.
40. The b*ir*d spoiled the c*ur*d.

Reduction of Vowels in Connected Speech

In the chapter on listening, we have already talked about the reduction of vowels in connected speech. Because of this characteristics, |ei| 'a' becomes |ə|, and |æn| 'an' becomes |ən|. Students can practise the use of strong and weak forms of determiners, pronouns, prepositions and auxiliary verbs in the class. (See Table 4 on p. 176).

PROMINENCE AND STRESS

In Chapter 8, we have talked about the prominence of a syllable in relation to its neighbouring syllables in a word. For instance, in the word *example* |igza:mpl| the syllable |za| is more important than |ig|, and in *instance* |instəns|, |in| is more important than |əns|. In connected speech, sounds are likely to be more like each other (because of 'assimilation'), as in *He wasn't there* |hiwɒnnt ðeə:|, w*as* becomes *wan*. Sometimes we leave a sound altogether (because of elision), as in *go away* |gʒ'wei|, ə is deleted. The process of stress-assignment is relatively fixed.

Words get stress, to a great extent, according to the speaker's choice but he/she is not entirely free to place stress on a certain word. There are some lexical and grammatical constraints. For instance, 'content words' (such as nouns, verbs, adjectives) get more prominence than 'function' words (such as articles, prepositions, pronouns and conjunctions). We have just seen in Table 4 on p. 96 how some 'function' words undergo vowel-reduction.

INTONATION

Intonation is closely related to sentence-stress. It is an important aspect of speech pattern and is concerned with tones. Tones are of three types: normal, high and low, which we can show by drawing the lines over and under the passage of a written utterance. A line drawn at the base of the letters of a word indicates that the word is pronounced with a normal tone. A line above a word makes high tone and a line some distance below the word suggests a low tone. For instance, in (41) *the situation is*, is spoken in a normal tone, '*to*' of *intolerable* in a high tone and *able* in a low tone.

41. The situation is in|tol|erable.

The teacher should familiarise his/her students with the normal tones of a declarative, a command and a *wh*-question sentence, as in (42), (43) and (44) respectively:

42. This is my son.
43. Come to see me.
44. What is the matter?

The key to the rising falling intonation is the location of the high note. What comes before the high note is spoken on a normal pitch and what comes after it is spoken on a low pitch. The fall of one's voice to a low tone at the end of a sentence is a sort of vocal punctuation mark; it indicates that the thought is completed. The rising falling intonation establishes a mood of certainty and completeness.

The rising intonation is normally used at the end of a question which does not have a *wh*-(question) word. It is a question which may be answered merely by *yes* or *no*. The voice normally goes to a high note on the last sentence stress and the syllables which follow the rise are pronounced on the high note too, as in (45-46):

45. Have you read the book?
46. Will he take note of it?

A statement may be turned into a question by the use of a rising tone alone, as in (47):

47. It's time for the meeting to end?

Sometimes there is a non-final intonation in a sentence which precedes the last important word, as in (48):

48. What do you know about me?
49. I think that it is a good idea.

In sentences with *or* or *and* the rising intonation is used for all except the last segment, as in (50-51):

50. You can say it in writing or orally.
51. He can speak Hindi English and Bangla.

There are other types of intonation patterns but the types given above are sufficient for the beginners learning normal conversational English.

In Chapter 8 we have already talked about the rhythmic pattern of speech which must be kept in view by a speaker learning English as a second language. We may reiterate that several words of a sentence form a rhythmic group and one or more than one rhythmic group may form an intonation pattern. The teacher is expected to demonstrate this point while speaking in the class. He/she should also pay attention to the rhythmic pattern of sentences as spoken by students.

COORDINATION OF LISTENING AND SPEAKING

Listening and speaking are two inalienable aspects of oral activity and teachers should plan them as complementary assignments. The spoken words in the class should be used to enhance one's listening ability which could be tested by asking questions. The listener must show that he/she has understood what the speaker said. It means he/she should be able to say what he/she meant by what was said. Mere reproduction of the utterance of the first speaker is not enough; it is not a sign of listening comprehension. In short, listening an utterance properly depends on w*ha*t has been spoken and how and, in an oral activity class, the listener must speak out what he/she has heard, otherwise the teacher will not know whether the listener has comprehended the spoken words.

SENTENCES AS THE STARTING POINT OF SPEAKING-LISTENING ACTIVITY

In the beginning small sentences should be used for conversation. The opener should ask a simple question based on the structures the listener has been exposed to either in the class when structures were drilled or a statement made elsewhere.

In India, it is a very common experience that when two strangers meet, they want to know about each other. They use sentences like 'who are you?' 'Where do you come from?' 'How long will you stay here?' etc.? Each of such questions can be answered in a simple, straightforward manner. For example, one can imagine a short conversation between 'x' and 'y'.

52. X : Who are you?
    Y : I am Ramesh and you?
    X : I am Paritosh. Are you new to Delhi?
    Y : Yes, I am. I am from Firozpur.
    X : I am from Delhi. Are you going to stay in Delhi for some time?
    Y : Yes, I am. I am now an undergraduate student in Sri Ram College of Commerce.
    X : Are you staying in a hostel?
    Y : No, I got no seat in the college hostel. I am looking for a private room.
    X : O.K. I will try to help you.
    Y : Thank you.

The pattern is very simple. X asks a question to which Y answers. He repeats the same question to X. X wants to know where Y is from and is told that he is from outside Delhi but is now a student of a college in Delhi. X wants to know where Y is staying, to which Y tells him that he has no place to stay. X promises to help him in finding an accommodation for him.

We may note that X and Y take turn in talking and the conversation goes on smoothly, X initiates the talk to which Y responses by telling him about himself and asking about him. The conversation opens well and goes on till a terminal point comes (i.e., X assures Y to help).

A conversation may be short or long but it needs at least two persons to carry on. There may be another scene in which the teacher tells a story which is a listening-comprehension exercise for students. At the end of the story, the teacher asks questions which students have to answer orally. A student responds to one of the questions which shows that he/she has understood the story. Suppose he/she has, the teacher can observe whether he/she has used the right pattern, rhythm and intonation while answering his/her question. The teacher can note the errors, if any, and point it out to the student in a friendly and encouraging manner. The knowledge about turn taking and topic management helps learners to understand the changing roles that speakers take up in conversation and the way meaning is negotiated at the micro-level of each turn.

Both interlocutors (i.e., the speaker and the listener) have to be clear when they should speak, when they should keep silent and when and how they should let the other person speak. Pitch and loudness of an utterance indicate when the speaker wants the listener to respond. The low pitch functions as a turn yielding device whereas a high pitch signals a bid for a turn. The topic management is closely bound up with turn-taking mechanism. It makes the listener realise whether further information is sought as a response. A second language learner ought to have the knowledge of these concepts from his/her experience of participation in a conversation in the first language.

STAGES OF DEVELOPMENT OF SPEAKING ABILITY

By the time the child goes to school, (s)he knows how to express himself/herself through talking, asking questions and listening to answers. (S)he learns by listening to the bed time stories and nursery rhymes in kindergarten and nursery schools. At the elementary school level, the goal of the teacher should be to let the child feel free so that he/she is comfortable. The language lesson should be short with a good programme. If the second language of the child is going to be the teacher's medium of instruction, it is a must since the child is not familiar with it, because it is not used at home at all. The children from the culturally disadvantaged homes need a great deal of time and opportunity to improve their listening and speaking ability in the language.

Participation by Children

Children should be encouraged to talk in English if it is the medium of instruction. Even if it is one of the content subjects, (s)he should be encouraged to talk in it. Opportunities can be offered by making them listen to music, rhymes, stories and conversation. Questions should be asked at the end, out of curiosity, and not as an exercise. The programme should encourage the child to narrate his/her own experience. The teacher should note the vocabulary and structures the child knows and try to build further programmes on that basis. The goal is to encourage the child to use clear, intelligible English. The teacher should help the child with his/her pronunciation, especially with his/her articulation of sounds and intonation so that he/she attains natural ease and fluency.

As the child advances through the grades, the teacher should make him/her aware of the fundamentals of the spoken language. The children of middle and upper grades should be asked to narrate stories, their personnel experiences of life and anecdotes. They should be able to carry on informal conversation, participation in discussions and debates. They should have something to say and say it in a clear and pleasant manner. They should learn how to be courteous and make their speeches acceptable. For that, they should listen to others with an open mind. Listening to the radio and television is a great experience in that direction. We should remember that spoken language precedes written language in all areas of language development. The teacher should note that the language acts develop together even at the level of second language learning and the work in oral communication is basic to all.

How to Improve Speaking Skills of the Learner

- First of all, the learner should think of ideas he/she wants to convey to the listener. He/she must have something to say.
- He/she should have confidence in saying what he/she wants or needs to say.
- The speaker should have enough stock of words, phrases and sentences to say what he/she wants to say.
- He/she should have the ability to say it in a manner that the listener can understand. For it, he/she should be able to pronounce his/her expressions correctly. That is, he/she should have correct pronunciation and intonation.
- He/she should be fluent while speaking. If he/she fumbles for correct expressions and takes undue time in articulating himself/herself, the listener may be bored, he/she may feel indifferent.
- The speaker has to consider the socio-cultural background and personality of the listener. In short, he/she should choose appropriate words for the person he/she is talking to.
- He/she should know the social conventions of interaction (e.g. turn taking, encourage the listener to speak and comment on what is being told to him/her).
- He/she must follow the norms of the society the listener belongs to and be polite and courteous.

- The teacher should choose such topics for discussion in the class which are motivating, interesting and exciting for the learner.
- He/she should encourage students to talk about their childhood experiences, hobbies and personal likes and dislikes.
- Discussion could be arranged around any subject discussed in the class, not necessarily in the English class, and found interesting.
- Word games, including the rephrasing of an expression the teacher uses, would enrich the vocabulary of the learner and increase his/her ability to rephrase and interpret.

To sum up,

- a speaker produces sentences which the listener processes.
- The speaker has to keep in view *who* he is speaking to amd *what* he is speaking. His/her utterances may be formal or casual.
- The speaker's utterance should be acceptable and intelligible.
- If a student speaks a wrong sentence or has pronounced an utterance wrongly, he/she should not be stopped in the middle. It should be pointed out to him/her later on.
- A learner should try to speak clearly by uttering the sounds of English correctly. He/she should practise the unfamiliar sounds well by using minimal contrasts in words and sentences.
- He/she should learn how to reduce vowel sounds in a connected speech and pay special attention to stress and intonation patterns.
- Speaking to a person means interacting with him/her. He/she should know when to give the other person a chance to speak.
- The practice of turn taking should be adhered to.
- The speaker should learn how to manage the topic he/she is speaking on, when to yield and when to stop the conversation.
- While speaking, he/she should try to be natural and fluent. He/she should not fumble in search of a grammatically correct sentence.

Development of skills in listening and speaking is a continuous programme. if it is not possible to assign a specific element to the course of study for a given class, the necessary skills must be introduced as and when children need them. They must be encouraged to express themselves in their chosen second language. However, the most important point is to motivate them to speak for which occasions need to be created. Recently many innovative and varied methods have been used to study the role of motivated conversation in second language acquisition. They suggest that oral interaction, which may include recast or reformulation of the speaker's utterance, leads to output enrichment or change. In short, it may mean enhancing the learner's power of speaking.

[To develop materials and resources for spoken English, see chapters 21 and 22.]

15

Exploring Reading: Processes and Strategies

A. PROCESSES AND STRATEGIES

Reading is to the mind what exercise is to the body.

—Richard Steele, *Tatler* 147

Reading maketh a full man; conference a ready man and writing an exact man. —Francis Bacon, *'Of Studies'*, p. 50

"Reading" means "the action or skill of reading", a written or printed matter which may be a literary or non-literary text, for example a short story, a novel, a drama or an article in a newspaper or magazine. As we read for a variety of purposes, it is difficult to interpret what we mean by 'reading'. Although it involves the same cognitive processes and resources, we use them with varying emphasis on these processes and resources depending on why we read a particular piece of written text. For example, when we read a newspaper, we usually read the headlines and subtitles to *skim* news stories. We slow down and read more carefully when we come across news or comments of our interest. When we read a good novel, we read more slowly with a view to finding out how the story develops or a character is portrayed. Even when we read a novel, we *skim* if we find the novelist belabouring a point in such a way that we find the details tedious or boring. Sometimes we *skip* some details but later on we realise that it is necessary to go through them carefully in order to appreciate what is discussed later. In such cases, we come back to the lines or passage which we have initially read in a hurry. If we read some instruction (i.e. on a bottle of medicine or on a household appliance), we read every word carefully. In other words, we read to understand what we read and acquire the information that we find relevant. In an academic setting, reading means reading to understand and learn. We read to integrate information and evaluate it critically.

LEARNING TO READ THE MOTHER TONGUE

By the time a child is ready to learn to read in his/her mother tongue, he/she has acquired some knowledge by listening and speaking it. It is the development of language in him/her that makes him/her ready to read. He/she has the knowledge of the sound system of his her mother tongue. He/she knows reasonable number of words and some grammar. He/she knows how to put words together to frame phrases and sentences. All he/she has to learn is the writing system of the language so that he/she can establish a relation between the sounds he/she knows and the symbols which represent them. As children know their mother tongue by the time they start learning to read, it is not a difficult task for them to pursue reading.

READING THE SECOND LANGUAGE

Reading in one's mother tongue involves 'reading to understand' and 'reading to learn'. The first is a process which involves perceiving the internal meaning of what is written or printed; it may be known to the reader from beforehand. The second process leads to the acquisition of knowledge. When one intends to learn to read the second language, one has the same goals; one aspires to understand and gain knowledge. However, there is a difference. The second language learner does not have the same language resource which he/she had when he/she started learning to read in the mother tongue. He/she does not have the ability to listen to or speak the second language. He/she does not have any knowledge of its grammar or vocabulary. Only if a child comes from a family where English words are freely used in everyday conversation in the mother tongue, he/she may have some limited vocabulary and if he/she has been to a nursery school or kindergarten, he/she may be familiar with some English sounds, their combinations and sentences. Likewise, if the child is growing up in an English-speaking neighbourhood, he/she may have picked up some spoken English.

LETTER-SOUND CORRELATION IN ENGLISH CONSONANTS

The student is first taught the letter of the alphabet of English, after that, the first task in teaching class I students how to read is to make them aware of the relation between the letter of the English alphabet (i.e. its graphemes) and its sound (phonemes). The task is a little difficult because one letters or a group of letter of English can represent various sounds and one sound can be represented by various spellings. Sounds such as /b, d, f, j, k, l, m, n, p, r, t 'l' are easy to comprehend because each one of them is represented by one letter of the alphabet. For example, *big, dog, fan, jar, kite, lamp, man, nose, pen, rat* and *tree* in which the letters stand for the sounds represented by these symbols. The letter *v* and *w* stand for the sounds /v/ and /w/ respectively, as in *van* and *wall*. The letter x stands for the sounds /z/, as in Xerox, and for |ks| as in the last sound of *Xerox* and *box* or the first sound of *X-ray*. The letter *j* is pronounced as the sound /dʒ/ and the letter z (zeal) as /z/. The letter c is pronounced as /s/, as in *ice* /ais/, and as /k/ as in *cat*/kæt/. The letter g is pronounced as the sound /g/ as in *goat*/gaut/and /dʒ/ as in gym /dʒim/ and general /dʒenaral. The letter s is pronounced as /s/ as in *miss*/mis/, as /z/ as in nose/nauz/ and /ʃ/ as in *sugar*/ʃugə:/.

The combination of *c* and *h*, is pronounced as /tʃ/ as in *child* /tʃaɪld, as /ʃ/ as in *challis*/ʃælɪs/ and as /k/ as in *chaos*/keɒs. The combination of *p* and *h* is pronounced as /f/, as in *phone*/fəun/and that of *t* and *h* is |θ| as in |θiŋ| thing or /ð/ as in *they* /ðe/. The combination of *n* and *g* is pronounced as /ŋ/ as in *sing* /sɪŋ/. The combination of *k* and *n* is pronounced as /n/ as in *knee*, and so is the combination of *g* and *n* as in *gnat* /næt/. The combination of *p* and n is /n/ as in pneumonia /njuməunɪə/ and that of *p* and *s* is /s/, as in *psalm* /sa:m/ and psychology/saɪkɒlədʒɪ/. The combination of *s* and *ch* is sometimes /sk/ as in *scholar* /skɒlə:/ and sometimes /ʃ/ as in *schedule* /ʃedju:l/. The combination of *w* and *r* is pronounced as /r/ as in *wrong* /rɒŋ/. The combination of *w* and *h* is pronounced either as */hw/* as in *when* /hwen/ or as *h* as in who / hu:/ or *whole* /həul/.

Vowels

English has only five vowels in its graphemes but 12 single vowels and 8 diphthong sounds. The table below gives a list of all of them.

Table 6: Relation Between Phonemes and Graphemes in English

Vowel Sound	*Letters (Spelling)*	*Examples*
i:	ee	tree, free
	e	be
	ea	leaf, sea
	ei	receive, deceive
ɪ	i	rich, with
	y	lily, pity
	e	pretty, wicked
	ie	ladies, cities
	a	village, private
e	e	bed, red
	ea	dead, head
	a	many

Vowel Sound	*Letters (Spelling)*	*Examples*
æ	a	rat, sat, hand
	ai	plait
ʌ	u	sun, fun
	o	son, one, colour
	ou	country, enough,
	oo	blood, flood
	oe	does
a:	a	pass, mass, father
	au	laugh
	ear	heart [ha:t]
	er	clerk [kla:k]
	al	calm [ka:m]
ɒ	o	dog, gone
	a	was, watch, want
	au	cough,cause
	au	all, talk
ɔ:	aw	saw, lawn
	ou, au	baught, cause
	a	all, talk
	oor	door, floor
ʊ	u	put, full
	o	woman, wolf
	oo	good, book
	ou	could, should
u	u	rude, crude
	oo	food, spoon
	ou	soup, group
ə: (ɜ)	ir	girl, bird, first
	er	her, heard, earth
	ur	turn, nurse
	our	journey, courtesy
ə	i	possible
	e	gentleman
	a	woman
	o	oblige
	u	suppose

Vowel Sound	*Letters (Spelling)*	*Examples*
	ou	famous
	er	mother
	or	doctor
eɪ	a	late, make, lady
	ai/ay	day, may, rain, aim
	ei/ey/	eight, they
	ea	great, break
ai	i/y	high, time, write, try, dry
	(e)igh	height
	ie	die, lie
	ei	either
ɔi	oi	noise, voice
	oy	boy, toy
əu	o	home, old
	oa	road, soap
	oe	foe, toe
	ou	soul
	ow	know, blow
au	ou	house, mouse
	ow	cow, town
iə	ea	idea
	eir/ier	weird, fierce
	eer	deer
	ear	dear
ɛə	are	care, mare, rare
	air	chair, air, pair
	ear	bear, wear, tear
uə	oor	poor
	ure	pure, cure, sure
	ur	curious
	ewe	sewer
	our	tour

Based on Gimson 1964: 93-94

The table given above illustrates the correlation between the vowel sounds of English and their spellings.

Word Recognition and Word Game

Though sound recognition is the starting point, it is word recognition that is at the centre of reading fluency. In fact, the recognition of sounds and sound combinations is an essential step towards words recognition. Recent research suggests that it is slower in L_2 than in L_1. If both languages have identical or the same graphic systems (e.g. both use the Roman script), then the word recognition process of L_1 affects that of L_2. As Indian languages have orthographic systems different from the system in English, this problem does not arise. It is a question of acquiring a new system without the interference of the practice used in the mother-tongue. However, some tribal languages of the North-East India use the Roman script and they may show the influence of their system while reading English.

Spelling Games

In order to facilitate word recognition process, the teacher may organise spelling games. The teacher says a word and the student spells it out. If the student fails to complete the spelling or misspells the word, another student is given a chance. The process continues till the word is correctly spelt. The winner gets a point. The teacher says another word and so on. A record is kept of success scores and the total is declared towards the end of the class.

Chain Spelling (antakshari)

Another game involves chain spelling. A student begins the game by spelling a word. The next student spells another word which begins with the last letter of the previously spelt word. Any student who begins his/her word with the wrong letter, misspells the word or mispronounce it is dropped from the game. If the game is divided into two opposite teams of students it ends when one of the teams loses all of its members.

Drills and Dictations

Other steps which can be taken to consolidate word recognition are spelling drills and dictation. The spelling drill may involve practice to spell out words with special attention to the words the spelling of which are tricky (e.g. *ei vs ie* as in *receipt, deceit, belief, achieve* etc.) or word with double final consonants (as *begin* but *beginning, equip* but *equipped, control* but *controller*, *occur* but *occurred* or words where *a k* is inserted, as in *panic* but *panicky, picnic but picnicking, traffic* but *trafficking*, etc.). Dictation will force the student to give concentrated attention to both the sound and pronunciation of words.

Vocabulary and Reading Development

The knowledge of vocabulary plays a key role in developing the reading speed of the learner. That is why the teacher tries to increase the vocabulary of his/her students in several ways. The beginners are shown the pictures of objects and living beings that they denote. Reading picture books is a very enriching exercise. One can show the pictures of *shoes* and ask students to name other items of footwear, such as *boots, chappals, slippers, sandals*, etc. If they fail to name an item, its picture can be shown; most likely they will be able to name it. Likewise, objects in the classroom can be pointed out so that students can name them. Food items can be easily named. If the student does not know the name of an item in English, the teacher can supply it. He/she can name adjectives like *good, better, best; bad, worse, worst; big, small, nice, fair, clean, dirty, hot, cold, full, empty, long, short* and make them practise sentences such as,

This room is big small, clean/dirty, hot/cold, etc.

The same sentences can be practised by adding intensifier to the adjectives, as in

This room is very nice/bad/dirty, etc.

It may be further increased in length, as in

My bedroom is very large.
My study room is relatively/rather small.
His blue shirt is very dirty.

The act of introducing various kinds of vocabulary will have its impact on the reading speed of the child. It is essential that he/she is able to read pronouns such as *I, we, you, he, she, it, they* and their various forms, *this, these, that, those,* various forms of the verb to be (*am, is, are, was, were, been, being*) and to *have*, articles *a, an,* and *the*, prepositions such as *of, in, at, on, for, with, by, from,* conjunctions such as *and, or, if, which, that, and, but,* modal verbs such as *can, could, would, should, shall and will,* and the negative words *no* and *not*. According to the British National Corpus they are among the most frequently used words. Vivian Cook (2009) gives a list of twenty most frequently used words as nouns, verbs and adjectives in English which are given in Table 7.

READING FOR COMPREHENSION

Students are usually asked to read a given passage and answer questions based on it. The type of exercise is called *comprehension*. It is given to find out whether the student has comprehended the passage, i.e. grasped it clearly.

Table 7: The 20 Most Frequent Nouns, Verbs and Adjectives in English (Taken from Vivian Cook (2008:48)

Position	*Nouns*	*Verbs*	*Adjectives*
1.	time	say	new
2.	people	know	good
3.	way	get	old
4.	year	go	different
5.	government	see	local
6.	day	make	small
7.	man	think	great
8.	world	take	social
9.	work	come	important
10.	life	use	national
11.	part	give	British
12.	number	want	possible
13.	children	find	large
14.	system	mean	young
15.	case	look	able
16.	thing	begin	political
17.	end	help	public
18.	group	become	high
19.	woman	tell	available
20.	party	seem	full

Whether he/she has done so is reflected by the answer he/she gives. In order to perform the task successfully, one should first read the whole passage carefully to find out what it is about, i.e., what the topic is and how it has been developed. It may be developed by citing facts, giving examples, narrating events or by giving arguments for or against the main proposition. A careful candidate reads the questions only after reading the passage at least once. He/she may read all the questions before he/she tries to answer them one by one. Now that he/she knows the questions, he/she reads the text again to find the appropriate answers in such a way that they do not overlap. He/she locates the cues and develops them in his/her own language. If he/she quotes the lines from the given text, he/she may not be able to convince the examiner that he/she has understood what he/she has gone through.

Some comprehension questions, especially questions for students of higher classes, may not have their answers directly given in the passage. They are to be understood on the basis of the inference from the given sentences. For example, if we get a passage which deals with the marital discord between a couple and a question is asked, 'Has the husband stopped beating his wife?'

How do we answer it if there is no reference to physical violence in the text? We can neither say 'yes' nor 'no' because either way we commit that the husband beat his wife. The correct answer is not given because it can be inferred, i.e. the question is irrelevant as he never beat her. Inferential questions are based on what is given in the text and can be answered correctly if the reader has not only understood the given text but also its implication. Briefly speaking, one not only reads and understands what is given but infers what lies in between the lines. Reading involves interpreting what is read. It also involves evaluating the given text critically.

READING SPEED

While talking about the rate at which the normal native speaker of a language reads, Carver (1992) observes that *scanning* is a process of reading fast at the rate of 600 words per minute and it does not usually involve the process of understanding the meaning of what is read. Reading for understanding is, the rate of 250 to 300 words per minute and reading for textual interpretation, at best, at the rate of 200 words per minute. We may point out that Carver's findings are based on the data obtained from the fluent native speakers of English in the U.K. It may be almost the same for the competent native speaker of any language but not for a person learning English as a second or foreign language. According to some researchers, the difference in the rate of reading and understanding of English texts between a native and non-native speaker of English is that of degree; according to some others, it is that of quality as well.

FIRST LANGUAGE VERSUS SECOND LANGUAGE READING

A reader of English as a second language has the same variables as the readers of English as a first language or mother tongue, namely variation in age, training, schooling, motivation, socio-economic factors and individual cognitive abilities of the reader but there are marked differences as well.

Second language learners do not have the same resources as the first language leaners-readers have. By the time a child native speaker learns how to read alphabets, he/she already knows thousands of words of the language. He/she also knows how to construct and use basic sentences, even compound and complex sentence, though their length may be short. He/she has already learnt some stories and nursery rhymes orally at home. All he/she has to learn is the orthography of the language, i.e., what is the relation between the sounds and shapes of the letters of the alphabet. When he/she is able to read and recognise words and sentences, he/she is delighted because it is nothing but a discovery of what he/she already knows.

The second language learner, on the other hand, has to learn not only the orthography of a new language, i.e. how sounds are combined and spoken but also what they mean when they form words and sentences. The task may be a bit easier if the child has grown up in a fully bilingual situation. In case, he/she has grown up in a society in which English is the second language, he/she already knows a lot of words and sentence structures of this language, as is the case of an Indian child in the UK or the USA. He/she may be as fluent in the spoken language as a native speaker, because that language is used in the home environment and in the playground. But a child learning to read English at school in rural India may not have such a privilege. For him/her, the spoken language is as strange as the written one. He/she may often wonder why *–u-* is pronounced as |ʊ| in *put* but as |ʌ| in *but*, why *sch-* is spoken as |*sk*| in *scholar* but as |ʃ| *sh* in *schedule*. Learning the conventional writing system is only a part of the problem. There are problems of other types. For instance, why does *there* have a meaning in *The book is there on the table* but not in *There is a book on the table*?

The psycholinguists (those who study the psychology of language learning) have found that a second language learner has a bilingual mental lexicon. For instance, when he/she comes across a rose flower, he/she is reminded of *gulab* in Hindi-Urdu; when he/she comes across milk, he/she is reminded of *dudh*. However, there may not be a mother-tongue equivalent for *custard* or *daffodils*. In such a case, he/she familiarises himself/herself with new objects and associates them with names as a native speaker does. In short, such instances pose not only linguistic problems but also cognitive problems. It accounts for processing differences between first and second language learner's reading rates. As word-recognition is at the centre of reading fluency, Koda (2005) emphasises, that it must be viewed as a major factor in its own right. She points out that the orthographic differences between the first and second language of the learner affects his/her word recognition efficiency in the second language. We can find support for her observation if we take cognizance of the initial tendency of a Hindi-speaking child learning English to opt for spelling pronunciation of English words. For instance, most students read *ghost* as |ghəʊst| rather than |gʊest| even though English has no |*gh*| sound. Sometimes even school teachers of English in India fail to point it out.

The Indian Learner

The implication of examples discussed above is that the teachers of English in India need to realise that most learners of English come from a different orthographic backgrounds. They feel handicapped in the beginning, not only because they have to learn a new orthographic system but also because they have to develop a new processing mechanism.

The same is true of acquiring vocabulary in English. In urban India, educated parents use a lot of English words in everyday conversation and students come to the class equipped with them. They may not be familiar with the spelling of *soup, bread, egg, pastry, cake, pudding,* etc. but they know what they are and learn to read them faster than students from rural India who have neither seen these items of food nor heard these words spoken. Perhaps an easy way out is to show them these items and spell out their names but it is not always possible to do so.

ROLE OF VOCABULARY IN READING DEVELOPMENT

Researchers have pointed out that adequate text comprehension is achieved only when the reader knows at least 98 per cent of the words used in a passage. It is true that context helps in guessing the meaning of some unfamiliar words but that is not always the case. In most cases, the student guesses the meaning on the basis of the context and he/she is not able to generalise it. It is also true that a word that is 'guessable' for a native speaker is often incomprehensible for the second language learner. Sometimes the meaning of a word may be guessed incorrectly from a given context. Even when it is guessed correctly, it may not be retained accurately by the learner. That is why the role of a dictionary is important, especially the dictionary that gives sentences for each meaning of an ambiguous word or each type of its use (for instance, *use* of a word as a noun and a verb).

One way to increase the vocabulary of the learner is to make him/her familiar with the way one word leads us to several words. It may not be suitable for all stages of language learning but can be definitely tried with advanced students. They can be told how from *use* we get the adjective *useful* and *useless*, abstract nouns *usefulness* and *uselessness* and adverbs *usefully* and *uselessly*. They can also be told that an object that is fit to be used is *useable* and the person who uses it is its *user*. An advanced student can be made familiar with expressions such as *user-friendly* and *user-hostile*. A *computer-user* student can be introduced with terms such as *user-oriented* (a system designed to give priority to the user's convenience) and *user-interface* (the means by which the user and a computer system interact). Of course, we are not saying that all these words should be introduced at one go; they must be graded and used only when a student is ready for them. In short, a number of related words can be introduced if the student is familiar with the basic word and the teacher finds that the words derived from its synonyms and derivatives are useful.

THREE APPROACHES TO READING

Phonic Method

The *phonic method* encourages learning to read with the help of phonic clues. The work starts with consonant and vowel sounds and covers all the basic sounds and spelling patterns of English. Attention is given to structural analysis such as 'read', 'reads', and 'reading'. Some people pay special attention to phonics in the first grade and ignore reading as a thought-getting process. The critics of the method say that because of heavy emphasis on phonics at the beginning, the child becomes slow in deciphering what he/she reads. Besides, he/she does not get accustomed to reading for comprehension because his/her reading is centred mainly on letters.

Linguistics Approach

Another approach is the *linguistics approach* which was initially championed by C.C. Fries (1963) a structuralist linguist. He said that learning to read something is not meant to know something but to do something. By 'something" he meant high speed recognition of letters and sequence of letters in words. He claimed that the recognition results in getting the meaning of what one reads. The approach advocates introducing the child to consonant vowel consonant combinations first, as in *cut, hat, pin, not* etc. it then leads to the blend of consonants like *spin, skin, stand* and *then to* other modified words. As it relies solely on the printed letters, its books have no illustrations.

The Basal Reading Programme

The third approach is the *Basal reading programme* for elementary school children after they have gained a clear concept of reading and have a fund of words they recognize with ease. The programme rests on the assumption that a set of essential and fundamental skills are generally known to the learner. The programme provides essential prerequisites to successful growth in word comprehension, interpretation and all aspects of reading. By and large, the child learns what he/she is led to learn in response to the content and structure of teaching materials. It implies the careful planning of reading materials in terms of (a) the values of sounds and letters that represent them, (b) the practice to recognise a word as a whole unit and, (c) the grasp of their meaning, both as single words and in larger units such as phrases and sentences. Besides, one should develop the suitable habit to adjust to reading in the light of one's purpose for reading. The Basal programme is essentially eclectic; it is designed to develop readiness of vocabulary, word recognition and word perception and comprehension skills.

Some Indian children learn to read a word letter by letter and some syllable by syllable but eventually they learn to read word by word. If the teacher reads the material phrase by phrase, using proper pause and intonation, children get used to them. Besides, their experience of reciting nursery rhymes in chorus or alone comes to their help. The success that a child attains in learning to read is closely related to the satisfaction he/she finds in his her experience with reading. Some teachers put children to read the passage again and again to enable them to gain rapid recognition of words but it tires them. Some other teachers report that they find children learning better when they are given new contents with the same words to read in various contexts. The teacher may use flash cards with words written/printed on them to renew the contact of children with words they have recently come across. He/she may ask the children to work with workbooks for reforcement. The child begins to recognize a word from a context or from its similarity with another word (e.g. he/she gueses the meaning of *cleanliness* on the basis of his/her knowledge of *clean*). Given a suitable book to read, the child may make rapid progress in independent reading. It is the duty of the teacher to give guidance and suggest suitable reading material at that stage.

IMPROVING READING SPEED

Recent research works suggest two alternative ways of improving learners' reading proficiency.

i. The language threshold hypothesis, and
ii. The linguistic interdependence hypothesis.

The Language Threshold Hypothesis

The word 'threshold' refers to a point of entry or beginning. It also means the magnitude or intensity that must be exceeded for a certain result. The language threshold hypothesis suggests that some minimal threshold of proficiency in the second language must be attained in order to enable the reader to transfer his/her first language reading skills to reading in the second language. In other words, L_2 reading development must take place in a learning context that promotes overall L_2 language proficiency. It is essential for the learner who belongs to the lower level (i.e. primary) classes.

The Linguistics Interdependence Hypothesis

It maintains that learning to read is accomplished only once. Once the learner has matured in their ability to read in the first language, his/her awareness of the reading process can be automatically applied to the second language. Thus, reading programme in the second language is supposed to share a common underlying efficiency with reading ability in the first language (Cummins, 1974).

Researches have been conducted on these lines of thought and their results have been compared. It has been found that general proficiency in second language is a better prediction of second language reading than first language reading ability. It implies that the threshold hypothesis is more reliable than the linguistics interdependence hypothesis.

The controversy is relevant if second language teaching starts later than the first language learning. Since our proposal is to start teaching both the languages from class 1, it is not so much relevant in Indian context. However, it does point out the need to prepare students who want to learn to read prior to the reading exercises start. In other words, exercises in listening and speaking must precede exercises in reading, for they will enable students to have some language proficiency in general when they start reading a text. It may be pointed out that this is not the practice in most schools in India, they start with the reading lessons and come to listening and speaking later. Recent researches suggest that the priority must be changed.

READING STRATEGIES

A good reader varies his/her reading strategies according to why he/she is reading. The following are the main strategies:

i) *Intense reading* for detailed information—it involves reading the whole text very carefully to understand every point mentioned in it.
ii) *Scanning*—it implies having a point in mind and looking for it in the text carefully in order to identify relevant information, e.g. to scan through the research material.
iii) *Skimming*—it involves reading a text quickly just to understand the main idea or important points. For instance, one usually skims through a newspaper to get the *gist* of important news.
iv) *Skipping:* It involves omitting portions of a text that one is reading. One can do so if one knows how to scan. In other words, scanning involves the art of picking up the relevant points and skipping involves the art of discarding or ignoring what is irrelevant from the point of view of the reader. For instance, when we look at the notice which mentions the time of arrival and departure of various trains at a railway station, we skip through information about other trains and concentrate on the one in which we are interested.
v) *Extensive Reading* involves reading a wide range of reading materials rapidly. In extensive reading, the reader is more interested in knowing the narrative contents than in how they have been narrated.

The goal of a reader is supposed to be well skilled in the arts of intensive and extensive reading so that he/she chooses the strategy needed at a particular moment.

HOW TO SPEED UP READING?

Given a reasonable stock of words (suitable for a specific level of learning) and sentence structures, one can expect a second language learner of English to increase his/her speed of reading and comprehension through repeated reading activities. Experiments have shown how multiple readings of a short text accelerates fluent readings of those who have already developed their word recognition skills.

The linguistic interdependence hypothesis (Cummins 1979) maintains that learning to read is learnt only once. If a learner has matured in his/her ability to read in the first language, his/her awareness of the reading process can be transferred to the second language. In short, the reading performance in the second language shares a common underlying proficiency with reading ability in the first language. Of course, it presupposes that the learner has crossed the orthographic hurdle and has reasonable ability to pronounce words and phrases with appropriate pauses and rhythm. As Dakin (1969) points out, people recognise words and patterns on a page in a such a way that they overlook errors and read sentences correctly. For instance, in an experiment, the readers were given a passage in which the word *passage* was deliberately spelt as *passige* and *since* as *sincee* but most readers read them as *passage* and *since*. The experiment suggests that most readers do not read letter by letter nor do they always read word by word. For instance, words like *the* and *and* can be repeated on a page without the reader noticing it (e.g. can can…). In the initial stage of learning, a child reads word by word (in some cases even letter by letter) but in the process of reading a text, he/she learns how to group words together and sees them as parts of a structure. The evidence of structuring can be found in the way children read aloud; they select words as parts of a phrase or a sentence. They select a particular intonation in the beginning of a sentence and follow it through to the end. The pattern they select depends on what they predict is going to come. For example, is it going to end as a statement or a question? Sometimes the prediction of the learner may be wrong which leads to a false grouping of words. In some cases, the learner may realise midway that he/she has chosen a wrong intonation. He/she may stop and reread the sentence with an appropriate intonation. If he does not do so in a classroom, the teacher may intervene and read the sentence correctly without admonishing the learner. Dakin points out how the eyes of the reader do not fall on grammatical words such as *of*, *the*, *at*, *and*, etc. but on content words like *boy*, *read*, *past*, *good*, etc. If a learner uses these strategies, he/she is on the way to be a skilled reader.

Recent research in some American universities has found that it is the monolingual English speakers who tend to ignore grammatical markers and pay much more attention to content words than non-native speakers of English do. It suggests that native speakers of English are able to supply these grammatical items from their prior knowledge of the language which the learners of English as a second language do not, initially. In other words, the native speakers have the ability to predict grammatical markers which the non-native speakers lack. That is why he/she pays so much attention to these markers, i.e. the structure words. If their predictability of these markers is improved, their reading speed would improve considerably.

Enhancing Linguistic Predictibility

Language experts have suggested ways to improve the lexical, syntactic and semantic predictability of learners. To increase their lexical predictability, students may be given a key word in the classroom and asked to supply its synonyms (i.e., other words that have almost the same meaning). Alternatively, they may be asked to give its opposite words. They may be encouraged to play a word-game in which one student supplies a word and asks others to give its synonyms and antonyms. For instance, given the word '*say*', students can respond by saying *tell*, *speak*, *state*, *express*, *pronounce*, *articulate*, etc. If they fail to state some of these words, the teacher can write them down on the board. If they are asked to give the opposite of *say*, they may mention *to be quiet|silent|mum*. The teacher may point out the fact that there is no one-word verb which is opposite of *say* but there are expressions to convey the idea. They may be told that *say*, primarily a verb, can be used as a noun (as in, he had his *say* (i.e.an opportunity to express his view). A noun derived from *say* is *saying* (a short commonly known statement of wisdom) and its derived adjective is *sayable*. A person who says something is a *sayer* (as in, sooth sayer 'a person able to foresees the future). Learning these associated words is very important for foreign learners of English. However, the teacher should see to it that he/she introduces only those associated words which are appropriate for the general level of students at a point of time.

Whenever possible, students should be asked to supply words on the basis of general association. One way to do it is to ask them to paraphrase a given expression. It will help them to answer comprehension questions in their own words. Expanding one's vocabulary by association can be a fun; it may help them acquire lexical predictability faster.

Practice in syntactic predictability goes hand in hand with semantic predictability. Increasing grammatical predictability enables one to understand what will follow a certain grammatical marker. For example, *the* predicts that a noun will follow it and so does an adjective in a noun phrase e.g. *the nice boy*. If it is followed by a relative pronoun such as *who*, it predicts that a relative clause will follow it e.g., *the nice boy who is standing in the corner*. A noun phrase in the beginning of a sentence predicts that a verb phrase will follow it, as in *The nice boy who is standing in the corner is a good athlete*. Students may be given a grammatical marker as a cue and asked to complete a noun phrase or a verb phrase, etc. If they practise building up structures with the help of grammatical markers, they learn how to group words in a phrase and read a phrase as a unit. Practising to read according to phrase marking gives cues to pauses and increases one's reading speed.

The understanding of syntactic units leads to the understanding of semantic units. For instance, usually a conditional sentence consists of two clauses but so do compound sentences. It is the syntactic unit marker that tells us that a particular sentence is a conditional sentence. In such sentences, the antecedent (conditional) clause is marked by *if* and the consequent clause by *then*. Even if *then* is not used but *if* is, we know that it is a conditional sentence. (i.e. *If I was offered the job, I would take it*). The familiarity with the distribution pattern of subordinate conjunctions associated with cause and effect helps students in processing such complex sentences faster. If two clauses are combined by *and* or *or*, they form a compound sentence.

PROCESSING SENTENCES

Just as structural words serve as clues to certain grammatical expectations, they serve as keys to discover the way a paragraph is organised. It helps learners to predict the pattern of thought and enables them to discover the main idea. This is an important step towards skimming for crucial information. It is important to realise that sentences are not processed in isolation but in relation to contexts.

Presupposition and Focus

The student may be made aware of the concepts of presupposition and focus so that he/she is able to discern what new information the sentence contains. For instance, if we have a sentence, *John broke the glass*, we generally presuppose the existence of a person called *John* and want to tell others what he did, i.e. *broke the glass*. Thus, the action, *broke the glass*, is in focus. If we come across the sentence *It is John who broke the glass*, we presuppose that someone broke the glass and assert that the person was *John*. The syntactic strategy of using *It is John* gives the clue that John is the person who did what is known already; it is new information. Suppose we have the sentence: *It is the glass that John broke*, we presuppose that John broke something and the new information is contained in *the glass*. If the sentence contains *John not only broke the glass but also damaged the tray*, the clause *John broke the glass* is presupposed and the additive expression *but also* signals that he did something else as well, i.e. he damaged the tray. The expression *but also* makes the reader alert and he/she looks for new information.

Sentence Cues

The teacher can make advanced students aware of what strategies a writer uses and what they signify. For instance,

- Disjunctive proposition have the structure 'not A but B'.
- Alternative proposition are given as 'either A or B'.
- Expressions such as *for example*, *for instance*, indicate that B is an instance of A.

- Expressions such as *because*, *since*, *therefore*, or *consequently* suggest that B is a cause of A or a reason for A.
- Expressions such as *in other words, that is, i.e.* indicate that B is a restatement of A or a clarification of A.
- Expressions such as *on the other hand*, *however*, and *but* suggest that B is different from 'A'.
- Expressions such as *likewise, in the same manner*, and *also* suggest that B is similar to A.
- Expressions such as *then, next, before, subsequently* suggest that A and B are in temporal sequence.

The presence of such cues enables the reader to understand what is likely to come next. If he/she is skimming a passage, he/she may choose to skip a sentence that begins with *for example*. If he/she is analysing it, he/she will pay attention to not only the examples but also the restatement of what he/she has already read.

Comprehension

Just as sentences are integrated in a paragraph, paragraphs are integrated in a text, be it a non-fiction narrative, an argumentative expository essay or a short story, drama or poem. Advanced students (for example, students of senior secondary classes) may be introduced to the technique of discourse analysis. Given a short story, they may be encouraged to locate its main theme and how it has been developed. A critical assessment of a text presupposes its comprehension which, as we have already argued, depends on the comprehension of sentences and paragraphs and an understanding of how they fit in the whole text. Comprehension of a text is the ideal goal of every reader though he/she may not be able to conclude whether he/she has comprehended it fully. The hints given above are intended to enable him/her to move towards the goal.

Deletion and Recoveribility

Another linguistic point that needs to be emphasised involves the concepts of deletion and recoverability. In certain cases a sentence may be the short form of a larger sentence. For instance, let us have a look at the following sentences:

Cows are domestic animals and buffaloes are too.

We find that the second clause of this compound sentence has been structured. It can be read as 'cows are domestic animals and buffaloes are domestic animals too'. The verb phrase *are domestic animals* has been deleted from the second clause because the deleted element can be recovered from the first clause. The teacher needs to make students familiar with the concept of deletion and how it can be recovered from the other part of the sentence or paragraph so that they are not left bewildered. If it is not taught, they may misunderstand a passage. For example, we may look at the following two sentences from a text:

> Among the people whom Columbus knew, it was believed that the earth was flat. The ocean was infested with terrifying monsters, which often devoured ships.

It is obvious from the first sentence that the writer does not believe that the earth was flat; he simply mentions what the friends and acquaintances of Columbus believed. But what about the second sentence? There is no overt syntactic cue but if it is read in continuation of the first sentence, it becomes obvious that it was also the belief of these people, and not of the writer. Allan (1975) refers to an experiment that he tried on his students. He gave them a passage that began with. *It is popularly believed that* ... and then asked them a series of questions such as 'Does the writer believe that'. He was surprised to find most of his students saying 'yes'. Obviously, these students failed to pay due attention to the sentence introducing the paragraph. '*It is popularly believed that* ... They missed the main instruction of the writer, which was to refute these beliefs later on in the paragraph and not to assert them.

CULTURAL PREDICTABILITY

So far we have discussed the role of the text in the process of reading and interpretation. We have talked about linguistic contexts and how their understanding can increase our linguistic predictability but that is not enough, especially for a non-native learner of English. Cultural predictability is an important factor in reading a piece of writing. A student unfamiliar with the socio-cultural background against which a text has been written finds it difficult to comprehend it fully. It is because the writer takes a whole body of cultural knowledge and attitudes for granted in so far as his readers are concerned. A native speaker of English has not only the intuitive knowledge of the syntax of the language and a large vocabulary, he/she is also aware of the socio-cultural conventions. It enables him/her to predict what is likely to follow in a given context more easily than a non-native speaker can; he/she can eliminate some alternatives in advance. His/her reading comprehension is faster. The solution lies in making the non-native student familiar with the relevant cultural contexts in advance of his/her reading the text. The teacher can fill in this gap in his/her introductory remarks.

To sum up, the speed of reading materials in English can be increased if the teachers of English plan it in a graded manner.

- At the initial stage a student should be encouraged to read word by word, rather than letter by letter.
- As he/she moves further up, he/she should be encouraged to read phrase by phrase, i.e., he/she should take a phrase, rather than a word, as a unit. The teacher can demonstrate how it is done and how natural pauses enhance the comprehension of the text.
- Efforts should be made to increase the lexical, grammatical, semantic and cultural predictability of the student.
- Lexical predictability can be enhanced by playing word-games. Students can be encouraged to take it as fun while they try to supply synonyms and antonyms of a word. They should be familiarised with the process of word formation, without exposing them to linguistic jargons.
- While reading a paragraph or a text, the role of syntactic cues should be emphasised.
- Advanced students can be enabled to learn how to skim in order to concentrate on central points and skip the details. At this stage the role of silent reading should be emphasised.

It may be pointed out that many Indian students going to the US universities find it difficult to cope with their reading assignments and depend mostly on classroom lectures. That is why they are not able to do very well. If they learn at school how to read fast, it will be a great asset to them when they go in for higher studies, whether in India or abroad.

B.
STAGES OF DEVELOPMENT OF READING HABIT

Learning to Read Imaginative Literature

> If you do not have the time to read, you don't have the time or the tools to write. As simple as that. —Stephen King

Children love to listen to imaginative stories much before they start going to school, much earlier than they can understand the difference between a real life story and an imaginative story. Much depends on how exciting a story is and how imaginative a story-teller is. A story may be absurd from the point of view of an adult but not for the child if it is told in an interesting manner. Very often parents tell their children the folk tales they have heard and enjoyed in their childhood. These are tales in which birds and animals behave like human beings. They love and fight with one another, play tricks and crack jokes. The writer has the experience of telling such a story to his son when he was very young. He heard it so many times yet he was never tired of listening to it. Once he did not feel like telling him any story but he insisted and asked him to narrate the same oft-repeated story. He did so but skipped some repetitive dialogues. The child stopped and asked him to repeat them by quoting some of the skipped lines. He knew what was omitted and wanted him to include it in his narrative. The point is: though the child had heard the story many a time, he wanted to listen to it again. Even though he remembered the dialogues, he wanted them to be included in the narrative every time he heard it.

Reading a Familiar Story

A child who has heard a story and retained it since his/her early childhood, loves to read it when he/she learns how to read. Reading such stories is a fun for him/her. He/she is familiar with the vocabulary and the narrative, and finds reading it easy, it does not strain him/her. He/she feels delighted to have discovered on his/her own what he/she already knows. One may argue that it is true of the stories he/she has heard in his/her mother tongue but not of what is given to him/her in a foreign language. But it is fallacious. The writer found his son and grandchildren enjoying stories from *Panchtantra* in English, published by Children's Book Trust, Delhi. He also found them insisting on buying a new book containing some of these stories and published from the UK or USA because they had better illustrations and print. As a matter of fact, he found four versions of the stories from *Panchtantra* in his second grandson's collection because he liked their illustrations, colour and print.

Cartoons and Comic Books

These days there is one more link between listening to a story and reading it later; it is the comic book. Children look at the cartoons in comic books very attentively even when they cannot read their dialogues in fine prints. Perhaps they imagine the dialogues or recapitulate what they have already heard. The comic books motivate, rather than deter, children from reading the full texts later, just as a very abridged, retold version of *Gulliver's Travels* motivates them to read a more elaborate retold story and, at an advanced level, the full original text. When the writer was doing English (Honours) in BA, he found it very easy to read the original text because he had read its abridged version at school. he enjoyed reading *Oliver Twist* more than *Far from the Maddening Crowd* because he had read the abridged version of the former, but not of the latter.

Stories on TV

Another factor that motivates young readers to read a book is his/her familiarity with its story on television. Once the writer learnt that the story of Vikram and the Vampire was going to be telecast. He wanted his second grandchild to be familiar with the story before he saw the serial. He gave him a book and asked him to read it but he returned it to him after a day saying that he did not like it. However, when he saw one or two episodes of the serial, he came to him on his own and asked him for the book. He read and enjoyed it. He liked how Vikram solved a riddle in every story. He was so excited about his prior knowledge of it that he often asked others what the solution was going to be. When they failed to satisfy him, he would give his solution which proved to be correct. It was this problem-solving exercise that kept him excited so long as the stories were telecast. These stories are very suggestive and the remarkable fact is that even a ten year old child could appreciate it. The point is that being exposed to an imaginative story on television and through comic books encourages a child to read the story on his/her own. It helps him/her in increasing his/her reading speed.

Children from an educated family in the urban area are more likely to be exposed to comic books than those from less privileged families in rural areas. However, even they are likely to be exposed to the children programmes on television. In any case, there are teachers in elementary schools who can play the role of story tellers. As much depends on the choice of the story and the technique of storytelling, the teacher should choose an amusing and entertaining story and present it in a natural and interesting manner. The power of the story teller over his/her young audience can hardly be overestimated. The more dramatic he/she is, the more he/she finds them involved in the story.

Dramatization

A teacher who uses an oral story to expose his/her students to English should never forget the fact that telling a story is an aid to the unconscious development of the child, and not a factor in planned conscious development. It means, no effort should be made to ask grammatical or comprehension questions at this stage. If the teacher concentrates on the dramatic presentation of the story and succeeds in sustaining the interest of the child, he/she should feel satisfied. He/she may try to find out whether the child liked the story. If so, why? Even the children who did not like it should be encouraged to tell why they disliked it. Those who do not want to respond should be left undisturbed; perhaps they are still in the make-believe world of the story and do not want to get out of it so soon.

GOALS OF STORY TELLING

We have argued that there are two goals of storytelling in the class: to facilitate students to concentrate on the story and to make them familiar with its broad outlines so that when they are asked to read it later, they feel comfortable. We have also argued that students should not be deprived of enjoying it by focusing their attention on the pronunciation, spelling or structures of the spoken words. The ultimate goal is to enable students to have a positive attitude towards the story so that they feel tempted to read it on their own.

From Oral Story Telling to Reading a Story Aloud

Priscilla Lynch, an education consultant in New York University, observes that reading books aloud is the most valuable support that parents can provide to help children learn to read.

She suggests that the parents should:

- be enthusiastic and cheerful while reading (The more enthusiastic the reader, the more the child will enjoy the story).
- run his/her fingers beneath the words he/she reads (It signals that the print carries the story).
- leave time for examining the illustrations more closely and encourage the child to find things in the picture.
- invite the child to join in whenever there is a repeated phrase in the picture.
- link up events in the book with similar events in child's life.
- answer the question the child asks in the middle of the story.

The practice of reading aloud to the child at the bed time is common among educated people in urban areas. It is rare in rural areas in India, partly because parents are not familiar with English and also because they have no energy left at the end of day's work to do so. In such a situation the teacher can play the role of a parent in the classroom and read the story aloud.

Initial Stage

While listening to the child reading a story aloud, a teacher (or parent) should enjoy it and praise him/her for his/her efforts. If the child stops in the course of reading and asks for a word, he/she should be helped immediately so that the meaning of the story is understood. If the child replaces a word, for instance, *street* by *road* (or vice versa) while reading, he/she should not be interrupted because the intended meaning is not lost. However, if he/she reads *horse* for *house*, the listener should say that he/she did not hear it correctly and ask the child to read it again. Most likely he/she will make the correction; if he/she does not, the teacher should help.

Fantasy Stories

The fact that children love to read imaginative literature, specially fantasy, is illustrated by the popularity of J.K. Rowling. She has written a series of children's fantasy stories concerning the exploits of Harry Potter, a boy wizard.

Some 325 million copies of its first six volumes have been sold world wide. The books have been translated into 64 languages. Samantha Shanoy, a 21 year old graduate from Oxford, has written *Bone Seran*, a fantasy novel which is in the tradition of Harry Potter. Millions of its copies have already been ordered for sale. For her, writing the book was like "a drug I could not help taking" and so is the experience of the readers of Harry Potter. If a student acquires the ability, both his/her interest in reading fiction and his/her reading speed are bound to improve.

Of course, some students are more imaginative than others; they are more ready to suspend "disbelief". But regardless of quickness of imagination, all students are capable of imaginative entry into the feelings and experience of other persons. They relate the fantasies of authors like Rowling with their own fantasies and this correlative experience enables them to get lost in the narrative. Once hooked up, they cannot get out of it till the narration comes to an end. If this habit is formed, it can be easily, perhaps automatically, transferred to whatever they read. The point is, students should be initially encouraged to develop the habit of reading and nothing can do it more effectively than reading imaginative literature.

Books based on fantasy, adventures and the desire to explore the unknown are popular among children. Sometimes they present an over-simplified picture of human characters and action but even such books have the underlying concept of cause and effect. They make readers aware of human values and of the significance of everyday life. Initially the enjoyment of reading literature is unconscious but as the child grows, it becomes conscious. Young children prefer narratives in which even natural objects and animals are humanised. This stage of unconscious enjoyment must not be bypassed because it leads to unconscious appreciation. Even if children read what the adults (i.e. parents and teachers) consider to be "trash", they should not be discouraged. We should remember that the reader of trash has a chance to improve his/her taste, but a non-reader has no taste to improve.

STAGES OF GROWTH IN LITERARY APPRECIATION

So far we have discussed three points:

(i) how listening to interesting stories can motivate children to read them;
(ii) how imaginative literature can keep them occupied and indirectly inculcate in them the habit to read faster for enjoyment; and
(iii) how enjoyment of reading leads children to literary appreciation.

The teacher plays an active role in the development of students in all of them. The interest of the student will be created in stories only if he/she is exposed to them in an interesting manner. His/her interest in reading books of fantasy and adventure will be triggered only if the teachers and/or parents make such books available to them. His/her capacity to appreciate what he/she reads will be strengthened if leading questions are asked and their answers are politely and indirectly evaluated. Even in this age of science and technology, the search for delight is as much alive as it was in earlier times and the nature of delight evolves as children grow up.

Interesting Text Books

Growing up physically and mentally go hand in hand and they affect the child's development of enjoyment in literature. Curriculum planners and teachers of English have to keep it in view while sorting out syllabus for language teaching. If formal teaching emphasizes too much on structural complexities in the initial stage of teaching, the student may find it a dull exercise. If he/she is deprived of pleasure, the desired result will not be achieved. At the stage when the child likes to read imaginative stories and be in the world of fantasy, the teacher can make a variety of books available to him/her which delights him/her. As the child grows up, he/she moves gradually away from the simple interest in what happened and he/she asks himself/herself why it happened. The physical development of the child is matched by his/her psychological development. If the reader finds answers to his/her *why* and *how* in what he/she reads, he/she enjoys reading even more. The complexity of problems and their solutions offered by the writers affects the young reader. He/she wonders what creates emotional response in him/her. It is one of the crucial factors that motivate reading.

INTENSIVE READING

As the reader's interest shifts from unconscious enjoyment to conscious appreciation of the text, the teacher's role increases. He/she tells his/her students to interpret what they have read. He/she directs their attention to details that reveal traits of characters and their mood. He/she familiarises them with narrative devices such as foreshadowing, flashback and the underlying point of view. He helps them in examining the interrelationship of form and ideas. Even if they are engaged in this intensive study, they should be encouraged to continue with the wide reading of text for enjoyment. However, he/she should encourage students for intensive reading only when the extensive reading for enjoyment has prepared them to do so.

Developing Critical Appreciation

While teaching the art of appreciation, the teacher should be careful so that students do not ape his/her response; he/she should inculcate in them a true sense of appreciation. They may develop a false sense of appreciation if they are forced to appreciate before they are ready to do so. Some students judge "literary" works on the basis of the general reputation of the writer, and claim to find a lot of attributes in the text even if it does not have them. Sometimes they write what they think the teacher will like. Sensitive teachers can detect these tendencies and help them to give an honest appraisal of the work by asking leading questions. Only when a student is able to know what has delighted him/her in what he/she has read and why, he/she would be considered to be consciously appreciative. It may be unrealistic to think that all high school students have come upto this level but the teacher should do his/her best to enable them to reach it.

WRITTEN EVALUATION

High school students can be asked to write an assessment of what they have read, i.e. whether they liked the story, its characters and the way they were presented. Such an exercise can enable the teacher to understand their level of conscious enjoyment of the text. Responses to such questions will enable him/her to find out whether students have simply recognised the content of the text or learnt to appreciate it as well.

Rikki Tikki Tavi

Before we conclude this chapter, we would like to look at the two versions of the same story, *RikkiTikkiTavi*, the original story written by Rudyard Kipling and its abridged version as retold by Sampurna Chatterjee. It is about the adventures of a young mongoose. He is swept out of his burrow in a flood and faints in a ditch. A young boy, Teddy, picks him up, brings him to his house and feeds him. The mongoose sneaks out of his room to explore his surroundings. He hears the sound of a tailor bird, Darzi whose, egg has been eaten up by Nag, a cobra. While he is confronted with Nag, Nagina, his wife, tries to attack him but he leaps and bites her. He is then confronted with Karait, another snake. Nag is now in the bathroom. Rikki Tikki attacks and bites him but he is not dead yet. The father of the boy shoots Nag dead. Darzee tells Rikki Tikki where Nagina and her eggs are. He crushes all the eggs except one. He stops when he finds Nagina ready to bite Teddy. He attacks Nagina but she escapes into her hole. Ricki Tikki goes inside and kills her. This is the story in brief.

The abridged version of the story makes it entertaining by adding on onomatopoic sounds to the narrative, such as *aaachhoo* for a sneeze. When the snake comes out of the grass, he makes the hissing sound, hisssssss. When Nag speaks, he says *musst* for *must*, *yesss* for yes and *mongoo*ses for *mongoose*. Instead of *comes*, he says *comesss*, Nagina says *friendsss* for *friends*. When Rikki Tikki talks to the tailor bird, he answers his questions as if sounds echo:

'Near the rubbish heap heap heap'
'Near the melon bed bed bed'

When Nag is killed, the tailor bird sings,

> 'Nag the snake is dead, dead, dead.
> Rikki Tikki bit off his head head head
> Tonight I can sleep sleep sleep'.

This device of playing with sounds is not there in the original story but it adds to the entertainment of the very young listener. The storyteller will succeed only if he/she can modulate his/her voice appropriately. He/she can add to it by encouraging the child to imitate him/her. The language of the story is simple. Even when its sentences are long, they are easily comprehensible.

The original story is much longer; it has more details of every event mentioned above. It begins dramatically with a song that warns Nag of his approaching death. Rikki Tikki, as soon as he regains consciousness, wants to explore the things around him because his motto is to "run and find out". In that process, he puts his nose in the ink, burns a bit of his fur by playing with the burning cigar and jumps on the shoulder of Teddy's father to see how writing is done. The huge garden around the bungalow tempts him to go out. He is confronted with Nag and injures him but he escapes. Nag and Nagina talk among themselves like human beings, and they do not make hissing sounds. Rikki-Tikki first kills Nag and then Nagina in a violent battle with her. The story ends with a chant by darzi, the tailor bird in praise of Rikki Tikki, the valiant mongoose. The narrative is upto the standard of grown-up children.

A teacher may narrate the story of Rikki Tikki to the students of elementary class. He/she may make them read it a few years later and make them read its full version when they are in the junior high school. He/she will find that what has been written about exposure to various versions of the same story above, is helpful in reading the original story later on.

The Blue Umbrella

There are stories like *The Blue Umbrella* by Ruskin Bond which are meant for junior school students. It has no abridged version because it is brief. It has no miracle or surprises and no non-human character speaking like human beings. It is the story of Binya, a hill girl who exchanges her pendant with a tiger's claw for a blue umbrella and becomes very fond of it. She makes all persons in her neighbourhood familiar with her proud possession. Ram Bharose, the petty shopkeeper, plays tricks on her but is condemned by all. She has several adventures because of the umbrella and children love to read about them. There are many examples of structural parallelism in the book, but it is better not to stop in the middle of reading to admire it. The goal of reading such books is to enjoy them and to increase one's reading speed indirectly.

- Reading story books is an exercise in extensive reading. It increases one's reading speed.

1. Some suggestions for story telling
   Stories from Panchtantra, especially 'The Monkey and the Crocodile', 'The Big Lion and the Little Rabbit', The Stork and the Crab', 'The Tortoise and the Geese', 'The Blue Jackel', 'The Brahmin and the Goat', 'The Elephants and the Mice', etc.
   In addition to it, local folk tales may be narrated in English.
2. Stories for the first stage of extensively reading.
   (a) Written versions of stories they have been told already.
   (b) Comic books such as *Power Rangers, The Lion King, Aladdin, Donald Duck, Micky Mouse* (Series), *Alibaba*, etc.
3. Stories Retold for the Second Stage of Reading, such as those in the Ladybird Series (e.g. *The Three Musketeers, Oliver Twist, Treasure Island, Peter Pan, Alice in Wonderland, Gulliver's Travels, Tales from the Jungle Book, Aesop's Fables, Goodnight stories*, etc.
4. Stories for Senior High School Students (Extensive Reading), *Stories of Sherlock Holmes, The Invisible Man* (H.G. Wells), Simple Science Fiction, Myths and Legends Extended versions of novels they have read earlier in a simplified form may be tried.
   Stories based on the plays of Shakespeare may be introduced.

To sum up, children are exposed to folktales, myths and legends by their parents orally. It is further enforced by reading such stories aloud to them.

- Children get interested in the printed texts when they look at cartoons, comic books and watch stories of their interest on television.
- They may be supplied with the simplified versions of stories they have already been told orally.
- Much depends on the style of the story teller or reader.
- When children grow up, they may be introduced to retold versions of children classics. Later on, they may read the unabridged classics.
- Such a gradual exposure to the written material makes children interested in extensive reading.
- Once they get used to extensive reading, they should speed up their intensive reading.
- While extensive reading should be used for comprehensive tests, intensive reading should encourage children to appreciate what they read. Their improved comprehension ability will prepare them to read texts on various subjects whereas the ability to appreciate the texts will train them to work on their own composition well. It will enable them to understand the implication of what they read and to draw inferences from it.

16

The Dynamics of Writing

Who often reads will sometimes wish to write. —*William Cowper*

The word *writing* refers to both the written text (as in 'Salman Rushdie's Writings') and the act of producing a written text (as in 'he is writing an autobiographical novel these days'). The elements of writing involve a series of cognitive activities. When we think of a written text, we think of its writer and potential readers. We think of the strategies the writer has adopted to develop and communicate his/her ideas to his/her readers. This relational aspect is a particular social and material condition under which a written text is produced. Just as an accomplished novelist is affected by his/her environments, so is a child writing a small piece of composition in the classroom or at home. A writer who is learning to write may not be conscious of the complex task he/she has undertaken but he/she is constrained by its complexity.

SPEAKING VS. WRITING

Both writing and speaking are used to express one's experience or ideas, but there is a basic difference. When one communicates one's thought orally, one not only speaks out stream of utterances but also uses features such as tone, intonation, volume and pauses to convey what one intends to express. Even gestures and postures (kinesics) come to one's aid. On the other hand, when one writes, only written words convey one's thoughts. Of course, there are non-linguistic devices, such as punctuation marks (e.g. comma, semicolon, colon, full stop, etc.) and the use of capital letters and italics. These typographical devices highlight the written text but they do not suggest anything new in addition to what is written. Nevertheless, the use of punctuation marks is unavoidable. We end a statement with a period (i.e. full stop), interrogative sentence with a question mark and an exclamatory sentence with a mark of exclamation, as in (1-3) respectively.

1. The writing system of English seems to be erratic.
2. How do you spell the word |nais|?
3. What a funny way to write it!

Commas, semicolon and colon indicate the duration of pauses in a sentence; they are used like pauses in the spoken language.

SPELLING AND PRONUNCIATION

The way a word is written in English does not give a cue to the way it is spoken. For instance, the sequence of letters *ea* is pronounced one way in *heard* |hə:d|, another way in *beard* |biəd| and yet another way in *meat* |mi:t|. We may like to recall a poem by T.S. Watt in this context.

I take it you already know
Of TOUGH and BOUGH and COUGH and THOUGH.
Others may stumble, but not you,
On HICCOUGH, THOROUGH, LOUGH and THROUGH.
Well done! And now you wish, perhaps,
To learn of less familiar traps.
Beware of HEARD, a dreadful word
That looks like BEARD but sounds like BIRD.
And DEAD it's like BED, not BEAD
For goodness' sake, don't call it DEED!
Watch out for MEAT and GREAT and THREAT
They sound like SUITE, and STRAIGHT and DEBT.
A MOTH is not a MOTH in MOTHER
Nor BOTH in BOTHER, BROTH in BROTHER
And HERE is not a match for THERE
Nor DEAR and FEAR for PEAR and BEAR
And then there's DOSE and ROSE and LOSE –
But look them up – and GOOSE and CHOOSE
And CORK and WORK and CARD and WARD
And FONT and FRONT and WORD and SWORD
And DO and GO, then THWART and CART
Come, Come, I have hardly made a start.
A dreadful language? Man alive,
I'd mastered it when I was five!

This poem highlights the way these words are written and spoken in English. For most people, these are words the spellings of which are always troublesome. We have already mentioned in the previous chapter how the combination of five vowels represent twelve vowel and eight dipthong sounds. Learning to know them is a matter of sheer memory; we repeat their spellings either orally or by writing. Some experts advocate the use of mnemonic principle which is based upon the association of ideas. For instance, one can remember that *repetition* has a *pet* and so has *competition*. We have to remember that there is a *mar* in gram*mar* or that if we spell the first half (*gram*) correctly, the second half is its repetition in the reverse order.

Spelling

The teacher should choose only those words for the exercise in spelling writing which the student is familiar with. However, care should be taken to include the words which the student will need in writing exercises elsewhere. He/she could explain specific spelling patterns that permit generalisation. For instance, the end consonants of certain verbs are doubled when they are in past tense, as in *drop-dropped, occur-occurred, equip-equipped*. They are doubled in words such as *red-redder-reddest*.

- It follows a simple rule. When words of one syllable and those of more than one accented on the last syllable ending in a single consonant is preceded by a single vowel, double the consonant before a suffix beginning with a vowel is added to it. For instance,
  - begin, beginning, beginner
  - control, controlled, controller
  - drop, dropped, dropping
  - occur, occurred, occurring, occurrence
  - plan, planned, planning
  - refer, referred, referring
  - run, running, runner
  - swim, swimming, swimmer
- However, words ending in a final consonant preceded by a vowel do not double their final consonant, as in
  - Need, needed, needy
  - Train, trained, trainer, training, trainee
- Likewise, words ending in two consonants do not double the final consonants, as in
  - bend, bending
  - turn, turned, turning
- Words not accented in the final syllable do not ordinarily double the final consonant, as in

  happen, happened, happening
- Words ending in *y* preceded by a consonant usually change *y* to *i* before any suffix is added to it. Examples:
  - city-cities, sky-skies, fly-flies

- ➢ beauty-beautiful, busy-business
- ➢ easy-easier, easily
- ➢ lucky-luckily
- ➢ marry-married, marriage
- ➢ merry-merrier, merrily
- ➢ try-tried, (but trying)

- Words ending in y preceded by a vowel do not change y to i before any suffix is added to it, such as
  - ➢ annoy, annoyed, annoyance
  - ➢ employ, employer
  - ➢ stay, stayed, staying

However, we have pay, paid; day, daily; lay, laid, etc.
Another generalisation can be made about final *e*.

- The final *e* is usually dropped before a suffix beginning with a vowel but it is retained before a suffix beginning with a consonant:

argue-argument	*but* bare-barely
come-coming	care-careful, careless
dance-dancing	hate-hateful
like-likable	safe-safely
love-lovable	excite-excitement

- However, in some cases silent *e* is retained even if a suffix beginning with a vowel is attached to it, as in

here-herein	mile-mileage
there-therein	shoe-shoeing

People are often confused about words containing *ei* or *ie*. The generalisation given below is helpful:

- when the sound is *i:*, put *i* before *e* except after *c*, as in achieve, belief, brief (exception, deceive, receive, perceive, ceiling)
- when the sound is not *i:*, put *e* before *i*, as in weight, neighbour, eight, either

However, there are several exceptions to it.
Another helpful tip could be added about the *inserted k*. The letter *k* is generally added to a word ending in *c* before a suffix beginning with *e*, *i*, or *y* is added to it.

Picnic-picnicking
politic-politicking
traffic-trafficked

The spelling of English words is difficult because of many reasons. The main reason is that the sounds in English have changed in pronunciation in course of time but the writing system has remained unchanged. Not only that, numerous words are not spelt as they sound, but many that sound alike are spelt differently. We have identical pronunciation for *no* and *know*, and for *cite, sight* and *site. Kernel* and *colonel* have the same sounds but are spelt differently. To spell may be treated as fun if we play word games. Besides, if one has discipline and concentration, one can acquire proficiency in spelling. Games like scrambles and anagrams help one in improving one's spelling.

There are several reasons why the native-speaker children make spelling mistakes. They first know the word orally and then learn to read and write it. They read the word *knock* correctly but write *nock* instead. They may write *by* for *buy, strait* for *straight, troup* for *troupe, waste* for *waist, ring* for *wring* and *yoke* to *yolk.* Vivian Cook (2008-94) reports some L_2 learners of English writing *wether* for *whether, sattisfaction* for *satisfaction, bussiness* or *busines* for *business* and *becaus* or *becuas* for *because.* We have some Indian students writing *priviledge* for *privilege, misshap* for *mishap, missionery* for *missionary, impretion* for *impression, zerox* for *xerox* and *defenite* for *definite.* Since most Indians learn English as a second language more often by exposure to a written text than by hearing them correctly, they tend to have their pronunciation of words influenced by their spellings. However, they have their own areas of confusion, for example, between *ei* (as in *receive, ceiling*) and *ie* (e.g. *achieve, brief*), between *–ar, -er* and or (as in *angular, particular, diameter, carrier, actor* and *aggressor*), between *–vise* (as in revise), *wise* (as in *likewise*) and between *–ise* (e.g. *advertise, despise*) and *–ize* (as in *criticize, civilize, localize*, etc.

Some Indians write *athaletics* or *athelatics* for *athletics, enterance* for *entrance, explaination* for *explanation, mischievious* for *mischievous, nerveous* for *nervous, simalar* for *similar* and *umberella* for *umbrella.* Some write *acept* for *accept, colum* for *column, fasen* for *fasten, lisen* for *listen, offen* for *often, rythm* for *rhythm* and *grammer* for *grammar.* Some write *begining* for *beginning, equiped* for *equipped, manish* for *mannish, prefered* for *preferred, transfered* for *transferred* and *benefitting* for *benefiting.*

Learners need to be told that sometimes a vowel is dropped in pronunciation, but not in spelling, for instance, *accidentally* |æksidentli|, *deficient* |difiʃnt|, *familiar* |fəmiljar|, *original* |əridʒnəl|, etc. Likewise a consonant may be dropped in pronunciation but not in spelling, as in *column* |kɒləm|, *empty* |em(p)ti|, *fasten* |fasn|, *landlord* |lænlə:d|, etc. Sometimes, a silent letter (in pronunciation) causes misspelling, as in *pneumonia* |nju:məʊnia|, *psalm* |sa:m|, *pseudo* |sju:dəʊ|, *psychology* |saikɔlodʒi|, *knee* |ni:|, *know* |nəʊ|, *knock* |nɒk|, *knot* |nɒt|, *plumber* |plʌmbə:|, *wring* |riŋ|, *wrap* |ræp|, *hymn* |him|.

USE OF DICTIONARY

Learners should use a dictionary to find out the meaning of a word and how it is built up. The knowledge of the ways in which prefixes and suffixes are added to words not only increases one's vocabulary but also improves one's spelling. *Un-* is added to a word to get its negative (e.g. *likely-unlikely*) but if a word begins with *r*, *l* or *m*, we add *ir-*, *il-* or *im-* as prefixes; for example, *irrelevant*, *illegal*, *immoral* etc. To get an adjective out of a verb, we may add *–able* at the end of a word but if it is not a complete word, we add *–ible*, as in *horrible*, *divisible*, *visible*, etc. The suffix *–ible* is added if a word ends in *miss* (as in admissible), |t| (as in *digestible*), g (as in *illegible*), c pronounced as s or k (as in *reducible*, *conductible*, etc.). Dictionaries should also be consulted for finding plurals of words (regular as well as irregular). It is easy to say that one should use only those words whose spellings are familiar but that suggestion is not enough to meet a writer's requirement. One should better consult a dictionary if one has a doubt about the spelling of a word. If one concentrates on some of the points discussed above and looks up a dictionary when necessary, one need not find the problem difficult to solve.

The dictionary can be used productively to support writing by looking at the synonyms of a word and finding out which of them is appropriate in the context in which one wants to use it. We usually talk about *a clear sky*, *a clear idea*, *a clear view* and *a clear note*. Suppose the writer has used the word twice in a passage and does not want to repeat it the third time. He/she is reminded of its synonym such as *definite*, *distinct*, *explicit*, *obvious*, *transparent*, *straightforward*, etc. but all of these cannot be used in a specific context. He can talk about *a transparent scene*, *an obvious statement*, *a definite or distinct opinion* and *a straightforward comment* but not a *definite* or *distinct sky* or a *transparent road*. As there are collocational restrictions on synonymous expressions, so there are restrictions on the use of their antonyms. We can think of the sky being *cloudy* or *foggy* but not being *vague* or *opaque*. One realises these restrictions when one sits down to write.

The method of connectionism which shows the relation of a word with its near-synonyms and antonyms also establishes a link between the word and its derivatives. It has been discussed earlier on pp. 158-160. For instance, *clear* (adjective) reminds us of *clarity* and *clearness* (nouns) and *clearly* (adverb). Compound words, such as *clear-cut*, *clear-sighted*, *clearup* and *clearout* come to our mind. If there is a reference to the word *clear* in a specific context, some of these points can be raised by the teacher to enrich the learner's vocabulary.

The words are connected not only on the basis of sameness and difference in their meanings, but also on the basis of relationships (e.g. *large-small*, *old-young*), continuum (e.g. colour terms such as *white, yellow, blue, green, black* or temperature such as *hot, warm, tepid, cool, cold*).

The selection of an appropriate word is one problem, the use of an incorrectly constructed word or phrase is another. For instance, one should talk about *a recipe for cooking* rather than *a cooking recipe, the shooting by the police* rather than *police firing, traffic jam* rather than *jam, book maker* rather than *book monger*. If one has a sufficiently large stock of words at one's disposal and knows their meanings, one finds it easy to express oneself precisely and fluently.

The ability to write presupposes not only the knowledge of words and their spellings, but also of how the words are combined into sentences and how sentences are manipulated to fit into a coherent paragraph. The knowledge of syntax helps immensely in this task but the ability to write well involves much more than writing grammatical sentences. It includes the ability to write coherent sentences in a piece of composition by using appropriate cohesive devices (The tips on grammar are given separately in chapter 9).

STEPS IN THE GROWTH OF WRITING SKILL

Before the child decides to share his/her ideas or expressions with others in writing, he/she has to learn the basic writing skills. A proper training in these skills has got to be sequential as given below:

i. Learning letters and how to combine them in words.
ii. Copying familiar texts
iii. Writing dictation.
iv. Writing controlled composition
v. Writing original composition

Learning to Write

Even if the child knows to speak the language, he/she may not be able to write in it if he/she does not know how to write the letters of its alphabet. An Indian child learning English as L_2 will not be able to write in English unless he/she learns its alphabet.

The first step is to learn how capital and small letters are written in English. He/she should have a workbook and practise cursive writing by trying to write the way it is written in it. While teaching the writing skills, the teacher should remember that letters *i, t,* and *l* belongs to the straight line group and *n, u, m, w* and *s* to the curve line group. Letters *a, o,* and *e* belong to the circle group while *f, p* and *z* belong to the hanging loop group. As soon as the student has practised writing the letters separately, he/she should be encouraged to write them in combination such as *am, be, mn, wh, qu* etc. As the next step, he/she should practise how to write words and then sentences. The mechanics of writing can be learnt by practising to copy sentences as written in the workbook.

Copying Familiar Texts

Children can begin to practise writing their own names. It will give them a level of muscular control and eye-hand-mind coordination. It is a gradual exercise. When they can write their names firmly in their workbooks, they can practise it on the books and workbooks they possess. That way they will declare their possession and learn to care for it. They can practise writing memoranda to remind themselves what they have to take to school the next day.

Copying is an indispensable part of writing exercise. It provides practice in relating sounds to their graphic representations. It is desirable that the student comprehends the sentence(s) he/she copies. It is a task which involves several sequential steps. While copying letters, students have to be careful that they are correctly ordered within a word and words are correctly ordered within a sentence. Apart from the word-order, the student has to pay attention to the spelling of everything he/she copies. Every sentence has to begin with a capital letter, should be well balanced and should have proper spacing between words. The letters should be placed properly so that the handwriting is legible. It must have a neat look. Every statement should end with an appropriate punctuation mark.

Punctuation Marks

The student should be told about punctuation marks. Every sentence ends with a period unless it is a question or an exclamation. If it is a question, it ends with a question mark '?'. If it is an exclamation or exclamatory sentence, it ends with a note of exclamation ' !'.

1. 'What are you doing?'
2. 'I am writing a story.'
3. 'Oh! What a nice idea!'

The first sentence is a question. The second is the answer to that question, a statement of fact. The third sentence expresses surprise. Each type of sentence has its unique punctuation mark. They are like traffic signals. They signal writers to stop for a while and then move. A comma ',' indicates a very short break and semicolon ';' makes one stop for a little longer period than a comma does, however, it does not permit one to stop as a long as a period (full stop) does. There are other signals but an elementary school child may not use them. However, if the child is telling a story, he should know what inverted commas mean. When a character speaks directly in a story, one puts whatever he/she says within quotation marks ("...")

He said "I am not going to school today."

There are rules involving the use of a capital letter. The first letter of the first word in a sentence is written in the capital letter. The first word of a proper name is also written in the capital letter. There are other occasions when a capital letter is used but they need not be mentioned to a child who has just started to write.

Dictation

In the beginning, a dictation exercise should be short. It may contain words, phrases or short sentences. As a student progresses, the teacher may dictate longer sentences. The sentences should be spoken or read at a normal speed. As a dictation is not a speed test, the teacher should allow enough time for the student to write the dictated material. If the student misses something to write, that portion should be reread at a normal speed.

WRITING A PIECE OF COMPOSITION

There are several approaches to the development of technique to learn how to write a piece of composition, at least in the initial phase of writing. One of them is to teach how to write a piece of controlled composition.

Controlled Composition

In a classroom students may be asked to write a piece of composition in a controlled situation. They may be shown strips of scenes describing a situation or narrating an event and asked to write down whatever they have seen. Likewise, they may be prompted to express their ideas on a particular topic in a question-answer session. The questions should be put in a systematic manner so that the responses to them are systematic. Sometimes a teacher may write down the outlines of a topic and ask students to develop them in the same order. While using any of these techniques, the focus is on the formal organisation of the structure of composition. The form is already given, it is the task of students to develop it by carefully constructing and manipulating sentences. Students are told how several questions are related and responses to them form a paragraph. The skeleton of the composition is already given; what the students has to do is to add flesh to it, so that an able-bodied text is produced. This technique emphasises the formal accuracy of the text and how to achieves it, though there may be variation due to individual responses.

WRITING STRATEGIES

A writer may choose one of the following to write on:

(i) his personal experience,

(ii) experience gained by reading or observation,
(iii) by looking out the critical issues around the writer,
(iv) by exploring the feelings and experiences of others.

He/she needs to identify a topic and organise his/her thoughts to develop it. He/she may note them down and then organise them in a systematic manner. If it is a narrative or descriptive writing, it could be chronologically ordered. Whatever the nature of the writing, it must be coherent. The outlines jotted down earlier have to be revised, keeping its consistency and coherence in view. Once the first draft is ready, it must be revised from this point of view.

During the discussion on the given assignment, students need to be told that a composition consists of several paragraphs and each paragraph has a topic which is mentioned somewhere in the paragraph, preferably, in the beginning. The topic sentence is usually developed by means of additional, detailed information to support the idea given in the sentence. It may be supported by facts, examples or arguments. A paragraph must be a coherent unit which is possible only if its details are logically and smoothly arranged.

Note Taking

The teacher should teach students how to take orderly notes. There are several reasons for learning to take notes.

- While reading, it trains the reader to concentrate on the main points. It is an exercise in scanning and skimming and getting to gist.
- It helps the reader from wandering away from the main points.
- The reader comes to see not only the main points of the writer but also the relationship of one point to another.
- It is a good training for reflection.
- It teaches, by practice how to take notes.

The most common method of taking notes is to prepare a running summary. Another method is to prepare notes by first outlining what one listens or reads. Though it is a difficult method, it has the advantage of showing how the writer or speaker has developed ideas and related them to one another.

- While preparing notes, one should familiarize oneself with the meaning of unfamiliar words from the context. If it is not clear even then, one should look up the dictionary.
- One should also learn to distinguish between facts and opinion. A fact is a statement of that which exists and can be seen whereas an opinion is a statement of what one believes or thinks about the topic.
- One should learn to distinguish between main and subordinate ideas.

The main ideas are discussed at length whereas subordinate ideas are just referred to. These points are common to written texts and orally delivered speeches and one can adopt the same technique for taking note of a speech.

- While taking notes, one should ignore unproved assertions, references to unproved cause and effect relation and generalization from insufficient evidence.

Summarising

The skill involving summarizing depends largely on the skill to take notes. Once the process of taking notes is completed, one should put them, in a logically proper order and then rewrite it. While doing so, one should be brief. One should follow the principles of préús writing and avoid figurative language and long expressions.

The wholeness of the summary is the focal point. Unless it is understood properly, a fair, comprehensive and balanced report cannot be prepared. It depends on one's ability to find out the main points and then organize other points in a logical manner to put them coherently. Only when it is done, a wholesome report will be ready.

Free Composition on Restricted Topics

As soon as the teacher is convinced that his/her students have gained self-confidence, he/she should encourage them to write whatever they feel on a given topic. However, they must be warned that they should not digress from the topic sentence. Though students will have freedom to write their composition without any given outlines now, they will be restricted by the topic.

Initially students will be asked to write about themselves, their family members or school. They may be asked to talk about games, books, places, festivals or objects they like. A favourable topic will encourage them to express themselves well. However, the teacher should assign only such topics that they can handle grammatically. In other words, they are not expected to use structures that they are not familiar with. They should be sufficiently equipped with the vocabulary and basic structures that they are expected to use while writing. They should get all the help they need to handle a topic.

Essay

An essay consists of several paragraphs. Suppose students are asked to write an essay on the concept of an 'ideal high school'. It may have the following outlines:

(i) the spirit of the school.
(ii) its administration.

(iii) its faculty members.
(iv) its programmes – (a) curricular, (b) co-curricular.
(v) its students.

Each of these topics (which are the sub-topics of the title of the essay) can be further sub-divided, as follows:

(i) the spirit of the school: friendly, democratic, loyalty to the school and its values.
(ii) its administration: democratic, respect for its discipline, positive responses to students' problems, etc.
(iii) its faculty: dedicated, friendly, competent, understanding.
(iv) its programme: diversified programmes for students of science, commerce and arts, co-curricular activities: cricket and football clubs, swimming club, debating society, dramatic society.
(v) its students – mixed group representing various sections of the society.

Given these outlines, it is easy to write an essay on this topic. Similar outlines can be discussed on other topics to encourage students to write their own composition.

Writing a Narrative

When we write systematically what happened, we have written a narrative essay. Whether it is a simple narration of chronologically related events or a carefully plotted elaborate description, it is a narrative. Children are fond of writing about objects or events they know very well. That is why they prefer to write about events which actually happened. Some people find it convenient to narrate an event around a person who experienced it. We can think of a real event and imagine a person who experienced it and develop our narrative around a third person.

While planning a narrative, we can plan to answer the following (or similar) questions:

i. How should the narrative begin?
ii. What should be its end?
iii. How should the narrative be brought to that end?
iv. Should the story be narrated in the first or third person?
v. Which part of the event is to be narrated in great detail?
vi. Should the flashback technique be used? If so, to what extent?

While narrating the story, one should be natural and write realistic dialogues. One should build the plot carefully and keep track of it while developing it. Such an outline will bring the narrative to the selected end.

Writing a Descriptive Essay

A descriptive essay involves the description of an object is a 'non-judgemental' (in, neutral) way. It is developed on the same line on which a narrative is, though there is some difference. For instance, it could provide the background information before an actual description begins. One can begin the description of an elephant after giving some details of how useful a domesticated elephant is in our life. The description may have details of a domesticated elephant's everyday behaviour and compare it with its wild life in a herd. It can refer to how elephants are shown in a circus playing football.

The Structure of an Expository Essay

An expository essay is written to inform, explain or clarify. It deals with facts and ideas and interprets them. It tries to present the point of view of the writer and persuade the reader to accept it.

Like descriptive or narrative essays, it has an effective introduction and a conclusive end. The introduction leads the reader directly to the topic. It clarifies what the topic is and does not leave the reader in suspense. It explains both sides of an issue and tried to come to a conclusion

Argumentative Essay

An expository essay is different from an argumentative essay only in one sense; in the argumentative essay, the writer takes a position in the introduction and marshals arguments in its favour. It refers to the opposite position in order to refute its arguments. It does not mention arguments that are in favour of the other side whereas in an expository essay arguments that are in favour of both sides are discussed. Both types of essays need coherence and logical consistency. They are supposed to arrive at a logical conclusion.

In both expository and argumentative essay, the writer is supposed to argue a case. He/she can cite inductive or deductive arguments or both of them. Besides, he/she can use analogy to make the arguments stronger.

Inductive and Deductive Reasoning

When one writes an argumentative essay or prepares an argumentative speech, one wishes one's readers or listeners to accept one's point of view. One proposes to support one's ideas with strongest possible reasons.

There are two kinds of reasoning: inductive and deductive. In inductive reasoning, one offers facts, statistics or instances and evidence. The more evidence the writer has in his/her favour, the stronger is his/her arguments. As the writer's generalisation depends on the strength of the evidence, its truth or falsity depends on it.

Another kind of reasoning is deductive. One reasons deductively when one is able to begin with a generalisation which is generally accepted. One applies it to a particular situation and draws conclusions. A deductive argument is offered in the form of a *syllogism*. It is in three parts. The first part consists of a broad generalisation. It is a major premise. The second part offers a particular situation to which the major premise applies. It is a minor premise. The third part of the syllogism draws the conclusion. If the first two premises are true, the conclusion is sound. For instance,

Major premise:	All normal children are born with an inherent ability to acquire language.
Second premise:	Ahmed is a normal child.
Conclusion:	Ahmed has the inherent ability to acquire language.

One can test the correctness of the syllogism by asking the following questions:

(a) Are the premises true?
(b) Does the conclusion follows logically from the premises?

If the answers to these questions are positive, the syllogism is sound and it yields a strong argument. The strength of an argumentative essay lies in the strength of the syllogisms.

Reasoning by Analogy

Sometimes people use analogy to clarify a point. Analogy involves comparison. This kind of reasoning depends on comparing one object or situation with another. Although analogy never proves anything directly, it clarifies a point. It is sound if two objects or situations that are being compared have a large number of points in common. If there are few or no points of similarity, analogy proves to be false.

Cause-effect Relations

If one can prove that in all (or most of the) situations there is a causal relation between X and Y, i.e. X causes Y, one succeeds in giving a sound argument. Here again, we should be careful. The fact that one event or condition follows another event or condition, does not necessarily mean that the second event or condition was caused by the first. Much depends on whether the fact (which is presumed to be the cause) is relevant to the context, i.e. it suits the situation or is considered "off the track" and has been used to cause confusion.

Students could be encouraged to write an argumentative essay. Since the goal of such a composition is to persuade the reader to accept the writer's point of view, students should be asked to present their strongest arguments clearly and logically. If a generalisation is to be made on the basis of evidence, it should be sound and convincing. In case the argument is deductive, the main premises of the argument should be sound. If the facts stated in the premises are true, the conclusion will be logical and convincing. The teacher should make these points clear to students.

Composition

After students have practised writing controlled composition, they should be encouraged to write free composition, i.e., a piece of writing for which no outlines are given. Such compositions are written "out of one's head" on a given topic. In the first step, the student should list all the ideas that come to his/her mind on the topic. They may not be in any order. Once the list has been completed, it should be examined carefully to remove points which seem to be unrelated to the topic or which need a detailed discussion but do not contribute substance to the topic.

In the second step the student should group related ideas together and arrange the groups in a logical order. It will lead to ready outlines for the given free composition and contain subtopics. Each subtopic can be developed as a paragraph or more.

When the outlines are ready, the student may begin to write the composition. The first point should be the introduction of the topic. it should make the purpose of his/her composition clear. It should arouse the interest of the reader so that he/she reads the whole thing.

The introduction should be followed by the main body of the composition which may have several paragraphs. The transition between the paragraphs should be smooth and clear. A new paragraph should have a link with the preceding paragraph. There are several devices to establish the link. For instance, the new paragraph may have a pronoun which refers to an event or an idea in the preceding paragraph, or it may directly refer to the previous idea.

The last paragraph will be the conclusion. It will summarize what has been discussed earlier or reemphasize the main point of the composition.

MAIN APPROACHES

There are two main approaches which a teacher can adopt to handle the act of writing a composition. They are the process approach and the production of the text approach.

The Process Approach

The process approach does not believe in giving an organised pattern to the class. It believes that the approach should be generative enough to encourage students to explore their ideas in a meaningful manner. It believes in providing and maintaining a positive and meaningful environment in which students work through their composing process. The interference of the teacher is minimum; it is to encourage students to develop an efficient and effective creative process. They learn on their own how to get started, prepare a draft, revise and edit it and finally have a well-written composition. In this approach it is the student who identifies the task and chooses an appropriate strategy to accomplish it. The focus of the enterprise is on the writer, and not on the teacher.

The Production of Text Approach

This approach is centred around the production of a text, and not the writer. The text is viewed as a conventional response to the task of writing in such a way that it is recognised by others. In this approach, the teacher concentrates on the rating of the text which includes variables of the text: linguistic and rhetorical and knowledge of the subject-matter. This approach has primarily been recommended for those students who use English as a second language. The product of the writing is evaluated to find out whether any remedial teaching is needed and if so, in what areas. The issues that emerge out of the assessment of written composition are topics on which the composition teacher is supposed to work. From the teacher's point of view, the text approach is the best method. The evaluation of the composition shows how well a student has performed. It is used to decide the next strategy.

LETTER-WRITING

Exercises in writing include letter-writing as well. A friendly letter is written in a natural and informal style, though the degree of informality depends on who the letter is addressed to. A letter written to one's parents will be a more formal type of friendly letter than the letter written to one's siblings or friends. The teacher should make students familiar with the format of friendly letters and point out the subtle difference in the style of various types of informal letters. For instance, social notes could be of various types, e.g. informal invitation, a reply to an informal invitation, thank you notes, etc. Students should be familiarized with formal invitation and its reply. They should be shown how business letters are written and replied. A letter ordering a business firm for certain merchandise should be different from a letter of enquiry or request. Students should be told how an application is written formally and how a complaint is made about a clearly defined requirement.

BOOK REVIEW

Students are usually asked to write the review of a book, which is different from writing a book report. The latter consists mainly of retelling the plot of a book. Students of junior classes could be asked to write a report on the contents of the book; those of the senior classes could be asked to write the review of a book. The review contains a critical appraisal of the book. It discusses its plot, the development of its characters, its social background and the reporter's reaction to all these points.

DIALOGUE

A dialogue is a conversation in a play, a book or a film. It takes place at least between two persons: a speaker and a listener. The participants in a dialogue take turns to speak; when one person speaks, the other listens. When he/she stops, the other person responds. In a civilised society, people take turns to speak; they do not interrupt the speaker unless he/she is saying something objectionable or intolerable. Here is an example.

JULIA :	…I am going to make you dine alone with me on Friday and talk to me about everything.
EDWARD :	Everything?
JULIA :	Oh, you know what I mean. The next election and the secrets of your cases.
EDWARD :	Most of my secrets are quite uninteresting.
JULIA :	Well, you cannot escape. You dine with me on Friday. I have already chosen the people you are going to meet.
EDWARD :	But you asked me to dine with me alone.
INDIA :	Yes, alone. Without Lavinia. You will like the other people. But you care to talk to me. So that's all settled.

The Cocktail Party by T.S. Eliot, p. 302

This dialogue is taken from a play. Julia has invited Edward to a party without Lavinia, his female companion, and that for her means being alone with him.

The dialogues should be in a colloquial language. It should be informed and should sound natural. It should sound like a piece of conversation in one's real life. Students should be asked to write dialogues on topics they are familiar with. They should be incidents that have really happened.

SPEECHES

A speech is a formal talk than a person gives to an audience. It is an oral exercise but if one wants to deliver a good speech, one should prepare a written speech. While organising a speech, the speaker should remember that it has to be given orally without any written script.

While preparing the written draft of a speech, the speaker should keep the following points in view:

- He/she should know whom he/she is going to speak to. The topic should be interesting to the *audience*.

- His/her *orientation* should depend on the nature of the audience. If the people he/she is going to address are friendly and known, his/her style should be informal. If they are going to be unknown, it should be formal.
- He/she should keep the purpose of the talk in view. Is it going to be informative or explanatory? Should he/she try to be argumentative and convincing?
- He/she should try to keep the audience entertained.

The speaker should keep all these factors in view while preparing his/her notes. He/she should organise his/her thought in a logical and coherent manner. Even if the speech is going to be merely entertaining, it should be systematic. It should have a definite beginning in which he/she should explain what he/she is going to talk about. The major portion of the speech should be devoted to the elaboration of the theme. The final portion should summarise his/her presentation and lead to a neat conclusion. The speech should be prepared keeping the time allotted to him/her in view and he/she should be able to wind up his/her speech in time.

In brief, the outlines of the speech should be similar to that of an essay but the speaker should not ignore the difference between the two genres. The essay is to be read by a reader whereas the speech is to be heard by a group of people. It is the duty of the speaker to keep the interest and attention of all members of audience in view. They should not be distracted at any point.

DIARY

A diary is a personal notebook which has space for each day of the year in which one has to write down things one has done or has to do in the future. Such diaries are called engagement diaries. It may contain information such as the following:

November 10

10 a.m. :	I have to attend the English class from 10 am to 12 noon. Mrs. Sharma will explain what the passive voice is and when it is used.
2 p.m. :	I will participate in the department seminar till 4 p.m.
4.30 p.m. :	I will go to the central library and consult a book on the advantages of keeping a diary.
7 p.m. :	Light refreshment and tea with Janardan, my classmate.
9.30 p.m. :	Dinner
10 p.m. :	I will watch the news bulletin on the television.
11 p.m. :	I will go to bed.

A diary is kept to write down the experiences one undergoes every day. It is also to record one's thought. Here is an example.

> I got up late and got ready in a hurry to catch the school bus. By the time I reached the bus stop, my school bus had left. I took an auto rickshaw. It got in a traffic jam and reached my school late. The assembly was already in session. I waited outside the hall and joined my classmates when the assembly adjourned.
>
> The first class was on mathematics. I realised that I had forgotten to take the home assignment with me. Mrs. Joshi was very angry. I did not like it, for I had missed my assignment at home for the first time today. I thought it was not fair on her part to equate me with those who are irregular very often.
>
> The science class was all right. I enjoyed the social science teacher. She is so knowledgeable. I could not enjoy my game class. The experience of the mathematics class came back to me. It haunted me. Any way, it was my own fault. Had I got up on time, it would not have forgotten the math notebook. I shall try to be punctual and careful from tomorrow.

TRANSACTIONAL WRITINGS

They deal with *notes*, *notices* and *letters* relating to financial transaction, including advertising. Below we reproduce some notices and advertisements to highlight their main features.

IPICOL

INDUSTRIAL PROMOTION AND INVESTMENT CORPORATION OF ODISHA LIMITED

(An ISO 9001-2008 Certified State Level Nodal Agency)

IPICOL HOUSE, JANPATH, BHUBANESWAR - 751022, ODISHA, INDIA,

Tel: (O): 0674 2542601 Fax: 0674 2543766

REQUEST FOR PROPOSAL FOR SELECTION OF AN AGENCY FOR INVESTMENT PROMOTION ADVISORY SERVICES

Tenders are invited from eligible firms for "Selection of an Agency for Investment Promotion Advisory Services".

The complete Request for Proposal Document shall be available on the website **www.investodisha.org** and **www.odisha.gov.in** from **30th October 2015** onwards.

Fig. 11: Notice (i)

A notice is written or printed information which is usually put in a public place. It is an announcement or advertisement in a newspaper or on television. It may be even a warning of something that is about to happen. Here are three samples of notification. The first is a request for a proposal for selection of an agency for investment promotion advisory services. The second and third pieces given below are tender notices. They formally invite certain agencies to do some services.

Preparing a notice is a specific task. The writer knows what the task is and what is expected of the person or agency which is going to respond to it. The notice should mention it in a clear and straightforward language. The notices cited above do not mention the task specifically. They ask the expected respondents to see the relevant website and get the details.

The notices and advertisements are written in a formal language as is clear from notices (ii) and (iii).

HINDUSTAN SHIPYARD LIMITED
(A Govt. of India Undertaking)
Ministry of Defence
Gandhigram (PO), Visakhapatnam-530 005
An ISO 9001 company

TENDER NOTICE

Sealed tenders are invited from potential and experienced contractors for Outsourcing of Supply of material for 06 x 10 T BP Tugs for IN. Further details, please visit hsl website : www.hsl.nic.in.

DGM (SBO)
949379 2004/2354

Fig. 12: Notice (ii)

TRAVANCORE TITANIUM PRODUCTS LTD
A Government of Kerala Undertaking
Kochuveli, Thiruvananthapuram -695021
PH: 0471-2502163, FAX: 2501533

E-TENDER NOTICE

Quotations are invited in two bid system for **"Fabrication, Installation, Testing and Commissioning of new 1600 Mts. capacity Acid Storage Tank in TTPL premises through e-procurement system of Govt. of Kerala"**. For more details visit : www.etenders.kerala.gov.in.

Tender ID: 2015_TTPL_40703_2

Sd/- , Chief Manager (Commercial)

Fig. 13: Notice (iii)

Fig. 14: Advertisement for Pond's BB+ cream

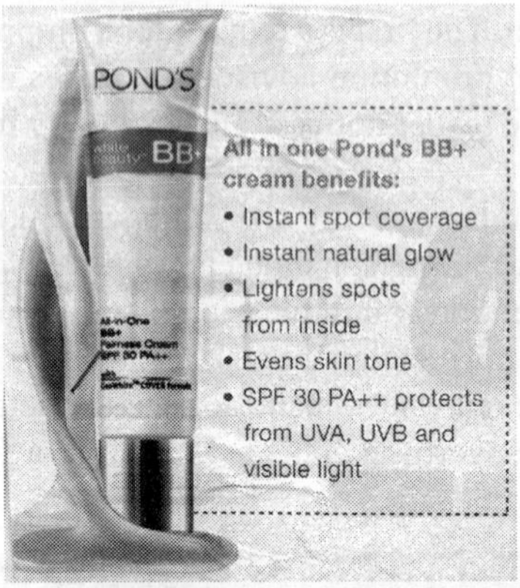

Fig. 15: Advertisement for Pond's BB+ Cream

Fig. 16: Advertisement for Pond's SPF 15 PA++ Cream

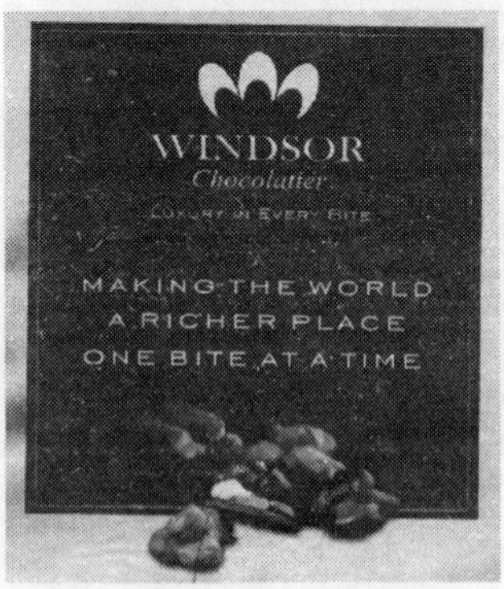

Fig. 17: Advertisement for Windsor Chololates

ADVERTISEMENTS

An advertisement is a kind of notice telling people about a product, job or service. It could also be about a picture or a film. It is written to highlight the quality of the product that is meant to be sold. Since it is connected with the buying and selling of a product, it is called 'commercial' as well. The main objective of the advertisement is to augment the sale of the product. The advertisement trier is to keep this objective in view and speaks of its high quality to make it saleable.

Three advertisements about a branded pond's cream (Figures 14-16) refer to the same item for sale: Pond's cream. They keep the obsession of an average Indian in view and promise an instant spotless fair complexion. Figure 14 suggests that Pond's BB + cream is the outcome of a breakthrough research by the Pond's Institute. Figure 15 tries to be more impressive by using medical jargon. It tells us how its SPF 30 PA protects a person from UVA< UVB and visible light. Figure 16 is more detailed and personal. It emphasises the need for a fair skin without any blemish during the festive season and highlights that Pond's SPF 15PA removes facial dullness and age spot. It uses medical jargon to impress the potential customers and sounds more impressive. It appears more like a medical expert's advice than an advertisement for the sale of Pond's cream and that is its success.

Figure 17 is an advertisement for Windsor chocolates. It is more sophisticated and subtle. It seeks the fairness of the corporate sector and appeals them to order for it as a Diwali gift. The advertisement uses only a few words but the photographs of almond, cashew nut and walnut are prominently displayed.

While writing an advertisement, the writer should highlight its quality.

- It should have a personal tone so that the reader feels that it is in his/her personal interest to use it.
- The quality should be highlighted in such a manner that the reader is tempted to buy it.

The style and quality of an advertisement depend on who it is meant for. If its aim is to draw the attention of the upper class, it uses sophisticated understatements. If it is for general public, it is more straightforward. It uses lofty expressions and promises, and appeals to the reader's sentiments. It is wordy and loud mouthed. Students should be able to appreciate the various types of advertisements. They should associate the styles with the purpose for which they have been published and talk about its success in relative terms.

The advanced high school students could be asked to present a written *report* of an event in or outside the school. It could be a report on a meeting or discussion session they have attended.

CHARTS AND DIAGRAMS

There are three types of charts: a bar chart, a flow chart and a pie chart. Each of them is useful in its own way.

Bar Chart

A bar chart shows a diagram that uses narrow rectangles of different heights that display comparative figures involving an item. For instance, figure (18a) shows the relative decline of the number of students studying in junior schools in Kerala.

It shows that the number was 52.44 lakh in 1990 which came down to 50.02 lakh in 2003 and 37.70 lakh in 2015-16. The figure shows the gradually declining number of students. It leads the news commentator to comment that the lack of enough children has turned many privately run schools into uneconomic institutions.

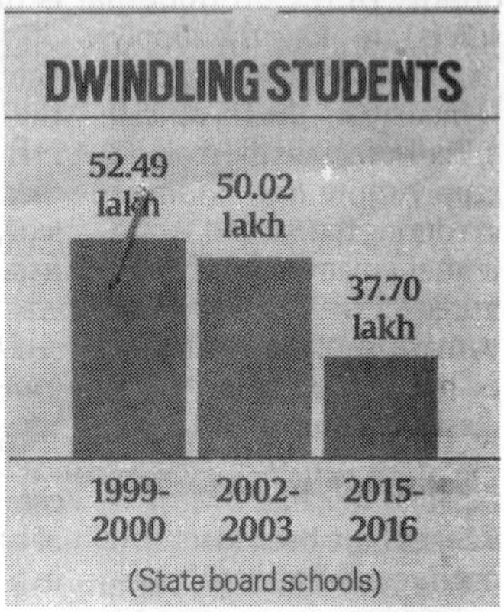

Figure 18(a): Number of School Students in Kerala

Figure (18b) is based on the Report of the Central Water Commission Government of India. It shows how the per capita availability of water is gradually declining in India. Both these figures compare the status of a single topic chronologically. There is another way of comparing the relative significance of bars, as in (18c).

Figure 18(b)

The bar chart in (18C) compares the public and private sector banks on various parameters, such as the number of ATMs, points of sale (PoS) devices, and credit and debit cards issued and used. The data show that the public sector banks have steadily increased their shares in most of these parameters over the last four years.

Flow Chart

A flow chart is a diagram that shows the connection between different stages

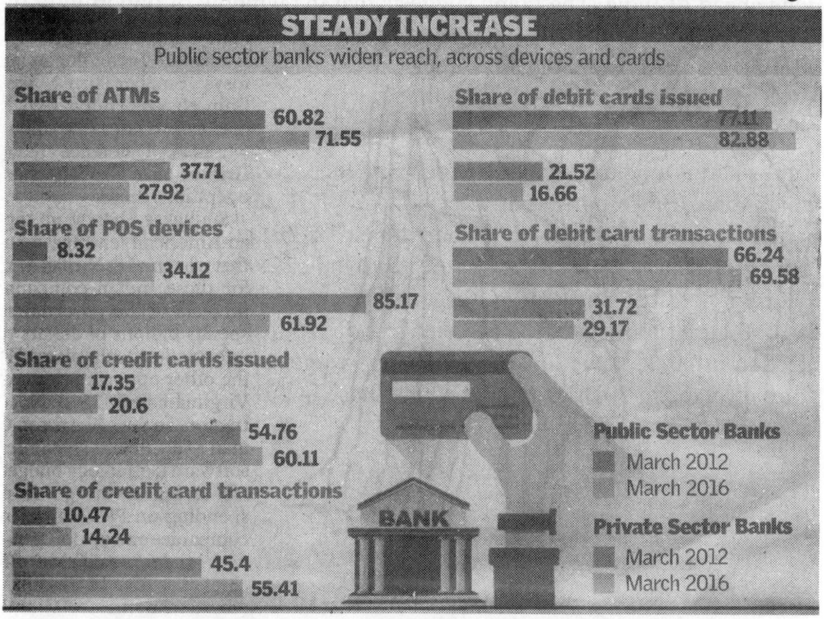

Figure 18(c)

of a process or parts of a system. It shows the sequence of movements or action of people or things involved in a complex system of activity.

For instance, the flow chart in (19a) shows the curves of the share in global apparel export by India, Bangladesh and Vietnam. It is clear from the

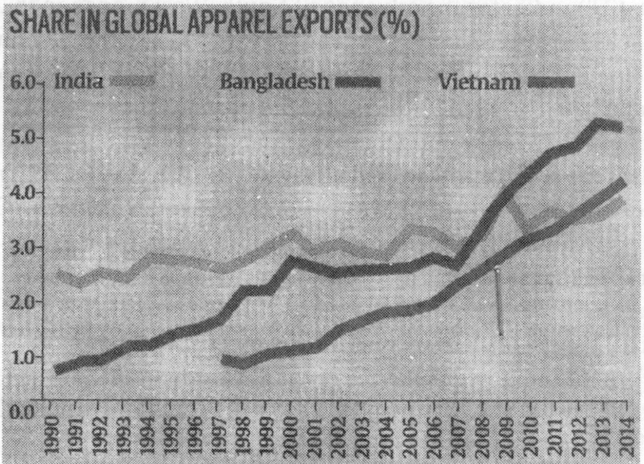

Figure 19a

chart that India started at a point higher than Bangladesh and Vietnam but is now it is a point lower than that of Bangladesh and even Vietnam has marginally gone ahead of India. The graph suggests that the window of opportunity of going ahead in the export of garments is narrowing and India needs special effort to regain its potential advantages.

Pie charts

A pie-chart is a type of graph in which a circle is divided into sectors each of which represents a portion of the whole. Each sector shows the size of the particular amount in relation to the whole. For instance, Figures (20a) and (20b) represent two pie charts, Figure (20a) indicates the percentage of votes that each political party got in the general election in assembly in Assam in 2016. Figure (20b) states the percentage won by these parties in the general election in 2011. If we look at the charts, we get an idea of how shares of votes changed in 2016 in comparison to those in 2011.

Fig. 20(a)

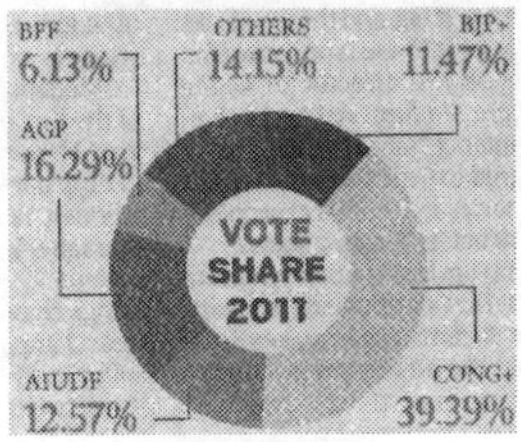

Fig. 20(b)

Maps

Sometimes facts are presented through the markings on a map. For instance, the map in (21) indicates the advance of South-West monsoon in 2016. The monsoon season started this year by the end of May. By the first half of June the deficiency in rainfall was about 25 per cent which was sufficiently compensated in the South of India by the end of June. Then it moved to Central India, Western UP, Delhi and Chandigarh and covered nearly the whole of Punjab, Haryana and Rajasthan. Till now (the first week of July) Central India was 12% deficient, North-India was 2% deficient and North-West 27 percent deficient. The Rainfall has been below normal in Bihar, Uttar Pradesh, Gujarat and Central Maharashtra but the Mat department is optimistic about better days ahead.

Figure 22 shows recent increase in the connectively of mobile service in those pockets of India which have left wing extremism.

Maps are used very frequently to locate something somewhere or to indicate the movement of something.

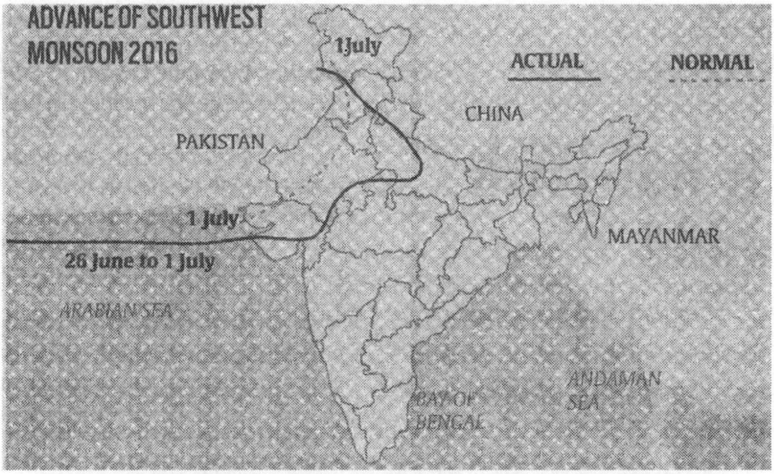
ADVANCE OF SOUTHWEST
MONSOON 2016
1July
ACTUAL
NORMAL
CHINA
PAKISTAN
1 July
MAYANMAR
26 June to 1 July
ARABIAN SEA
ANDAMAN
SEA
BAY OF
BENGAL

Fig. 21

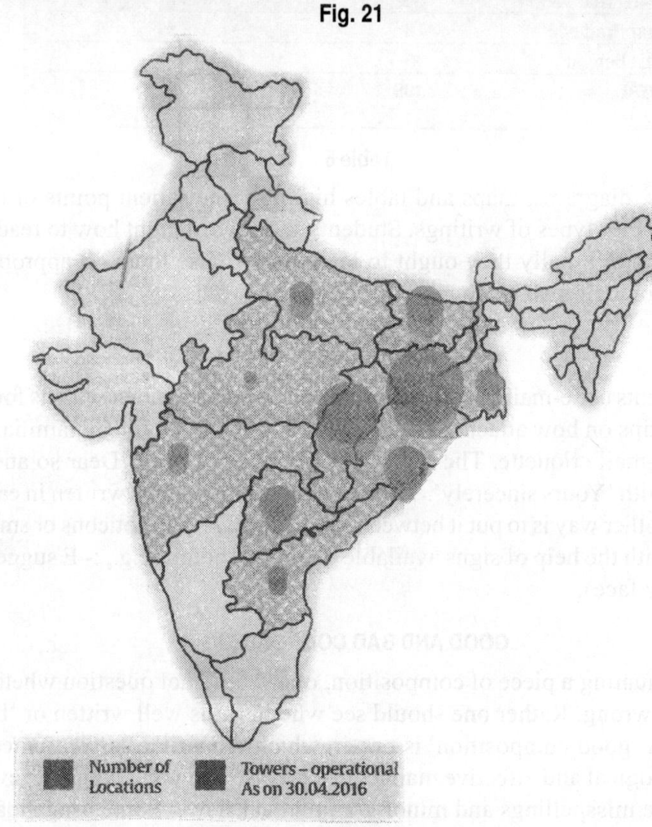
Number of
Locations
Towers – operational
As on 30.04.2016

Fig. 22

Tables

Tables are used to mention facts. It may be noted that the map in (22) does not give a concrete picture though it points out specific locations. The table in (8) completes the task.

OPERATIONAL TOWERS		
STATE	NUMBER OF LOCATIONS	TOWERS OPERATIONAL AS ON APRIL 4, 2016
Andhra Pradesh	54	45
Bihar	184	184
Chhattisgarh	497	489
Jharkhand	782	561
Maharashtra	60	56
Madhya Pradesh	22	22
Odisha	253	149
Telangana	173	77
Uttar Pradesh	78	78
West Bengal	96	87
TOTAL	2,199	1,748

Table 8

Charts, diagrams, maps and tables highlight the salient points of one's essay and other types of writings. Students should be taught how to read and interpret them. Finally they ought to learn how to use them on appropriate occasions in their own writings.

E-mails

Since students use e-mail services, they should be made familiar with its format, including tips on how attachments are e-mailed. They should be familiarised with the e-mail etiquette. The message usually starts with 'Dear so and so' and ends with 'Yours sincerely'. The most important point is written in capital letters. Another way is to put it between asterisks (*...*). Emoticons or smileys are used with the help of signs available on the keyboard (e.g., :- E suggests a very happy face).

GOOD AND BAD COMPOSITION

While evaluating a piece of composition, one should not question whether it is right or wrong. Rather one should see whether it is well written or 'badly written'. A 'good composition' is one in which the writer has presented his ideas in a logical and effective manner in a precise and vivid language even if it has some misspellings and minor grammatical flaws. Some usage may be questionable, but if the writer makes his/her point clear and interesting, most readers will consider it "good", regardless of its flaws. A correct composition, on the other hand, has no misspellings, grammatical flaws or errors in usage. The writer's presentation may not be logical and effective, but it is judged to be "correct" if it is grammatically correct. Ideally, a presentation should have a worthwhile content as well as flawless style of writing.

While going through a piece of composition, the teacher emphasizes, knowingly or unknowingly the mechanics of the language – its spelling, grammar and usage. While a reasonable teacher does not ignore them, his/her chief attention is on what is said. He/she emphasises the "wholeness" of the composition, the entire process by which its parts (words, sentences and paragraphs) are put together. He/she tries to see whether the sequences in which the contents are arranged are logical and interesting. He/she knows that good paragraphing is largely a matter of organising and structuring one's major ideas on a given topic.

Failure to teach effective writing is often a result of failure to relate verbal expression to its deeper roots in feelings and thought. Rigid compositional demands often inhibit the internal process involving perceiving, experiencing, feeling and thinking. The personal reality occurs first as an internal formulation and then as a verbal realisation. In fact, the act of writing is a process of realisation of verbal expression rather than a specialised verbal activity. The emphasis should, therefore be more on the relation of written expression to mental activity, on craftsmanship. When children give expression to their felt responses, their writing will be worthwhile.

DIFFERENCE BETWEEN THE COMPOSITION OF L_1 AND L_2 WRITERS OF ENGLISH

Most British experts make a distinction between those who have English as their mother tongue and those who use it as a second language. They argue that those who use English as L_2 are already proficient in writing their composition in L_1 and it has its impact on what they try to express in L_2. However, this claim is disputable because no one is the native writer in a language by birth. A L_1 speaker has to acquire the skills of writing at school the same way as a L_2 speaker of English. The only difference is that he/she may have the knowledge of a larger vocabulary and structures of the language than the person who has acquired it as L_2 has. In short, the difference between L_1 and L_2 writers is largely a matter of degree. All writers continue to improve their language and knowledge of the subject-matter. If a person acquires the knowledge of L_1 and L_2, there is little difference between their writings in L_1 and L_2. If the knowledge of L_2 is acquired later than that of L_1, there is bound to be a difference in their quantum of knowledge and, consequently, their writing ability. However, if there is a strong motivation to acquire English as L_2, the difference will be minimum. The skills acquired for writing in English is the same whether one uses English as L_1 or L_2. It is the knowledge of the subject-matter that makes the difference. If one has acquired the writing skill late, one may be proficient in composition-writing in L_1 and it may impact one's efforts to write something in L_2, but it need not be the case. In this context, one may look at Cumming and Silva (2008) who provide a comprehensive overview of research on second language writing in English.

To sum up, the student has to plan how to write a piece of composition. He/she should see how the work is going on and then check how well he/she has finished the job. The teacher could monitor the task.

- The student should revise what he/she has written in order to improve its language and content.
- He/she could get the feedback from the teacher to redo the text, if necessary. If he/she reads his/her piece aloud in the class, he/she can get the reaction of his/she peers, which could also be of much value while revising the text.

UNIT 6. LANGUAGE, LITERATURE AND AESTHETICS

17

Different Creative Forms of Language

> "Literature is the better part of life. To this it seems inevitably necessary to add, provided life is the better part of literature."
>
> —Wallace Stevens

WHAT IS LITERATURE?

When English derived the word *literature* from Latin *litters* (letter of the alphabet) via French in the fourteenth century, it meant 'book learning' in general. This generalised sense of literature meaning 'anything written on a subject' persists even now in expressions such as 'scientific literature' or 'advertising literature'. Hazlitt (1825) considered the writings of Issac Newton (a physicist) and John Locke (a philosopher), great literature. It was in the nineteenth century that the term started being used only for creative and imaginative writings (e.g. poetry, drama, novel short story) and all other writings (e.g. fictional and historical writings) were called non-literary. Even now it is debatable whether biography, autobiography and travelogue should be called literature. We are not clear whether cultural studies (including writings on feminism) are literary pieces or not. We keep on debating whether products of popular media broadcast (e.g. soap opera, pop songs pulp fiction) are literary. While Rene Wellek and Austin Warren (1963) observed that only works with the creative function are literature, Peter Widderson (1990) thinks the proper study of literature is "everything else". The debate will continue but it will not prevent the common man from studying what he/she considers to be literature.

LITERATURE IN THE SCHOOL CURRICULUM

In many parts of the world today there is a growing demand for teaching English as a language of international communication. It is argued that people need functional English for trade, commerce, administration and higher academic activity, and the study of literary English does not contribute much to it. We consider such a view erroneous. Literature provides the L_2 learners of English with necessary impetus to gain proficiency in the language. It reinforces all the *four basic skills* that language teaching emphasises. When a piece of literature is introduced to a class, it is first read aloud by the teacher or one of the students. It provides an exercise in listening. After listening to the lesson, the student reads it quietly to understand its content. The reading is followed by a question-and-answer session which provides him/her with an opportunity to speak. The group discussion on the topic gives him/her another chance. When he/she is given an assignment to write answers based on the lesson, it gives him/her a lesson in writing.

When a student thinks about the lesson he/she has read, he/she interprets it in a new light. Reading literary pieces awakens and enlarges his/her perception of the world around him/her. It encourages him/her to explore and appreciate feelings and emotions in an appropriate way. He/she comes across various types of conflicts, frictions and clashes in the world of literature which enrich his/her sensibility and social awareness. They enable him/her to have an effective understanding of the culture that is represented in a literary work and prepares him/her better to face life. At least for these reasons, the study of literature needs to be pursued.

NEED FOR LITERATURE IN THE SCHOOL CURRICULUM

To talk about the place of literature, especially English literature, in the contemporary school curriculum in India is to talk about a subject and a programme which are in a state of flux. It is more fashionable to talk about English for Special Proposed (ESP) (for example, business, like writing advertisement, reportage of events as is done in newspapers, radio and television) than about it as a piece of literature. But is that all? Language is not a commodity which can be bought, used and disposed of. It is an inescapable part of our life, and the most effective means to communicate our thought. It articulates our analytical ability and rational faculty. As Edward Sapir, a distinguished linguist of the first half of twentieth century, observed "It is primarily a vocal actualisation of tendency to see realities symbolically". As Sussanne C. Langer comments, "...our primary world of reality is a verbal one. Without words, our imagination cannot retain distinct objects and their relation. The transformation of experience into concepts is the motive of language." This view places language at the centre of human experience; it places imaginative rather than logical faculty, at the centre of linguistic life and growth. The goal of learning a language should, therefore, be the imaginative verbal experiences, i.e. literature. As imagination is vital to human life, so is literature, its verbal manifestation. As creative impulse is a part of our imaginative reading and creative composition. Our language curriculum should include books of great variety of values and vision. It should open to students a variety of possibilities. As literature offers an effective opportunity for such a study, it liberates both students and teachers from narrowness of mundane technical knowledge; it offers an opportunity to teachers to draw their ingenuity and students, the power to broaden their vision and to think and act creatively. It makes teachers informal and flexible and offers them an opportunity to improvise. The need of the hour is to have a student-centered, response-oriented teaching to explore, rather than teach, literature with students.

OBJECTIVES OF STUDYING LITERATURE

As discussed above, the main objective of discussing literature at school is to let students learn how to appreciate imaginative and creative writings. It means they have to acquire the ability to analysis the language of a written text to understand what is distinctive and significant about it.

The specific objectives are:

- to approach the text analytically and critically;
- to acquire the ability to compare a specific text with other texts and find out whether they represent different cultural contexts;
- to apply different critical approaches to unravel its complexity;
- to understand unfamiliar terms and difficult idioms so as to interpret the text accurately and adequately;
- to learn to enjoy reading literary pieces;
- to develop a personal response, i.e. to be able to react personally (and not to reproduce the reaction of the teacher, the guide or the peers).

Literature is primarily meant for enjoyment and the reader must be able to infer, interpret and evaluate what he/she reads to enjoy it. He/she should be able to discover the theme of what he/she reads and work out how it has been developed. Only then a proper interpretation is possible.

LITERATURE AND MEDIA

The term *media* is the plural of Latin *medium*, meaning 'middle' or 'between'. The media means two interrelated yet distinct things. In one sense its means 'modes of communication' which enable people to communicate. We have *print media* such as newspapers and magazines, *tele media* such as telegraph, telephone, television, etc. The term *electronic media* includes films, videos, cables, satellite and the internet.

Media have both technological and sociological dimensions. We have popular media and high-tech multimedia. Print media is a popular media; it comprises newspapers and magazines. Electronic media have audio or audio visual dimensions. They create a real and a virtual world, a world of sounds created by a computer in which people can communicate with each other, play games and pretend to live another life. It creates a world of illusions, a world of make-believe. In a broader sense, the world of literature is also a world of make-believe. To an extent, both create similar effects.

Language is a code which is used as a means of communication. The basic code is the same but it is realised differently in different media. We have the spoken language and the written language, and the spoken language within the written language. There is a difference between casual conversation and formal speech, between dialogue and monologue. And we have written literature (e.g. novels, stories, plays) which contain both formal and informal languages, oral and written. We have the language of the real world and of the virtual world, the languages of a chat in our drawing room and in a classroom. The words on the page may contain one's well-considered thought as well as a fantasy. The world of literature rolls all of them up. And it is true not only of an advanced language like English but of any language, howsoever primitive or underdeveloped it may be. It becomes obvious when literature available in these languages, whether oral or written, is translated into English. Translation, then, is a medium of understanding the world of those spoken languages we do not know and understand.

CREATIVE WRITINGS

Reading someone's writing is a unique and complex experience because a writer is an interpreter of experience. His/her writing is a creation which reflects the peculiarities of his/her perception. His/her interpretation of the world reveals his/her own image of the world.

Differences in experience become even more evident when we read the creative writings of writers of different cultural backgrounds. Language provides the way of conveying chunks of experience. It is difficult to tell how deeply it is involved in the ways people understand the world. But we know that people have personal biases which are subtly revealed in their use of the language. A writer tries to discover how others differ from him/her and thus perceives how he can write something interesting and significant. His/her messages come out of the unique features of his/her perception of the world. We read his/her writings to understand his/her message. If every writer perceived the world the same way, he/she would be interpreting the same world and conveying the same message. Then there would be nothing new or original to read. While reading a piece of writing, we contrast it with similar writings we have read. It is the uniqueness of the contrasting features that catches our attention.

CONVEYING SHARED EXPERIENCE

We may say a writer's message is an unshared experience. His/her whole effort is to share it with his/her readers. He/she tries to describe a man, a scene, an act, a thought or any experience as truthfully as he/she can. However, he/she knows that he/she is limited by the subject he/she has chosen, by his/her own knowledge of the subject and by his/her ability to convey that knowledge to his/her readers. In spite of his/her limitation, he/she tries to convey his/her personal experience to us in an imaginative and intelligent manner.

A work of literature is not merely a set of sentences grouped in paragraphs which are integral parts of a text. That is what we find in a book on physics or chemistry as well. What makes literature different from non-literary works to the impact it leaves on us. Like a book of science or social science, it informs us. But that is its least important target. Its aim is to stir our feelings. It does not just make a statement about the world, it exemplifies an attitude, a point of view towards it. In this way, it gives us an insight into our lives and helps us to understand ourselves as well as others. It enlarges our acquaintance with human motives and feelings and sharpens our perception about them. It deals with profound and universal human problems in a way which enriches our understanding. A good moral requires us to understand human nature and social values. It may also make us feel indignant against social injustice, brutality and exploitation which a powerful news dispatch may not be able to, in spite of the social commitment of the reporter.

There are various ways of studying literature, out of which socio-psychological approach seems to be more appealing. Historical approach helps us in understanding a piece of literature which discussed some aspects of social development at a particular point of time. The formalist approach is a refined version of the textual approach. It focusses on words, images, symbols and the theme of the text. However, sometimes it is so much preoccupied with the treasure hunt that it overlooks its social relevance.

RELEVANCE OF THE TEXT

While trying to analyse and interpret the text accurately, the reader is bound to find out whether the experience of reading it is relevant to him/her. It is specially so for the reader whose mother tongue is different or who belongs to a different culture. Sometimes he/she may come across a piece of literature which provides a completely different background. Understanding even such pieces is relevant for two reasons. First, it exposes the reader to a different culture and broadens his/her vision. Secondly, even a piece written against a different cultural background may represent the same human values though they may be communicated somewhat differently. That is what we find in the literary contribution of speakers of English living in South Africa, Australia, New Zealand and India. A more diverse example is found in English literature translated from other languages. It is heartening to note that they represent the same basic human values as literature produced by the native speakers of English.

THE SPEAKER AND THE SITUATION

In every piece of literary work, there is someone talking about something. That someone is the speaker, implicit or explicit, and that something is the situation about which he/she is speaking. For instance, in "Lucy Gray or Solitude", the speaker is a lover of nature, possibly the poet and the situation is the solitary environment in which Lucy grew up. She was lost in the wild world but, in the eyes of the poet she is immortal because she has become a part of nature.

ATTITUDE

An important component of a piece of literature is the attitude of the author, Lucy has lost her life, because she did not get the kind of protection she could have got in an urban society. The attitude of the speaker is clear. He mourns her loss but is happy that she has become a part of nature and is presumably, happy to be so.

In a literary work the speaker may focus his/her attention upon something in the situation that makes us think of an abstract concept. Thus, he/she makes the concrete image symbolic which carries a broader meaning.

THEME/THESIS

When we come across a book of fiction we have not read, we want to know what it is about. In answer to this question, one can talk about the situation and character. That is a specific answer. But one can talk about its general concept, i.e. the *theme* which is the abstract subject of the novel. All works of art have themes but they may or may not have a thesis. The work has a thesis only if it has a profound and deep meaning and it explains a significant aspect of human experience. The thesis of the work is revealed when we have a deeper understanding of the text.

STRUCTURE AND TEXTURE

A work of art has many parts, some of which are dominant and some are subordinate. The relationship among the dominant parts constitutes its *structure* and the relationship among the subordinate parts is its *texture*.

PLOT

The main role of the structure is to bind the development of the work together, to connect its beginning with its end. The result of what lets things together is its *plot*. It may be complex or simple.

MODES OF LITERATURE

Out of four modes of literature, poetry, drama, fiction and essay, *poetry* is hard to define. Some poems are regular, they are metered. Some are irregular, they are free verses. For instances, all poems prescribed in *Literature Reader* (for class X) are regular. When the stressed syllables of a discourse occur regularly and form a pattern, the poem is regular. Metrical discourse emphasises the sounds of words to a greater extent than is normal in an ordinary discourse. Free verses do not have such recurrence of stressed syllables but they do exhibit rhythmic organisation. Sometimes it relies on repetition, as in "The Hollow Men" by T.S. Eliot.

We are the hollow men
We are the stuffed men
hearing together
Head piece frilled with straw.

A poem, whether regular or blank verse, conveys feelings. It is rich in figures of speech and other poetic devices.

A prose *fiction* is a narrative with a plot. Unlike a newspaper dispatch or a narrative on the television, it tells a story which could have happened but did not actually happen. It has a spatial and temporal perspective upon the event it describes. Usually it describes conflict, sometimes between two or more people, sometimes within the single individual. The conflict takes place within a particular background. The narrator has a distinct position from which he/she observes the conflict.

Plays, like fiction, are narratives which develop into a situation and have conflict. However, they are different from fiction. When the fiction is dramatized, its pure narrative passages disappear. The dramatist depends mainly on dialogues. What cannot be conveyed by dialogues is compensated by stage direction, action and costume of actors. In a drama the speaker is withdrawn to the background but he/she controls the play by the scene she/he selects, the dialogues he/she uses through characters and the action that takes place.

Essays include narrative, descriptive, expository and argumentative writings. However, a literary essay is different from essays on history, social science and science. It is different from reportage and news analysis. A literary essay is evocative even if it is a narration or description. It has some complexity which non-literary essays do not have. Scientific writings which have these qualities may claim to be literary, though the readers may not agree. Whatever we may think of non-literary writings, they contain important information and knowledge. A student is supposed to have the habit of reading and interpreting them as well.

TRANSLATION AS A CREATIVE ACTIVITY

While translating from one language into another, good translators follow the principle of *equivalence* i.e. as nearly as possible. The translated work should create the same effect on the reader as was produced by the original. Experts say that translation is a "search for approximate analogies". The translator should first find out whether unconditional (i.e. literal, faithful) translation is possible. If not, he/she looks for adaption (i.e. free and natural translation). As Gertrude Steiner points out, "The complete, penetrative grasp of the text is an art whose realisation can be precisely felt but is nearly impossible to paraphrase or systematize". The translated text should have approximately the same communicative power that the original has.

In the process of selecting an appropriate word or expression, the translator faces several problems especially in translating cultural terms. For instance, the word *dharma* has been translated as *duty* or *right* (righteousness) by some and *discipline*, *piety*, *rule* or *system* by others. While translating *Samskar*, a Kannada novel by Anand Murty, A.K. Ramanujan had little difficulty in handling its occurrence in the text, he chose context bound appropriate words in English but he had enormous difficulty in translating the title of the novel because it represented all those connotations and more. He left it untranslated. If an exact equivalent is not available, the translator has to look for some compensatory devices for its restitution. If needed, he/she can add notes to clarify the significance of the original metaphors or other literary devises used in the original text. As every language has its own mechanism to present a notion, a strict adherence to the form of the original language may not be desirable. Perhaps translators from Indian languages to English are so much culture-bound that they tend to stick to the literal translation as much as possible. They do not feel that their main concern should be to translate the thought contained in the text as naturally as possible. We are not advocating the case for adaptation or recreation. What we want to emphasise is that the translated material should be able to create the same effect that the original does.

For understanding the creative process of translation of a poem, we produce below a stanza from *Subh-e-Azadi* (Freedom's Dawn) by Faiz Ahmed Faiz.

> Ye dagh dagh ujala, Ye shab-gazida sahar
> Vo intazar tha Jiska, Ye wo sahar to nahin
> Ye wo sahar to nahin jiski arzu lekar
> Chale the yar se mil jaege kahin na kahin

LITERAL TRANSLATION

> This stain covered day break, this night bitter dawn
> This is not that dawn of which there was expectation

This is not that dawn with longing for which
The friends set out (convinced) that somewhere it would be met with.

TRANSLATION BY V.K. KIERNAN

The leprous day break, dawn night's fangs have mangled
This is not that long looked for break of day,
Not that clear dawn in quest of which those comrades
Set out believing that in heaven wide void....

TRANSLATION BY DAVID MATTHEWS

This pitted down, snake-bitten sky of morning
We waited for this day. It came at last
But this was not our hope of heaven's dawning –
The dreams of our comrades cherished in the past
(Hope against hope, we looked towards the sky...)

SARVAT RAHMAN'S TRANSLATION

This blemished light, this half dawn by night half devoured
Is surely not the dawn for which we were waiting
This cannot be the dawn in quest of which hoping
To find out somewhere friends, we all set out

The three versions of the opening lines of the poem are different on surface but there are some common points. They all try to capture the spirit of the poem. The poet and his comrade had hoped for a bright day break when India would gain freedom but when it came, it was stained with the blood of those who were victims of communal riots.

The first translation calls it 'this leprous day break', the second, "the snake-bitten sky of the morning' and the third, the blemished light this half dawn by night half devoured.

Each translator has tried to capture the idea, behind '*Ye dagh dagh ujala, ye shab-gazida sahar*' (literally, this stain-covered day break, this night bitten dawn) in his own way.

Mr. Rahman calls the dawn of freedom 'the blemished light... half devoured by night'. *Blemished* means spoilt that is beautiful. It captures the main point of the poet but only partially. Matthews calls it 'pitted dawn snake-bitter sky of morning. 'To pit' is 'to make a hole'. To be the pits is used to refer to the worst example of something. The 'snake-bitten sky' is a contrived expression and is not a natural expression in English. Compared to these two, Kiernan's 'this staincovered daybreak' sounds more natural. 'This might bitten dawn' is also approximately appropriate. Faiz repeats the line '*ye wo sahar to nahin*'. 'It is not that dawn' to emphasise the point that this was not the freedom that people had longed for. Kiernan captures the point by repeating the line 'this is not the dawn'. This emphasis is missing from the other two translations. For these reasons we consider Kiernan's translation better than the other two. It may be pointed out that some other translators have also tried their hands on this poem but we have selected only these three for comparison. We have kept our comments confined to the appropriateness of the translation while keeping the intentions of the original lines in view.

The teachers may select some Indian language poems which have been translated in English and encourage students to discuss their appropriateness.

NEED FOR TRANSLATION

Those of us who have read English literature have not only read eminent novelists, story teller, poets and dramatists of English but also famous novelists, poets, dramatists and literary essayists of French, German and Russian. We have read Gustan Flanbert, Emile Zola, Victor Hugo, Honoré de Balzac, Andre Gide Marcel Proust, Albert Camus, Jean Paul Satre of France, Thomas Mann, Gunthar Grass and Franc Kafka of Germany and Leo Tolstoy. Turgenev Iyodor Dostevasky, and Anton Chekhov of Russia. We have read the plays of Nikolai Gogoi and Turgenev, the poems of Goethe, Rainer Rilke, Baudalair, Paul Valery and Mallarmé, none of them in the language in which they wrote them. We have read their English translations and become familiar with the socio-cultural situations they are referring to. It is difficult for an average reader to have a mastery over all other languages to read and appreciate original works but it is not difficult to read their English versions, appreciate them and be even influenced by them. Translations of literary works into English have enabled the first and second language learners of English to widen their knowledge and emotional experience.

As India is a multilingual country, it is not possible for an average speaker of Hindi to learn Bangla, Marathi, Gujarati, Kannada and Tamil to read famous literary works written in these languages but it is easy to read them if they are available in Hindi or English. There are individual collections and anthologies published by Sahitya Academy and National Book Trust but they are not always to the mark. While preparing an anthology of Indian writings in English during the fifty years of independent India (1947-1997) Salman Rushdie went through dozens of translations in English, but could select only one translated text, S.H. Manto's Toba Tek Singh. Rushdie regretted that he had to ignore good writers of Indian languages because of "their translations inadequacies rather than their own". The lack of first rate writing in translation can only be a matter of regret, he observed. There are English translations of Tagore, Premchand, Mahasweta Devi, Rahi Masoom Raza, Srilal Shukla and others but their translations do not come up to the level of the originals. On the other hand, some Indian writers who write originally in English have produced literature which has distinctly Indian flavoure and can stand the list of international writings in English. In short, we need good translations of literary works of Indian languages in English.

VARIETY OF ENGLISH LITERATURE

Till nineteenth century, literary historians and critics talked about only British writers when they discussed English literature. In twentieth century, American authors also started being discussed even in England. In recent years, we have started discussing writers in English from Canada, Australia, New Zealand, South Africa, India and other countries as well. Patrik White (Australia), Coetzee (South Africa), Chinua Achebe and Wole Soyinka (Nigeria), V.S. Naipaul (Trinidad) and Salman Rushdie (India) are internationally acclaimed English authors who have retained the flavour of the country they originally come from. It has led people to think about not only varieties of English language but also English literature. It has added richness and colour to English literature. The high school students may not have opportunity to study their works but they need to be told about these new trends.

The post-colonial non-British/American writers have indigenous themes which they develop sometimes in indigenous idioms. For instance, the stylistic feature of complex Indian English that native English critics have noted are lengthy sentences, bookish (rather than colloquial) vocabulary and habitually formal expressions (Platt 1984:149, Jenkins, 2015) and the use of modal *could* and *would* for *can* and *will* respectively [Trudgill and Hannah (2002)].

Chinua Achebe, a Nigerian English writer, observes, "the African writer should aim to use English in a way that brings out his message best without altering the language to the extent that its value as a medium of international exchange will be lost. He should aim at fashioning out an English which is at once universal and able to carry his peculiar experience". (as quoted in Jenkins 2015:209). Similar opinion has been expressed by Nguagi wa Thiong'o (1986), another Nigerian, Samuel Abidi (2011) of Cameroon and some others. Indian writers in English also hold similar views. In short, English has reached a stage in the post-colonial, globalised world where it has to maintain its international standard and incorporate as much regional flavour as is in consonance with it.

CONTEMPORARY CREATIVE WRITINGS IN INDIAN ENGLISH: POETRY

The tradition of writing poems in Indian English began with Toru Dutt and Michael/Madhusudan Dutt and was developed by Rabindranath Tagore,

Aurobindo Ghosh, Sarojini Naidu and others. Tagore's *Gitanjali*, Aurobindo's *Savitri* and Sarojini Naidu's '*The Golden Threshold*' made their mark. Harendranath Chattopadhyay continued the tradition and gave it a realistic twist.

Among the contemporary Indian poets in English Don Moraes, Nissim Ezekeil, Kaki Daruwala, A.K. Ramanujan, Jayant Mahapatra, Gieve Patel, Keshav Malik, Arun Kolatkar, Kamla Das, Arun K. Mehrotra, Adil Jussunwala R. Parthasarthy, Pritish Nandi and P. Lal have made significant contributions. Their poems deal with changing social structure and values as well as personal conflicts. Salman Rushdie (1999:XI) commends some of them (esp. Ramanujan, Kolatkar and Mahapatra) for coming up to international standard. As Kaki Daruwala observes, "While poets observe to hone the language to his purpose, the language also has its way in poetry," Kamla Das knows it well when she writes.

> "... Why not let me speak in
> Any language I like. The language I speak
> Becomes mine; its distortions, its queerness
> All mine, mine alone.
> It is half English, half Indian,
> funny perhaps, but it is honest.
> It varies my joy
> My longings, my hopes
>
> —*Introduction*

In spite of inadequacies that Kamla Das refers to Indian poets try their best to accomplish real poetry. *Modern Indian Poetry in English*, edited by P. Lal (1969) represents typical samples of such poets. Poets like Vikram Seth have explored new ground.

FICTION

While discussing fiction in Indian English we cannot ignore Mulk Raj Anand, the author of *Two Leaves and a Bud*, *The Untouchable* and *The Coolie* who treated the underprivileged section of Indian society with sympathy and respect. Nor can we ignore Raja Rao, the author of *Kanthapura* and *The Serpent and the Rope* who tried to communicate some aspects of Indian culture to the English speaking world. However, it was R.K. Narayan who made a significant contribution by referring to the conflict between traditional static India and modern India eager to progress. His *The Vendor of Sweets* is a beautiful example of this effort. He created Malgudi, an imaginary town and made it vividly real. *The Malgudi Days*, *The Man Eater of Malgudi* and other similar books deal with Indian situations in a mildly funny manner. G.V. Dasari, wrote a funny novel *All About Mr. Hatter* in which he made "the first genuine effort to go beyond the Englishness of the English language" (Rushdie XVI), I. Allan

Sealy's *Trotter Nama* is directly influenced by Desani, and so is Rushdie, to an extent. Ved Mehta's autobiographical fiction is also impressive. Anita Desai's *In Custody* and *Games and Night* are very acute and poignant. Salman Rushdie's *Midnight's Children* is undeniably a part of the story of India since independence. It is unique in many ways and so are *The Satanic Verses* and *The Moor's Last Sign*. Ruth Prawer Jhabvala's novels are the voice of a rootless intellectual in search of regional identities. Rohinton Mistry has a kind of realism that sets him apart and so is the charming prose of Vikram Seth in *A Suitable Boy*. Arundhati Roy's '*The God of Small Things*' has a charm of its own and so has Jhumpa Lahiri's '*The Interpreter of Malodies*' and Upamanyu Chatterji's '*The Incredible American*", Amitabh Ghosh's '*Son of Poppy*' (triology) Aravinda Adiga's '*The White Tiger*' and Kiran Desai's '*Strange Happenings in the Guava Orchards*' are highly original works. The number of fiction writers in Indian English is increasing every year but many of them are social chronology rather than fiction.

DRAMA

Though classical Sanskrit literature is well-known for plays and every educated Indian is familiar with them either in original or translation, contemporary Indian writers in English have not made any significant contribution. Rabindra Nath Tagore is well-known for his plays such as *Sanyasi* or the Ascetic, *Chitra*, *The King and the Queen*, and *Karna and Kunti*, their English version is hardly popular. Gieve Patel's *Princess*, Gurucharan Das's *Larrin Sahib*, Erna Watchgandhi's *Asylum* and Dinu Mehta's *Mythmakers* have some good points and have been staged well. Nissim Ezekiel's *Marriage Poem* is a tragi comedy, *Sleepwalks*, a one act farce, and *Nalini* and *Songs of Deprivation* are also well known. Some critics view him more favourably than other Indian English playwrights. Though Indian society is full of conflicts and contrasts, no writer has tried to exploit them suitably in his/her play. Pritish Nandy has also written some plays which have been staged well.

MISCELLANEOUS LITERATURE

Mahatma Gandhi's *My Experiments with Truth* and Jawaharlal Nehru's *My Autobiography* are fine contribution to this genre. No less significant is Nirad C. Chaudhuri's *The Autobiography of an Unknown Indian*.

The non-literary creative essays, travel accounts, memoirs and the like should provide models for students to think afresh and practise writing similar pieces.

The teacher should encourage students to narrate their own experiences orally as well as in writing. The oral narratives of personal experience can motivate students to write them down Experience comes to us from actual circumstances of our life as well as from the world of imagination, primarily from the works of literature. The type of non-literary texts we have referred to in this chapter can provide a solid background for writing free composition.

Students should be made aware of the way a creative writer goes through the process of writing. He/she makes a hypothesis and verifies it for its consistency and usefulness. He/she tries to have a rapport with his/her reader by enriching his/her immagination. His/her arguments are either inductive or deductive which should have sound logical basis but sometimes they fail to be so. A clever writer appeals to the emotions of his/her reader or misguides him/her by hasty or complex, misleading arguments. Students should be warned against such pitfalls when they come across such writings. They should be helped in developing a judicious and natural outlook. Only then they can interpret any writing objectively.

ENGLISH TRANSLATION OF CONTEMPORARY INDIAN LITERATURE

Apart from the contribution of Indian writers in English, there are others who have produced significant literature in various Indian languages and are available to English-speaking public in India and abroad through their translation. Among the Bengali writers we may mention Premendon Mitra, Samar Sen, Naresh Guha, Buddhadeva Bose, Subhas Mukhopadhyay, Shankar Ghosh, Jivanand Das, Saumintro Sengupta and Tarak Sanyal, Ananda Shankar Roy, Bonophul, Sunil Gangopadhyay, Tarashankar Banerjee and Amiya Chakravarty. They are available in English translation and so are Badal Sirkar's plays. Among Hindi writers translated into English are Premchand, (*The Gift of a Cow* translated by Gordon Rodermal), Rahi Masoom Raza (*The feuding families of village Gangauli* tr. by Gillian Wright), Shrilal Shukla (*Rag Darbari* translated by Gillian Wright), translated by (#), Yash Pal (Short stories, translated by Corinne Friend), Ramdhari Singh 'Dinkar' (The Sun Charioter translated by Paul Stanslow *et al.*) and many others. Anthologies like Modern Hindi Poetry (by Vidya Niwas Mishra) have also made their mark. Mohan Rakesh's short stories, plays and novels are also available in English. Specimen of both *Nai Kavita* (New Poem) and *Nai Kahaniyan* (New Short Stories) have been published in the *Journal of South Asian Literature* published from East Lansing, USA.

In Urdu, we have the English translation of Faiz Ahmad Faiz by V.G. Kiernan who has also published poems from Iqbal. *Hundred Poems* by Faiz translated by Sarvat Rahman, '*An Anthology of Urdu Verse in English*' translated by David Matthews, '*The Golden Tradition, An Anthology of Urdu Poetry*' by Ahmad Ali are also available. Besides, English versions of some other poets have been published in the *Journal of South Asian Literature*. In prose Saadat Hussan Manto has been translated by several persons, including Lelie A Fleming and Douglas Brown. 'Qurratulain Hyder' has translated her own novel *Aag Ka Dariya* as *River of Fire*.

18

Understanding Different Forms of Literature

I. POETRY

Poetry [is] the best words in the best order. —S.T. Coleridge

Poetry is the record of the best and happiest moments of the happiest and best mind. —P.B. Shelley

The study of poetry' means, 'a detailed investigation and analysis of a poem' with its thorough understanding. The process involves arousing and directing one's curiosity to understand and appreciate its contents and style of presentation. Some poems are easy to comprehend, others are puzzling or complex. Poems are usually written in a language which is chosen and organised with great care and skill. It may be very close to the spoken form, but developed in an effective expression. Its close analysis is an indirect exercise in the students' power of self-expression. We may look at "This is just to say" by William Carlos Williams:

I have eaten
the plum
that were
in the icebox
and which
you were probably
saving
for breakfast.
Forgive me
they were delicious,
so sweet,
and so cold.

The poem refers to an ordinary event in a simple language. The poet has eaten the plums that somebody had kept in an icebox. He apologises for doing so without permission but in what an innocent way!

Another poem, an extract from "Burnt Norton" by T.S. Eliot gives us a profound message:

Time present and time past
Are both perhaps present in time future,
And time future contained in time past.
If all time is eternally present
All time is unredeemable.

It is written in a simple language and has a straightforward logic. What appears to be 'future' right now will be 'present' after sometime and 'past' after a while. Future, thus, is potentially past and past is another form of present. It means future and past are contained in present. It implies that time is unable to be regained. The given extract illuminates the complex philosophy of time in a simple language. Its logic provokes our mind. That is how a simple statement becomes evocative.

If we look at a two-line poem 'The Fly', by Ogden Nash, we are simply charmed:

God in his wisdom made the fly,
and then forgot to tell us why.

We often wonder what the utility of the fly is; for it seems to be of no use. The poet has alluded to the theory of creation, as given in the Bible. Every creature God has created serves some purpose but for the fly. The poet wonders why God forgot to tell us why he created it. The statement is short but its implication is not, for it makes us doubt the assumption behind the theory of creation. Compared to it, his poem, "The Pig" makes a categorical observation:

The pig, if I am not mistaken,
Supplies us sausage, ham and bacon.
Let others say his heart is big –
I call it stupid of the pig.

We get sausage, ham and bacon out of the flesh of the pig when it is killed. Rather than calling it the generosity of the pig, the poet calls it its stupidity.

RHYME AND RHYTHM

The two poems of Ogden Nash have another marked feature. In the first poem, 'fly' rhymes with 'why'. In the second poem, 'mistaken', rhymes with 'bacon' and 'big' with 'pig'. The phrases have been arranged in such an intelligent way that they rhyme. The rhythm binds the lines into a pattern and contributes the sense of the poem.

One point a child notes, perhaps sub-consciously, is that the words of a poem move in rhythm. He/she finds it in nursery rhymes, such as the following:

One	two
Buckle	my shoe;
Three	four,
Knock	at the door;
Five	six
Pick up	sticks.
Seven	eight
Lay them	straight;
Nine	ten
A big	fat hen

The child not only observes that the first line rhymes with the second, the third with the fourth (and so on) but also that there is a pause almost in the middle of each line which accounts for the arrangement of stress.

"In the Bazaars of Hyderabad"[1] by Sarojini Naidu, the second line rhymes with the fourth (displayed… brocade) and sixth (Jade) and the third with the fifth (silver…. amber) in the first stanza. The same rhyme scheme is there in the second stanza, except that the fifth line rhymes with the first (vendors…. peddlers). All other stanzas have almost the same pattern; the second line rhymes with the fourth and sixth.

In "Daffodils"[2] by Wordsworth, each stanza has six lines in which the first line rhymes with the third (cloud…. crowd) the second line rhymes with the fourth (hills…. Daffodils) and the fifth with the sixth (trees…. breeze). All the four stanzas have the same pattern. This rhythmic arrangement makes the poem symmetrical.

In "Two's Company"[3] by Raymond Wilson, the first line rhymes with the second (but…. tut), the third with the fourth (tattle …. rattle) and so on until the end of the poem.

SOUND IN POETRY

The structure of sounds has an important place in the structure of a poem. Expression through sound structure involves pitch, stress, duration, voice quality, articulation, the phonetic timbre (a distinctive musical quality) and pattern in time.

Alliteration is the repetition of the same sound (s) or syllable in two or more words of a line. It has a noticeable artistic effect. It produces emphasis or euphony. The most common type of alliteration occurs at adjacent or closely connected words, as in 'full fathom five thy father lies' or in 'To sit in solemn silence in a dull, dark, dock'.

1-3 All these poems are presented for Class VII in *Oxford Pathways*, approved by the CBSE.

Assonance is the resemblance of sounds between syllables of nearby words. For example, in "slopping mast and dropping prow", there is assonance (slopping … dropping).

The *reduplication* of phonetic pattern is another device to produce sound-effect, as in 'hickory, dickory, dock' or 'goosey, goosed, gander.' *Repetition* of a sound, syllable, word, line, stanza or metrical pattern is a basic unifying device of poetry. For instance, in "Never seek to tell thy love", William Blake says:

"I told my love, I told my love,
I told her all my heart"

In 'Rime of Ancient Mariner', Coleridge repeats parts of an expression:

"I looked upon the rotting sea,
And drew my eyes away;
I looked up the rotting deck,
And there the dead man lay.

In "Stopping by the woods in a snowy evening", Robert Frost repeats the entire line to bring out the meaning:

And miles to go before I sleep,
And miles to go before I sleep.

To grasp a sense of the stanza, one should read it aloud and trust its rhythm. It gives pleasure in its own right but the pleasure is at its highest when the rhythm cooperates with the sense of the poem.

IMAGERY

Another point that strikes the mind while reading a poem is its *imagery*. An image is the reproduction in the mind of a sensation produced by a physical perception. In literature, it is treated as a figure of speech. It is regarded as a special poetic device which is used as a part of a larger whole. It explains, clarifies and makes vivid what the poet is talking about.

Similes and metaphors are used as imagery. A *simile* is a comparison of one thing with another, explicitly mentioned by the word 'like' or 'as'. In 'Daffodils' the poet compares himself to a cloud that feels lonely and moves along valleys and hills.

I wondered lonely *as* a cloud…

A *metaphor* is a condensed simile. Instead of saying 'X' is like 'Y', it says 'X' is 'Y'. It shows the relation involved in the identity of X and Y. It is usually used to clarify, define or describe something relatively unknown in terms of something well-known. For instance, the ripples on the surface of the water have been identified with the movement of flowers; they both appear to be dancing in the breeze. It makes an expression intelligible while retaining its conceptual independence.

Personification is a manner of speech endowing things or abstract ideas with life. In 'Daffodils' the flowers have been personified and so have been the stars in the sky; they dance and toss their heads like human beings. In "Mirror"[4] by Sylvia Plath, the mirror on the wall has been personified and is expected to answer the questions put to it.

Lexis

The most common exploitation of words in poetry is the use of *collocation* to produce new ideas and interesting images. The combination of words is generally guided by 'selection restriction' which demands semantic compatibility. When Vikram Seth refers to 'moonlight cold and pale' or Shakespeare talks about 'guilded monuments' 'unswept stone' or Shelley refers to 'colossal wreck, boundless and bare', Coleridge points out the 'bright' and 'glittering' eyes of the mariner', they all have the semantic compatibility of expressions in view. Sometimes the collocational restriction is deliberately violated to create a kind of poetic effect which will not be created if it is adhered to. In Seth's 'The Frog and the Nightingale', the frog admires his own 'splendid baritone'. He persuades the nightingale to sing like him by puffing off her lungs with her passion. When she puffed up, burst a vein and dies, the frog calls her 'a stupid creature' far too nervous, far too tense, far too prone to influence.' The choice of collocation is rather unexpected but it creates the desired effect. Thus, in a poem, adherence to collocational restriction is as effective as its deviance.

Ambiguity of words is another aspect exploited in poetry. In 'Subject, Object, Sentence' Stephen Spender takes advantage of the ambiguity of these words.

> Subject thought, because he had a verb
> With several objects, that he ruled a sentence.
> ....
> *Subject*, the dictionary warned, means someone ruled by person or thing
> ...he must be *objective.*
> Thus, with a shock he realised that sentence
> Like subject-object is treacherously double...
> A sentence is condemned to stay as stated
> As in life sentence.

Syntax

Dislocation of the word-order is a special feature of some poems, for instance, the poems of E.E. Cummings. The use of fragments of a sentence linked by

---

4. This poem is a part of the CBSE text book, 'Literature Reader', for class X.

simple repetition is the special features of Ezra Pound's poems. In 'Daffodils' by Wordsworth we come across:

' Ten thousand saw I at a glance'

It has an object-verb-subject order which has been effectively used. And so is the line

And then my heart with pleasure fills
And dances with the daffodils.

We may look at a stanza from Phorb Cary's 'A Legend of North Land'

'So up she went through the chimney,
Never speaking a word
And out of the top flew a woodpecker,
for she was changed to a bird—'

'Up she went' is definitely more poetic them 'she went up'.

So far, we have discussed the way a poem is written, especially its style. Let us now look at its form.

NARRATIVE

A narrative poem is one that tells a story. It has two basic types: epic and ballad. Originally an epic was performed by an individual and a ballad by a dancing and singing group. Initially the narrative was about gods; later on it involved demi-gods and human beings as heroes. S.T. Coleridge's *The Rime of the Ancient Mariner*[5] is one of the best narrative poems of the romantic period. It displays his artistic sense of the ballad. He creates a situation in which he presents weird tales with an uncanny ability. The intensity of his feelings lends an air of its own to his narrative. The style seems to be more important than the story. The first two parts of this long ballad-style poem have been prescribed for students of Class X. Parts of the poem (in quotation marks) have been written in the first person (supposed to have been spoken by the Mariner) and the rest in the third person (where the narrator comments on the event). Wordsworth's *The Prelude* is a narrative in which he tells us the stories of local events.

PLOT

The succession of events in the poem is its plot. Look at the following poem of Edward Lear:

There was an old man of Nepaul,
From his horse had a terrible fall;

5. A portion of the poem is prescribed for Class X by the CBSE.

But, though split into two, by some very strong glue,
They mended that Man of Nepaul.

Each line of this poem draws us on to the next. When we reach the last line, we know that the story is complete and we do not need to have another line. This forward movement, line to line, from the beginning to the end of the poem is its plot. The most common means of carrying the plot forward is its narrative. The poem tells a story and is finished when the story is finished.

Wordsworth's "Lucy Gray" is a poem of sixty four lines. The story of Lucy begins at line 13 and ends at line 56. The plot of the poem begins with line 1 and ends with line 64. The title of the poem is "Lucy Gray or Solitude" and its end is,

O'er rough and smooth she trips along
And never looks behind;
And sings a solitary song
And whistles in the wind.

In between is the story of Lucy but the story is not the plot of the poem. What happens between the title and the end of the poem is the slow emergence of an image of solitude: a solitary person, as inaccessible as a ghost. In this independence, there are loss and pathos for other people, but the solitary person has achieved a kind of freedom. The last line presents an image of a happy, independent life. There are changes in the vividness of narration, which indicate shifts in focus. They are events in the plot of the poem which are different from the events in a story.

"In the Bazaar of Hyderabad" is a descriptive poem which presents scenes in the shops of a merchant, a vendor, a goldsmith, a fruit seller and a weaver. The plot comprises all these and contains no story. Vikram Seth's "The Frog and the Knighingale"[6] contains a story but Sylvia Plath's "The mirror"[7] has no story but it has a plot. It consists of a series of questions which presuppose certain truths. "Snake"[8] by D.H. Lawrence describes the appearance of a snake at a water pool. The poet is simply charmed by its graceful movement but his educated mind tells him to kill it.

The plot of a poem demands an appropriate 'form' which gives shape and pace to it. It demands a mechanism of syntax that facilitates an arrangement of words in such a way that it moves without any impediment.

PRESENTING THE THEME

The aim of a poem is to present its theme in such a manner that it moves the reader. It depends on the mastery of the poet over his/her style. It also depends

6-8 All these poems are included in *Literature Reader* prescribed for Class X by the CBSE.

on his/her knowledge of the subject. If he/she knows it, he/she can find out appropriate words, images and rhythms he/she needs to use. He/she is confident that nothing else that comes to his/her mind belongs to the poem.

In "Not Marble, nor the Gilded Monuments"[9] Shakespeare compares poetry with monuments. In the first stanza he states that gilded marble monuments cannot outshine the bright contents and powerful rhyme of a poem. In the second stanza he points out that a devastating war can overturn the statues and well-built mansions but it cannot destroy the poem, for it is retained in people's memory. The poet has praised his friend in the poem which the future generations will remember till the world ends. The end-couplet asserts that the poem has immortalised his friend.

This poem is a sonnet which has three quatrains of four lines each. The first quatrain lets the theme of the plot and the next two quatrains elaborate it. It leads to the conclusion in the last couplet. The quatrains have the rhyme scheme of 'a, b, a, b' and the couplet, of 'c, c' which make the poem a sonnet. Each quatrain conveys a unit of 'meaning'. The poet uses alliteration such as 'marble.... monuments', 'princes.... powerful', 'stories..... sluttish', 'wasteful war', 'pace...... praise', posterity', etc. It personifies 'monuments' as well as 'poetry', war 'as well as 'Mars'. The poem focuses throughout on a definite theme and vividly describes an area of human imagination; it is an area of experience that its plot names and handles.

So far we have discussed some formal aspects of poetry which the teacher should keep in mind while discussing a particular poem in the class. Here are some general outlines which he/she should pay attention to.

1. Preliminary assessment

The teacher should make a preliminary assessment of the poem before introducing it to the class. He/she has to decide which aspects should be given attention to and what points need special explanation. He/she should find out whether the poet is addressing a particular person or people in general, whether the poem is in the form of a monologue or a dialogue, and whether it carries an underlying meaning. He/she should be practical in deciding how much background information should be given to a specific group of students.

2. Introduction

The necessary background against which the poem was written should be given. Special attention should be paid to socio-cultural factors if the L_2 readers are not aware of them.

---

9. The poem is prescribed for Class X and is in Literature # recommended by CBSE.

3. Presentation

The teacher should read the poem to the class because its true effect is obvious only when it is read aloud properly. That way its dramatic and rhythmic quality can be demonstrated. If available, a recorded version of the poem can be presented to the class. A repeated recitation can be arranged to make them grasp and appreciate the poem.

4. Discussion

A discussion can be initiated on general lines, such as

(i) Who is speaking in this poem?
(ii) Who is he speaking to?
(iii) What is the situation?, etc.

A specific discussion can centre around the poem, with special reference to its plot and the way it has been unfolded, its style (including its syntax) and its rhyme-pattern. The use of similes, metaphors, personification and other rhetorical devices, if any, should be illustrated during the discussion.

When the teacher is sure that all the details of the poem have been grasped, evaluative questions can be taken up. He/she can ask:

(i) Why did the poet choose this topic?
(ii) Do you experience the same thought/feeling?
(iii) What effect does the poem have on you?
(iv) Does it remind you of any other poem?
(v) Is the background of the poem different from yours? If so, in what sense?

Questions may be asked about the language of the poem, particularly about its unusual syntactic pattern, if any.

5. Reinforcement

Students should be given a chance to read the poem aloud to get a 'feel' for it. Not all students should be asked to read it aloud, for it will make the exercise dull and monotonous. Some poems may need dramatized reading which can be arranged by students.

6. Assignment

To reinforce the comprehension of the poem further, students could be given a written assignment on its plot and style and on the student's personal reaction to them.

To sum up, the process of teaching a poem involves making students familiar with its background, plot and style.

Students should be made acquainted with the rhyme scheme and rhythm of the poem. They should be made aware of:

- its sound pattern,
- its imagery
- its syntax
- its plot, and with
- how the theme has been presented.

The teacher should make a preliminary assessment and give the necessary background of the poem.

- He/she should present the poem orally.
- The discussion should aim at making the plot as well as style of the poem clear.

The question-answer session should meet this task.
If necessary, the presentation can be reinforced.

- Written assignment will further consolidate the comprehension and interpretation of the poem.

II. FICTION

The word 'fiction' involves imaginary literature in prose. It includes novels, novelettes and short stories. This genre constitutes fictitious prose narratives, typically representing characters and action with some degree of realism. The novel established itself with the works of Fielding and Richardson in the eighteenth century. Though character study was a major preoccupation of the novel, the element of romance was also prominent. Later on, the rudiment of realism developed. Some novelists paid special attention to socio-cultural reality; others were preoccupied with psychoanalysis of characters. Novelettes or short novels were written by distinguished novelists, such as Henry James, Joseph Conrad and D.H. Lawrence.

A short story is a prose narrative which is briefer than a novelette. It is more restricted in characters and situations. It is usually concerned with a single effect. Unlike in novels, characters in short stories do not develop fully. They concentrate on a single aspect of personality which is revealed or undergoes a change as a result of the development of the plot. The climax occurs usually at the end, though other arrangements are also possible.

Edger Allan Poe, an American writer, threw much light on the structure and purpose of the form. O'Henry popularised the surprising end of a short story, involving an ironic reversal of expectation. Some other writers showed the sordid reality and truth of life. Some concentrated on the inner psychological processes of characters and reduced action to a minimum. Novelists such as D.H. Lawrence, Katherin Mansfield and Ernest Hemingway became distinguished short story writers as well.

Detective stories are narratives of mystery, frequently involving a murder or a crime. In a detective story a perfect crime is reported which the detective solves by initially examining the situation and asking searching questions. He explains by the deductive process how the crime was committed and solves the puzzle, if any.

The Central Board of Secondary Education in India has not prescribed any novel for intensive study in English though it has prescribed short stories at various stages of school education. It has occasionally prescribed detective stories as well. There is a practical advantage in choosing a short story over a novel; the former is easier to handle in the class than the latter. A story can be read to a class in a single sitting, and studied as a single assignment. The whole class can experience reading a story in one go which makes it easier to discuss.

THE STUDY OF SHORT STORY

While discussing a short story the following elements can be taken into account:

(i) its setting
(ii) characters
(iii) narrative
(iv) narrative techniques
(v) language
(vi) theme

(i) The setting

It refers to the background in which the story is set. Sometimes it is discussed explicitly in the beginning of the story. For example, the story "The Enemy"[1] by Pearl S. Buck gives the description of the house of Dr. Sadao Hoki, a Japanese surgeon, in the very beginning. It is a stone house built upon rocks well above a narrow beach. It is a warm night, full of heavy fog. The garden is full of fog. It is in this atmosphere that an injured American flings out of the mist. 'The Third Level'[2] by Jack Finney does not set the background at all. Actually, the so-called third level of Grand Central Station in New York confuses people other than the narrator because they do not believe it exists. They consider it his fantasy. Rather than being the setting, it is believed to be the theme of the story.

(ii) Characters

The word *character* refers to an individual in a novel or story. It also refers to

1-2 Both the stories are included in *Vistas*, a supplementary reader in English for Class XII published by NCERT, New Delhi.

the mental or moral qualities distinctive of an individual. A short story has at least one individual whom it tries to perceive, assess and understand. Sometimes a character is presented as being good or bad but very often he/she is perceived as having various degrees of goodness and badness. A character in a fiction is what his/her author makes him/her to be. A student should be able to make up his/her mind about the intention of the author regarding the character of the individual he/she has created. For instance, in 'The Enemy', Pearl S. Buck creates the character of a Japanese doctor in the context of a war. An American prisoner is washed ashore in a dying state and is rescued by the doctor near his cottage on the beach. As a Japanese, he hates the American, but as a doctor, he considers it his duty to give him medical aid. He brings him home, operates upon his wound and nurses him back to health. His acts are against his patriotic sense and he reports it to the local military general to ease off his conscience. However, he does not want him to be handed over to the army and be kept as a prisoner. He conspires with the general to get him killed but it does not work. Finally, he helps him to escape to an island. Though he treats that American as an enemy he also remembers his own life as a student in America and fondly recollects how nice his professor was. On the surface level, it is the story of an injured American which tells us how he was rescued, nursed and made to escape but underlyingly the story represents the inner conflict of the Japanese doctor; even his wife shares this conflict.

'The Third Level' by Jack Finney explores the mental state of Charley, the protagonist, who imagines the third level of Grand Central Station in New York, a level which for others does not exist. The story is a study of human psychology through the puzzling characterisation of Charley who is lost in his fantasy.

The interpretation of a character is a valuable exercise while reading a story. Students may be encouraged to undertake it by answering questions as the following:

(i) What does the author tell us about the character?
(ii) What is the character supposed to convey about himself/herself?
(iii) What do other characters say (or think) about that character?
(iv) What does the character represent by his/her thought and action?

The student should be reminded that his/her assessment is to be based on what the author conveys in the story, and not outside its frame. Otherwise it will represent a distorted picture.

(iii) Narrative

In any short story the narrative, i.e., what happened and why, is of primary importance. The student needs to understand the intention of and motive behind the narration but he/she has to remember that social and historical forces also play their roles. In 'The Enemy', the background of the Second World War cannot be ignored; it is because of it that every American and Japanese hated each other. The hatred was so deep-rooted in the society that every servant of Sadao's household deserted him when he gave shelter to an injured American. 'Seventeen Oranges'[3] by Bill Naughton is written against the background of the prevailing poverty of the working class people which compelled the protagonist, Pongo, to commit small thefts.

(iv) Narrative Technique

There are various ways of narrating a story. In many stories, events normally follow one another in a strict chronological sequence. "The Enemy" is one such story. The injured American emerges in front of Dr. Sadao Hoki, a Japanese surgeon standing near the cottage. He is brought home, given first aid, nursed, operated upon and he leaves the cottage when he recovers. The sequential order has been maintained. In 'Patol Babu, Filmstar' by Satyajit Ray, no such order is maintained. When introduced, Patol Babu is an ordinary citizen who is offered a small role in a film. Later on, we are told, that he had been a successful stage actor in local theatres. Patol Babu goes to the place of shooting and then he recalls in a flashback what a famous stage actor had told him. Encouraged by those words, he plays his role well and comes back home without waiting to receive any payment.

In some of the stories (e.g. in 'The Enemy'), the story is told in the third person; in some, it is partially in third person and partially in the form of a dialogue between the characters, and in some others, in the first person. In 'Patol Babu, Film Star', the events are partially narrated by the author and partially conveyed through dialogues. In "Seventeen Oranges" it is mostly in the first person, in the words of the protagonist, and in 'The Third Level' it is entirely in the words of the main character.

(v) Language

The most straight forward type of short stories maintain a straight forward style throughout. In some cases the language reflects the thought and feelings of the characters of the story. For instance, in "The Enemy" Sadao gives reasons for considering the injured man his enemy in the following manner:

"I care nothing for him. He is my enemy." All the conflict in Sadao's mind is communicated in the following lines:

"I do not know myself what I shall do with you… I ought of course to give you to the police".

---

3. The story is included in *Pathways*, a textbook recommended for Class VII.

The character of the injured American is reflected in the language he uses. When Sadao asks him, "who gave you permission to leave your room?" he replies, "I am not used to waiting for permission".

"The Third Level" begins with the statement of facts: "The Presidents of the New York Central and the New York – New Haven and Hartford Railroad will swear on a stack of timetables that there are only two levels. But it crosses the world of reality when it says, "I say there are three, because I have been on the third level of the Grand Central Station". Charley speaks to his psychiatrist who calls his assertion "a waking dream wish fulfilment". This phrase is an apt expression for the mind of a man who wishes to escape the insecurity of his surroundings. It is "a temporary refuse from reality" as stamp collection was for him. The language of the story is a nice mixture of statements of fact and suggestiveness.

A short story may have allusions and understatements. It may use a complex language to indicate an intricate situation. We are more conscious of the language of a poet than of a fiction writer because in the latter we are pre-occupied with plot, action, situation, setting and characters. However, we cannot forget that all these are communicated through language and it is the teacher's task to demonstrate how it is done.

(vi) Theme

A short story has a certain theme. Sometimes the theme may be obvious, as in "Seventeen Oranges" but sometimes there may be an underlying theme which is parallel to the obvious narrative. "The Enemy" is the obvious story of a Japanese doctor and his handling of an escaped American prisoner of war but underlyingly it is the study of a person's professional commitment when it comes into conflict with social expectations; it is a conflict between one's nationalism in its narrow sense and one's humanist outlook. The classroom discussion should aim at clarifying these undertones. The student should be enabled to grasp simple concepts, as character, plot, events and surface themes before they come to the underlying theme. The technique of moving from the known to the unknown needs to be adhered to.

A detective story has a slightly different format. First, the issues to be investigated are put before the detective who asks the complainant a few preliminary questions. Then he and his associates, if any, visit the scene of the crime which is carefully scrutinised to make some inferences. Then the suspects are carefully interrogated, finally it zeroes down to one suspect who confesses the crime when he is confronted with fact. The hypothesis of the detective is based on the evidence and all escape routes are logically ruled out. That is how the problem is solved. "The Adventure of Three Students"[4] by Arthur Canon Doyle is one such story.

---

4. The story is included in *Pathways*, a course book approved for use in Class VII.

Mr. Hilton Soames, a lecturer at the college of St. Luke's complains to Mr. Sherlock Holmes, the detective, that a question paper for use in the examination the next day was missing from his table. He also asserts that it could not have been done by Barrister, the watch man.

Mr. Soames lives on the ground floor of a four storeyed building. Three students live in the rooms upstairs. They are going to appear at the examination. Mr. Holmes visits the scene of the crime and questions Barrister. Then he decides to visit the rooms of these students. He is welcomed by Gilchrist and Daulat Ras but the third resident refuses him entry to his room. However, Mr. Holmes does not suspect him. He suspects Gilchrist who is tall enough to see through the window the question paper lying on the table. He is copying the question when Mr. Soames approaches the room through the side door. Gilchrist hides himself in the bedroom of the Soames and sneaks out as soon as Soames is gone. Mr. Holmes reconstructs the event correctly. When confronted with the fact, Gilchrist confesses the crime.

METHOD OF PRESENTATION

The method of presenting these points are, more or less, the same as in presenting a poem to the class. As a preliminary assessment, the teacher should read the text before he/she goes to the class. He/she should be clear in his/her mind about the plot of the story, its narration, characterisation, language, etc.

The classroom presentation should be preceded by the cultural background of the story. The presentation involves the reading of the story in the class. It should be followed by a discussion on all aspects of the story: its plot, characters, expansion of the theme and the language used in it. For reinforcement another discussion may be held which should usually follow students' responses to the assignment. If the story has long dialogues, students may be encouraged to play roles and go through the dialogues. It will clarify the story further.

To sum up, while discussing a short story, including a detective story, the student should try to understand its following components:

(i) setting
(ii) character
(iii) narrative
(iv) narrative technique
(v) language, and
(vi) theme

Before presenting the story,

- the teacher should make a preliminary assessment of the text.
- He/she should discuss the socio-cultural background of the story.
- The story should then be presented to the class.
- It should follow a discussion of the story in the form of questions and answers, comments by students, and, if possible, by dramatizing the whole story.
- For reinforcement students should be given written assignments.

III. THE STUDY OF DRAMA

'Judge not the play before the play be done' —*John Davies*

Drama means a play for theatre, radio or television. It is a genre of literature designed to be represented on a stage by actors. There are many types of dramas, for example, comedy, comedy of manners, miracle play, morality play, mystery play, historical play, tragedy, etc. Drama is an ancient art form which has undergone many changes in course of time.

An one-act play is a short, unified, dramatic work. As a distinct dramatic type, it is generally limited in the number of characters as well as sequences. Usually there are two or three characters in one setting. A single incident with sufficient amount of exposition leads to a chain of events, without any subplot. The climax usually occurs at the end of the play. One act plays are favourite items on television and radio and for small amateur theatre groups.

Most texts in junior and senior high schools in India prescribe one-act plays. Sometimes they prescribe one act or sequences of an act from a larger play. For instance, *Literature Reader*, published by the Central Board of Secondary Education, has an extract from *Julius Caesar* by Shakespeare recommended for Class X.

THE SCOPE OF DRAMA

The study of a drama does not just involve the description of or discussion on events from real life; it is the recreation of life, as visualised by the dramatist. As such, it constitutes all the elements of real life. It includes not only the language used by actors but also their movements, positions, gestures and postures. The language it uses is supposed to be the spoken language of that period. It does not constitute merely the expressions uttered by the characters but also how they are uttered. In other words, it takes note of intonation, pitch, volume, emphasis, hesitation and other modulations of utterance.

Short (1996) talks about two levels of a dramatic discourse. At one level, we have the playwright and the reader/audience and the dramatic text conveyed by the playwright. At another level, there are characters and the message that is conveyed by their performance (i.e. dialogue and non-verbal messages). The discourse can be conveyed in the form of the following diagram:

Addressor 1 (Playwright)	→	Message (Text)	→	Addressee (Reader/Audience)
Addressor$_2$ (Character)	← → ←	Message (Dramatic Action)	← → ←	Addressee$_2$ (Character)

Fig. 24: Short's (1996) Model of Dramatic Discourse

The constant interplay between the text/performance and reader/audience and the characters or actors in the dialogue interaction creates meaning. These complex discourse aspects of drama and action, speech and perception need to be brought to the attention of students. They have to realise that dramatic discourse is similar to everyday conversation, though in the play with a historical background, it need not be the representation of present day speech. The dialogue conforms to the norm supposed to be present in the society in which the play is located. For instance, *Julius Caesar* is located in the history of the ancient city state of Rome and written against the background of Caesar's conquest of Pompey. "The Dear Departed"[1], an one act of play by Stanley Haughton, was written against the background of early twentieth century and highlights the moral degradation of the British middle class. "Michael"[2] is an adaptation of Leo Tolstoy's short story "What Men Live by" and has a feudal Russian background.

DISCOURSE: TURN-TAKING

The dialogues in all the plays follow the social convention of turn-taking and in all of them there is regular exchange between two persons. For instances, "The Dear Departed" begins with a conversation between Mrs. Slater and Victoria, her minor daughter, which is joined by Henry, her husband. When Mrs. Jordon, her sister, comes to the stage, she joins the conversation and so does Ben, her husband. None of them speak simultaneously except in extra-ordinary circumstances. Even when Victoria comes with the news that the grandfather is not dead, she does not interrupt abruptly. First she draws the attention of her mother and when she gets the permission (e.g. "what is it, child?"), she conveys the news. When the grandfather, Abel, appears on the scene, he speaks, what appears to be, abruptly but it is not so. When Mrs. Slater wants Mrs. Jordon to be quiet, she does not. Towards the end of the play she does not stop, even when Henry and Mrs. Slater request her to do so simultaneously. Ben and Henry are surprised when Abel announces that he is going to get married and they both speak simultaneously 'what?' In short, when turn-taking is broken, it is for a purpose and it serves it well.

In *Julius Caesar*, Caesar, Calpurnia, Brutus, Cassius, etc. take turn to speak. In the meeting that Brutus addresses after the assassination of Caesar, the citizens take turn to pass remarks but when they agree to what Brutus says, they speak in one voice. When Antony speaks, the citizens react one by one but, at one point when citizens need to be quiet, they say in one voice, "Peace, ho!"

---

1. Recommended for Class X by CBSE in *Literature Reader*.
2. Recommended for Class VII in *Oxford Pathways*.

DIALOGUES AND COOPERATIVE PRINCIPLES OF CONVERSATION

Dialogues are carried on the cooperative principles of conversation. Usually the characters follow the maxim of quantity and give the right amount of information to let the communication proceed. The maxim of quality demands that characters do not speak what they believe to be false. The maxim of manner demands clarity of expression and the maxim of relation demands the speakers to be relevant. Usually all the dialogues of a play follow these norms and, even if they are violated, they serve some purpose. For instance, when Abel, the grandfather of Victoria, comes to the stage, Victoria says innocently 'Oh, grandpa, I'm so glad you're not dead'. Mrs. Slater tells a lie, "Victoria says she is sorry about your head'. She violates the maxim of quality to adhere to other maxims. When Abel finds all others in the mourning dress, he asks Ben whether he was going to the funeral, he first says, "Oh, Yes" and then "No, of course not".

In the extract from *Julius Caesar*, the dialogue develops on a logical pattern. Caesar wants to go to the senate to address the citizens but his wife persuades him not to. She refers to a bad dream which alludes to Caesar's murder. When Brutus comes to persuade Caesar to go to the Senate, he interprets the dream in a different way and Caesar agrees to accompany him. On the way to the senate, he is stabbed to death by Brutus, Cassius and some others. When Antony comes to the scene, he wants to know the reason. Brutus addresses the citizens and persuades them by his reason that Caesar deserved death, for he was ambitious and wanted to be a dictator. Then Antony is permitted to speak. He repeats the charge against Caesar as levelled by Brutus, whom he calls an honourable man. Antony proves logically that Caesar was not ambitious. He brought all the plundered property and captured slaves to Rome, refused to be the king when he was offered the crown, and left a will in which he promised to give all his personal wealth to the state. When the citizens listen to Antony, they turn against Brutus and other killers of Caesar and call them traitors. They now want to avenge Caesar's death. All the dialogue is carried on in a civilised manner, according to the norms of polite discourse.

THE STYLE OF DIALOGUE

In *Julius Caesar*, the conspirators are very civil and polite while speaking to Caesar. They are neither abusive nor threatening. Even though Brutus knows how Antony feels after Caesar's murder, he is very polite to him and permits him to speak after his own funeral speech. In his speech, Brutus appeals to the citizens to believe him for his "honour" and listen to him with "awakened sense". He says that he admired Caesar for his bravery but hated him for his ambitions. He asserts that Caesar was killed to save Roman citizens from being enslaved. When Antony comes to speak, he says that, if Caesar was ambitious, it was his "grievous fault". He points out that Caesar had brought ransoms and slaves to the state, had thrice refused to be crowned and had bequeathed all his property to the state in his will and yet he was called ambitious. After listening to his speech, the citizens turn against the conspirators. It is because of the way facts are put before them. After every point Antony makes, he asks the citizens whether that was the sign of Caesar being ambitious, yet, very cleverly he goes on saying.

> "*But* Brutus says he was ambitious
> And Brutus is an honourable man".

He repeats this point and says,

> *Yet* Brutus says he was ambitious
> And, *sure* he is an honourable man".

When the citizens feel outraged, he says,

> "…. If I were disposed to stir
> Your hearts and mind to mutiny and rage,
> I should do to Brutus wrong, and Cassius wrong,
> Who, you all know, are honourable men
> I will not do them wrong; I would rather
> To wrong the dead, to wrong myself and you.

Antony shows Caesar's wounds to the citizens and points out where Brutus had wounded him. He calls it "the most unkindest cut of all". The skill of Antony's oratory lies in his recounting things what Brutus called his ambition in such a way that it shows his selflessness. The the sentence "he is an honourable man" becomes even more ironical because of the way Antony repeats this expression:

> "And Brutus is an honourable man"
> "Yet Brutus says…. "
> "And, sure, he is an honourable man."

He says that he did not intend to 'stir them up in mutiny' and asserts that he had "neither wit, nor words nor worth" to do so but the overall impact of his style is such that people are provoked to rise in mutiny against Brutus.

As against the oratory of Brutus and Antony, we have the cool, matter of fact dialogue of Abel in "The Dear Departed". He understands fully that none of his daughters likes him and that they pretend to show their love to him out of greed. He says that he would leave all his property to whosoever he lives with and then tells them that he is going to marry Mrs. Shorrocks and live with her. He does not say directly that he is going to disinherit his daughters but makes it clear to them by the declaration of his future plan.

In "On the face of it" Susan Hill draws the portrait of an alienated young man and a lonely old man without uttering any word of her own. It is the conversation between the two persons that brings out their characters. Both of them are disabled; the old man has a tin leg and the young man has an acid-burnt face. The old man observes the world with a positive outlook; the young man wants to keep himself aloof from the world. They talk about various things. The old man explains his philosophy of life; it is to see, find out and hear things around him. The young man goes home and tells his mother that he is going back to the old man "only to look at things and listen". And he does go back to the old man, in spite of his mother asking him not to. The old man has kindled the mind of the young man and aroused his curiosity, his will to look around and understand. The end has a philosophy behind the story, a positive attitude to life but it all comes naturally to the young man. It is the casual conversation between them that brings the play to the climax.

We have seen above how the plot of a drama is built with the help of its dialogues. But speech is not the only thing in a drama; it involves action as well. In *Julius Caesar* the action consists of the arrival of Brutus and his friends at Caesar's residence, their departure for the senate with Caesar, the murder of Caesar and the display of the dead body to the citizens.

Antony uses the wounds on the body of Caesar to incite anger among citizens and it leads them to move out to take revenge upon Brutus and his colleagues. The actions are well-synchronised with the utterance and the integration of the two elements creates the desired effect. However, it is not necessary that every play should be packed with action. For instance, there is not much action in "On the face of It", or in "The Dear Departed", yet they are meaningful and thought-provoking plays.

Like the novel, the drama has setting, characters, narratives, techniques, language and theme but the drama is more complicated than the novel. The names of the characters are given by the author but what they are like is to be reconstructed by the reader or viewer; it is never given directly by the dramatist. In other words, the printed words have to be converted into a live performance, whether it is done on the stage or imagined by the reader.

CLASSROOM PRESENTATION

Students should have an authentic impression of the play. It is necessary that they see a good performance of the play on the stage. Alternatively, they may be exposed to its film version, if available. In any case, the teacher should encourage the students in the class to have careful rehearsals of the play so that they can enact it on the stage. A good performance or even a good reading of the play can help a lot to bring the text close to the audience. The spoken language, with all its elements, can bring the effect of the drama to them.

Elaborate staging may not always be possible but even a rudimentary presentation is better than not doing it at all. When such dramatic activity is developed, the job of studying and interpreting the play becomes easy.

Discussion

After a reasonable presentation of the play, the class is ready to discuss its many aspects. Questions of searching type will encourage students to have insights into the meaning and implications of various speeches. The teacher can help students explore the interdependence of speech and action. While discussing these aspects, a reference to the actual text should not be lost sight of. The discussion should lead to a comprehensive and connected account of what happened in the play and what it means.

Background

Either before presentation or during discussion the teacher should provide the historical and socio-cultural background against which the play is written. The spoken text of the play is important but so is its background. While discussing *Julius Caesar*, the democratic nature of the citizen state of Rome should be made clear. While discussing 'The Dear Departed" a picture of modern world in the West should be presented to make it clear that the concept of joint family does not exist anymore and even the father is considered to be a burden. However, there is a deep-rooted desire to inherit his property.

Reinforcement

The characteristic form of reinforcement for a play is to prepare students to act it on the stage. It translates the printed text into action. In this process, attention is to be paid to the minutest details and their significance should be brought out. The teacher should encourage students to develop their analytical ability so that they can not only appreciate the movement of the play but also realise how it reaches its climax. They should be encouraged to write a critical appraisal of the play at the end of the whole exercise.

To sum up, a play should be enacted before its critical appreciation is attempted. That way, students can realise how speech and action go hand in hand to present a complete picture. The dialogues should be practised in a proper manner, paying attention to the necessary gestures and postures. The background of the plot should be discussed adequately and the setting should be realistic. The teacher should make students realise that a play is closer to life than any other form of literature because of its contextualised presentation. An analysis of the dramatic discourse involves highlighting the interaction between speech, action and perception. Students should be made to understand the role each of them plays in conveying the message of the play. The study of drama allows students to explore the analytical, linguistic and sociocultural aspects of life displayed in the text visually.

IV. OTHER LITERARY FORMS

So far we have discussed the problems involving the study of poetry, fiction and drama. However, a great deal of literature does not belong to any of these categories. For instance, there are biographies and autobiographies which are significant pieces of literature. There are travel accounts which are as interesting as fiction. Besides, theré are literary essays which are persuasive, argumentative, polemic or edifying. There are writings on personal accounts which are of great human value. Sometimes such writings are included in textbooks and studied at the high school level. Some scholars hold the view that no course on literature will be complete without some introduction to such works.

AUTOBIOGRAPHICAL PIECES

Vistas, the core course book, recommended for Class XII by CBSE, has a piece entitled "Memories of Childhood", one by Gertrude Simmons Bonnin (who wrote under the pen name 'Zitkala Sa') and another by Bama, a Tamil dalit woman. Bonnin writes about her early days in a boarding house in an American school. As a native American Indian, she was fond of her freedom but in the hostel she led a regimented life. For instance, when she went to the dining hall, she was supposed to keep standing till a bell rang. Even when she sat down, she was not supposed to start eating till another bell rang. She gives a vivid account of how she was forced to have a hair-cut. The account is as lively as a short story.

The second piece is a vivid account of the experiences of a dalit girl from Tamil Nadu. She gives a detailed account of what she saw on the roadside while going to or coming back from school. She tells her experience to her brother who is studying in a college. He makes her aware of the fact that they are dalits and are looked down upon by people of upper castes. She is told that the only way to rise up in the society is to have good education and to do well at it. She listens to her brother, works hard and stands first in the class.

The student should be made aware of the fact that autobiographies and biographies give the accounts of events in real life and there is nothing imaginary about them. Both these pieces have clear portrayal of the personality of their writers. They have a distinctive style and they narrate honest and undistorted human experience which might create genuine interest in students. Personal narratives encourage students to become critical readers and users of their style.

TRAVELOGUE

Sometimes travel accounts are included in the prescribed texts. They have the actual experience of travellers, which are of interest to students. A travel account includes not only the accounts of the places one visits but persons one meets and objects one comes across. It is usually entertaining and arouses the curiosity of readers to visit similar places. "A Pilgrimage to Tawang" is one such travel account by Verrier Elwin. It offers a graphic description of the natural beauty of Arunachal Pradesh and is marked by the high degree of empathy for the inhabitants of the region. "My Endless New York" is not a travel account but a sketch of life in New York, a multi-coloured cosmopolitan city. It gives an interesting account of migrants from different countries living together, tasting various ethnic food and enjoying a varied cultural life.

HOBBY

Some writers have written very perceptive pieces on their interests and hobbies. For instance, Salim Ali's "The Thrill of Bird Watching" is an absorbing account of the life of the bayas. It tells us how male bayas build their nests and invite female bayas to come and live with them. A male baya can build several nests, each for one of his several wives. If a female baya fails to accept a nest, it remains deserted.

POPULAR CULTURE

There may be an essay on popular culture like the current cinema, theatre or art. For instance, Brendan Gill's essay on the current cinemas gives a panoramic view of cinemas in the USA in 1970s. Russel Lynes's essay talks about the revolution in men's clothes in the USA and Gore Vidal's 'The Waking Dream' talks about the World of Tarzan.

OTHER TOPICS

Some essays talk about current social problems, some about education and some about science. Some are speculative and some are practical. Essays may be argumentative, discursive and thought-provoking.

EFFECTIVE AND CRITICAL THINKING

When a writer picks up an area to explore, he/she is initially aware of difficulties in his/her way to explore. He/she makes a careful exploration of the problem in the form of a *hypothesis*. He/she wants to test it to provide an adequate solution to the problem. His/her attempt at its *verification* may reveal an inadequacy in the hypothesis and the process of enquiry resumes further. It may involve both conscious and sub-conscious activities. They lead to several hypotheses which are checked against each other. At this stage, the writer adopts a *heuristic procedure* which is not a rule-governed procedure. It does not specify a finite set of steps that can be carried out in a mechanical manner and results in a correct answer. It provides questions or aspirations that guide enquiry and increase the chances of coming up with a working solution.

HOW A HYPOTHESIS IS MADE

A hypothesis is a tentative solution to a problem. It may be true or false, reasonable or unreasonable, acceptable or unacceptable. There may be several hypotheses which come to the investigator's mind that he/she is most likely to opt for. The one that stands the test of experience and is consistent with reliable knowledge is accepted. A hypothesis may have many consequences and if these consequences are borne out by experience, it is likely to be sound. Immediate *correspondence* gives credibility to the hypothesis.

Another test of a sound hypothesis is its *consistency*. A hypothesis is accepted or at least considered tenable, if it does not violate what is believed to be true about the world. It is also evaluated in terms of its *usefulness*. If more than one hypothesis seem to offer solution to a problem, they are comparatively evaluated. The hypothesis that does least violence to accumulated reliable knowledge is usually chosen.

EVALUATIVE WRITINGS

Before writing his/her pieces the writer tries to guess who are going to his/her readers and what their backgrounds are, so that he/she could build bridges with them. He/she guesses about their knowledge and values and adopts a style that would suit them. If he/she is writing an *evaluative* article, he/she describes the basis of his/her judgment so that his/her conclusions become convincing or at least palatable. If he/she is *dogmatic*, he/she is aggressive in his/her style of communication. Dogmatic writings lead often to conflicting positions. They become rigid and reduce the possibility of cooperation. A provisional writing, on the other hand, focusses on the process of enquiry and acknowledges the tentative nature of its conclusion. It implies that more than one reasonable conclusion is possible. It encourages careful, open-minded reading. Such a writer makes an assumption of similarity with regard to his/her readers. He pinpoints agreement on crucial matters and tries to extend the area of agreement.

Usually the *intention* of a writer is to change or reconstruct the image that the reader has in his/her mind. However, the reader tends to resist such changes, sometimes marginally, sometimes very vehemently. The reader's image influences his/her evaluation of the alternatives offered by the writer. When a writer formulates a new hypothesis, he/she develops a new way of interpreting problematic data. In other words, he/she constructs a new image of certain features of the world which may be vague and tentative or clear and certain. The clearer the message is, the better is the chance of its acceptance or serious consideration by the reader.

ARGUMENTS: INDUCTIVE OR DEDUCTIVE

While trying to seek acceptance, the writer is reasonable, and presents his thought according to the rules of logic. Arguments are either inductive or deductive.

Inductive arguments are empirical. They start with observations about particular things and lead to the generalisation about such things.

Deductive arguments proceed from generalisation or premises and lead to inferences about particulars. A categorical (deductive) argument is usually in the form of a **syllogism.**

A syllogism has a major premise and a minor premise. The minor premise asserts that it is a relevant aspect of the major premise. The relation between the two premises leads to the conclusion. The conclusion could be faulty if one of the premises is erroneous.

DEFECTIVE ARGUMENTS

Not all writers employ categorical arguments. Some of them may employ arguments which are logically less consistent but they are persuasive. They exploit people's fixed beliefs and evoke their feelings arising out of faith. Such arguments are called *Argumentum ad Populum.*

Besides, an *Argumentum ad Populum* is an appeal to the emotions of the people; it amounts to playing to the gallery. Worse than it is the abusive argument or argument by force or threat of force. Sometimes people tend to give *circumstantial arguments* when clear cut arguments are not available to them. Sometimes an argument is based on one's *ignorance.* Sometimes they are based on *hasty generalisations* and sometimes on *false causes.* Some arguments are *accidental* i.e. a general argument is applied to a particular case to which it is not applicable. All such arguments fail to convince a discerning reader. Such readers can see through the game a writer is playing while using *petitio principli* (begging the question). In such a case, the same proposition is used as the major premise and the conclusion. Propositions which contain complex questions are also irrelevant. In such a case an Yes/No question is asked in a situation where it is irrelevant (e.g. Have you given up smoking' to a person who never smokes). Besides, there is thus *fallacy of irrelevant conclusions.* It refers to a case in which an argument which is supposed to lead to a particular conclusion is directed to prove a different conclusion. Arguments that lead to logically irrelevant conclusions are used primarily because, in some cases, they appear to be convincing. A clever writer may use it in a cold, neutral language.

So far we have discussed the structure of reasoning. We have seen how one reason flows naturally from the one before and how they lead the reader to an overall conclusion. A logical conclusion follows naturally from the premises. However, sometimes the procedure is deliberately or unknowingly ignored. Erroneous conclusions are drawn which seem to be convincing. Sometimes arguments are based on false premises and they fall apart when scrutinised rationally. That is why one needs to be precise about the use of one's argument and careful about one's assumptions. While making counter arguments, one should be fair and balanced. Besides, one should ensure that one's argument carries more weight than one's adversary's. One should be judicious in selecting one's sources and careful while evaluating them. No point can be proved by quoting an authority; it can, at best, provide supportive arguments. One should not misrepresent other's claims or draw a conclusion from a distorted version of history. Factual claims and statistical evidence should be carefully cited; their credibility should be taken into accounts with due care.

NON-LITERARY WRITINGS

The points discussed above apply to any kind of writing, whether they are essays or newspaper articles or comments. They are applicable to advertisements and reviews as well. We may keep them in mind while reading any book, be it on science, social sciences, philosophy, history or applied sciences.

Whichever type of essay is prescribed or recommended as the text, the teacher should enable students to find out what the topic is and whether the title reveals the topic. They should examine whether the introduction and conclusions are effective and the main points are organised and interlinked. The teacher should point out whether the transition between paragraphs is natural or abrupt and the paragraphs fit well in the complete text. The paragraph structure should be examined to find out whether there is a clear movement of ideas and they are organisationally coherent. Within a paragraph, the structure of sentences should be well knit and coherent. They should not be unduly long and should not contain superfluous expressions. There should be a logical sequence of ideas, leading to the main topic of the essay.

The essays are supposed to inspire students to write their own composition. They should read the selected pieces critically so that they can analyse the writer's method and techniques. Such essays can inspire them to write their own pieces well. The teacher could ask them questions that suggest ways to start creative writing.

UNIT 7. SYLLABUS AND TEXTUAL MATERIALS

19

Development and Analysis of Syllabus and Textual Materials

CURRICULUM AND SYLLABUS

According to the *Oxford Dictionary of English* (2005:426) *curriculum* refers to 'the subjects comprising a course of study in a school or college'. *Syllabus* is also 'the course of study or teaching' (ibid, 1787). According to Webster's New World Dictionary, *curriculum* is a fixed series of study required, as in a college. It also means, 'all of the courses collectively, offered in a school or college, etc. or in a particular subject. *Syllabus*, in American usage, means a 'summary or outlines containing the main points, especially of a course of study'. In short, *curriculum* and *syllabus* are near synonyms. However, pedagogues make a distinction between the two. Though both of them provide comprehensive guidelines and readings for a courses, curriculum refers to something more than that; it involves a way of viewing an instructional programme 'as a functioning instrument of education' (Tyler, 1949:1).

According to Tyler, a curriculum must answer the following questions:

1. What educational purpose should the school seek to attain by adopting it?
2. What educational experience can be provided that is likely to attain these purposes?
3. How can these educational purposes be effectively organised?
4. How can we determine whether these purposes are being attained?

The curricular developers should be clear about the objectives. They become the criteria by which materials are selected, contents are outlined, instructional processes are developed and tests are prepared. As objectives are a matter of choice, a comprehensive programme of education should be the guiding factor in making value-judgements. Tyler thinks that the study of the learners themselves should be used as a source of educational objectives.

It suggests the kind of changes in behaviour that an educational programme seeks to bring about in its students. The need of students can be ascertained by the information about the learner compared with the standard norms, Needs also indicate certain knowledge attitudes, skills and psychological needs of students, including their interests.

Another important factor involves the study of contemporary life outside the school. It includes job analysis. It is important to know what kind of job is available in the market and what training is needed to get it. It can be on regional, national and international basis. In regard to the teaching of English, it can be done in terms of various functions an English knowing person can perform. The development of language competence can enable students to get certain kind of jobs. It can also help them in performing larger educational functions. The objectives of the curriculum should be such that they can be easily attained to a significant degree in the time available. Two other points are needed educational philosophy behind teaching that subject and the psychology of learning. The objective should be stated in a form that is helpful in selecting learning materials and in guiding teaching.

Learning experiences should be used to develop thinking, both inductive and deductive. Inductive thinking involves drawing generalisation from the data and deductive involves applying generalisation to specific cases. Learning experiences should be helpful in acquiring information and developing social attitude and personal interest of students.

The National Focus Group on Teaching English organised by the NCERT, Delhi (2005) realised the need for a coherent curriculum policy for the teaching and acquisition of English along with other Indian languages. It argued that it should be considered in relation to other subjects and have a *language – across the curriculum* perspective. It should also aim at the creation of multilingual students who will have a broader perspective on language use. It should aim at a minimum level of proficiency for the comprehension and production of language in real life. It means students should have the ability to speak English fluently outside the classroom to fulfil social requirements. Thus the objective of English language teaching has shifted from knowing the grammar of English and passing the examination with a minimum ability to acquiring a native—like language skill to transfer knowledge across language.

CONNECTING THE KNOWLEDGE OF ENGLISH TO THE WORLD OUTSIDE

It has been already pointed out in chapters 4 and 5 that there are external influences on the learning of English in India, (such as interstate and international availability of jobs, better access to learning resources and wider mobility). Internal factors include students' desire to improve their academic and occupational efficiency and to have better communication with Indians who do not know the mother tongue of the student. An important factor is to compete with students from English medium schools for entrance into all Indian institutions of science, medicine and technology. The world-wide demand for English-knowing Indians in information technology (IT) is an immediate impetus which may not be permanent but is likely to continue as long as English is a global language. In view of such perspectives, the objective of the English language curriculum should be for candidates to acquire ability to speak and understand English nationally as well as internationally. It may be noted that the Kothari Commission has set the objective of acquiring English as a 'library language' and had emphasised the target of acquiring reading and writing ability. Those targets are still valid but the priority has shifted to spoken English. That is how a student can get successfully connected to the world outside. Now that every Indian child has right to six years of education guaranteed under the Right to Education Act (RTE), the target of the curriculum should be basic English language proficiency for all.

CURRICULUM PROCEDURE

The National Focus Group on the teaching of English has chalked out the following procedure for the teaching of English.

At the initial level the curriculum should emphasise the building of familiarity with English, initially through spoken English and later on through both spoken and written English. It can be done by exposing students to rich language input by teachers as well as by electronic media (e.g. radio and television). That way they will be exposed to adequate data in English.

This scheme needs a change in teaching strategy. At present the emphasis is on master-learning of limited data; from now onwards it will be regular exposure to a variety of spoken language in meaningful contexts. The emphasis should be on the exposure of students; their oral comprehension will increase gradually. The learning of nursery rhymes and nonsense verses and listening to stories and dialogues can help in attaining the objective further.

The objective of learning to speak English is a major intellectual exercise in the context of India because in most cases, especially in rural and tribal areas, the student will not be exposed to English outside the classroom. The classes will have to be organised in such a way that pupils talk in English. It will make individual learning overt. The classroom strategy should, therefore, be to engage students in dialogues about day to day experience. They may share jokes and anecdotes and tell stories, howsoever, brief or trivial they might be. They may be engaged in rhythmic speech and voice modulation. In short, the learners should play the role of participants rather than spectators.

The task of language acquisition and development is enormous. Much depends not only on giving proper orientation to curriculum but also on the innovative skills of the teacher. To provide comprehensive input is essential but to get comprehensive output is also necessary.

At the later level: The initial emphasis on speech will expose students to many types of structures and a wide range of vocabulary which will need refinement at a later level. The Students must gain lexical competence for further development of their communicative skills. The first task is to enable them to have command over whatever words they have become familiar within the course of acquiring oral skill. They can be further developed if students get interested in reading extensively. The 'incidental' vocabulary they have acquired should gradually become 'instructed' vocabulary. That can be done by associating words with appropriate contexts.

TEXTBOOK MATERIALS

Textbook materials should be carefully chosen keeping in view the curriculum objective and the environment in which learning takes place. The selected pieces should be culturally appropriate. They should have functional orientation. That means the materials used in the text should be not only pieces of literature (e.g. stories, poems, plays, etc.) but of historical, geographical and scientific interests. That is how students will be prepared to read books on these subjects in English and the range of their vocabulary will be diversified. The process of inducing the range will be strengthened if books on various subjects in English are made available in the class libraries. Science fiction and detective stories are of absorbing interest for upper level school children. While children literature should be used in elementary classes, adolescent literature should be made available to senior high school students.

Selecting materials to obtain specific objectives is a major problem for textbook writers. As the wealth of material increases, the problem becomes more complex. It is not necessary to select only well-known or overused literary pieces from English. Suitable materials well-translated from regional languages should also find their place.

Selection has always implied a careful examination of possible materials by professionally competent teachers. They should have a balanced choice of classical as well contemporary literary pieces, both from original sources and also in translation. As far as practicable, the selected materials should not be controversial, i.e. they should not be target of community or political interests. They should remember that students are not only a part of the local community but also of a secular, democratic society and of the community of humanity.

LEARNER-CHOSEN TEXTS

The National Focus Group has recommended the learner-chosen texts. They include stories, articles, jokes and cartoons that students may be encouraged to choose and bring to the classroom. The selection of such texts will depend on the initiative of the teacher and will encourage students to read materials of their wider reading interests. They will fill in the gap left by the carefully chosen texts compiled by textbook writers and editors. Students could be encouraged to create their own materials which can be compiled and computer-typed in the form of class magazines. The objective of such an endeavour is to motivate students to write whatever they want to write and share with others. It will be a meaningful step, different from the routine exercise of writing essays and letters. The art of note taking while reading anything relevant and making one's own notes to write composition should also be one of the objectives.

MULTILINGUALISM IN THE ENGLISH CLASS

While the Report of the National Focus Group has not mentioned the possibility of adopting a bilingual teaching method for the teaching of English, it has opened the door for bilingual education in a controlled way. While the teacher will supply a comprehensive teaching input in English, students may not be asked to respond to it in English. Such students may be permitted to respond in the mother tongue. It is an appreciable point but it may indirectly discourage students from responding in the target language. *The National Curriculum Framework* (2005) and the *Knowledge Commission* have discussed the use of English to impart education in English in a selected subject, it has not recommended such a bold step. While we are in favour of using the mother tongue to make an English word comprehensible, its explanation in English is complex, we do not favour the use of the mother tongue in this fashion. Of course, the student can express himself/herself by using an expression in the mother tongue if he/she does not have the required vocabulary in English at his/her command but that is a different matter.

In short, the new curriculum should put emphasis on imparting students all the four skills and the initial point should focus on oral comprehension rather than written comprehension with emphasis on the textbook. The latter has led more Indian students to rote-learning to pass the examination and get a good grade. But that is not really acquiring the language. The real acquisition means having the ability to handle the language well both orally and in writing in any situation in real life. To be able to handle it in the real world is to be able to practise interpersonal communication and to enjoy programmes on mass media. As English plays a significant role in shaping our social attitude, it is imperative to have such a programme. If better understanding between people is to be achieved on an all India basis, English is bound to play a pivotal role till it is replaced by an Indian language. The overall objective of teaching English should be to create such an understanding among all Indians, and not to add to an exclusion class of English-knowing elite.

20

Development of Textual Material

Planning the Teaching of English

The problem of planning the teaching of English at high school is a major one, especially for a new teacher. One of the major problems is to keep students of superior ability gainfully engaged while paying special attention to students of low linguistic ability or of culturally disadvantaged background. Another is to have a balanced attitude towards the contents of the English curriculum. Though specific texts are prescribed by the Board of Secondary Education on the recommendation of the National Council of Educational Research and Training (NCERT), there is some scope for the teacher to have a dynamic approach. He/she has to decide how to balance the four communication skills while teaching literature. Since Indian high schools have no separate reading improvement course, its goal has to be incorporated while going through the prescribed literature texts. The planning of the text is not in the hands of the teacher but planning of units within each course is.

A new teacher could consult senior teachers who teach the same subject. He/she should follow the instructions for teachers given with the text, if any. As far as possible, he/she should provide a significant context for the study of the text and should keep the interests of groups of students in view. The individual teacher should always be working within the local context.

UNIT PLANNING

The term 'unit' implies 'unity' and unit teaching implies the search for unity in an English programme. There is nothing more central to the teaching process than a concern for unity.

There are three types of units in English:

(i) the unit organised around a segment of subject matter;
(ii) the unit organised around an activity or process; and
(iii) the unit organised around a theme or topic.

The 'Subject-Matter' Unit

The unit that finds its unity in a segment of the subject matter is most familiar. It accounts for much of the teaching in English classrooms. The teacher seeks unity by centering his/her attention on a clause or a sentence or some other element of grammar or story or some other aspect of a specific literary work or on a chapter or section of the text book. Though this type of unity is safe, it may prove to be unimaginative and pedestrian.

The 'Activity' Unit

It finds its unity in a language activity or process, for instance, acting out the dialogue of a story or an one-act play in the class or narrating the event of the prescribed text orally in a lively manner. The more students participate in such an activity, the better it is. Students may be encouraged to write up the content of a text that is being discussed in the form of a letter addressed to a friend or produce it in the form of a news report. The subject matter of the activity may vary; the unity is found in the process of skill.

The "Idea-Centred" Unit

A unit may take its unity from an idea or theme. The thematic unit permits the unity of an idea through oral discussion of its ramification or through writing on the aspects of the idea.

These three types of units are not mutually exclusive; a given unit may combine these approaches. There is no magic in any type of unit; the success depends on its apt handling by the teacher. However, there are two advantages of the idea-centred unit: (i) it provides a natural means to deal with individual differences, and (ii) it offers a vital context for the teaching of skills and content. The theme of an idea provides an opportunity to gain unity in the class in spite of opening doors for diversity of views.

Steps to Plan a Unit

Once the teacher has chosen the general topic or theme of the unit, he/she should plan specifically for certain outcomes. The objectives of the unit should be stated specifically and realistically. The teacher should be clear about the understanding of the concept he/she wants his/her students to have.

Classroom activity should be chosen to accomplish the objectives of the unit. Whether it is a classroom discussion, an oral report or a written assignment, it should have direct bearing on the objective of the unit. The four activities – reading, writing, speaking and listening – are complementary to one another but only one should be stressed at a time.

The teacher should work out a logical sequence for the unit. As far as possible, each subsequent activity or assignment should grow naturally out of the last. The teacher should see to it that the unity of the unit is not lost in course of the progress of the activity.

The teacher should keep a check on the unit plan. He/she should determine procedures to do so. He/she should monitor his/her plan to see that its objectives are not lost. For this purpose, he/she needs to administer the tests. Besides, he/she should be a keen observer and keep a check list. Successful teachers find ways to attend to individual needs of students while maintaining the necessary unity in the class.

The routine of giving assignment offers excellent opportunity to provide remedy for individual differences even though all students are to do the same assignment.

People often think of good teaching in terms of the image of a dynamic teacher who performs dramatically before a rapt class. Though the oratorical skill is important, it is only one aspect of teaching. A careful and effective planning of lessons is equally, perhaps more, important than a dramatic presentation.

SPECIFIC OBJECTIVES

A good lesson plan sets up specific aims to be achieved. It delimits the material to be taught and indicates the most economical procedure. It relates each lesson to what has been taught and what will follow. It makes room for orderly progress. It should be brief but should have sufficient detail to convey the main idea. It should indicate exactly what facts or items are to be learnt. It should provide for all four skills of language learning and make room for a variety of classroom activities.

As there is no best procedure to be recommended, the teacher should rely on his/her skill and intelligence and take the intelligence level of the class into consideration. *The Herbertian scheme* of five steps are extremely useful for planning a lesson. They are: (i) motivation, (ii) presentation, (iii) explanation, (iv) application and (v) summarization. The teacher should try to motivate students towards the lesson by his/her introductory remarks. The body of the lesson consists of presentation, explanation and application. The summary or evaluation may include oral questions or a brief written quiz. The effectiveness of instruction is measured largely by the nature of the question that the teacher asks and the care with which he/she frames it. The questions should measure students' achievement, and stimulate their interest.

A good question should be clear and concise. It should require thought and extended response. It should involve a single idea and reflect a definite purpose. it should catch the general attention of the class. It should be distributed as evenly as possible and not addressed to bright students only.

The teacher should use a device that creates interest in students and sustains it. He/she should use a variety of activities including texbook reading, board work, and question and answer sessions.

The homework assignment is absolutely essential to understand how much learning has taken place. The teacher should emphasize how important it is for students. After giving an assignment, the teacher should ask students if any clarification is needed. If there is something difficult or new in the question, it should be clarified. The teacher should correct some homework, distribute them among good students who may correct the rest with the help of the corrected homework as their model. The teacher can make a spot check of assignments already corrected by students.

SEQUENTIAL PLANNING

A basic issue in English language teaching is to provide for sequential planning. In some schools and syllabi the same sequence in grammar is repeated from standard four or five to twelve. Some other systems make provision for the teaching of grammar piecemeal, rather incoherently. Some have planned sequence for improving writing but they assign topics for composition at random. In literature, a poem (e.g. 'Lucy Gray') is found anywhere from grade eight to grade twelve. No plan exists in prescribed textbooks to teach students the skills they need to interpret a literary text.

It is essential to highlight the main characteristics and uses of the English language and to give students an understanding of how to write. For an incremental curriculum, the teacher needs detailed information about the types of grammatical information a student requires at a specific level. Those who compile textbooks and syllabi are supposed to be guided by such considerations but these guidelines should be clear to the teacher as well.

A sequential curriculum requires a planned writing programme from the grade at which English is introduced to grade twelve. There should be an agreed programme on the kind of writing skill that needs to be stressed at each grade level. One needs to emphasize composition much more than grammar to enable students to write well. But a large amount of writing will not by itself assure excellence, it must be followed by proper correction and editing.

In recent years there have been loud pronouncements about planning curriculum that is built step by step. We need to follow such pronouncements sincerely and build the structure meticulously. A good curriculum should have an observable sense of direction so that the teacher focuses on the learning activities necessary to accomplish its objectives.

PLANNING COMMUNICATIVE ENGLISH TEACHING

The Central Board of Secondary Education in India recommends the teaching of communicative English with focus on the following tasks: Reading, Writing and Speaking.

Reading requires the learner to focus on factual as well as inferential comprehension of the text. The learner should be closely engaged with the plot of the lesson, sequence of events and character analysis. In case of poetry, the formal and linguistic characteristics of the poem should be emphasized.

Writing sustains the interest of the learner in the lesson he/she has gone through and encourages his/her creative thinking.

Speaking should start with a classroom discussion on the lesson one has read and lead to the presentation of the same and/or similar items in learner's own words.

These steps should be accompanied by suitable *activities* related to the lesson. The focus of such an activity should be on the application of newly learnt concepts and skills in different situations and contexts. The learner should explore and interpret the lesson from all possible angles and that is what is ultimately needed for the successful completion of a lesson as a unit. The next six lesson-planning units will discuss a fiction, a poem, a drama and a non-literary text, grammar and composition to illustrate what needs to be done.

LESSON PLANNING: SAMPLES

'A'
PLANNING THE READING OF A POEM

Class: X (CBSE)
Subject: English (Poetry)
Topic: '*Snake*' by D.H. Lawrence

General Aims

Reading a poem should help students—

- understand, appreciate and enjoy a poem,
- develop their literary sensitivity,
- sharpen their interpretive skills so that they become discerning readers.

Immediate Objectives

- Students will be able to understand the main idea of the poem.
- They will be able to appreciate the conflict in the mind of the poet on seeing the snake: the natural instinct to admire the majestic

movement of the snake and the educated voice to kill the poisonous creature.

General Teaching Aid

A well-equipped classroom, pieces of chalk, chalkboard, duster, etc.

Specific Teaching Aid

A picture or sketch of a snake drinking water at a water pool.

Previous Knowledge of Students

- the knowledge of what a poem is and how it is different from a prose piece.
- familiarity with snakes.

Introduction

- The teacher will make some introductory remarks about the poet.
- He/she will discuss briefly the difference between a rhymed verse and a free verse.
- He/she will draw their attention to some new expressions in the poem.
- He/she will summarize the poem briefly.

Introductory remarks

D.H. Lawrence was one of the best novelists of twentieth century. Besides, he wrote short stories and poems. His novels are known for his insightful study of human relations between a man and his mother, and the lover and beloved. His novels express the right kind of tenderness and passion between individuals and negate the spirit of industrial civilization. His short novels and stories display richness and intricacy of human life and are known for his achievement of form. They have clear objectives and a fluent style.

Lawrence's earlier poems are rhymed verses on subjects taken from nature. There is hallucinatory quality in the images of these poems. Some of them are poems of conflict whose images are always polarized. The accuracy of his observation haunts the mind. A later collection of his poems—*Birds, Beasts and Flowers*—has a supernatural luster that shines through the figures of men and animals. The work of mature Lawrence has complete control of his medium. Its poems are in free verse which move with a gripping sonority. Its music has a pattern of vibrations; it is a living thing, evolving from the flesh of the virtuoso. He would move about a theme, enveloping it in constantly growing spheres of influence.

The poem—*Snake*—is about his fascinating encounter with a snake. In it, he is confronted with a dilemma: his educated voice calls him to kill it but his natural intuition admires its majestic personality and feels honoured that it has offered him an opportunity to play the host.

His blank verse has a definite rhythmic pattern supported by alliteration, assonance and similar other devices. Lawrence uses onomatopoeia, repetition and simile to brighten the effect of his poems.

Theme and Substance of the Poem

The teacher will point out the theme of the poem. It concerns the confrontation of the poet with a snake at his water-trough.

One hot summer afternoon the poet comes down the steps of his cottage and goes to the trough to fill water in a pitcher. He finds a snake ahead of him at the trough to quench its thrust. The snake is at the edge of the stone trough. It rests its throat upon the stone bottom and sips water with its straight mouth. It lifts it head from drinking, looks at the poet vaguely, stoops and drinks a little more. After drinking enough, it licks its lips, slowly turns its head and proceeds towards the broken bank of the wallface. It climbs the bank and puts its head into the hole, slowly withdrawing itself into it. The poet picks up a small piece of log and throws it at the water trough. The part of the snake that was still out convulses and it goes completely inside the hole in a haste.

That is the narrative part of the poem.

Procedure

Reading the Poem Aloud (by the teacher)

The teacher reads the poem aloud. If a taped voice is available, (s)he plays the tape and later on, asks students to identify its rhythmic pattern. If necessary, he/she plays the tape again.

The teacher asks all students to read the poem slowly and silently. While they are engaged in reading, (s)he notes down difficult words used in the poem on the board and gives their meanings.

Vocabulary

Carob tree = a red flowering tree, originally grown in the Mediterranean area.
Pitcher = a type of container with a handle.
fissure = crack
mused = thought about
bowels = bottom of the earth
venomous = poisonous
to finish someone off = to kill someone
depart = leave,
Pacified = satisfied
perversity = the quality of showing a deliberate device to be unreasonable
longed = desired,

flickered = made small, quick movements
drew up = came to a halt
convulsed = moved violently
writhed = made twisted, squirming movement, responded with great emotional or physical discomfort.
palling = worthless
albatross = a source of frustration of guilt, an encombrance
expiate = make amends.

Reading the poem aloud, stanza-wise by students

As students read a stanza, one by one, the teacher draws their attention to *poetic devices* used in each stanza.

Alliteration, i.e. the occurrence of the same letter or sound at the beginning of adjacent or closely connected words, as in 'strange-scented shade', 'slackness soft bellied…', 'sipped, straight … softly … straight … slack … silently', 'mused a moment', 'earth-brown, earth golden, 'burning bowels', 'Sicilian … smoking', peaceful … pacified', 'drunken … dreamily', 'uncrowned in the underworld'.

Assonance: resemblance of sound in syllables in nearby words arising particularly from the rhyming of two or more stressed vowels but not consonants, also from the use of identical consonants but different vowels.

Repetition: the action of repeating what has been said or written as in;

'must wait, must stand and wait',
'I was afraid, I was most afraid',
'slowly, very slowly',

Simile: the figure of speech involving the comparison of one thing with another thing of a different kind to make a description more vivid or emphatic as in:

He lifted his head from his drinking *as cattle do*,
And looked at me vaguely as *drinking cattle do.*
'he lifted his head dreamily, *as one who has drunken*
flickered his tongue like a *forked night on the air*
looked around like a god unseeing into air
Writhed *like lightening*
'he seemed … *like a king*'

Presentation

The poem will be presented to the class with active participation of students. It will be discussed in the form of questions and answers:

Teacher Q.: Where and when did the poet see the snake?
Student Ans.: He saw it one summer afternoon when he went down the

steps of his cottage to get a pitcher of water. The snake was at the edge of the stone trough. Its throat was rested upon it.

Q.: What was the snake doing there?

Ans.: It was drinking the water that dripped from the tap.

Q.: What did the snake do when it saw the poet?

Ans.: It lifted its head, saw the poet and started drinking water again.

Q.: What did the snake do after it finished drinking water?

Ans.: It licked its lips, looked around, turned its head and started moving towards the hole in the wall in which it lived.

Q.: What did the poet do when he saw it moving?

Ans.: He picked up a crude log and threw it at the water trough.

Q.: Was the snake hurt?

Ans.: Probably yes, it was partially hit. The part of the snake that was out of the hole moved violently. In a moment, it had gone into the hole.

Q.: Was the poet satisfied?

Ans.: No, he regretted it, He thought the act of throwing the log was perverse on his part.

Q.: Why perverse?

Ans.: The snake had done no harm to the poet. It came to drink water. When its thirst was satisfied, it was going back.

Q.: What did the poet feel when he saw the snake withdrawing?

Ans.: The poet felt that the snake was an honoured guest who behaved majestically. As soon as its mission was over, it withdrew itself elegantly.

Q.: What does the poet compare the snake with?

Ans.: The poet considers it as an uncrowned king in exile.

Q.: Why?

Ans.: Because the poet thinks that the snake is also a creature of the earth but it has deliberately withdrawn itself into the dark hole of the earth. Had it chosen to live in the open world, it would have lived a royal life.

Q.: What is the impact of the presence of the snake on the poet?

Ans.: It causes a conflict in the poet's mind. The rational in him tells him to kill it because it is poisonous but his intuition prevents him from doing so. He is charmed by the majestic look of the snake.

Q.: What does the poet treat it to be like?

Ans.: The poet treats it like an honorable guest who should be treated well; he ought to be hospitable to it.

Q.: What impression about the poet is formed by you?

Ans.: I feel the poet is an admirer of nature. He loves all natural objects, even if they are deadly snakes. He is taken in by the beauty of the snake, rather than its poison.

Recapitulation

The teacher will help students to recapitulate the contents of the poem by asking them to summarize it in parts so that many of them could participate.

Home assignment

The teacher will ask students to write the summary of the poem as a home assignment. She/he will ask them to spell out the conflict in the mind of the poet clearly.

'B'
PLANNING THE READING OF A FICTION

Class: X (CBSE)
Subject: English (Fiction)
Topic: '*Two Gentlemen of Verona*' by A.J. Cronin

General Aim

- to let students 'understand, appreciate and enjoy' fiction
- to help them develop their fiction reading sensibility
- to improve their interpretive skills

Immediate Objective

The immediate objective is to enable students—

- to understand the plot and theme of the story.
- to appreciate the values of faith, trust and love.
- to be aware of family values contained in this story.

General Teaching Aids

Pieces of chalk, chalkboard and duster.

Specific Teaching Aids

A photograph or picture of a scene of a room in a hospital with a patient and nurses.

Previous knowledge of students

Awareness of the disease of tuberculosis and how its patients are kept in isolation.

Introductory Remarks

- The teacher will explain some features of fiction in general.
- He/she will point out how novels are different from short stories.

- He/she will summarise the story and emphasise its important features.
- He/she will make some observations on the writer.

About the Writer

A.J. Cronin was a doctor by training who became the victim of a disease. When his first novel, *Hatter's Castle* was a huge success, he gave up practising medicine and became a full time writer. *The Citadel* and *The Key of the Kingdom* are his famous novels. His short stories are equally successful. In this story he talks about the two brothers who face hardship in the treatment of their sister. The story is known for their sense of devotion to their sister.

Nicola and Jacopo, the two young brothers, were the sons of a widower-singer, who was killed in a bomb raid. Their home was completely destroyed. Their sister, Lucia, was left alone when the brothers joined the resistance movement against the German occupation of Verona, a small town in Italy. When the war was over and they returned home, they found their sister suffering from tuberculosis of the spine. They got her admitted to a hospital in a village called Poleta and decided to earn enough to pay for her treatment. They took up any job they happened to come across: shined shoes, sold fruit, hawked newspapers, conducted tourists around the city and ran errands. They lived very frugally, saved money and paid Lucia's bills on time.

When the narrator of the story came across them, they were dressed shabbily and were selling wild strawberries. Next day he found them shining shoes briskly. They volunteered to take him around Verona and showed him the tomb of Juliet. When they expressed their desire to go to Poleta, he drove them to the hospital. They went to meet their sister while he waited outside and got the relevant information from the hospital nurse. When the boys had finished talking to their sister, they came to the narrator who took them back to Verona. The boys were tight lipped about the noble sacrifice they were making for their sister. The narrator was touched by this nobility and humanely behaviour.

Procedure

- The teacher will first narrate the story and then read the text aloud.
- Then he/she will ask his/her students to read the text quietly.
- Meanwhile he/she will explain the difficult words on the writing board and ask students to copy them in their notebooks.

Vocabulary

Outskirts = the outerpart of the city.
worn = old and damaged
cut off = shorts made by cutting off the legs of a pair of trousers
tunic = a sleeveless, loose outer garment

take along = to carry with someone
demeanour = appearance and behaviour
artless = innocent, natural and simple
coloured = showed embarrassment
vaxation = state of being annoyed
vestibule = lobby next to the outer door of the building
intrude upon = to put oneself deliberately in a situation where one is not welcome.
keep going = provide for sustenance

Comprehension questions

Q. (Teacher): When did the narrator meet the youngmen for the first time?

Ans.: (Student): When they were selling wild strawberries.

Q.: What did they look like?

Ans.: They looked shabby in their ill-fitted dress. One of them was in a worn jersey and cutoff khaki pants; the other in a shortened army tunic which was loosely hanging on his skinny frame.

Q.: What were their names?

Ans.: The elder brother was Nicola, he was 13. The younger was Jacopa, he was hardly 12.

Q.: What were they doing next morning?

Ans.: They were shining shoes.

Q.: What did they say when they were asked what their profession was?

Ans.: They said that they did anything: sold fruit, shined shoes, hawked newspapers, acted as tourist guides and ran errands.

Q.: What were they doing one night when the narrator saw them at the pavement?

Ans.: They were waiting for the arrival of a bus to sell newspapers.

Q.: When asked what for they were working so hard, what did thy say?

Ans.: They evaded the question and merely said that they had a plan.

Q.: What made Jacopo ask for a ride to Poleta?

Ans.: He said so when the narrator volunteered to do something for them before leaving Verona.

Q.: Where did the boys go when they reached Poleta?

Ans.: They straightway went to a hospital to meet Lucia, their ailing sister.

Q.: How did the narrator discover it?

Ans.: The nurse told him the whole story about the death of their father in a bomb raid and the sister getting tuberculosis. She told him that the brothers got her admitted to the hospital and paid the bills on time.

Q.: What did the narrator feel?

Ans.: He felt that they could not have done better.

Q.: What is the impression that the story leaves on you?

Ans.: That the brothers were deeply devoted to their sister and earned by working hard to help her. They were selfless and noble and did not want to publicize their noble act. The narrator was deeply touched by their wholehearted devotion to their sister and felt that only such people enrich human life.

Recapitulation

- The teacher will ask some students to narrate the story in the third person.
- The major portion of the story can be written in the form of dialogues and enacted in the class. It will reinforce the message further.

Notes on Language

The teacher may note that the story has several phrasal verbs in it, such as *put off, put on, break down, set off, put up with, come in, come across, come up against, turndown, turn in, turn into.*

He/she should draw the attention of students to their usage and encourage them to use them in their own sentences.

Home Assignment

The teacher will ask students to rewrite the story in their own language.

'C'
PLANNING THE READING OF A DRAMA

Class: X (CBSE)
Subject: English (Drama: One act play)
Topic: *The Dear Departed* by Stanley Houghton.

General Aim and Objectives

- To make students familiar with the language of the drama, i.e., the language of everyday use.
- To let them have the experience of dramatisation, i.e. staging a drama.
- To make them learn how to act and speak in a given situation.

Immediate Objective

- To read aloud to make students familiar with the play.
- To enact it in the class in collaboration with students.

- To let students know how to modulate their voices.
- To make them aware of the significance of physical movements, gestures, facial expressions in consonance with the development of the plot of the drama.

General Teaching Aids

Pieces of chalk and chalking board.

Specific Teaching Aids

Costumes needed to enact the play.

Introduction

The teacher will give introductory remarks about the playwright and the play.

William Stanley Houghton, the playwright belonged to the late nineteenth and early twentieth century. He was a realistic playwright who believed that every play must present an idea. In "The Dear Departed" he looks at the condition of the old member of a family, the greed of his children to grab his properly and their selfishness in relation to one another. He satirises the degradation of their moral values in simple colloquial English. The dialogue is pretty convincing.

The Play

Henry Slater, his wife Mrs. Amelia Slater and daughter, Victoria live with Mr. Abel Slater, an old genteman who is in his seventies. One night Abel sleeps so soundly that he fails to wake up the next morning. Mrs. Slater thinks that Abel has passed away and starts preparing for the funeral. She informs Mrs. Amelia Jordon, another daughter of Abel, about his death. She arrives with Ben Jordon, her husband on the scene. Befor they come, Mrs. Slater and Henny bring the bureau that was is Abel's room down to their own room so that when it comes to dividing the property of Abel between Slaters and Jordons, it is not counted as his.

The two families decide to have tea before going to Abel's room. At the dining table, Mrs. Slater wonders whether Abel had paid the latest installment of the insurance. In order to be sure, she asks Victoria to go upto Abel's room and bring the bunch of keys. When Victoria goes up, she finds the old man getting up. She reports it to Slaters and Jordons. While they are questioning the truth of Victoria's remarks, Abel walks into the dining room. He is amazed to find Jordons there so early in the mourning dress. Abel wonders who is dead but gets no clear answer. Eventually he realises that they thought he was dead. He declares that he is going to change his will and leave all his property to the person he will be living with. He feels that he is unwanted by Jordons and Slaters and declares that henceforth he will live with Mrs. John Shorroks, a widow, whom he is going to marry soon. His announcement shatters the dreams of Mrs. Slater and Mrs. Jordon to share his property after his death.

The Theme and Development of the Plot

The teacher will point out that the *theme* of the play is to expose the hypocracy and selfishness of the two daughters of Mr. Abel, Mrs. Slater and Mrs. Jordon with whom he has been living by turn. They are not interested in him. All the time their eyes are on his property which they intend to grab as soon as he is dead.

The *plot* of the play gradually unfolds itself. First, we find Mrs. Slater and her husband removing the bureau from Abel's room to their room so that it looks like it is in their possession and Jordons cannot claim it. Everything is done in a hush-hush manner. They grab his clock as well.

When the Jordons arrive, they want to know whether the doctor has visited him. They are told that he has not. The two families decide to have tea before going upstairs to see Abel. Meanwhile they discuss how to announce his death in the newspaper and whether he has paid his overdue insurance. When Victoria is told to go upstairs and bring the bunch of keys, she comes back to report that her grand pa is getting up. When Abel comes down, they feel embarrassed. Abel wants to know why Jordons are in the mourning dress. Ben tells a story which is not convincing.

Abel claims that he was not asleep when Amelia and Henny Slater went to his room but he was dazed. He finds his bureau and clock downstairs and wants to know what they were doing there. Mrs. Jordon accuses Amelia of stealing them from Abel's room assuming that he was dead. Abel accepts that he was not fair to Amelia in his will but has decided to change it. He has decided that all his property will go to the person he will be living with at that time. He further says that none of his daughters welcomed his staying with her. They show their willingness to keep him with them but he is not convinced of their sincerity. He tells them that he is going to marry Mrs. John Shorrocks, a widow and live with her. All his property will go to her according to his new will. Disinherited and disillusioned, they all are shocked by the news.

Vocabulary

(*to speak*) *sharply* =	suddenly and abruptly.
precocious =	(of a child) having developed certain abilities or inclination at an early age.
gallivanting =	going around seeking pleasure
in colours =	wearing colourful dress
traitcoat =	(male) blackcoat worn on formal occasion and having a long, rounded and split tail.

till ovr new black is ready = till a new dress of mourning is ready.
bureau = a writing desk with drawers.
to drive a hard bargain = to argue aggressively and force the other party to agree on the best possible arrangement.
pinch = take without permission.
ostentatiously = with pretension and showy display with a view to impressing someone.
complacent = showing uncritical satisfaction with oneself
crushed = felt overwhelmingly disappointed.
Piqued = aroused interest or curiosity.
as merry as a sand boy = extremely happy and carefree
poetic license = freedom to change normal rules of language.
hang-about = loiter
what the dickens = used for emphasis or surprise or annoyance.
to be gone = to be dead
merry = cheerful and lively
snug = warm and cosy, comfortable
hearthrug = a rug spread in front of the place to protect the carpet or floor.
public-house = a pub
disparagingly = regarding it as worthless.
transfixed = became motionless with wonder and astonishment.
gingerly = in a cautious manner
tomfoolery = foolish behaviour
Consternation = a feeling of anxiety or dismay typically at something unexpected.

Presentation

In the first stage of presentation, the teacher will read the dialogues aloud, modulating his/her voice, according to the role he/she is playing.

In the second stage, the roles of Mr. and Mrs. Slater Victoria, Mr. and Mrs. Jordon and Abel are assigned to different students. They speak the dialogues according to the plot. The teacher shows them how to modulate their voices. He/she also directs them how to play their roles through gestures and postures.

In the third stage, the students play their roles on a well-equipped stage. They are supposed to behave like professional actors.

The teacher highlights inconsistency in the behaviour of Mrs. Slater and Mrs. Jordon by drawing the attention of students to the change in their attitude. When they presume Abel to be dead, Mrs. Slater grumbles that she had to put up with him in the house for three years. She calls it a sort of 'swindling'. To this remark Mrs. Jordon retorts, "I had to put up with him for five years."

When they find him alive and he announces that he will make a new will and leave his property to whomsover he is living with before he dies, they change their attitude and each of them wants him to live with her. Abel understands their real motive and says, "It seems to me that neither of you has any cause to feel proud about the way you have treated me." He knows that both of them want him to live with them because of money. Since they considered him a burden, he has decided to live with someone who considers it a pleasure to look after him. That is why he decides to marry Mrs. John Shrrocks and leave her his fortune. The hypocrisy of his daughters is thoroughly exposed and he decides to cut off his connection with them.

Recapitulation

After the final enactment of the play on the stage, a student comes to the stage to recapitulate what the audience has already seen. He puts special emphasis on the message the play is supposed to convey.

Finally, the teacher comes to the stage to speak about the disintegration of the joint family and the condition of the elderly people in modern society. He draws the attention of the class towards the colloquial language of the play.

Finishing Touch

Before the discussion on the lesson is concluded, the audience is asked to come forward and express their views on the relevance of the play against the contemporary social background.

'D'
PLANNING THE READING OF A SUPPLEMENTARY LESSON

Class: XII
Subject: Supplementary Reader in English (*Vistas*)
Topic: Journey to the end of the earth by Tishani Doshi

General Aim

The general aim is to make—

- reading a supplementary book: An enjoyable experience,
- students appreciate the writing,
- they understand the social milieu against the background of which such pieces are written.

Specific Aim

To enjoy the experience of the author while he went on journey to Antartica.

General-Teaching Aids

Chalk board, pieces of chalk, duster.

Specific Teaching Aids

A map of Antarctica, photographs taken by travelers to the continent (south pole) pictures of the Antarctic landscape.

Introduction

The teacher will point out the location of Antarctica on the map of the world, and introduce the photographs of the expeditions to students. He/she will tell them about various expeditions to *Antartica.*

Summary

The writer boards a Russian research vessel going to Antarctica, the coldest, driest and windiest continent in the world. It crosses nine time zones, three bodies of water and three ecospheres. After he reaches there, he feels relieved in Antarctica's white landscape and uninterrupted blue horizon. He is wonderstruck to find it so frigid and desolate.

A super continent called Gondwana existed in the south of the universe about 650 million years ago. It comprised present day Arabia, Africa, South America, Antarctica and the peninsula of India. Gondwana was much warmer and it had a wide variety of flora and fauna. It thrived for nearly 500 million years. It was the time when dinasours gave way to mammals. It is mind-boggling to think of phenomenal geological changes and the significance of cordilleran folds and pre-cambrian granite shields and of ozone and carbon. it is equally remarkable to think of South America drifting towards North America, opening up the Drake passage to create a cold circumpolar current that keeps Antarctica frigid and desolate. While in Antarctica, one forgets all about human civilization. It has only midges and mites, blue whales and gigantic icebergs. One can spend uneventful days in Antarctica, occasionally disturbed by avalanche or calving ice sheets.

Human civilization has been barely 12,000 years old which is a very short period of time in geological clock. But in this short period, people have exploited nature ruthlessly and endangered global temperature by burning fossil fuels. While environmental pollution has endangered life, Antarica remains unpolluted. It shows how little changes in environment can have favourable repercussions. If the lives of Phytoplankton, the grasses of the sea, are affected, they will affect the lives of marine animals and birds and disturb the global cycle.

In Antarctica, the author's ship could not move beyond a point. The author walks on the thick ice pack, 180 metres underneath it is live salt water. The author wonders whether it would became a warm place again.

Procedure of Presentation

The teacher will summarize the essay first.

He/she will ask students to read the lesson.

It will be followed by comprehension questions and answers.

Q.: What is the weather like in Antarctica?

Ans.: As the surface of Antarctica consists of very thick layer of ice, the weather is chilling cold throughout the year.

Q.: What is the impact of this type of weather there?

Ans.: Antarctica is frigid and desolate. There are no trees and vegetation. There is no human population. As there are no polluting agents, it does not have the thick layer of carbon dioxide. If the polluting elements go there, the temperature will go up and the snow will start melting.

Q.: What is the significance of this kind of environment?

Ans.: It is an ideal place to study the present, past and future of the earth. As the threat of global warming is gradually increasing, such a study is badly needed.

Q.: What is the significance of its simple ecosystem?

Ans.: Because of its simple ecosystem, it lacks biodiversity. It is a perfect places to study how little changes in the environment can have big repercussions.

Recapitulation

Students will provide the summary of the essay to recapture its main points.

Rapid Reading

Students should be asked to read the essay again, silently and keep time. They should repeat the practice to read faster.

Assignment

Students should be asked to read the report of Indian expedition to the South Pole and write his/her own report as though (s)he has been there.

'E'
PLANNING THE LEARNING OF GRAMMAR

Class: X
Subject: English (Grammar)
Topic: Tense (The difference between Simple Past and Past Perfect)

General Objective

- to enhance students' comprehension of English grammar'.
- to enable them to handle tense forms well
- to understand when they are used

Specific Objective

- To make students aware of the difference between Simple Past and Past Perfect
- To enable them to use these tense forms correctly
- To encourage them to recognise whether they have been used correctly is a given situation/context.

General Teaching Aids

Chalkboard, pieces of chalk, duster.

Specific Teaching Aids

- a chart showing various forms of past tense and how they are formed.
- A flow chart with sentences of both tense forms in a passage (i.e., a connected text)

Previous knowledge

Knowledge of various forms of past tense

Introduction

- The teacher will read the connected sentences on the flow chart.
- (s)he will underline the sentences which have verbs in simple past and past perfect.
- (s)he will explain whether they have been aptly used.
- He/she will change the forms of the verb in the given sentences (i.e. use simple past in place of past perfect and past perfect in place of simple past)
- The students will be asked whether the changes are correct in the given context. If not, why?

Presentation

The teacher will build up his/her discussion on the basis of students' responses. If the responses are wrong, he/she will point out why they are considered to be wrong.

Highlights on Discussion

The teacher will motivate students to be active participants in discussion. Look at the following sentences:

1a. She *paused* to take a quick break.
1b. She *paused* and *took* a quick breath.

In (1a) *paused* is used to suggest past action; it is in the simple past tense form.

(1b) has two verbs-*paused* and *took* and each of them *indicates a past action.* The verbs are used in the sequence in which the actions happened.

(1c) She *took* a quick breath after she *had paused.*

In (1c) as well *took* and *had paused* indicate two past actions but their sequence is disturbed. The first action (she *paused*) is mentioned after the second. Hence it is in the past perfect form. If the sequence of tense expressions are different from the sequence of events, the verb that is mentioned later but refers to the first action, is in the past perfect form; as in (2).

2. I *knew* they would prefer to feel that they *had kept* the secret.

Keeping the secret occurred earlier than knowing it; hence its form is in the past perfect. The same is the situation in (3);

3. They *were* quite alone in the world. A bomb *had* destroyed their home and *thrown* the children into the streets. They *had* always *known* a comfortable life.

The second and third clauses are in a sequence but they occur later than the first clause. Hence they are all in the past perfect.

Now look at the clauses in (4):

4. During these summer days, under the hot sun, they *shined* shoes, *sold* fruit, *hawked, conducted* tourists round the town and *ran* errands.

These five verbs have been used in a sequence but the actions may not be in sequence as they are unrelated. Hence, they are in simple past.

5. We *bought* their biggest basket, then *set off* towards town.

(5) has two verbs reporting the actions in the past and they are mentioned in the order in which the actions took place. Hence, they are in the simple past.

Generalisation

The following conclusions are drawn:

1. A past action is expressed by the verb in its simple past form.
2. If there are two or more verbs referring to past events in a sentence and they are unrelated, each of them takes a simple past form.
3. If there are two or more verbs and they are mentioned in the order in which actions took place, we use simple past for them.
4. If there are two or more verbs and the action that occurred later takes an earlier position in the sentence, it occurs in the simple past and all verbs that are mentioned later are in the past perfect form.

Stage 2

Another aspect of the use of the past perfect is in the reported speech, as in (b).

6a. He *went* home (simple past)
6b. I was *told* that he *had gone* home.
6c. She *told* me that he *had gone home.*

In (69) the verb is in the simple past.

In (6b) and (6c) it is in the past perfect because the action of going took place earlier than the action of reporting but it is mentioned later.

Stage 3

Sometimes simple past is used in the sense of non-past, as in (7a)

7a. I demanded that he *apologised.*
b. I demanded that he *should apologise.*
8a. She suggested that I *bought* a car.
b. She suggested that I *should buy* a car.

In (7a) *apologised* has been used in the sense of *should apololise.*

In (8a) *bought* has been used in the sense of *should buy.*

There are examples of the use of a past tense form in a sentence the reporting verb of which is *demand, insist, suggest, recommend* or *propose.*

This type of construction is sometimes called subjunctive.

Another use of the past in the sense of non-past (i.e., present)

a. It is late. It is time we *went* home.

Recapitulation

The teacher will discuss sentences like those given above and make generalisations about the use of Simple Past and Past Perfect in an appropriate context.

Classroom Exercise

- The teacher will write sentences with verbs in the infinitive form.
- He/She will ask students to use the given verbs in the correct form.
- The answer will be checked.

The teacher will use the correct form only when students are unable to solve the problem.

Assignment

- The teacher will give the assignment asking students to supply correct simple past and past perfect forms *of verbs* in a connected text.

'F'
PLANNING PARAGRAPH-WRITING

Class: XII (CBSE)
Subject: Composition in English
Topic: Planning How to Write a Paragraph

General Aim

- to make them realise what a paragraph in an essay (or any creative writing) is.
- to develop the skills to appreciate a well-written paragraph.

Specific Objective

- to make students feel what a paragraph is. (It is a series of sentences developing one topic)
- to enable them to find the topic sentence in a paragraph.
- to make them aware of the fact that the topic sentence occurs at or near the beginning of a paragraph.
- to show them how a paragraph is developed by supplying detailed information on the idea expressed in the topic sentence.
- to show that every paragraph has a conclusion.

General Teaching Aid

Chalk board, pieces of chalk and a duster.

Specific Teaching Aid

A chart displaying three paragraphs, one with the topic in the beginning, one in the middle and one at the end.

Introduction

The teacher will explain what a paragraph is.

A paragraph is a carefully organized unit of sequence of sentences. Each paragraph has a topic sentence which it develops by means of detailed information given in support of the idea expressed in the topic sentence.

- It may be developed by facts or examples. It may be developed by narrating an incident or by arguments in a line of reasoning.
- A paragraph is an organized unit which is formed by discussing only one topic in it. It should have an interesting beginning, a well-developed main body and a conclusion. The arrangement of details should be coherent. They should follow one another logically and smoothly. They may be arranged in the order of time or importance of task or arguments.

Procedure of Presentation

After giving the introductory remarks, the teacher will proceed with the chart to illustrate the strategies developed in a paragraph. He/she will go through the first extract.

Extract 1

> *The similarity between the human body and a machine is really rather superficial.* it can be summed up in the statement that both require fuel and oxygen and obtain energy by slow or rapid combustion; both require systems of elimination for the waste products of combustion and the ashes of unified; moving many parts of each consisting of mechanical levers, if one considers the wheel as a continuous lever, and each contains secondary structures which can be crudely described as 'tubes', 'triggers', 'straps' and 'wires', some of which are by no means indispensable to the healthy working of the whole. Beyond that, the comparison fails. No machine can grow in size; no machine sees, hears or feels; no machine reproduces its kind or repairs its own broken or worn out part, no machine thinks.

The teacher will use this paragraph to point out its theme and show how it develops. The theme shows the similarity between the human body and a machine. The writer mentions the similarities, one by one and then highlights the differences. The teacher will show the close link between the sentences and the marshalling of facts.

Extract 2

> Future generations may look upon the harnessing of atomic energy as the greatest single milestone in man's material progress in the everlasting battle to control nature's forces to make possible a decent life for himself on this earth. But *while the development may mean man's greatest scientific triumph, it may also mean the most tragic moment in his history, a moment in which we may be standing on the brink of the greatest abyss.* For all the man's recent ills have been *brought* about by the misuse of products of man's genius. If mankind sees to it that atomic energy is properly controlled, this new cosmic fire can bring him new lights, new warmth and new freedom. If he allows it to get out of control as was the case with man's other inventions, it will mean a conflagration that will engulf the earth and its inhabitants, leaving abysmal chaos.

The teacher will point out that the topic is in the middle of the passage. It refers to the triumphs and tragedy of atomic exploitation. He/she will explain how the paragraph has been developed.

Extract 3

> What is the meaning of the value of cultural survival? Does it mean valuing people of distinct backgrounds or valuing the diversity of background itself? The notion that the people ought to be respected as equals regardless of their ethnicity, race, gender and other distinguishing characteristics is an essential part of modern democratic philosophy. But it hardly follows from this philosophy that we must preserve diversity itself. Cultural groups have no moral claim to eternal existence, especially against the rights of choice of their own individual members. What they do have is the right to be free from circumstances under which their continued existence is made impossible because of injustice. The proper focus of our moral concern is the *rights of the individuals* that constitute them. While current threat to aboriginal cultures should be of moral concern, it should emerge from the rights of its individual members and not from any questionable moral claims made on behalf of the cultures themselves.

The third extract has mentioned the topic at the end of the paragraph. The teacher will point out how it emerges as the conclusion of the sentences mentioned earlier and how they are all interlinked.

Stage 2

After discussing the organizational patterns of these paragraphs, the teacher will choose a paragraph from the textbook and ask students to find out its topic.

- He/she will ask questions about how the paragraph has been developed. He/she will let several students have a chance to answer him/her and finally make his/her own observation.
- He/she will ask them to explain how the paragraph fits into the longer text from which it has been taken.

The same exercise can be gone through involving another passage.

Recapitulation

The points mentioned in the introduction will be reiterated with reference to the illustrations discussed in the class.

Students will be now asked to answer:

- What a paragraph is
- how it develops, and
- how it fits into a larger text.

Assignment

Students will be asked to write a paragraph on each of the following topics:

i. narrating an experience, (e.g. a day full of surprises)
ii. describing a favourite place
iii. factors to select a favourite course at school
iv. Advantages of being a bilingual
v. Clothes do make a difference in life.

Given above are the samples of lesson planning, one each for poetry, fiction, drama, non-literary prose, grammar and composition. What is common to each of them is that they have the same basic structure: general aim, specific objective, introduction, presenting and discussing the text step by step. Individual characteristics differ in accordance with the genre to which the selected piece belongs.

Students are advised to look at the genre of the piece they have selected for lesson planning and introduce variation in the planning to suit the topic they are going to discuss. Only then special features of each genre and each lesson in that genre will come to light.

UNIT 8. PLANNING LEARNING AND TEACHING

21

Dramatization and Other Modes of Language Representation

Listening with care and attention and understanding what is spoken is one the primary tasks of the learner of a second language. As words are combinations of sounds and the printed word is a graphic representation of sound sequences, one should be able to synchronic sound sequences with printed words. It means, one should be able to coordinate their spellings with their spoken sounds. The learner of English as a second language should be able to hear the clear and distinct pronunciation of spoken words by the teacher in the classroom and by a speaker on radio or television. He/she should be able to mark the rhythm and pattern of the language. A young learner in the elementary class should have an opportunity to listen to the recorded sounds. He/she can imitate them individually or collectively in a classroom.

CHORAL READING

Reading or speaking collectively, as in a chorus, improves one's pronunciation. One learns the beat, rhythm and pattern of the language automatically. A student who is hesitant about imitating his/her teacher's voice alone, imitates it with great pleasure in the group. The beginners can use nursery rhymes which are often full of sound combinations, alliteration and assonance. For instance, let us look at the following nursery rhyme:

1. Mary, Mary, quite contrary
   How does your garden grow?
   With silver bells, and cockle shells
   And pretty maids all in a row

The speaker has to take a short pause after *Mary* in the middle of the first line and *contrary* at its end. He/she has to repeat similar pauses in the third line at *bells* and *shells*. The second and fourth lines are spoken without any internal pause but one cannot ignore to note that *grow* and *row*, the last words of the second and fourth lines rhyme. The poem suggests where to pause and make one associate such pauses with rhythm.

One of the "Nonsense Alphabets" of Edward Lear runs as follows:

2. A was once an apple-pie,
   Pidy
   Widy
   Tidy
   Pidy
   Nice insidy
   Apple-pie

The nonsense words—*pidy*, *widy* and *insidy* fit in with the word *tidy* and they all need brief pauses as against the first line which ought to be spoken in one stretch. In the following nonsense verse, the end of the first line rhymes with that of the second and fourth and third line has an internal rhyme.

3. There was an old man of Nepaul,
   From his horse he had a terrible fall;
   But though split into two, by some very strong glue,
   They mended that man of Nepaul.

The lines tell us where to pause while reading.

While practising choral reading in (3) the class may be divided into two; one group reads lines (1) and (2) and another, (3) and (4).

SAYING AND DOING

It involves describing an action while carrying it out. A student says, "Get up. Go to the door." Another student describes this act as he does it, "I get up and go to the door." A third person describes the act using the third person. "He (or she) gets up and goes to the door." Though the task is meant for the beginners, this pattern can be used at a higher level as well. For instance, the second person may say, "I got up and am going to the door" and the third person may report, "he got up and went to the door." While listening, the learner associates the object and the action directly with the spoken words or expression. The teacher could think of several classroom activities in this fashion and make his/her students practise them.

DIALOGUE

The dialogue is the most fundamental activity in language teaching. It provides the context for what is discussed. Turn-taking is an essential part of dialogue and students should be asked to take turns while talking.

The dialogue may be a very useful form of exercise for teaching vocabulary and grammatical constructions. However, its successful use depends on the imagination, ingenuity and resourcefulness of the teacher. A successful use of dialogues may make the class lively and enjoyable. The students should be able to speak without consulting the book and use appropriate gestures while speaking.

Each dialogue should be a small unit portraying a scene from daily life or dramatizing an anecdote. The range of talk is practically unlimited if the teacher is a little imaginative. Some of the topics are: the weather, the family, a scene at breakfast, lunch or dinner, meeting someone on the street, on way to school, on the way back home, at the movie, in a hotel, etc.

In the beginning, the teacher should work out a dialogue and ask participating students to follow it. However, as students gain confidence, they should be given a topic and left free to work out their own dialogues. The activity could be quite effective and lifelike if the selection of topics is not like a classroom assignment. The dialogue should have elements of individuality, surprise and pleasure. At the same time it should be relevant.

DRAMATIZATION

Children are keenly interested in acting. A play needs guidance at many points, although basically it is children's own work and can be carried out without interference. Dramatizing an episode from the text helps children to organize their thinking, have clarify of meaning and enter in imagination into the life they are reproducing. It all leads to the deeper understanding of the text they reproduce.

Children of eight and nine, very readily can turn the material they are studying into dramatic plays. They gain the idea from radio, television and movies. Small children would like to dramatize nursery rhymes like 'Jack and Jill', 'Little Miss Muffet', 'Hickory, Bickory, Dock' and 'Little Jack Horner'. Stories such as 'Three Bears', 'Little Duckling Tries His Voice', 'The story of Dobbin', 'The Poppy Seed Cake', and the 'Little Indian Boy' are popular and children will love to dramatize them.

Stories for dramatization must fit the interest of students. Children should be allowed to select the stories they like because they can interpret only those characters and actions which they can enter into with pleasure and understanding. Short stories appeal most if they have clearcut action and dialogue. Stories from Kipling's *Jungle Books* appeal to them a lot.

Learning lines and parroting them make children stiff and self conscious; getting the feel of the play and coming up with their own lines make them natural and creative. A child who has memorized lines but forgets what he/she is supposed to say feels miserable on the stage. If he/

she speaks naturally, he/she will come up with something that fits the situation; it will help him/her to regain confidence. As participation in a play calls for careful thought for timing and attention to the sequence of events, the child gets trained in consistent sequential thinking which helps him/her in other areas of thinking.

The staging of an one-act play or scenes from a play in the classroom has its own value but it has its limitation as well. Usually the best actors are selected from among the best students of the language class keeping their personality, pronunciation and fluency in view. The actors should be able to use proper gestures and facial expressions to interpret the roles they are playing. The play should appeal to students so that they engage themselves in it enthusiastically. The dialogue should be simple, natural and lively. It should become familiar to all, the actors as well as the audience. The dramatization of events of daily life, anecdotes and dialogues taken from the stories included in the reading text, is also welcome.

Oxford Pathways, a textbook recommended for class 7 by NCERT, contains a short one act play which can be enacted by the students of that class very easily. It has four main characters and five minor characters. It can be staged with some preparation. Alternatively, it can be used in the classroom only for dialogues. *Literature Reader*, a textbook for class X, contains the assassination scene from *Julius Caesar* by Shakespeare. It contains powerful speeches by Brutus and Antony which can be of much interest to students, especially those who want to practise how to speak in a debate. The scenes can be staged after some preparation. Dramatization can follow oral practices.

PUPPETS, MARIONETTES, PANTOMIMES AND SHADOW PLAYS

Serving as actors is the children's fovourite way of carrying out dramatic interpretation of what they have read. There are other ways as well that can add to the variety of experience. Puppets of a number of kinds can be used with younger children while older ones may develop skilled performance with marionette.

Puppets made with bottles are pushed around a table as though they are acting. Children talk for those characters. This game is for very young children. Upper primary and middle grade children use hand puppets made of paper bags or scraps of fabric. Some children manipulate them and talk on their behalf. Senior students can create their own marionettes and manipulate them by strings to produce popular plays. They can act in pantomimes and shadow plays. They have to think in terms of action and grouping. The medium requires them to give attention to clear portrayal of mood and action of characters without the use of words. These creative activities get students interested in what they read. Besides, they help them build life-time values in attitudes, habits and real mental power.

A primary school teacher in Kakinada, Andhra Pradesh uses puppetry to attract students from fishermen hamlets to his school. He explains his lessons with the help of puppets who talk like two individuals, or a man and an animal. He uses shadow puppets, glove puppets, rod puppets and puppets along with ventriquial puppets whose voice appear to come from a distance. He converts waste materials into attractive puppets and uses them for academic purposes. Every innovative language teacher can follow his example.

FELT BOARD AND FELT CUTOUTS

The board made of felt mounted on soft board can be used for many purposes. It is an excellent medium for building up conversation and developing vocabulary.

Sets of cutouts made of felt are commercially available. There are sets of felt cut outs of wild and deomestic animals, water creatures, birds, insects, means of transport and traffic signs. They can be used while telling a story or narrating an event to children of junior classes.

READING A TEXT

A text can be *read* out first by the teacher and then by students. The teacher should pronounce new words carefully and explain their construction and meaning. It could follow *silent reading.* Supplementary readers should be read silently and followed by comprehension tests. The usual method of testing comprehension is by questioning on the text. In a language class, the question has a double purpose. One wants to know whether the student has understood what he/she has read. At the same time, one wants to see whether the student can express his/her thought correctly in English. The question should therefore be in a simple language so that they are easily comprehensible. They should follow the logical sequence of the text.

INTENSIVE (CLOSE) READING

Intensive reading is usually practised in the class. The teacher should give the substance of the lesson orally to motivate students. Then he/she can read the piece aloud slowly and clearly. He/she should note down the new words and expressions on the board, pronounce them correctly and tell their meanings. It should be followed by reading it aloud by students, paragraph-wise. Once this task is done, they should read it silently and answer questions written by the teacher on the board.

EXTENSIVE (WIDE) READING

Extensive reading is generally done outside the class, because it is essentially silent reading. In order to prepare them for silent reading, the teacher need not explain all difficult expressions in advance. He/she may write comprehension questions which students may try to answer. Supplementary reading materials are to be read silently. Students should orally present a summary of what they have read.

COMPREHENSIBLE INPUT

An alternative view of language pedagogues is that the emphasis should shift from mastery learning of limited input to regular exposure to "a variety of meaningful language inputs". The goal should be to expose students to adequate amount of data in English. In other words, input should include not only textbooks but other print materials such as children's magazines, popular cartoon books, audio cassettes, film strips containing interesting and entertaining dialogues, etc. Early exposure to natural language, aided by illustrations, gestures and postures can increase students' comprehension of the language. Even in non-English medium schools students can be encouraged to have exposure to subject textbooks in English. One need not worry about the meaning of all the words and expressions they will come across; they will get the sense of what they read and guess the meaning contextually. They may faulter often but it does not mean that the exposure to language should be controlled. Continuous familiarity with the language will make them feel at home and will help them in building up a working knowledge of the language.

EXPANDING VOCABULARY

One of the sure ways of expanding vocabulary is the use of *cards*. On one side of the card there is a new word, on the other, there is a picture or drawing denoting what the word stands for. If the word does not denote an entity but suggests an idea, feeling or concept, its mother tongue equivalent can be given. Usually such cards are commercially available. Alternatively, the teacher could prepare his/her own cards. The English and Foreign Language University, Hyderabad has prepared reading cards words of a hundred and four which can be easily obtained. Each of these cards contains a short passage containing the use of a word. Students could have a look at them individually as often as possible. Its use is a sure way to improve their stock of words.

There are several ways in which the learner's vocabulary can be enriched. One of them is to play a word game, another is to have a quiz competition.

Word Game

A word game can be played in many ways. Suppose a student says the word *happy* and wants to know which other words are close to it in meaning, one can say *cheerful, delighted, delightful, jolly, jovial,* and many other words. We talk about a *happy* or *cheerful* or *delightful* or *joyful* occasion. A *happy* person is a *cheerful, delightful, gay* or *jolly person.*

A student can ask what is the opposite of *happy*. Of course, another student will say, *unhappy*. But others may use words such as *sad, dejected, depressed, distressed, sorrowful, melancholy,* etc.

Games may be played involving collocation of words. The word *happy* reminds one of *happy family, happy moments, happy-go-lucky, happy couples,* etc. It also reminds one of *happiness, happily, unhappy, unhappily, unhappiness,* etc.

In short, given a word, one may be asked about its synonyms, antonyms, collocations and derivatives. One may be asked to infer the meaning of a word which is almost obvious from the context in which it is used. The game could be passed from one student to another to get the whole class involved.

QUIZ

Students may be quizzed about the words they know. Some typical quizzes may be as follow:

1. To give way to someone is to ....
2. To overcome and take control of a place or people by military force is to ....
3. To gradually become faint and disappear is to ....
4. The distinctive taste of a food or drink is its ....
5. To show approval or preference for something is to .... it.
6. That which is absolutely deprived of light is ....
7. The surface that reveals no curves, bumps or holes is ....
8. Acute mental pain resulting from loss, misfortune or deep distress is ....
9. A person who works without being paid is called a ....
10. A person who spends a lot of time reading is ....

[The answer to these questions are: 1. yield, 2. conquer, 3. fade, 4. flavour, 5. favour, 6. dark, 7. flat, 8. grief, 9. volunteer, 10. studious]

CHARTS, GRAPHS AND MAPS

While teaching, a teacher may use pictures, charts, graphs and maps to illustrate his/her points. The pictures may show paintings or drawing of scene or character or an object. They may help students in visualising what they read or are told about.

Charts may contain pieces of information that are relevant to the texts but not included in it. They may complete the picture and put the text in a context. It may contain figures and/or diagrams. They may be in the shape of *bar charts*, *flow charts* or *pie charts*. *A bar chart* is a diagram that has lines or narrow rectangles or bars with different heights to show different amounts so that they can be compared.

A *flow chart* is a diagram that shows connections between the different stages of processor parts of a system. A *pie chart* is a diagram consisting of a circle divided into sections to show the size of a particular amount in relation to the whole.

A *graph* is a planned drawing, consisting of lines showing how two or more sets of numbers are related to each other. A *map* is a drawing or plan of something. It is the diagrammatic representation of an area of land or sea showing some features. Some charts and maps are commercially available. They can be bought and used on relevant occasions in the class. Other charts, maps, diagrams and graphs needed for specific lessons should be prepared by the teacher concerned with the lessons. (see pages 170-173 for more details.)

To sum up,

- Various modes of textual representation – choral reading and singing, dialogues, dramatization, handling puppets and marionettes, displaying pantomimes and shadow plays – should be used to make students familiar with the lesson.
- Appropriate meaningful input should be provided to enrich communication environment of learners so that they are familiarized with the language imperceptibly.
- Various types of word games – anagrams, *antakshari*, giving synonyms and antonyms, definitions and use of prefabricated expressions should be practised to enrich one's vocabulary.
- Pictures, charts, graphs and maps should be used to highlight a point and make it familiar.

22

Audio-Visual Aids

'Sound brings language to life, and life to language'.

—*Elton Hocking*

Audio-visual materials have been used for classroom teaching for quite sometime. Under the name "audio-visual" we think of those devices, techniques and materials which appeal directly to the ears and eyes of the learner. The simple devices consist of pictures, cards, charts, diagrams and maps. The elaborate devices include the use of radio, phonograph records, lingua phones, language laboratories, motion pictures, films, television and computers. They are considered to be effective in teaching because they tend to hold the interest of the learner and contribute to the efficiency, depth and variety of learning. By appealing to various senses, they have an enduring effect on learning; their aesthetic characters make learning pleasant and enjoyable. They are used to support the classroom activity and are not a substitute for the teacher.

FLASH CARDS

The easiest device is the use of flash cards. It is particularly useful in the beginning classes for teaching words and their pronunciation. They are used for rapid and lively review. The teaching items are printed or written neatly on the pieces of cardboard. The printed words should be large enough so that they can be easily read from any part of the classroom. The cards have lexical items and, if possible, their pictures or sketches on them. They may be used to drill their grammatical forms and uses or to test their knowledge of vocabulary.

In bilingual classes, the meaning of the words could be printed on the reverse-side of the cards. The teacher may show the reverse side and ask for its English equivalent or vice versa. He/she may show the word and ask for its synonyms or antonym in English. He/she may ask the student to use the words in an indicative sentence or a question.

CHARTS

Charts are specially useful in the beginning classes. They present materials in a systematic manner and can be permanently on display in the classroom. A flip chart consists of large sheets of paper fixed at the top to a stand so that to be turned over. It is usually used for presenting information in a meeting but can be used in a classroom as well. Commercially available picture charts can be purchased and used. They should be handled with care so that they are not spoilt. (For types of charts, see pp. 171-172)

HANDOUTS

Handouts usually contain a summary of the talk/lesson to be discussed in the class/seminar. They are documents that guide the teacher and students in the course of discussion and can be useful in higher classes.

CARTOONS

Cartoons of children's interest can be collected and displayed in the class. There are several books which tell well known children's stories through cartoon. *Amarchitr Katha* publish his cartoom stories regularly. They may be made available for their benefit. Audio visual picture cartoons can be seen on television.

PICTURES

Pictures depicting scenes from the English-speaking countries, especially the UK and the USA could be used for the decoration of the rooms to create a favourate environment for the lessons. The pictures and photographs on temporary display could be contributed both by teachers and students. Besides, there should be pictures which could be used for conversational purposes. Snapshots of relevant scenes, costumes and aspects of civilization and culture should be used while going through such lessons. Pictures can be used to review vocabulary or to expand an idea or a scene. Travel posters can be used for room decoration as well as for instruction.

SLIDES

Slides could be used for presentation. The images of the transparencies can be projected on the screen with the help of an *overhead projector*. The projected materials are manipulated by the presenter, where necessary, to highlight a point.

Flash cards, charts, pictures and slides are all visual materials. Besides them, other auditory materials can also be used.

PHONOGRAPH RECORDS

The magnetic records, long playing records and tapes can be used effectively for aural as well as oral learning. They have many advantages. They can be stopped at any time for the teacher to make comments, ask questions and clarify a point. The recording can be heard as many times as the teacher deems appropriate because they are under the control of the handler. Many types of records are available, such as basic records for language learning, phonetic exercises and for literary appreciation.

TAPE RECORDER

The tape recorder is an extremely valuable device. The teacher can record the learner's voice while he/she speaks and play it back for correction. The tapes can be stored without difficulty and can be relayed without losing quality. Dobbyn (1966-67) discusses the use of the tape-recorder in Indian schools in detail.

The English and Foreign Languages University, Hyderabad has prepared some *talking books* which contain cassettes plus books. Each of them has a model speech accompanied by a printed text. The new (ninth) edition of *Oxford Advanced Learner's Dictionary* (2015) has a DVD which contains exercises in speaking and writing skills. It can be used by high school students. Though *e-books* are available in the market for advanced readers, *talking books* are yet to be commercially available.

RADIO

The radio is an easily available form of audio-communication. The teacher can switch on the BBC Channel to have students an experience of how English is spoken in Britain. The language programme of the channel is specially meant for foreigners learning English. The newsbroadcast on Indian channels can be heard to get used to standard Indian pronunciation.

MOTION PICTURE

The motion picture is a very effective teaching medium. It demands attention and provides an intensive experience. It reaches even those who do not know the language and helps the learners of a language. It often offers a pleasant experience and students love to watch it. The use of the film in the classroom facilitates better learning and retention of what is learnt.

TELEVISION

The television is the most effective medium of communication since it combines the advantages of radio and motion pictures. As it engages both the eye and ear, it brings the observer in contact with an event in an exciting manner. Like radio, it is a medium of one way communication. While watching the programme, the student can ask no question and the teacher cannot interrupt it to explain a point. He/she cannot tell in the middle how much his/her students have grasped. He/she must wait till the programme is over to ask or answer questions.

The TV can be used to show video clippings of various events that are relevant to the lesson. They can be used to show cassettes of scenes and cartoons.

As television is now the dominant mode of communication in India, it has to be adjusted to the requirement in the classroom. The point is to think of ways to approach it creatively. The new generation has taken to television in an entirely different way. The teacher should appreciate its potential freely and help students develop visual literacy.

LANGUAGE LABORATORY

The laboratory usually contains mechanical equipment by means of which students hear and repeat materials recorded in English (or any other language). They listen through earphones, repeat sentences through a microphone and record their voices on a disc or a tape. Later on, every student can play back his/her own recording and compare it with the model voice. If he/she is alert, he/she can find out his/her own shortcomings and remove them. In modern laboratories, the teacher can listen to the student's voice and suggest corrections. The laboratory may have a monitoring system which is centrally controlled. They give students a chance which they do not get in a usual classroom, the chance to listen and speak in a systematic manner.

The language laboratory is effective if the tapes are of good quality and students practise regularly. It is necessary that the material is played at the normal speed. The material should be varied, otherwise it would not catch students' attention. The laboratory provides regular practice in listening to model voices and enables students to imitate and drill them repetitively. Such a practice strengthens the learner's ability to understand the natural language at a normal speed. It helps him/her to enrich his/her vocabulary and increase his/her ability to speak. It is the teacher's task to see that the student comprehends what he/she practises. If the student can comprehend what he/she has learnt to speak correctly; his/her voice is easily intelligible in the areas where English is spoken as the mother tongue. A practice in the laboratory can not only improve his/her pronunciation and comprehension but also his/her oral self-expression.

Though a language laboratory is an effective means of improving student's learning, there are several difficulties in India. First of all, high quality course materials are not easily available for use. Secondly, there are serious financial problems because of which language laboratories cannot be established in every school. Even if efforts are made to have a central laboratory which several schools can use, there is the organizational problem. There could be the problem of co-ordination between schools regarding the use of time and space which is equally convenient to all. Equipment and software have to be made available on time and provisions have to be made for their proper maintenance. In short, infrastructural facilities are not available to have language laboratory in every school or for clusters of schools. The large number of students in every class poses another challenge.

COMPUTER

Recent advance in technology has enabled people to make use of personal computers for *Computer-assisted Language Learning (CALL)* where learners could work on individual computers at their own pace. It has facilitated the incorporation of audio and video input into learning programmes on a scale which was previously unimaginable. The best of the current programmes are interactive; they tailor to the progress of individual learners.

While most CALL programmes deal with the grammar and vocabulary of English, programmes for listening comprehension, reading comprehension and translation skills are also available. The computer has a programmed instruction which has the following characteristics:

- Each lesson has a precise description of the target language behaviour.
- The course content is divided into small, closely-linked units, called *frames.*
- The learner goes through the programme at his/her own speed.
- The learner is immediately informed of his/her achievement after the completion of each unit.

The initial programmes were based on Skinner's behaviourist model which did not give the desired result. Language presupposes communication and in a truly communicative situation the reaction of the participants is not easily predictable. As Valdman (1969: 50-51): observes, natural communication is not programmable. However, programmed lesson units on some aspects of phonetics and syntax can provide language learners with tools to enable him/her to attain fluency in the language. Some researches prefer *Programme-assisted instrument* to *programmed instruction.* In short, the computer has more to offer in the area of written skills and less in the area of oral productive skills. Even in the area of written skills, it is not of much help to creative writing.

MOBILE

Agnieszka Palalas (2011) explains how *mobile-assisted language* (MALL) offers flexible language learning texts which is interactive, engaging, authentic and contextualised and is connected with and supported by appropriate feedback and scaffolding.

INFORMATION AND COMPUTER TECHNOLOGY (ICT)

Information and Computer Technology (ICT) has helped in the development of multi-media portfolios which are being used offline or online or both ways. It is used for organizing, compiling and synthesizing information. It encourages self-directed learning and creativity. It enables one to have access to online libraries to enrich oneself intellectually.

Thouesny and Bradley (2011) point out how different interactive technologies in CALL have been widely used to promote language learning. Wood (2011) reports how tutorial CALL software enables learners of a foreign language to become independent only to a limited extent. He recommends a shift to natural language processing (NLP) technologies to promote independent language learning at an advanced stage.

Cadric Surre (2011) records the findings of a comparative investigation of the potential of these three different computer-mediated negotiated interactions—discussion board, text chart and video conferencing. He reports that all computer-mediated communication (CMC) modes allow negotiations but video conferencing is conducive to more meaning than others.

The book, *Second Language Teaching and Learning with Technologies: Views of Emergent Researchers* (2011) discusses various aspects of computer-assisted language learning. It reports that no final conclusion can be reached at in regard to the learning effects of a multi-media approach in second/foreign language teaching. However, one point can be safely asserted: the results of the complex media approach depends on the quality of the learning materials used. As the media have become technically more advanced, they have necessarily become more effective.

CORPUS LINGUISTICS

Corpus linguistics involves the study of computerized corpora and the methods of their analysis. This empirical approach to language analysis is based on natural spoken or written data as they occur in the text. The use of computer has made the analysis of data faster and much more efficient than it was ever before. The computer-based corpus data are the principled collection of the lexicon of natural texts which analyses the actual patterns of use. It makes it easier for linguists and language pedagogues to decide what information is useful to prepare second language textbooks and other teaching materials. The corpus gives us not only high frequency word lists but also samples of complex grammatical patterns and frequently used sequential patterns. The information on their frequency of occurrence makes the task of grading easy and reliable. In addition, they provide concordance packages which give additional information on lexical co-occurrence pattern. For instance, with the help of 'key words in contexts, one can explore the context of occurrence of those words.

The corpus-based findings (e.g. Paul Nation's Vocabulary programmes and Baber *et al.'s The Longman Grammar of Spoken and Written English,* 1999) serve the language teachers well. *Exploring Spoken English* (1997) by

Carter and McCarthy has been widely used for two decades to combine the use of corpus material with language instruction. There are several useful websites for corpus linguistics which can be relied on.

Multimedia Approach to Language Learning

A multimedia approach to language learning involves the use of sounds, pictures and films in addition to the text on the screen. It involves the use of CDROMs. In short, using several different audiolingual ways of giving information on several different materials for communication (as discussed above) is a multimedia approach to language learning.

As non-print media technologies continue to develop and have their impact on the lives of students, it should be used fruitfully to develop language programmes.

To sum up, visual aids like flashcards, pictures and slides are available to teachers and students to illustrate the points in the text. An overhead projector is needed to use the slides. The first two aids can be used in any school even in the remotest corner in India, where electricity is not available yet. Phonograph records, tapes and radio are audio aids whereas television, motion pictures and computers are audio-visual aids. Language Laboratories, CALL and MALL serve very useful purpose for self-improvement of one's pronunciation. As infrastructure develops, computer assisted language learning is gaining strength. At very advanced centres of language learning, information and computer technology is used to develop multi-media portfolios. With the passage of time, newer technologies are being fruitfully used for language learning and appreciation of literature.

UNIT 9

23

Language Assessment

Its Role and Importance

To *test* means to take measures to check the quality, performance or reliability of someone or something before putting it into widespread practice or use. In the context of language, it means to take a short written or spoken examination of a person's proficiency or knowledge. To *assess* means to evaluate or estimate the ability of a person. Although some scholars treat 'testing' and 'assessment' to be synonymous, many use the latter in a broader sense to include both formal measurement tools and other qualitative assessment of the overall fitness of the person being assessed. However, both involve the process of making inferences about the learner's language ability on the basis of his/her performance.

Language testing is a complex matter. The actual testing procedure takes several factors into consideration: why a test is set, what is tested, who is tested and when a test is set. Test developers have several presuppositions which their testees are supposed to share. They should know what contents will be tested, how it will be tested and what criteria will be used in rating.

PURPOSE OF LANGUAGE TESTING

Specific or general language tests may be used for different purposes and all of them have to meet the standards set for tests used in different contexts. These tests measure the language ability of learners. Besides, they are used to evaluate the language programme by means of an analysis of the results of a whole group of students. The following types of tests are popular:

APTITUDE TEST

An aptitude test provides information on the likelihood of one's success or failure in language learning. It has a predictive function. It is designed to determine a person's ability in a particular field of knowledge.

PLACEMENT TEST

This test is administered before the start of a programme to determine the initial level of proficiency of the learner who has been enrolled for a particular course. He/she is assigned an elementary, intermediate or advanced level group on the basis of this test.

FORMATIVE TEST

Formative evaluation takes place during the programme. It is intended to adjust or guide the programme. It is administered to an individual to determine what he/she has or has not learnt so that the programme can be adapted to the specific needs of the learner. It is called assessment for learning designed to improve students progress during the learning process. It is used in a highly sequential learning situation. A formative test can be conducted after each separate unit so that the learner is motivated to make necessary effort at the appropriate time to make up for his/her deficiency. Besides, it provides a feedback to the teacher. It helps him/her to find out the weak points of the learner and enables him/her to take corrective measures. Formative evaluation procedures are most effective when they are kept separate from the grading process.

ACHIEVEMENT TEST

An achievement test tries to find out what exactly a learner has learnt in a given teaching context. It is clearly related to a curriculum and only tests what has been taught. It may be used to measure progress in smaller units within a curriculum. Such tests are called *progress tests* as well.

Language evaluation need not be limited to achievement list, with respect to a specific syllabus; it should try to measure language proficiency.

SUMMATIVE EVALUATION

If the evaluation takes place at the end of the programme to evaluate the programme as a whole, it is called summative evaluation. *Summation* means the sum total of adding things together. The summative test of an individual measures what he/she has learnt by the end of a programme. It has profound effect on the learner.

DIAGNOSTIC TEST

A diagnostic test is closely related to a particular curriculum. It not only provides an impression of the level of proficiency that one has achieved but also establishes what a learner has not learnt. It always has a follow-up programme of revising what the learner has failed to learn. It provides much more specific information than an achievement test does. An achievement test answers the question how much a learner knows whereas a diagnostic test answers the question what the learner knows or does not know and helps the evaluator in predicting why. It is used to test skills in isolated areas.

PROFICIENCY TEST

A general proficiency test indicates what an individual is capable of doing as a result of his cumulative learning experience. It measures skills for real life purpose. If predicts, for instance, whether a person is proficient enough in a foreign or second language to pursue a certain profession. Proficiency test in English as a foreign language is administered to find out whether a candidate is proficient enough to pursue higher studies through the medium of English in an English-speaking country.

Each type of test has certain objectives behind it. It is the job of the test designer to specify these objectives in terms of the contents of the test so that the test results could be interpreted accurately. The more precisely the norm is laid down, the better the test scores can be measured. A teacher or a team of experts who are assigned the job of setting test papers should be clear about the objectives of the test. There are two factors which each test must meet: it must be reliable and valid.

RELIABILITY

The extent to which a test is internally consistent over time is referred to as its reliability. A test is reliable if it provides the same result when administered to two different persons of the same ability. It is also reliable if it is administered to the same person twice and yields the same result. This method indicates the stability of the test score. The higher the correlation between the two test scores, the higher is the reliability of the test. There are a number of factors which contribute to a greater degree of reliability. One is its objectivity and the other is the length of the test. If the number of test items is large, it increases the information about the testee. Another important point is to keep an eye on the quality of the item because poorly written tests do not give an accurate measurement of the attribute under observation. Of course, the quality of test items is very important. The reliability of the test is a prerequisite for its validity but a reliable test is not always valid. Once a test is determined to be reliable, it has to be shown that it is also 'valid'.

VALIDITY

The validity of the test is the most important factor for any test. A test is valid if it measures what it is supposed to measure. It is important for the test-users to decide what precise information they want to obtain from a test before deciding whether it is valid or not. An important factor in validity procedure is to investigate the extent to which inferences can be properly drawn from the performance of the testee.

Validity consists of three sub-types:

(i) *Content validity*, i.e., whether the content of the test questions is accurate and appropriate;

(ii) *Criterion-related validity*, whether other tests measuring similar linguistic abilities correlate with the test in question;

(iii) *Construct validity*: whether research shows that the test measures the 'construct' which involves all aspects of the testing process. A construct is an idea containing various conceptual elements typically considered to be subjective. It is the construct that influences the test-developer's choice of testing method, the intended meaning of test scores and the appropriateness of the test use.

Messick (1989) defines validity as a process of constructing an argument about the interpretation and uses of test scores. As an argument, validation may draw upon a number of different types of data to see whether the procedures of the test item correspond to learning targets (i.e. its content coverage).

Objectivity

A test should be not only reliable and valid but also objective. It should be structured and standardized. One way to be objective is to select several different types of procedures; another is to select several procedures of the same type. Both ways the degree of consistency of the assessees can be objectively determined.

TYPOLOGY OF TEST FORMATS

Broadly speaking, there are three types of test formats:

(i) close-ended, (ii) restricted and (iii) open-ended.

(i) A characteristic of *close-ended test* is that in which the testee does not have to formulate answers. The most frequent types are:

True/False: a condition for the type of question is that the statement has to be absolutely true or false within the given context;

Q. If a common noun begins with a letter which is a vowel, it is preceded by the article an.

T	F

The answer is F (false). For instance, the word *European* begins with 'e' which is a vowel but it does not take *an*. It takes *a* because it begins with a consonant sound *jʊrəpian.*

Matching: in which the correct combinations have to be selected from two columns of options;

Q. Match the words in the first column with those in the second column.

alarm	food
junk	bag
tea	jam
credit	tax
income	card
kitchen	clock
traffic	knife

The correct answer is:

alarm	clock
junk	food
tea	bag
credit	card
income	tax
kitchen	knife
traffic	jam

Multiple-Choice Questions (MCQ): in which the learner has to select the correct answer from among the given alternatives:

Fill in the blank by any of the four alternatives:

I do not like to be angry .... the situation I cannot change.

(a) by, (b) with, (c) in, (d) at

The answer is (d) *at*.

Multiple choice questions are objective. They are easy to score and take little time to answer but they take much time to construct, for it is not always easy to find good distractors (i.e., plausible wrong answers). Another problem is that the examinee can take a gamble on the correct answer. It is possible that he/she gets the right answer by eliminating the wrong answers. Many scholars hold the view that close-ended tests should be used on a limited scale.

(ii) Restricted response tests. In such a test, the response is formulated by the examinee. As answers of such questions are short and predictable, their scores can be objectively evaluated. They are easy to construct and expect short and precise answers, for instance, '*fill in the blank*'. Such tests are more reliable and valid; they yield more diagnostic information.

[The questions refer to the scene in the senate hall of Rome after the assassination of Caesar]

Q. What reasons does Brutus give for murdering Caesar?

[Here the examinee is supposed to talk about the reasons that Brutus gave and nothing more i.e. his ambitions.]

(iii) *Open-ended tests*: In general, such tests are considered to be very valid from communicative point of view. The problem is that responses to such questions vary considerably and it is very difficult to compare responses of various candidates.

Why is the speech of Antony more effective than that of Brutus?

[The answer depends on the comparative evaluation of the two speeches by the examinee. It is more likely that two candidates will not give the same answer.]

The *openended* questions can be used fruitfully to test the creative and critical thinking ability of the candidate. It may give him/her an opportunity to show his imagination and critical awareness. Such questions should be used to discourage him/her from relying solely on memory. Inferential questions lead the student to apply his/her mind; they can be answered only if the candidate has read the text analytically and critically. The evaluation of such questions may not be cent per cent objective but they test the intelligence of the candidate in a most important way.

CLOZE TEST

The cloze test was introduced by Taylor (1953) to determine the readability of texts and to test the reading skills of native speakers of a language but now it is used for the learners of a second language as well. This test provides a text in which every *n*th word (e.g. fifth or tenth word) has been deleted. The examinee has to restore the text by filling in as many deleted words as he/she can. In so doing, he/she will use his/her linguistic and textual knowledge as well as knowledge of the world. Cloze tests tend to correlate moderately to highly with standardised texts. They relate more to tests on grammar and vocabulary than on comprehension. The nature and degree of difficulty of the text in question has a certain effect on the cloze test. The distance between the deleted words can play a role in scoring procedure. There are two methods for deleting words: (a) "fixed ratio method" in which every *n*th word in a passage is deleted and (b) "variable ratio method" in which only content words are deleted.

The following is the sample of a cloze test.

Q. Choose the most suitable word for each blank in the passage.

It was Mr. Ram Kumar's ......(1)...... to shoot a tiger. Not that the lust to ......(2)...... had descended on him but that he wanted the locality to .....(3)....... safe. Circumstances offered him an ......(4)...... to fulfil his mission. The authorities announced a handsome ......(5)...... of money for the persons who would capture or ......(6)...... that wild tiger who had ......(7)...... terror in the area.

[Answer: 1. desire, 2. kill, 3. feel, 4. opportunity, 5. amount, 6. kill, 7. caused.]

A variation of the open cloze test is the multiple choice cloze test. Oller (1975) points out that the cloze procedure is sensitive to discourse constraints and the possible point of diminishing returns for increasing order of approximation is well beyond fifty words of context. It implies that discourse-based communication testing can be profitably used for cloze-tests. Discourse-based performance tests are integrative tests.

INTEGRATIVE VS. DISCRETE ITEMS TESTS

The types of tests that we have discussed so far test only one item at a time. They are called *discrete items tests*. The tests that test a number of things at a time (e.g., vocabulary, collocation, grammatical tests, etc.) are called *integrative* tests. They are more subjective than discrete item tests.

OTHER MEANS OF ASSESSMENT

Observation

Informal observation of learner's language use is one of the most widely used methods of assessment in a language classroom. It is believed that experienced teachers' estimate of students' ability is highly correlated with formal test results. Types of observation that can be used to monitor progress and identify individual learning difficulties range from anecdotal records to checklists of learners' performance. However, one needs a great deal of care and attention to yield valid and reliable data.

Portfolio

As discussed earlier, the teacher can have a separate portfolio for each of his/her students in which he/she records the progress made by them.

The teacher keeps separate records of each of his/her students mentioning therein his/her achievements and failures in performing the task given to him/her, the willingness with which it has been performed and the impression it has made on the teacher. He/she also notes the pattern the student has behind his/her successive assignments.

Personal and Peer Evaluation

Each student of a group of learners gives his/her assessment of his/her own achievement as well as the achievement of his/her peers. It adds to the teachers assessment of the student and enables him/her to have a holistic view of each student's progress.

Observational evaluation can be done not only by a teacher but also by the students themselves. If a student keeps the record of his/her own personal achievement, it is *personal evaluation*, if he/she is evaluated, by his/her peers (i.e. other students of the same group) it is *peer evaluation*. A *group evaluation* involves the evaluation of a candidate by a group of evaluators or the collective evaluation of a group of students.

In a personal evaluation, the candidate has to answer questions like:

- can you understand what you hear or read?
- can you summarise the information you come across?
- can you express yourself precisely and clearly?

The candidate may find himself/herself in an embarrassing situation while trying to answer such questions. It is not easy to assess one's own achievement dispassionately and objectively. Nevertheless, one should try to do it so that one can correct oneself and acquire more.

Can do type questions can be asked by the assessor during a peer assessment. A peer assessor should try to find out whether the candidate can

- understand the text he/she goes through in the class;
- answer comprehension and critical questions fluently without searching for expressions;
- can communicate in L_2 freely, using simple, colloquial expressions, etc.

The evaluators should choose both *discrete items tasks* and *integrative tests*. The latter is very useful to find out how well the candidate can communicate. The integrative questions should be such that they bring out the analytical and critical ability of the candidate. The candidate should be not only reflective but also imaginative leading to creative answer. They should bring out the problem solving ability of the assessee.

COMPREHENSIVE AND CONTINUOUS EVALUATION (CCE)

Scholars who emphasize the significance of assessment for the improvement of an ongoing coursework are in favour of comprehensive and continuous evaluation (CCE). It means one should not depend entirely on periodic discrete evaluation to find out what has been learnt and what is yet to be learnt out of what has been already taught. It should closely watch the cognitive growth of the learner in terms of his/her language use inside and outside the classroom, his/her interaction with peers and other persons. Such an evaluation cannot be made by the teacher's dependence on formative and summative tests. It can be done only when the teacher keeps separate portfolios for every child in the class and goes on noting down his/her day to day observation.

The teacher may assess the listening and speaking ability of a student by noting whether he/she can hear and speak all sounds and their combinations clearly and correctly. Those who can should be grouped together. Those who cannot should be in another group. There may be students who can listen to an expression well but cannot speak it out well. There may be others who can neither listen nor speak correctly. They may be kept in separate groups. Comprehensive and continous evaluation (CCE) should be practised to note the progress of such students. CCE can be used to keep track of progress in the reading ability of students.

RATING OR EVALUATION

Close-ended tests are easy to rate. Restricted response tests are fairly easy to rate but open-ended questions are problematic; their answers are less predictable and may vary considerably. The evaluator has to consider how appropriate an answer is within a given context. To make the rating more reliable, it is suggested that the response should be evaluated by more than one person. The training of evaluators increases the reliability of their rating. There may be individual differences between the evaluators but, by and large, they are reliable.

The effect of evaluation can be maximized if it is conducted *objectively*. The examinee must feel that he/she has been judged in terms of what he/she has been able to achieve and not in terms of the subjective opinion of the evaluator.

OUTCOME-BASED ASSESSMENT

In recent years, the governments of several countries have realised the need for system-wide indicators for monitoring the outcomes of educational programmes. This has led to the widespread introduction of 'outcome based', programmes of assessment and reporting. As a result, the performance assessment developed by teachers are used as the basis for reporting students' learning outcomes against pre-specified attainment standards, known as 'frameworks', 'benchmarks', 'bandscales' or 'competencies'. This type of approach has been adopted by the Common European Framework of Reference in Europe, the Canadian Language Benchmarks Assessment in Canada and the certificates in spoken and written English in Australia. In many cases the development of such assessment systems is driven more by government policy and ideology than by educational considerations. The politicisation of language testing has prompted the emergence of '*critical language testing*' which advocates greater attention to issues of fairness and equity for test-takers.

The fundamental concepts and practices in language testing have changed in recent years because of the shifting relationship between assessment and teaching. Now there is a widespread recognition of the need for close link between the desired outcome of instruction, curriculum contents and testing.

This new emphasis is closely reflected in testing policies, materials and methods. However, one needs to investigate whether the classroom assessment is done to ensure that the tests that are used in language programmes are optimally fair and valid.

SITUATION IN INDIA

In India, the National Council of Educational Research and Training (NCERT) has acknowledged the significance of *continuous and comprehensive evaluation* (CCE). It emphasises that assessment influences what is taught and how teaching and learning take place. The focus has now shifted from testing to learning, by perceiving assessment to be an overall process of learning. Thus, continuous and comprehensive evaluation has become a critical component of classroom practices.

Now that the active involvement of students has become a central part of learning, matching related items, sentence completion and multi-choice questions have become an integral part of formative assessment.

Each text book of English is accompanied by a workbook which includes formative and summative tests, the latter include reading comprehension and answering questions based on grammatical structures recommended by the Central Board of Secondary Education. Thus, efforts are being made to incorporate the latest methods of language testing in Indian system.

For instance, Alan Davies (1990: 89-92) reports on the evaluation system adopted by the Banglore/Madras Communicative Teaching Project which uses test questions involving (a) grammar, (b) grammar in context, (c) cloze test, (d) reading comprehension (for proficiency test) and (e) questions involving tasks and problems (for achievement test), Davies was also involved as a consultant in the evaluation of the Communicative Teaching of English Project of the first year undergraduate course in the University of Bombay. He found the examination reliable though he had several reservations. He suggested that the examination should include a listening question and a cloze question. He wanted the reading comprehension questions to be graded in terms of difficulties and general summarizing questions to have a variety of formats.

We endorse his recommendations and hope that the testing system adopted by the CBSE will soon be innovative and diversified. Some schools have already adopted a system of comprehensive internal assessment which is a welcome step.

The questions set for the secondary and higher secondary students by the CBSE board of examiners include many of the points mentioned above but Davies's recommendations are yet to be implemented.

REMEDIAL WORK

The net result of an assessment is that it highlights the areas in which the learner has done well and the areas in which his/her achievements are below the accepted norms. The areas in which the learner is deficient need remedial work. The teacher should revisit these areas in a new way and let students practise some more exercises. If there are areas in which the whole class is deficient, it makes sense to go over them, discuss the relevant structures and let the students do the exercises orally in the class. The effort can be strengthened by asking them to do the assignment at home, which can be evaluated and discussed again. If necessary, students must be given adequate feedback to work on. Only then the remedial work will have its desired impact.

FEEDBACK

The feedback can be in the form of correction. The best way is to give the student a chance for self-correction. Immediate self-correction means to give a student a chance to correct himself/herself as soon as he/she makes a mistake. Though it means an interruption in the speech of the student, it will draw his/her full attention. The alternative is to let the teacher wait till the student stops and then intervene. In this case, the flow of the speech of the student is not stopped but some students get tired when they stop finally; they become indifferent to what the teacher says. It is for the teacher to judge what is most effective in a given situation. Some teachers do not stop and correct the student. Instead, they prefer to comment indirectly on the error by using the correct form in several ways.

Another remedial method is *peer correction.* A student makes a mistake in his/her utterance, the teacher stops him/her and asks another student to correct it. If he/she succeeds in correcting it, the task is over but it may not have a favourable impact on the one who makes the error. His/her attention may not be on the incorrect expression but on the personality of the person who corrected him/her. Though the end result of both the steps is the same, i.e. the error is corrected, it is for the teacher to see that no adverse psychological impact is made in the class. Much depends on how he/she judges the situation and monitors the case. He/she should decide how to deal with the diversity in the class, and caters to different needs of students of different ability. He/she should make sure that there is something for every student in the class.

A child may be good at formal tests and answer all the formal questions well, but may not be able to use those features of language correctly or even satisfactorily otherwise. On the other hand, there may be students who use certain features correctly in casual conversation but fail to respond to formal test-questions well. Comprehensive and continuous evaluation demands that such anomaly should be taken into account. In short, a successful trainee should be able to handle the language well inside and outside the classroom, in formal as well as informal situations.

To sum up,

- Language testing is a complex matter based on several pre-suppositions.
- There are several types of evaluation: summative, formative, aptitude, achievement and diagnostic tests.
- Any type of test must satisfy two conditions: it must be reliable and valid.
- There are three types of test format: (a) close-ended test (b) restricted response test and (c) open-ended test.
- The close-ended tests have three types of questions: (a) true/false, (b) matching, (c) multiple choice.
- Written and oral cloze tests are significant.
- Teachers' informal observation is also an important means of assessment.
- Outcome-based assessment is emerging as a parallel test pattern and is yet to be practised on a large scale in India.
- Indian system emphasises continuous and comprehensive tests. It favours formative and summative tests.

Glossary of Terms

Accent: a distinctive way of pronouncing a language, especially one associated with a particular region (e.g. southern accent) or social class (e.g. lower class accent).
: a distinct emphasis given to a syllable or word in speech using stress or pitch.

Accented: spoken with a particular accent.
: (of a word or syllable) stressed.

Acquisition: the learning or developing of a skill. In developmental psycholinguistics, it is treated as a subconscious process of learning.

Affect(n): In psycholinguistics, it refers to learner's motives, needs, attitudes and emotional states.

Alternation: the use of the members of one grammatical class for another (e.g. singular for plural and vice versa), also called alternating forms.

Analysis: the process of separating a linguistic unit into its constituent elements (e.g. *isn't* is analysed as *is not*).

Aptitude: innate language learning ability.

Attainment: a term associated with 'acquisition', 'development' and 'learning', implying 'learning from within' (rather than 'coming from outside').

Attrition: another term for 'language loss', divergent from the norm of the language, while acquiring a new language, the process of reducing effectiveness.

Authentic reading material: genuine texts rather than those intended solely for language teaching purposes.

Automacity: 'fluent use', swift and automatic use of a given linguistic structure.

Automatic process: opposite of 'controlled process'. According to the information processing theory, learning, typically, begins with slow controlled processes which may be transferred into efficient, automatic routine processes.

Average: a measure that represents the central core in the distribution of data; mean, median.

Baby talk/motherese: incomplete child-like talk used specially by a mother to talk to children. Also called motherese.

Basic English: a modified form of English promoted by C.K. Ogden and supported by I.A. Richards in 1930s. They promoted the use of BASIC English for use of teaching English as L_2. BASIC is an acronym for British American Scientific International Commercial English.

Behaviourist theory of language learning: a theory initiated by Watson and developed by Pavlov, Thorndike and B.F. Skinner. It defines learning as habit formation. Language learning takes place by practising the repetition of an utterance till it becomes one's habit.

Benchmark: It refers to something that can be measured and used as a standard that other things can be compared with. Academic tests (e.g. proficiency in English as L_2) of a certain standard is a benchmark with which the achievements of individual students can be measured. It is a universally applied method to measure the performance of an institute or an individual.

Berlitz: the name associated with many language schools worldwide, employing a particular direct method of language teaching in which only the target language is used in the class.

Bilingual acquisition: the acquisition of two languages simultaneously from infancy.

Bilingualism: speaking two languages fluently.

Brain Storming is a way of making a group of people (e.g. teachers and students) think about a problem in order to solve it. In a brain storming session, the teacher solicits the views of his/her students on a topic, encourages them to discuss them and leads the group to a solution. The purpose is to generate as many ideas as possible.

CDA: *Critical Discourse Analysis* which analyses how linguistic changes are made in texts to create and maintain social inequalities.

Child language learner: a learner who begins to learn a language from childhood (i.e., before puberty).

Code alternation: a construction that includes lexical and syntactic items from more than one language.

Code switching: rapid shifting from one language to another by bilinguals.

Communication: an exchange or transmission of messages between two or more persons.

Communicative competence: knowledge of how to use a language appropriately as well as the ability to actually to do so.

Complexity: the amount of knowledge (or difficulty) in a linguistic structure. The same as linguistic complexity.

Comprehensible input: Language addressed to L_2 learners to convey meaning to them so as to maximize their understanding.

Connectionism: a way of information processing. It reduces knowledge to a vast system of interconnected nodes. The networks of nodes are many and varied and they are typically activated in parallel associated notions. It sees learning as establishing the links between vast number of connections in the mind.

Construct: a concept that linguistics has given to identify some quality that is thought to exist (i.e. language proficiency); an idea or theory that contains various conceptual elements.

Constructivism is a teaching and learning theory formulated by Piaget. It believes that students are the creators of knowledge and meaning through their interaction with one another, their environment and with their teachers. In a constructivist approach there is maximum interaction between teachers and students.

Contrastive analysis hypothesis: a hypothesis stating that where structures of L_1 differ from those in L_2, errors in L_2 will refer to the structures of L_1.

Contrastive analysis: the comparison and contrast of the linguistic structures of two or more languages to determine their similarities and differences.

Creative construction: the learner's internal intuitive organisation of input. It is reflected in the appearance of specific rules found in L_2 learners to generate and understand sentences.

Critical period hypothesis: The idea that there is a time limit within which a language can be easily acquired, i.e. around puberty. Beyond this period the learning of a second language is not so easy as language learning mechanism is atrophied by then.

Cross-linguistic influence: the influence of the mother-tongue in the learner's performance and development of a given target language. Also called *language transfer*.

Curriculum: the subject comprising a course of studies in schools or colleges. Sometimes it is used synonymously with syllabus.

Declension: the variation of a form of a noun, pronoun or adjective in Sanskrit, Greek, Latin and several other languages through which grammatical case, number and gender are identified.

Deficit grammar: the grammar of those persons whose language development seems to be incomplete.

Developmental errors: the errors of L_2 learners which are similar to those made by children learning their first language.

Deviant: departing from accepted standard or norm. Deviant expressions are ones that are not according to the norms.

Direct method: a method that relies on the teaching of second language through that language throughout.

Discourse analysis: analysis that studies conversational interaction by close analysis of transcription. It deals with repair, i.e. how the participants deal with things that go wrong. It involves analysis of connected texts, written or oral.

Discourse domain: is the area of interlanguage with its own particular linguistic characteristics. It is not a monolithic entity but a cluster of varieties based on different interlanguages.

Double marking: an error in which a concept is expressed twice when the language requires its expression only once, e.g. double plural *mens*, double negation, as *in we hardly never do it*.

Drill: a form of mechanical practice in which words or phrases are substituted within a sentence and practised until they become automatic expressions of the learner.

Empathy and language learning: those students who are able to empathise with the feelings of others, are better at learning the pronunciation of the second language than those who are not.

Empathy: the ability to understand and share the feelings of others.

English as lingua franca (LFE): it is the name for the kind of English that is used globally by non-native speakers for many kinds of international purposes.

English for special purposes (ESP): the varieties of English that are used for specific purposes, in business and trade, sports, education, scientific studies, etc.

Error: some aspects of conversation or composition that deviate from the norms of users of a standard language (see interlanguage).

Error-analysis: Listing and classification of the errors contained in samples of learners' speech or writings.

Evidence: Positive or negative evidence for the language learner or learning device that either serves to confirm or refute an assumption already held about L_2 learning.

Feedback: the response given to specific aspects of the learner's speech/writing during a verbal interaction; the teacher's evaluation of the student's response. It should be objective, even if it is negative. The feedback from students refines and enriches the teaching method.

Filter: that part of the internal processing system that subconsciously screens incoming language based on motives, needs, attitudes or emotions.

Foreign language: a language not used by the residents of the country or community in which that language is being learnt, e.g. Russian in India.

Formal language environment: the environment in which the focus of the speaker is primarily on the standard form of the language.

Fossilisation: Selinker's (1972) term for the apparently final stage when development in some areas of language learning stops despite repeated exposure and attempt to learn; errors that are very difficult to get rid of.

Four skills: language teaching can be divided into four skills of listening, speaking, reading and writing. Listening and reading are called passive (receptive) skills, speaking and writing are active (productive) ones.

Function words: are structure words such as articles (*a*, *an*, *the*) and prepositions that exist to form parts of phrases or structures.

Functions: functions comprise the reasons for which people use language, e.g. for informing, persuading and arguing.

Global error: it affects overall sentence organisation and causes confusion.

Grading: the arrangement of teaching materials according to some pre-determined order, e.g. the order of difficulty.

Grammar-translation method: the traditional academic style of teaching a second or foreign language which places great emphasis on grammatical explanation and translation in the mother tongue as a teaching method.

Grammatical competence: the knowledge of a language stored in the person's mind. It is the stage that encompasses all aspects of form and meaning and their relations.

Grammatical judgment: the competent native speaker's decision whether a sentence is grammatical or not.

Habit formation: according to behaviourists, language learning is acquiring a set of habits which are learnt by doing it repeatedly.

Host language: the language used by the residents of the country or community in which that language is being learnt, for instance, Hindi being learnt in Hindi speaking areas in India.

Idealisation: Regarding a language as perfect, the extent to which variability in a language is ignored.

Immersion programme: a programme of teaching a foreign or second language by exclusive use of that language (for teaching all or some subjects at school), a form of education where children speaking one language are instructed through the medium of another language, as in an English medium school in Hindi-speaking areas.

Informant: the person whose knowledge as the native speaker of a language is sought

Input: language data which the learner is exposed to.

Intake: that which is actually processed and turned into knowledge intake.

Interference: the influence of the habit of the old language (e.g. the mother-tongue) while learning a new language. It may be psychological or sociocultural.

Interlanguage: a term used to refer to the speech or writing of a second language learner in the second language before one learns the standard form. It refers to the non-native speaker of a given language where the focus is on conveying meaning and not on the formal correctness of the utterance.

Interlingual error: the error that reflects the influence of the first language in one's second language utterances.

L_1: first language of a person.

L_2: second language of a person.

LAD (Language Acquisition Device): it refers to language development strategy or mechanism that follows the principles of universal grammar and allows the learner to have competence in a language.

Language learning strategies: conscious or sub-conscious attempts to learn a language

Language transfer: another term for cross-linguistic influence. It refers to the influence of the mother-tongue or any known language on learning the target language.

Macro-environmental factor: broad overall characteristics of the language environment

Matching Problem: the learner's attempt to notice discrepancy between their own output and the native speakers' input. The learner needs to match their deviant forms against equivalent target forms for further development in learning.

Maturational: concerning the mental development of the language learner. At certain points during language acquisition, certain language principles may not be available to a learner. For instance, the universal grammar becomes available in stages as a child develops.

Meta-language: is used to refer to the ways in which a language system is exploited for the description or analysis of another language. The linguist and the language teacher use the formal properties of a language as a meta-language. For instance, we can use English as a meta-language to discuss the formal properties of Hindi or Tamil.

Meta-linguistic awareness: the awareness of language as an object of analysis. Its formalized awareness allows one to talk coherently about a language. It is also called meta-linguistic knowledge.

Minimal pair technique: the technique of making learners aware that the phonemes of a language are parts of a system of contrasts, for instance, between |i:| and |i| (as in *ship* and *sheep*) and between |s| and |θ| (as in *sink* and *think*).

Minimalist programme: the latest version of Noam Chomsky's generative grammar. It is his latest attempt to simplify syntax to minimum necessary principles and their applications to develop a system to connect sound and meaning according to certain parameters.

Modularity: breaking down a large system in a number of small systems. According to Chomsky, the language module refers to a special ability area obeying special properties. What is grammatical is determined by several modules of principles, each of which takes care of a specific aspect of grammar.

Monitor: a mechanism whereby language users inspect their own language output during performance to see whether it conforms to the given rules. It is a kind of censor that checks and repairs one's utterance, if necessary. According to Krashen, it is a conscious checking system.

Monolingual mode: in which the bilingual speaker uses a single language, whether it is his first or second language.

Motherese: see *baby talk.*

Motivation: refers to desire or willingness to learn a second language. It may be an integrative motivation to participate in the life of a community which speaks that language or instrument for utilitarian reasons (e.g. to get a job, etc.)

Multi-competence: the knowledge of more than one language

Native speaker: a person who has spoken a certain language since early childhood. A language later learnt even in early childhood cannot be one's native language regardless of how well one speaks it.

Nativist: the theory that concepts, mental capacities and mental structures are innate rather than acquired by learning. The person who believes in nativism is a nativist.

Natural approach: It is a communicative teaching method and is not to be confused with the Natural Method of Lambart Sauveur. It provides for initial communication in the target language in a restricted manner. The learner may use L_2 whenever his/her self-image and ease in the classroom prompt him/her to do so. Meanwhile his/her listeing input is gradually increased.

Natural communication task: a task that focuses on the ideas or opinion being discussed than on the language forms used.

Natural communication: a communication situation in which people focus on the ideas being discussed rather than on their grammatical structures.

New concurrent approach: is a highly controlled bilingual method of teaching. For instance, in a class where English is taught to Hindi-speaking students, the teacher can switch to Hindi when he has to explain important concepts. He can also switch to Hindi when students are getting distracted or when the teacher has to praise or criticise his/her students. He/she should switch over to English when he/she is revising a lesson.

Objectivity: the degree to which the data are not influenced by the bias of data collector due to his attitude, emotion, etc.

Obligatory occasion: a configuration of one or more linguistic items that require the use of certain other items.

Observational procedure: the procedure that captures data through visual observation.

Omission error: error due to the omission of an item that must be there in a well-formed utterance

Operational definition: one that defines a construct in terms of observation.

Organiser: the part of the internal processing system that is responsible for the learner's gradual and subconscious organisation of the new language system.

Output: it is usually used to refer to the learner's performance, i.e. in his speech and writing.

Overgeneralisation: when a learner organises some principles on the basis of his/her input to create new structures which are not sanctioned by established principles, it creates the problem of overgeneralisation.

Parameters: in linguistics refer to the ways in which language systems may vary. For instance, some languages are subject to the pro-drop parameter, some are not. Those that are within the pro-drop parameter, can drop their subject (e.g. in Hindi) and those which are not, cannot (e.g. English). Chomsky claims that parameters are parts of universal grammar.

Paraphrasing: rewording of something written or spoken; expressing the meaning of something using different words, especially to achieve greater clarity.

Parsing: the art of resolving a sentence into its component parts and describing their syntactic roles

Pattern: an arrangement found regularly in comparable structures.

Pedagogical grammar: a grammar describing a language for teaching purposes.

Performance: actual instances of linguistic behaviour which can be recorded for analysis. It takes place in real time and implies special mechanisms for producing and interpreting utterances.

Phrase structure: in a structural grammar; a sentence consists of two phrase structures – a noun phrase and a verb phrase – which can be further split into smaller structures

Positive transfer: the behaviourists used the term 'transfer' to refer to the automatic, uncontrolled and subconscious use of the previously learnt behaviour while attempting to produce new responses (e.g., the use of L_1 behaviour – while producing L_2). If the transfer results in correct performance, it is called positive transfer.

Pragmatic competence (also called pragmatic knowledge): it refers to the knowledge underlying the appropriate use of language in different contexts of use. It essentially means matching language with specific intention of the speaker.

Prefabricated pattern: superficially complex linguistic items which function like simple units. A language learner may use such items without analysing their components parts, e.g. 'I would like to …'.

Prescriptive grammar: a grammar prescribes what people should or should not say. For instance, it says one should not use *it is me* even though everyone says so now. Such a grammar has become irrelevant these days.

Principles and parameters grammar: this model of Chomsky's 'universal grammar' states that the knowledge of grammar that human mind has consists of two components: principles that all languages have in common and parameters on which they vary.

Principles: it permits or prohibits certain features of structures from occurring in languages. A language principle covers a large linguistic area. For instance, Chomsky's case theory is a universal principle which says that every language must have case attached to a noun phrase.

Programmed Instruction Method: In this method of teaching, students are asked to take specific steps to perform a task, if possible with the help of a computer. The students respond to the directions and proceed through the exercise until they learn the target specific skill. It is a self regulated method. The teacher's task is to provide the feedback, if necessary.

Prototype theory: It is an approach to categorization. It claims that children first learn words that are 'basic' because they reflect aspects of the world; rest of them are based on the partial resemblance with their prototypes. For instance *bird* is a superordinate level word of which the basic type is 'sparrow'. All other birds resemble sparrows to some degree.

Received pronunciation (RP) : the accepted (standard) pronunciation of British English given in the books about English. It is spoken by a small minority of British speakers of English.

Recreation: in Chomsky's generative grammar, L_1 and L_2 learning are essentially identical in the sense that universal grammar supplies exclusively to L_2 and that there is no transfer or any other kind of trans-linguistic change except in areas where universal grammar principles are subject to different parametric variations.

Register: a variety of language defined according to its social use.

Reliability: consistency of good quality performance.

Repair: the act of speaker or listener to get the interaction back on course when something goes wrong.

Repetition and rote learning: a common sense approach – to learn a new expression is to repeat it again and again until one knows it by heart.

Rule: a rule is a formula or an instruction which applies to a specific grammatical situation. It prompts one to add, delete, move, replace or substitute some forms. Rules are considered to be parts of a person's knowledge, a psychological reality.

Salience: the ease with which a structure is heard or seen.

Second language acquisition (SLA): the process of learning a second language. It may be learnt formally (in a classroom) or informally (in a community) or both.

Second language: a language learnt after the basics of the first language have been acquired. It may be a native language or a foreign language

Semantics: the study of meaning.

Sensitise: to make sensitive (to language), to cause someone to respond to certain stimuli.

Sensitive period: see critical period.

Silent way: of teaching concentrates on the expression of meaning abstractly through coloured rods.

Simplification: the process of making teaching materials easy by controlling their vocabulary and grammatical structures.

Standard language: is the dialect selected and codified for official purposes.

Strategy: an organised way to approach a task whether or not the learner is aware of applying it to a given context. The idea behind it is to facilitate acquisition. Communicative strategies that serve to make up for perceived gaps in the learner's knowledge is called *compensatory strategies*.

Submersion teaching: an extreme form of assimilationist teaching in which minority language children are put in majority language classes.

Synchronic: the study of a language at one point in time.

Task: a piece of work to be done or undertaken.

Task-based learning: the notion that learning and teaching should be organised around a set of classroom tasks. It requires students to use language to attain a particular non-linguistic goal. For instance, the goal of a shopping list task is the shopping list. When the list is completed, the task is over. The task requires students to work together and to report back but it does not tell them how to interact nor does it supply the vocabulary.

Teachability hypothesis: it asserts that, with certain type of constructions, learners can benefit only from intervention by teachers. However, teachers have to wait for natural processes of acquisition to take place before they can help the learner.

Total physical response: claims that listening to commands and carrying them out is an effective way of learning a second language. The students' social interaction with the teacher is unlike that found in any normal language exchange. This technique emphasises the listening first approach.

Traditional grammar: the old style school grammar concerned with labelling sentences with parts of speech and so on. Modern grammarians feel that their approach is outdated and unscientific.

Transitional form: (*See* 'developmental pattern')

Unanalysable chunk: (*See* 'Prefabricated pattern')

Unit: a self-contained part of an educational course, a number of lessons or activities built around a topic.

Unitory Competence Hypothesis: the view that there is one general factor underlying language ability. It is a part of a person's biological endowment which comes into operation when the person is exposed to the appropriate input. It directs the person to hypothesise about the structures of a language on a particular line.

Universal grammar: a set of principles which exist in a person's subconscious mind. It generates and limits in certain ways the grammar of a language (be it L_1 or L_2) in human mind on the basis of evidence provided by inputs. It comprises 'the system of principles, conditions and rules that are properties of all human languages'.

Validity: the true value of a text, the quality that establishes whether it is evaluating what it claims to evaluate

Washback: the influence of a language test on teaching and learning

References

Acharya, Poromesh (1997), Educational Ideals of Tagore and Gandhi: A Comparative Study, *Economic and Political Weekly* 32:12-601-606.

Aggarwal, J.C. and S. Gupta (2014), *Curriculum Development*, 2005, Delhi: Shipra Publications.

Aitchison, Jean. 2003, *Words in the Mind*. Oxford: Blackwell.

Aitchison, Jean. 2008, *The Articulate Mammal*. London: Routledge.

Alatis, James E. and Kristie Twaddell (eds.). 1976, *English as a Second Language in Bilingual Education*. Washington: Teachers of English to Speakers of Other Languages.

Allan, K. 1977. Classifiers. *Language* 53: 284-310.

Allen, Virginia F. 1975, Some Insights from Linguistics for the Teaching of Literature, in Burt and Dulay (eds.) 1975: 319-326.

Allwright, Richard L. 1975, Problems in the Study of Teachers' Treatment of Learners' Error, in Burt and Dulay (eds.) 1975: 96-109.

Anderson, Roger W. (ed.). 1984, *Second Language: A Cross-Linguistic Perspective*. Rowley, Mass: Newberry House.

Angelis, Paul J. 1975, Sentence Combining, Error Analysis and the Teaching of Writing, in Burt and Dulay (eds.) 1975: 292-299.

Arena, Louis A. 1975, A Method for Improving the Writing Skills of Foreign Students., in Burt and Dulay (eds.) 1975: 281-291.

Asher, James. 1986. *Learning Another Language throught Action: The Complete Teachers Guidebook.* Los Gatos, CA: SKY Oak Productions.

Auerbach, E.R. 1995. The Politics of the ESL Classroom: Issues of Power in Pedagogical Choice, in Tollefson (ed.) 1995.

Budheka, Gijubhai 1991 [1932 original Gujarati ed.] *Divasvapna* <Daydreams>: Delhi: National Book Trust.

Baker, William E. 1967, *Syntax in English Poetry*. Berkeley, Los Angeles: University of California Press.

Bansal, R.K. 1967. A Study of the Intonation Patterns in Educated Indian English. *Bulletin of the C.I.E.* 6. 117-122.

Bansal, R.K. 1967. Spoken English in India: Suggestions for Improvement, *Bulletin of C.I.E.* 6: 95-116.

Bever, Thomas G, Jerrold J. Katz and D. Terence Langendon (eds.). 1976, *An Integrated Theory of Language Ability*. New York: Thomas Y. Cornwell.

Biber, D., S. Johansson, G. Leech, S. Conradan E. Fienegan 1999. *The Longman Grammar of Spoken and Writer English.* Harlour: Longman.

Birdsong David. 1999, *Second Language Acquisition and the Critical Period Hypothesis*. Mahwah N.J.: Lawrence Erlbaum.

Bloom, Benjamin S. 1976. Some Theoretical Issues Relating to Educational Evaluation, in Ralph Tyler (ed.) 26-50.

Bond, Ruskin. 1981, *The Blue Umbrella*, New Delhi Students Store.

Brains, Martin 1971. On Two Models of the Internalization of Grammar, in Slobin, D. (ed.) 1971.

Brismont, Jean and Julie Franck (eds.) 2010, *Chomsky Notebook.* New York: Columbia University Press.

Brock, Peter, 1995. *Mahatma Gandhi as a Linguistic Nationalist.* Columbia, South Asia Publications.

Brodon, V. (1984), *Indian Philosophy in Modern Times*, Moscow: Progressive Publishers.

Brown, H.D, C. Yurio and R. Crymes (eds.) 1977, *Teaching and Learning English as a Second Language: Trends in Research and Practice.* Washington DC: *TESOL.*

Brown, H.D. 1973. , Affective Variables in Second Language Acquisition, *Language Learning* 23: 231-241.

Brumfit, Christopher (ed.) 1983. *Language Teaching Projects for the Third World.* Oxford: Pergamon Press.

Brumfit, Christopher and K. Johnson, 1979. *Communicative Approach to Language Teaching.* Oxford: Oxford University Press.

Bruner, J (1960), *The Process of Education*, Cambridge, Mass.: Harvard University Press.

Bruner, J.S. (1966), On Coping and Defending, *Towards a Theory of Instruction*, Cambridge, Mass.: Belkapp Press and Harvard University Press.

Bruner, J.S., J.J. Goodnow and G.A. Austin (1956), *A Study of Thinking*, New York: Wiley

Bruner, Jarome S. 1964, The Course of Cognitive Growth, *American Psychologist* 19.

Bruner, Jerome S., R.R. Oliver and P.M. Greenfield (1966), *Studies in Cognitive Growth*, New York: Wiley

Burns, Anne and Barbara Seidlhofer. 2009. , Speaking and Pronunciation, in Schmitt (ed.). 2009: 197-214.

Burt, and C. Kiparsky. 1972, *The Gooficon: A Rapid Manual for English*. Rowly. Mass: Newbury House.

Burt, Marina and Heidi C. Dulay (eds.). 1975, *New Directions in Second Language Learning, Teaching and Bilingual Education.* Washington: TESOL.

Burt, Marina K. 1975, Error Analysis in the Adult EFL Classroom. *TESOL Quarterly*: 9:53.63.

Burt, Marina, Heidi Dulay and M. Finocchiaro (eds.). 1977 , *Viewpoints on Second Language Learning*. New York: Regent.

Burton, Dwight L and John S. Simmons (eds.) 1965, *Teaching English in Today's High Schools: Selected Readings* New York: Holt, Rinehart and Winston.

Calci-Murcia, M., 1991. Grammar Pedagogy in Second and Foreign Language Teaching. *TESOL Quarterly*, 25(3) 459-480.

Cenkner, William (1976), *The Hindu Personality in Education*, New Delhi: Manohar.

Carrell, Patricia. 2009, Reading, in Schmitt 2009: 215-231.

Carroll, J.B. 1958. A Factor Analysis of Two Foreign Language Aptitude Batteries, *Journal of Genernal Psychology* 59: 3-19.

Carter, R. and M. McCarthy. 1997. *Exploring Spoken English.* Cambridge: Cambridge University Press.

Carver, R. 1992, Reading Rate, Theory, Research and Practical Implications. *Journal of Reading*. 36: 84-95.

Chappelle, C. and Geoff Brindley. 2009, 'Assessment' in Schmitt (ed.) 2009: 247-267

Chatterji, Sampurna. 2003, *Rikki Tikki Taki*. New Delhi: Penguin Lady Bird Book

Chiercia, Gennaro. 2010, Language, Thought and Reality after Chomsky, in Bricmont and Franck (eds.) 2010. 142-169.

Chomsky, Noam. 1959, A Review of B.F. Skinner's 'Verbal Behaviour'. *Language* 35: 26-38.

Chomsky, Noam. 1995, *The Minimalist Program*, Cambridge, Mass: M.I.T. Press.

Chomsky, Noam. 1997, *Language and Thought*. Wakefield: Novel Bell.

Chomsky, Noam. 2000, *New Horizons in the Study of Language and Mind*. New York: Cambridge University Press.

Chomsky, Noam. 2003, *On Nature and Language*, London: Cambridge University Press.

Cook, G. 1989. *Discourse*, Oxford: Oxford University Press.

Cook, Guy and Sarah North (eds.) 2010, *Applied Linguistics in Action*. London: Routledge.

Cook, Vivian. 2008, *Second Language Learning and Language Teaching*. London: Hodder Education.

Corder, S. Pit 1983, *Error Analysis and Interlanguage*, Oxford: Oxford University Press.

Corder, S. Pit. 1967, Error Analysis, Interlanguage and Second Language Acquisition *Language Teaching and Linguistics* 8: 201-218.

Corder, S. Pit. 1967, The Significance of Learner's Errors, *International Journal of Applied Linguistics* 5. 161-170.

Crystal, David, 2003. *English as a Global Language*. Cambridge: Cambridge University Press.

Crystal, David. 2009. *Language and the Internet.* Cambridge: Cambridge University Press.

Cummins, J. 1979, Linguistic Interdependence and the Development of Bilingual Children. *Review of Educational Research* 49: 222-251.

Cummins, James, 1984. *Bilingualism and Special Education: Issues on Assessment and Pedagogy* Clevadon: Multilingual Matters.

Curtiss, Susan 1982. Developmental Dissociation of Language and Cognition, in Obler and Menn (eds.) 1982: 285-312.

Dakin, Julian. 1969, 'The Teaching of Reading' in Fraser and O'Donnell (eds.) 1969: 99-120.

Davies, Alan. 1990, *Principles of Language Testing.* Oxford: Basil Blackwell.

Davies, Alan. 2007, *An Introduction to Applied Linguistics*, Edinburgh: Edinburgh University Press.

Davies, N. 1976. Receptive and Productive Skills in Foreign Language Learning. *The Modern Language Journal* 60: 440-443.

Dewey, John (1909), *Moral Principles in Education*, Boston: Houghton Mifflin.

Dewey, John (1910), *How We Think*, Boston: Health.

Dewey, John (1920)(1948), *Reconstruction in Philosophy*, Chicago: University of Chicago Press.

Dillion, George. 1979, *Language Processing and the Reading of Literature*, Bloomington, Indiana University Press.

Dobbyn, Michael N. 1967. Tape Recorder Methods and Materials, in *Bulletin of the Central Institute of English*, Hyderanad : C.I.E.

Dulay, Heidi and M. Burt. 1977a, You can't learn without goofing: An analysis of children's second language errors'; in Jack Richards, (eds.) 1972: 95-123.

Dulay, Heidi and M. Burt. Natural Sequence in Child's Second Language Acquisition, *Language Learning*. 22: 37 53.

Dulay, Heidi, M. Burt and Stephen Krashen. 1982, *Language Two*, New York: Oxford University Press.

Elias, Jo Anne. 1975, Predicting Your Way Through Written English, in Burt and Dulay 1975: 307-318.

Ellic, R. 2002. Frequency Effects in Language Processing. *Studies in Second Language Acquisition* 24(2) 143-188.

Ellis, N. and R. Schmidt. 1997. Morphology and Longe Distance Dependencies. *Studies in Second Language Acquisition* 19: 145-171.

Ellis, R. 2003. *Task-based Language Learning and Teaching*. Oxford: Oxford University Press.

Elman, J.L. 2001. Connectionism and Language Acquisition. In Tomasello, M. and E. Bates (eds.) *Language Development: The Essential/Readings*. Oxford: Backwell 295-306.

Els, Theo, Theo Bongaerts, Guus Extra, Carleo Van Os and AnnM-Mieke Janssen-van Dieten. 1984, *Applied Linguistic and The Learning and Teaching of Foreign Languages*, London: Edward Arnold.

Ervin-Tripp, Susan. 1974, Is Second Language Learning Like the First? *TESOL Quarterly*, 8.111-127.

Fabricio, Brenca F. and Denise Santos. 2010, *(Re-) Locating TEFL*: The (re) framing process as a collaborative focus for changes, in Guy Cook and Sarah North (eds.). 89-103.

Faignbaum, Irwat (1975), *The Use of Non-standard English in Teaching Standard: Contrast and Comparison* in Stoller, Paul (ed.) 1975, 143-157.

Ferguson, Charles and Dan Slobin (eds.). 1973, *Studies of Child Language Development*, New York: Holt, Rinehart and Winston.

Fillmore, Charles and Paul Kay 1988. *Construction Grammar*. Stanford: CSLL

Fillmore, Charles, Paul Kay and Mary Cattumine O'Connor 1988. Regularity, Idiomacity in Grammatical Constructions. The Case of let alone. *Language* 64:501-538.

Fodor, Jerry, Tom Bever and M. Garrett. 1974. *The Psychology of Language*. New York: McGraw-Hill.

Fraser, Hugh and W.R. O'Donnell (eds.). 1969, *Applied Linguistics and the Teaching of English*. New York: Humanities Press.

Fries, C.C. 1945, *Teaching and Learning English as a Foreign Language*, Ann Arbor, Michigan: University of Michigan Press.

Gardner, R.C. 1960, Motivational Variable in Second Language Learning, in Gardner and Lambart (eds.) 1972. *Attitude and Motivation in Second Language Learning* Rowley, Mass: Newberry House.

Gardner, R.C. 1983. *Frame of Mind and the Theory of Multiple Intelligence*. NewYork: Basic Books.

Gardner, R.C. 1999. Are there additional intelligence? in Kam, J. (ed.) 111-131.

Gattegno, Celeb. 1972. *Teaching Foreign Language in Schools: The Silent Way*, NewYork: Educational Solutions.

Goffman, Ervin. 1974. *Frame Analysis*. New York: Harper and Row.

Goldberg, Adale 1995 Constructions. A Construction Grammar Approach to Argument Structure. Chicago: University of Chicago Press.

Grittner, Frank M. 1969, *Teaching Foreign Languages*, New York: Harper and Row

Halliday, M.A.K. 1985, *An Introduction to Functional Grammar*, London: Edward Arnold.

Harley, B., P. Allen, J. Cummins and M. Swain (eds.) *The Development of Second Language Proficiency*. Cambridge: Cambridge University Press.

Honey, John (1977), *Language is Power*, London, Faber and Faber.

Howatt, A.P.R. 1984, *A History of English Language Teaching*, Oxford: Oxford University Press.

Ingnam, David (1989), *First Language Acquisition Cambridge*; Cambridge University Press.

James, William (1958), *Talk to Teachers*, New York: W.W. Norton.

Jasso-Aquilar, Rebeca (2010). Sources, Methods and Triangulation in Needs Analysis, in Cook and North (eds.), 2010: 171-194.

Jenkins, Jennifer (2015), *Global Englishes*, London: Routledge

Johnson, J.S. and E.L. Newport, 1989. Critical Period Effects in Second Language Acquisition: The Effect of Maturational Stage on the Acquisition of ESL. *Cognitive Psychology* 21: 60-99.

Kaplan, R. (ed.) 2002. *The Oxford Dictionary of Applied Linguistics*. Oxford: Oxford University Press.

Kasper, G. and E. Kellerman (eds) *Communication Strategies: Psycholinguistic and Sociolinguistic Perspective*. London, Longman.

Kenner, Hugh. 1959. *The Art of Poetry*, New York: Holt, Rinahart and Winston.

Khanna, Gayatri. 2012, *Oxford Pathways*, New Delhi: Oxford University Press.

Kipling, Rudyard. 1948, 'Rikki, Tikki Tavi' in *The Jungle Book*. Vol. 2.

Kodak, K. 2005, *Insight into Second Language Reading*, New York: Oxford University Press.

Kothari, D.S. 1966. *Report of the Education Commission*. New Delhi: Government of India.

Krashen, Stephen and T. Terrell. 1983. *The Natural Approach*, New York: Pergamon.

Krashen, Stephen. 1977a, The Monitor Model of Adult Second Language Performance, in Burt, Heidi and Pinocchiaro (eds.) 1977: 152-161.

Krashen, Stephen. 1977b, Some Issues Relating to the Monitor Model, in Brown, Yorio and Cryme (eds.) 1977. 144-148.

Krashen, Stephen. 1985. *The Input Hypothesis: Issues and Implications.* London, Longman.

Kroll, B. (ed.). 2003, *Exploring the Dynamics of Second Language Writing*, New York: Cambridge University Press.

Kroll, J.F. and T. Dijkstra, 2002. The Bilingual Lexicon, in R. Kaplan (ed.) 2002:301 321.

Kumar, Krishna (1986), Textbooks and Educational Culture, *Economic and Political Weekly* 21.30: 1309-1311.

Kuper, A. and J. Kuper (eds.) *The Social Science Encyclopaedia.* London: Routledge and Kegan Paul.

Lado, R. 1957, *Linguistics across Cultures*, Ann Arbor, Michigan University Press.

Lakoff, Robin (1975), *Language and Women's Place*, New York: Harper Colophon Books, Faber and Faber.

Lambert, Wallace. 1990. *Persistant Issues in Bilingualism*, in Harley, B. et al. (eds).

Lear, Edward. 1957, *The Complete Nonsense of Edward Lear*, New York: Dover.

Lenneberg, Eric. 1967. *Biological Foundations of Language.* New York: Wiley and Sons.

Linn, R. 1989, *Educational Measurement*, New York: Macmillan.

Lozanov, G. 1978. *Suggestology and Outlines of Suggestopedia*, NewYork: Gorden and Breach.

Lynch, Tony and David Mendelsohn. 2009, 'Listening', in Schmitt (ed.) 180-196.

Matsuda, P.K. 2003, Second Language Writing in the Twentieth Century: A Historical Perspectives in Kroll, B. (eds.). 2003: 15-34.

McCarthy, M.J. 1991. *Discourse analysis for Language Teachers.* Cambridge: Cambridge University Press.

McCarthy, M.J. and R.A. Carter. *Language as Discourse: Perspective for Language Teaching.* London: Longman.

McCarthy, Michael, Christian Mathiessen and Diana Slade. 2009, 'Discourse Analyses' in Schmitt (ed.). 53-69.

McCarthy, Michael. 2000, *Issues in Applied Linguistics*, Cambridge, Cambridge University Press.

McClelland, J. and D. Rumelhart (eds.) 1986. *Parallel Distributed Processing Explorations in the Microstructure of Cognition*, Vol. 2. Cambridge, Mass: MIT Press.

McNeill, David. 1966, 'Development of Psycholinguistics' in Smith and Miller (eds.). 1966.

McNeill, David. 1970, *The Acquisition of Language*, New York: Harper and Row.

Mendelsohn, D.J. and J. Rubin (eds.). 1995, *A Guide for the Teaching of Second Language Listening*, San Diego: Dominic Press.

Messick, S. 1989, Validity, in Linn, R. (ed.) 1989: 13-103.

Michaelis, Laura and Knud Lamborccht, 1996. Towards a Construction based theory of language function – the case of Nominal Extraposition. *Language* 72: 215 247.

Miller, Cassy and Kate Swift (1972), *Words and Women*, New York: Anchor Press.

Milon, J.P. 1975, 'Dialect in the TESOL Program' in Burt and Dulay (eds.). 1975: 159-167.

Mitchell, W. Kreith. 1990. On Comparisons in a Notional Grammar. *Applied Linguistics.* 11(1) 52-72.

Moody, H.L.B. 1971, *The Teaching of Literature with Special Reference to Developing Countries*, London: Longman.

Mother, Pondicherry: *Education Part II, Pondicherry*: Sri Aurobindo Ashram.

Murray, John. 1961. *Rabindranath Tagore: Pioneer of Education*, London.

Nandkumar, Prema (1977), *The Mother*, New Delhi: National Book Trust

Nash, Ogden. 1945, *The Selected Verses of Ogden Nash*, New York: Modern Library, Random House.

Nation, Paul 2001. Learning Vocabulary in Lexical Sets, *TESOL Journal*, 9: 6-10.

National Education Policy and the Programmes for Action 1986. New Delhi: NCERT

National Focus Group, NCERT (2006), *Teaching of English*, New Delhi: NCERT.

National Steering Committee, NCERT (2005), *National Curriculum Framework*, New Delhi; NCERT.

NCERT, CCE (*Continuous and Comprehensive Evaluation*), New Delhi: NCERT

Nemeser, William. 1971, Approximative Systems of Foreign Language Learners, *International Journal of Applied Linguistics*. 9: 115-124.

Newell, S. (ed.) 1969. *Proceeding of the Third Southern Conference on Language Teaching*. Atlanta: Spartanburg, SC.

Norris, J. and L. Ortega. 2000. Effectiveness of L2 Instruction. A Research Synthesis and Quantative Meta-analysis, *Language Learning*, 50: 417-528.

Obler, Loraine and Lise Menn (eds) 1982. *Exceptional Language and Linguistics*. New York: Academic Press.

Oller, J.K. 1973, Cloze Tests of Second Language Proficiency and What They Measure, *Language Learning*, 23: 105-118.

Oller, J.K. 1977, Attitude Variable in Second Language Learning, in Burt *et al.* 1977: 172-184.

Oller, J.K. and Murakani Parkins. 1980, *Research in Language Testing*, Rowley, Mass: Newbury.

Oller, John W.Jr. (ed) 1983. *Issues in Language Testing Research.* Rowley, MA: Newburg House.

Palalas, Agnieszka, 2011. Mobile-assisted Language Learning, in Thouesny and Bradley (eds.) 2011 (chapter 6).

Pandya, Mamta (2008), *Giju Bhai on Education*, From learningnetindia.org

Piaget, Jean. 1953 (1974), *The Language and Thought of the Child*, New York: The New American Library.

Piaget, Jean. 1975, *Biology and Knowledge*, Chicago: University of Chicago Press.

Pinker Steven. 2000, *Words and Rules*, New York: Perennial.

Prabhu, N.S. 1987. *Second Languge Pedagogy*. Oxford: Oxford University Press.

Quirk, Randolph (1990), Language Varieties and Standard Language, *English Today*, 21:3-10.

Ramachandran, Padma and Vasantha Ramkumar (2014), *Education in India*, New Delhi, National Book Trust.

Ravem, R. 1968, Language Acquisition in a Second Language Environment, *International Review of Applied Linguistics* 6:175-185.

Ravem, R. 1974, The Development of *wh* questions in first and second language learning, in Richards, J. (ed.). 1974.

Report of the Knowledge Commission, New Delhi: Government of India, 2007.

Richards, Jack (ed.), *Error Analysis: Perspective on Second Language Learning*, London: Longman.

Robinson, P. (ed.) 2002. *Individual Differences and Instructed Language Learning*. Armsterdan: John Benjamins.

Ross, S. 1997. An Introspective Analysis of Distance Inferencing on a Second Language Listening Test, in Kasper and Kellerman (eds.) 1997: 216-237.

Rumelhart, D. and J. McClelland. 1986. On Hearing the Past Tense of English Verbs, in McClelland and Rumelhart (eds.) 1986: 216-217.

Salkar, Kalyan, R. (1990), *Rabindranath Tagore: His Impact on India Education*, Delhi Sterling Publishers.

Saraswathi, T.S. (2009), Giju Bhai Badekha: Second Memorial Lecture, New Delhi, NCERT.

Sarre, Cedric, 2011. Computer-Mediated Negotiated Interaction: How is Meaning Negotiated in Discussion Boards, Text Chat and Video Conferencing?, in Thouesny and Bradley (eds.) 2011 (chapter 10).

Schmitt, Nobert (ed.). 2009, *An Introduction to Applied Linguistics*, London: Hodder Education.

Seely, C. and E.K. Romijn. 1993. *TPR is more than command.* Berkeley: Command Performance Language Institute.

Selinker, L, M. Swain and G. Dumas. 1975, The Interlanguage Hypothesis Extended to Children, *Language Learning*, 25. 139-155.

Selinker, L. 1972, Interlanguage, *International Review of Applied Linguistics*, 10: 209-31.

Selinker, L. 1992. *Rediscovering Interlanguage*. London: Longman.

Shapiro, Michael (ed.) (1984), *Language and Politics*, Oxford: Basil Blackwell.

Sharma, Pravin. 2011, *Teaching of English*, New Delhi: Shipra Publications.

Short, Mick, 1996. *Exploring the Language of Poems, Plays and Prose.* London: Longman.

Singh, Karan (1980), Sri Aurobindo: The Two Phases, in *Indian International Centre Quarterly*, 7:4, 243-261.

Sinha, Anjani K. 2013. English Language Teaching in Asia; Issues and Challenges. *Aligarh Journal of Linguistics*. 3: 1-9.

Sinha, Anjani K. and Usha Kiran. 1977, Error Analysis as an Aid to Second Language Acquisition, *CIEFL Bulletin* 13:2:23-40.

Sinha, Anjani, K. 1967 *An Analysis of Errors made by Undergraduate Students from Hindi-Speaking Areas (a monograph)* Hyderabad: Central Institute of English.

Skinner, B.F. 1957, *Verbal Behaviour*, New York: Applentea-Century-Croft.

Slobin, Dan. 1971, *Psycholinguistics*, Glenview, Ill.: Scot, Pressman.

Smith, F. and G.A. Miller (ed.). 1961, *The Genesis of Language: A Psycholinguistic Perspective*, Cambridge, Mass, MIT Press.

Smith, Michael S. 1994, *Second Language Learning: Theoretical Foundations*, London: Longman.

Smith, Neil. 1985. "Chomsky, Noam" in Kuper and Kuper (eds.) 1985: 105-106.

Smith, Neill. 1999, *Chomsky: Ideas and Ideals*, London: Cambridge University Press

Sri Aurobindo and the Mother (1967), *On Education: General Principles Part I, Education: Teaching Part II.* Learning Part III, Pondicherry: Sri Aurobindo Ashram.

Sternberg, R.K. 2002. The Theory of Successful Intelligence and its Implication for Language Aptitude Testing, in P. Robinson (ed.) 2002: 13-44.

Stoller, Paul (ed.) (1975), *Black American English*, New York: Delta.

Swain, M. and S. Lapkin, 1982. *Evaluating Bilingual Educating: A Canadian Case Study*, Clevedon: Multilingual Matters.

Swain, M. and S. Lapkin. 2000. Task-based Second Language Learning. *Language Teaching Research* (4)3: 251-274.

Tagore, Rabindranath *Shiksha.* Santiniketan, Vishwabharati.

Tagore, Rabindranath (2006), *Boundless Sky*.

Taylor, William. 1952, 'Cloze Procedure: a new tool for measuring readability', *Journalism Quarterly* 415-433.

Thornton, Geoffrey. 1980, *Teaching Writing: The Development of Written Language Skills*, London: Edward Arnold.

Thouesmy, Sylvia and Linda Bradley (eds.) 2011. *Second Language Teaching and Learning: Views of Emergent Researches*, Dublin: Research Publication.

Tollefson, R. (ed.) 1995. *Power and Inequality in Language Education*, Cambridge: Cambridge University Press.

Tollefson, R.W. 1991. *Language Planning: Planning Inequality.* New York: Longman.

Tomasello M. 2003. Constructing Language: A Usage based Theory of Language. Acquisition. Cambridge, MA: Harvard University Press.

Tyler, Ralph W. (1949), *Basic Principles of Curriculum and Instruction*, Chicago: University of Chicago Press.

Tyler, Ralph W. (ed.) 1976. *Educational Evaluation: New Roles, New Means:* Chicago: University of Chicago Press.

Valdman, A. 1969. The Limits of Programmed Instructions in Foreign Language Acquisition, in S. Newell (ed.) 41-54.

Vigotsky, Les Samanovich, 1962, *Language and Thought*, Cambridge Mass, MIT Press

Vivekananda, *The Complete Works*, Volumes, I, II, IV, Calcutta: Advait Ashram, Publication Division.

Watson, John B. 1925, *Behaviourism*, Chicago, University of Chicago Press.

Widdowson, H.D. 1979, *Explorations in Applied Linguistics*. London: Oxford University Press.

Widdowson, H.D. 1990. *Aspects of Language Teaching,* Oxford: Oxford University Press.

Wilkins, David, 1976. *Notional Syllabuses*, Oxford: Oxford University Press.

Wood, Peter, 2001. Quick Assist Reading and Learning Vocabulary Independently with the Help of CALL and NLP Technologies, in Thouesry and Bradley (eds.) (chapter 3).

Name Index